Praise for
Joy and Fear

"Just when I thought there was nothing more to write about the fabulous era when the Beatles made rock and roll history and invaded America in the mid-sixties, along comes John Lyons with a rich and fascinating stew of revelations and inside detail about the Fab Four in the Windy City. Facts I never knew. About irascible Mayor Richard Daley who did not want to hold the Beatles' hand. George Harrison's fervent and single-minded sister Louise, a one-woman band frantically promoting her brother out of her home in Benton, Illinois. In *Joy and Fear* Lyons captures the sixties and the stories behind the stories so perfectly. Those are just a few of the multiple ingredients that make this book must-reading for anyone who loves the Beatles. And who doesn't?"

—**Ivor Davis**, author of *Manson Exposed: A Reporter's 50-Year Journey Into Madness and Murder* and *The Beatles and Me on Tour*

"I thought I knew a lot about the Beatles and the Chicago music scene of the 1960s, but John Lyons' book is filled with wonderful tidbits totally new to me. He has certainly done his homework here and I would swear he was living in Chicago when Beatlemania landed on the American shores."

—**Dean Milano**, author of *The Chicago Music Scene: 1960s and 1970s*

Praise for Author's Previous Work

Teachers and Reform: Chicago Public Education, 1929–70

"…a masterful study."

—**Maurice Berube**, Old Dominion University, Virginia

"It should be read by anyone interested in labor, education policy, urban politics, or Chicago history."

—**Joseph E. Slater**, University of Toledo College of Law

America in the British Imagination, 1945 to the Present

"This important study, genuinely original in its focus and range, describes and assesses US influence on postwar Britain."

—**Michael J. Moore**, Appalachian State University

"…recommended as a hugely enjoyable read and one that contributes to a better understanding of Anglo-American relations"

—**Alan P. Dobson**, Swansea University

"Outstanding Academic Title, 2014"

—*Choice: Current Reviews for Academic Libraries*

JOY
AND
FEAR

THE BEATLES, CHICAGO AND THE 1960s

JOHN F. LYONS

PERMUTED
PRESS

A PERMUTED PRESS BOOK

Joy and Fear:
The Beatles, Chicago and the 1960s
© 2020 by John F. Lyons
All Rights Reserved

ISBN: 978-1-68261-932-2
ISBN (eBook): 978-1-68261-933-9

Cover art by Cody Corcoran
Cover photos courtesy of the Chicago History Museum.
Interior design and composition, Greg Johnson, Textbook Perfect

Unless noted otherwise, interior photos are courtesy of the author.

PERMUTED
PRESS

Permuted Press, LLC
New York • Nashville
permutedpress.com

Published in the United States of America
1 2 3 4 5 6 7 8 9 10

Contents

Introduction

On Monday morning, February 10, 1964, war broke out in Chicago. In factories, offices, department stores, construction sites, and classrooms, the young and the not so young argued vociferously over the startling performance of the musical group from England that they had witnessed on Ed Sullivan's television show the previous evening. "The arrival of the Beatles divided the students like nothing else before," Bernie Biernacki, who attended an all-boys Catholic high school on Chicago's Southwest Side, recalled of those early days of Beatlemania. "One group looked upon the Beatles as a subversive element, interlopers on good old American rock 'n' roll. This group were defenders of Elvis, Jerry Lee Lewis, even Pat Boone. They spoke of the Beatles as, to put it kindly, long-haired foreigners. Not real men. The Beatles had their defenders. This group began wearing their hair a little shaggier. Pointy shoes started being seen on some feet. Style of clothes took on a more European flair. Conversations in this crowd even mimicked the style of the Beatles' televised interviews." This division initially led to some name-calling and even cussing among these ever-so-holy schoolboys; but soon, as tensions escalated, scuffles erupted in the hallways between those who clung on to the old and those who embraced the new. The conflict Bernie witnessed seemingly concerned the superficial, but it ultimately revealed deeper scissions that would convulse the nation in the 1960s and reverberate up to the modern day.[1]

Nobody doubts the importance of the Fab Four. Emerging out of a thriving music scene in the English port city of Liverpool in the early 1960s, John Lennon, Paul McCartney, George Harrison, and Ringo Starr formed the most successful group in music history. First phenomenally successful in their homeland, they arrived in America in February 1964 and made their television debut on *The Ed Sullivan Show*, watched by a record audience of seventy-three million. The Beatles went on to push the boundaries of popular music, write songs that have become pop standards around the globe, and inspire some of the cultural and social changes of the '60s. By the time the group split in April 1970, they had scored nineteen number one singles and thirteen number one albums in the United States and were the best-selling musical act of the decade.[2] The further the '60s recede into the mists of time, it seems that the more importance is attached to the group. The number of books published on the Beatles reaches into the thousands, university departments churn out PhD dissertations on every facet of the group's story, and the number of college courses devoted to their music is multiplying at a rapid rate.

As Bernie's observations illustrate, however, the Beatles severely divided opinion when they first appeared in the United States. The long hair, the exhilarating music, and the excited reaction of the girls in Sullivan's studio audience brought squeals of delight from many youngsters and amused smiles from their parents as they sat and watched the talented Liverpudlians on their small black and white TV screens. Subsequently, young Americans rushed to the stores to buy Beatles records and Beatles-themed merchandise, formed local fan clubs and Beatles-influenced musical groups, and exhibited a willingness to embrace ideas and perspectives outside the prevailing cultural norms. Boys grew their hair obscenely long, and girls raised their hemlines enticingly high and indulged in unladylike behavior in the concert hall and on the streets.

The spectacle that they witnessed that fateful Sunday night stirred an entirely different emotion in others who feared that the mop-top haircuts, the vulgar music, and the wild screaming girls were a harbinger of unwelcome social and cultural changes to come. Newspaper editorials condemned them as an idiotic fad, religious leaders denounced the immoral behavior of their fans, and death threats and bomb scares marred their tours of North America. Many black teenagers, like their white counterparts, had little problem embracing the long-haired Englishmen but, in a decade of civil rights activism, other black youngsters decried the white intruders for cultural appropriation and preferred their own musical heroes. These worries and complaints gained traction among wider sections of the population as the decade wore on and as the Beatles adopted countercultural values, contributing to a wane in their popularity. When the Beatles broke up, they did so with much less fanfare than their joyous arrival in the US had caused only six years earlier.

Joy and Fear: The Beatles, Chicago and the 1960s examines the Beatles phenomenon through the lens of a singular city in the center of America. By exploring Beatlemania at the regional level, *Joy and Fear* offers a more nuanced and revealing story than a discussion of events in a national context could provide. In the '60s, America was a diverse country with distinct regional politics, media, music scenes, traditions and cultures, and the reception the Beatles received varied from place to place. Yet, Chicago is the ideal locality to use as a laboratory to study the Beatles phenomenon in depth. It began as a simple trading post in the late eighteenth century but, as the nation's transportation hub, the City by the Lake grew to become a thriving metropolis and America's Second City. Chicago provides not only a sizable population to assess the reaction to the Beatles but a varied one, with its substantial black constituency, large number of college students, and burgeoning suburbs.

The Windy City has a unique place in Beatles' history. Chicago-based Vee-Jay Records released the first Beatles single and album in the US. Chicago's Top 40 powerhouse WLS became the first American radio station to play one of their records, and their deejays claimed to have launched the first Beatles fan club in the US. With its 50,000-watt signal, WLS broadcast all over the country, as well as into Canada, and played a significant role in breaking the Beatles in North America. The group performed in Chicago five times, on three different tours. Only New York City staged more of their concerts in the US. When the Beatles appeared at White Sox Park on August 20, 1965, they played to more people than they did on any other single day on any of their North American tours. The most infamous press conference they ever undertook, when John Lennon explained his claim that the Beatles were more popular than Jesus, took place in Chicago in August 1966. In November 1968, the Chicago International Film Festival premiered John Lennon and Yoko Ono's first movie. In the same month, Chicago became the scene of the first obscenity case involving John and Yoko's scandalous *Two Virgins* album.

A City of Modernity and Traditionalism

From its humble beginnings, Chicago developed into a foremost commercial and manufacturing center, and it was home to some of the most influential musicians and sounds in American popular music. Hundreds of thousands of African Americans left the southern states in the Great Migration of the early twentieth century, bringing their musical traditions to the Windy City. Jazz was born in New Orleans but came of age in Chicago in the '20s as southern musicians found work in the city's restaurants, hotels, theaters, and dance halls. Chicago became the jazz capital of the world as jazz greats Jelly Roll Morton and Louis Armstrong, and the "King of Swing" and Chicago-native Benny Goodman, produced some of the most thrilling and innovative sounds in the city's nightclubs and recording studios.[3] Chicago, too, was the birthplace of gospel music in the interwar period, and legends like the "Father of Gospel" Thomas Dorsey and the "Queen of Gospel" Mahalia Jackson called the city their home.[4] Dinah Washington and Nat King Cole, who both attended DuSable High School on the South Side of the city, developed into two of the most successful entertainers of the '50s.

A second great wave of African-American migration from the southern states to Chicago profoundly influenced the evolution of rock 'n' roll music. In 1940, 277,731 African Americans lived in the city, comprising 8.1 percent of Chicago's population; by 1960, the number had risen to 812,637, or 22.8 percent of the city's residents.[5] In the bars and clubs on the South Side of the city, African-American musicians cultivated a distinctive style of blues music, commonly referred to as Chicago blues or electric blues. Instead of a solo singer playing with an acoustic guitar, a format that held sway in the southern states, in Chicago's nightspots, groups of musicians played electric guitars and percussion with a feverish energy.[6] Chess Records, founded by Polish immigrant brothers Leonard and Phil Chess in 1950, began to release this music from its headquarters at 2120 South Michigan Avenue. Indicative of the impact of the Great Migration, Chess included on its roster three Mississippian-born legends: Muddy Waters, who was born McKinley Morganfield; Chester Arthur Burnett, better known as Howlin' Wolf for his booming voice; and Willie Dixon, who became an outstanding songwriter and producer on the label. Chess also released early rock 'n' roll records such as "Rocket 88" by Jackie Brenston and his Delta Cats, which many claim to be the first of the genre, and recorded the music of rock 'n' roll pioneers Chuck Berry and Bo Diddley.[7]

"If you tried to give rock 'n' roll another name, you might call it Chuck Berry," the ever-quotable John Lennon said on the *Mike Douglas*

Show in February 1972, attesting to Berry's influence on rock 'n' roll and the Beatles.[8] Born in St. Louis, Missouri, in October 1926, Berry played his guitar in the clubs of his hometown where he started to integrate country sounds into his rhythm and blues repertoire. He headed north to Chicago looking for a record deal, and there he met Muddy Waters, who introduced him to the Chess brothers. Berry's first single on Chess, "Maybellene," reached number five on the *Billboard Hot 100* in the summer of 1955, and he enjoyed four more Top 10 hits before his star began to wane at the end of the decade.[9] Yet, his influence on other musicians continued. Elvis Presley appeared on stage with an acoustic guitar, and Fats Domino, Little Richard, and Jerry Lee Lewis played the piano; but Berry stirred many youngsters by strumming the relatively new and exciting electric guitar. Even more inspiring, he wrote his own songs, using humorous and poetic lyrics to tell stories about the everyday concerns of teenagers. The Beatles performed a number of Berry tunes and recorded versions of "Roll Over Beethoven" and "Rock and Roll Music."

Ellas Otha Bates, yet another Mississippi migrant, moved to Chicago as a child in 1934 and in the '50s became a fixture in the bars on the South Side of the city. As Bo Diddley, he began recording with Chess in 1955, releasing several classic 45s, including his first single, "Bo Diddley," a tune that introduced the influential chugging Bo Diddley beat to the world. His records failed to reach the upper echelons of the charts, but other musicians, including the British Invasion groups of the '60s, recognized his brilliance. Diddley's "Road Runner" was part of the Beatles' repertoire, and a live version of the song was recorded at the Star-Club in Hamburg, Germany, in 1962. The Rolling Stones and the Yardbirds recorded his music, and the Pretty Things took their name from a Diddley song as did the famous Crawdaddy Club in Richmond, England, where the Stones, the Yardbirds, and other British blues acts first started out.

There was far more to Chicago music than just Chuck Berry, Bo Diddley, or Chess Records. Vee-Jay, named after the first letters of its African-American owners, radio deejay Vivian Carter and her husband James Bracken, played an equally significant role in the evolution of rock 'n' roll. Headquartered on South Michigan Avenue across the street from Chess, Vee-Jay included on its roster blues artists John Lee Hooker and Jimmy Reed, doo-wop greats the Dells, the El Dorados, and the Spaniels, and soul giants the Impressions, Jerry Butler, Curtis Mayfield, Dee Clark, Gene Chandler, and Betty Everett. Other labels, such as Brunswick, Chance, Constellation, and King, opened premises on a ten-block stretch of South Michigan Avenue that became known as Record Row. Mercury, headquartered on Wacker Drive, opened a pressing plant in Chicago and competed for talent with major recording labels such as Columbia, Decca, and RCA Victor.[10]

Chicago gave the world much more than just groundbreaking music. When the city was rebuilt after the Great Fire of 1871, an architectural gem of gleaming steel, glass, and stone skyscrapers rose on the southwestern edge of Lake Michigan. Its wide boulevards, neat lines of alleys, and detached houses, all arranged on an orderly grid, were so different from the cramped terraced houses and narrow streets of European cities. "[T]he most profound aspects of American modernity grew up out of the flat, prairie land next to Lake Michigan," author Thomas Dyja asserts in his book on Chicago's vital contribution to modern-day America, *The Third Coast*. In addition to its world-famous music and innovative architecture, a rich literary tradition, mail-order retail, improvisational comedy, McDonald's, *Playboy* and softball all emerged from this most forward-looking of American cities.[11]

In spite of its innovative architecture, world-renowned popular culture and cutting-edge business practices, Chicago remained a city with one foot firmly planted in the modern world and one in traditional America. The city retained its strong links to the rural past, with the Union Stock Yards sprawling on the South Side and farmers transporting their grain, lumber, cattle, and hogs from the fertile land of the Midwest into the city, and from there, on to the rest of the nation. Those hardy immigrants able to endure Chicago's frigid snowbound winters and sweltering unforgiving summers established their own tightly knit ethnic neighborhoods that nourished customs from the old country. Streams of white migrants from the surrounding areas and the southern states journeyed to Chicago and, like their black counterparts, maintained their cultural traditions through their music. The *National Barn Dance* radio show, recorded in front of a live audience in downtown Chicago and a model for the *Grand Ole Opry*, aired on WLS on Saturday nights between 1924 and 1960. The program became an institution as the station's powerful 50,000-watt signal reached into the homes of Midwestern and southern farmers. A study undertaken in 1965 still identified Chicago as the city containing the greatest number of "country-western music households."[12]

The metropolis on the prairie also prided itself on being the City of the Big Shoulders, a tough town tied to traditional cultural values. While New York enjoyed its reputation as the cultural capital of America, and Los Angeles reveled in the glitz of Hollywood, Chicago had its roots securely placed in common sense Midwestern values. It became the first city to censor motion pictures in a systematic way as far back as 1907 when the local government appointed a censor whose job it was to cut scenes from films and ban others deemed inappropriate. By the '50s, the courts even began to question the city's eagerness to censor, but in 1961, in *Times Film Corp. v. Chicago,* the United States Supreme Court found in favor of Chicago's right to gag.[13] Chicago's Roman Catholic Church, with the largest diocese and parochial school system in the nation, exerted enormous influence on the life of the city. Under pressure from Archbishop Albert Gregory Meyer, Mayor Richard J. Daley barred the first Playboy Jazz Festival, scheduled to take place in August 1959 in Soldier Field. Comedian Lenny Bruce, who sprinkled his show with attacks on the Church, was arrested for obscenity at Chicago's Gate of Horn club on December 5, 1962. "It's possible that Bruce's comments on the Catholic Church have hit sensitive nerves in Chicago's Catholic-oriented administration and police department," *Variety* noted. A Chicago jury rendered Bruce guilty in March 1963.[14] Chicago sued Hugh Hefner, native of the city and founder of *Playboy* magazine, under obscenity laws for publishing nude pictures of actress Jayne Mansfield in the June 1963 issue of the magazine. The case, however, eventually collapsed.[15]

The local Catholic Church led the opposition to rock 'n' roll music when it first arrived on the scene in the '50s. In 1955, Chicago Inter-Student Catholic Action started a campaign to remove objectionable records from jukeboxes, television, and radio. They demanded that the music industry establish a review board that would listen to new records, furnish those that passed the review with a seal of approval, and then encourage jukebox operators, radio broadcasters, and television stations to refuse to play the unapproved music. As part of their "Crusade for Decent Disks," the group sent fifteen thousand letters to radio stations in the Chicagoland area demanding self-censorship. Radio station WIND professed innocence, declaring that they had been vetting records for years while WGN Radio and WGN-TV caved into the pressure by establishing a review panel to vet the records before they reached the airwaves. With a combination of deep analysis and wild imaginations, the records that WGN found to be a threat to the morals of the nation included "Dim, Dim the Lights," "I Wanna Hug You, Kiss You, Squeeze You," "Rock and Roll, Baby," "After the Lights Go Down Low," and "Live Fast, Love Hard, Die Young."[16] In March 1957, Cardinal Samuel Stritch, Roman Catholic Archbishop of Chicago, urged schools and church recreation centers to stop playing rock 'n' roll music. He condemned the music's "tribal rhythms" that could provoke unseemly behavior in young listeners. Record retailers in the city, however, reported no falloff in record sales because of the cardinal's remarks.[17]

Musicians continued to face censorship on Chicago radio in the '60s. Clark Weber, who became program director at WLS in 1965 and, without any prompting, called himself "Old Mother Weber," refused to air Them's "Gloria" because it discussed the singer's nocturnal encounters with a girl.[18] He also rejected Lou Christie's "Rhapsody in the Rain," a song about a young couple's dalliances in a car. Weber still refused to play the song even after Christie rerecorded it and removed the offending lyrics. "The inference still is there," insisted the eagle-eyed Weber.[19] Gene Taylor, Weber's predecessor as program director, concurred about the filthy nature of the Christie song. "There was no question about what the lyrics and the beat implied—sexual intercourse in a car, making love to the rhythm of the windshield wipers."[20] The 1967 debut single by the local band the Mauds, a remake of the Sam and Dave hit "Hold On, I'm Comin'," peaked at number fifteen on the WLS survey but not without enduring censorship. The station demanded that the Mauds record a clean version of the song that replaced the offending "Hold on, I'm comin'" with the rather confusing "Hold on, don't you worry." WLS broadcast the clean version while record stores sold the original.[21]

To understand how this city of modernity and traditionalism responded to the Beatles phenomenon, this book utilizes the voices of a diverse cast of characters: the unyielding figure of Mayor Richard J. Daley, who deemed the Beatles a threat to the rule of law; *Chicago Tribune* editor W. D. Maxwell, who first warned the nation about the Beatle menace; George Harrison's sister, who became a regular presence on Chicago radio; the socialist revolutionary who staged all of the

Beatles' concerts in the city and used much of the profits from the shows to fund left-wing causes; the African-American girl who braved a hostile environment to see the Beatles in concert; a fan club founder who disbelievingly found herself occupying a room opposite her heroes when they stayed at her father's hotel; the University of Chicago medical student who spent his summer vacation playing in a support act on the Beatles' last tour; and the suburban record store owner who opened a teen club modeled on the Cavern in Liverpool that went on to host some of the biggest bands in the world. With these stories and many others, *Joy and Fear* takes the reader back in time to experience the invigorating pleasure and discouraging anxiety that the Beatles engendered in America's Second City.

CHAPTER 1

"Four Haircuts and Four Unusual Jackets"

The Origins of the Fab Four

"In the far distant future, when our descendants study their history books, they will see one word imprinted against the year 1963 in the chronological table of events—Beatles!" leading music newspaper *New Musical Express* (NME) predicted at the end of the year that saw the emergence of the biggest sensations in British entertainment history. "For just as convincingly as 1066 marked the Battle of Hastings, or 1215 the Magna Carta, so will this present year be remembered by posterity for the achievements of four lads from Liverpool."[1] Setting aside the hyperbole expected of a pop music publication, the ascent of the Beatles, who had only released their first single "Love Me Do" in October 1962, was certainly unprecedented. Their second 45, "Please Please Me," issued in January 1963, reached number one in most British pop charts; and by the end of the year, their singles had topped the hit parade a further three times. Their debut long-playing album, *Please Please Me*, sat at the top of the charts in May and stayed there for thirty weeks until their follow up, *With the Beatles*, knocked it off the summit. The group started the year playing in small clubs and halls, and they ended it headlining sold-out shows in theaters up and down the length and breadth of the country in front of thousands of delirious fans. Because of regular appearances on radio and TV, and favorable coverage in the national newspapers, John Lennon, Paul McCartney, George Harrison, and Ringo Starr quickly

1

became household names in their homeland. The Beatles reached the pinnacle of success for a British entertainment act when they performed in front of a bejeweled and bemused Queen Mother at the Royal Variety Performance in London in November.

Their rapid climb to the top is even more remarkable considering that all four Beatles hailed from modest circumstances in the provincial Northwestern seaport of Liverpool. Richard Starkey, who later adopted the stage name Ringo Starr, was born on July 7, 1940, and raised in the deprived Dingle area by a divorced mother who worked as a barmaid. Because of illness as a child, Starr missed months of schooling, and when he finished his education, he labored in various menial jobs until he began work as an apprentice machinist. John Lennon entered the world on the ninth day of October 1940. His mother worked as an usherette in a movie theater and his father as a waiter on a ship. With his parents unable to care for him, Lennon's Aunt Mimi and Uncle George raised their precocious nephew in the lower-middle-class suburb of Woolton. His uncle died in June 1955, when John was only fourteen, and he suffered more misfortune at the age of seventeen, when his mother, with whom he had recently rekindled his relationship, was killed after being hit by a car. A failing student at school, John attended the Liverpool College of Art, drifting and unsure of his future. Mary and Jim McCartney celebrated the birth of their first child, James Paul McCartney, on June 18, 1942. Jim worked as a cotton salesman and Mary as a midwife. When Paul was fourteen, Mary died of an embolism leaving Jim to raise Paul and his younger brother, Mike, alone. Paul first met George Harrison, some eight months his junior, when they rode the same bus from their homes in Speke to their school, the Liverpool Institute. George's father drove a bus for a living and, like Paul, lived in government-subsidized housing. Paul worked as a coil winder in a factory after he left school, and George became an apprentice electrician.[2]

They may have been raised in Liverpool, but like so many youngsters born in postwar Britain, the imaginations of the four Scousers were located not in the Northwest of England but in the United States of America. The older generation regaled their children with tales of the smartly dressed GIs stationed in the United Kingdom during World War II. Some jealous Britons, mostly male, may have dismissed the Americans as "oversexed, overpaid, and over here," as the local females succumbed

John Lennon's childhood home at 251 Menlove Avenue, saved as an historic landmark by the National Trust and an attraction for tourists from all over the world. In the 1950s, Liverpool was seen as a musical backwater by the music industry based in London.

to the charms of their Hollywood idols made flesh, but they could not deny that the Americans were generous with their chocolate, chewing gum, cigarettes, and nylons. So-called Cunard Yanks—local seamen who worked on the ships that sailed from Liverpool to New York—and the soldiers stationed at the American Air Force base at nearby Burtonwood continued to bring the American influence into Liverpool after the war. "My so-called 'Americanization' started at birth because by that time—1943–44—the whole world, especially the West, was becoming Americanized," John Lennon stated in an interview in 1975, referring to the American movies, television shows, comics, fashion, food, and music that began to dominate British life. "I was brought up on Coca Cola, Heinz beans—which we thought were English—Heinz ketchup, and Doris Day movies. Arriving in the States was a great thrill, but there weren't many surprises since I'd seen so many Hollywood films."[3]

"American culture was there all the time," Paul McCartney said of his youth. "You would be seeing things on television like early Fred Astaire films, Bob Hope and Bing Crosby, that kind of thing, of our parents' generation. So a lot of what they liked was American; a lot of what we liked was, therefore, American."[4]

"We used to look to America for all those great records, and clothes and guitars, and anything good seemed to be from America," George Harrison admitted to disc jockey Scott Muni.[5] Hollywood movies, in particular, grabbed the imagination of Ringo Starr, who later pursued an acting career. Rather surprisingly, Starr revealed that Gene Autry, who he first saw in the movie *South of the Border* in the Saturday morning pictures, became the most significant musical influence in his life. "It may sound like a joke. Go and have a look in my bedroom. It's covered with Gene Autry posters. He was my first musical influence. He sent shivers down my spine when he put his leg over the horn on the saddle and sang, 'South of the border, down Mexico way.'"[6]

Seeing the singing cowboy Gene Autry sing "South of the Border" in the movie of the same name, inspired Ringo Starr's love of music.

This early exposure to the United States touched off a lifetime fascination with the country and a reverence for its popular culture. Richard Starkey and a friend wanted to immigrate from the United Kingdom to Texas, but the two young men soon tired of the endless form filling and resigned themselves to staying in Liverpool. If Starkey could not move to America, he could at least live like an American. Starkey joined a rock 'n' roll band called the Raving Texans, which became Rory Storm and the Hurricanes and, already nicknamed "Rings" because of the many rings on his fingers, he adopted the cowboy-sounding "Ringo."[7] According to Paul, Ringo introduced his friends to many American treasures. "It started off as Bourbon and 7 Up which Ringo drank, being the sophisticat amongst us. He always was. If there's anything American, like Lark cigarettes, Ringo knew it all. He had a big car. He might have been a GI, Ringo, the way he lived. He had a GI kind of lifestyle. He had a Ford Zephyr Zodiac."[8]

Lennon, in particular, imitated the rebellious slouches, the sullen pouts, and the gum-chewing swagger of American actors like Marlon Brando and James Dean who exuded an enticing disrespect for authority, so different from the deference that reigned in the UK. "I used to dress like a Teddy Boy and identify with Marlon Brando and Elvis Presley, but I was never really in any street fights or down-home gangs. I was just a suburban kid imitating the rockers," Lennon recalled of his youth. "I wanted to be the tough James Dean all the time."[9]

In January 1964, one month before the Beatles first came to the States, they told an interviewer about their admiration for the US. "America's the place, isn't it?" said Paul when asked why they wanted to visit the US. When asked if they were going to perform the Isley Brothers' hit "Twist and Shout," John replied, "No, we don't want to be doing it in America. We did it here 'cause they haven't heard it over here. And then their versions are a hundred times better than ours anyway. You know the Americans."[10]

American music, television, and movies fired the imagination of the four Liverpool lads and, like most British youth, they could not avoid comparing these golden images with the uninspiring world surrounding them. Liverpool seemed colorless and lifeless compared to the breathtaking images of the US they saw in Hollywood movies. Blue skies, sunshine, beaches, and palm trees contrasted sharply with the unrelenting rain, gray skies, and dampness of austere Britain. The sweeping landscape of the West and the endless highways disappearing into the distance suggested escape and freedom when compared to over-populated Britain with its narrow roads and cramped living spaces.

George Harrison confirmed these positive views of the country when he became the first of the four to set foot on American soil. "I just can't tell you how much I enjoyed America," George excitedly told an interviewer when he returned home from a trip to see his sister Louise in Benton, southern Illinois, in September 1963. George gazed in wonder at the dazzling skyscrapers he saw on his visit to New York City and the spectacular sandstone cliffs and expansive woodlands that surrounded him when he camped overnight at the Garden of the Gods in southern Illinois' Shawnee National Forest. "Their standard of living is so much higher than ours in every way," George exclaimed, "they all have central heating and air-conditioning, and every home has a big

George Harrison's childhood home at 12 Arnold Grove. No wonder America looked so glamorous!

television." He enjoyed the novelty of drive-in movies and waitresses on roller skates, and he envied the luxurious Cadillac driven by his sister's friend, the plentiful amount of ice in drinks, and the multitude of television channels and radio stations. This affluence, together with the hot weather and blue skies, convinced George that he would want to "live there for ever."[11]

The skiffle music craze of the mid-'50s, from which the Beatles emerged, had its origins in this infatuation with the US. Skiffle, a term that originated in 1920s America to refer to impromptu music-making, became all the rage in 1950s Britain as bands adopted the songs of American blues and folk artists like Leadbelly and Woody Guthrie. Glasgow-born Anthony Donegan, who took the name "Lonnie" from blues musician Lonnie Johnson and scaled the charts with Leadbelly's "Rock Island Line" in 1956, inspired thousands of young people to pursue their musical interests. Skiffle was affordable to cash-strapped young Britons unable to purchase expensive musical instruments. Budding musicians simply needed a single acoustic guitar or banjo and someone who could keep a basic rhythm on a washboard or an upright bass made from a tea chest, a broom handle, and a rope. The "skiffle craze blossomed and groups were formed from Land's End to John

O'Groats," musician Chas McDevitt wrote in his book on the history of skiffle. "Every town could muster a dozen groups; every barrack room, youth club and church hall echoed to the pounding of the washboard....At one point in 1957, it was estimated that there were between 30,000 and 50,000 groups in the British Isles. The sale of guitars was booming and it was reported that more music shops than jewelers were being broken into."[12] Skiffle music became so popular that the British Broadcasting Corporation (BBC), which held a monopoly on radio broadcasting in the UK, bowed to the demand, and in June 1957 began to broadcast the *Saturday Skiffle Club*. More bizarrely, Kellogg's began to give away a Skiffle Whistle with each box of their Rice Krispies breakfast cereal.

Each of the four boys began their musical careers in local skiffle combos. In the summer of 1956, John Lennon formed the Quarrymen, named after his school, Quarry Bank High School for Boys. Paul McCartney joined in the summer of 1957, and shortly after, Paul's school friend, George Harrison, who had previously been in the skiffle band the Rebels, became a member of the fledgling group. Before he joined Rory Storm and the Hurricanes, Ringo Starr played percussion in his first band, the Eddie Clayton Skiffle Group. By the late '50s, however, the skiffle craze had petered out. In October 1958, the BBC renamed the *Saturday Skiffle Club* the *Saturday Club*, and Kellogg's moved onto the next fad and replaced the Skiffle Whistles with colored marbles.

While skiffle proved to be a fad, another American sound, rock 'n' roll, enjoyed much greater

"Rock Island Line," which became a UK hit in 1956, instigated the skiffle craze that gave birth to the Quarrymen, the forerunners of the Beatles. Young Britons inspired by this song were probably unaware that the title referred to the Chicago, Rock Island and Pacific Railroad line that ran southwest out of Chicago.

longevity. Rock 'n' roll, derived from African-American rhythm and blues music, began to cross over to an enthusiastic young white audience in the mid-'50s because of its unconventionality. The young relished the not so subtle sexual innuendo in many of the lyrics, but the words of many rock 'n' roll songs were simple or incomprehensible and remained of less importance than the exciting sound and attitude of the performers. Teenagers loved the simple riffs and chugging rhythms of the music that emanated aggression and defiance. American rock 'n' rollers were outsiders, rebels who radiated wild abandon, epitomized by the screaming and hollering vocal style and the raucous stage antics of stars like Little Richard and Jerry Lee Lewis. While the big bands and popular balladeers of the decade remained slick, staid, and restrained, rock 'n' roll was full of raw power and exhilarating rhythms that touched young people on an emotional level.[13]

As the sounds and images of rock 'n' roll stars began to drift across the Atlantic, one man captured the imagination of the British public like no other. Born on January 8, 1935, in Tupelo, Mississippi, Elvis Presley moved with his poverty-stricken parents to Memphis, Tennessee, when he was thirteen years old. At the crossroads of American music, Elvis absorbed the sounds of gospel music in the Church and country and western, and rhythm and blues music on the radio. In 1953, Elvis, then aged eighteen, entered Sam Phillips' Sun Studios to make a recording as a present for his mother. Phillips liked his unique sensual voice and asked Presley to record "That's All Right (Mama)," which Sun Records released as his first 45 in 1954. In May 1956, his debut single in the UK, "Heartbreak Hotel," entered the charts, rising to number two, and in the summer of 1957, Presley had his first number one single in Britain with "All Shook Up." Once they saw magazine photos of the exotically named star, young Britons became even more thrilled as they observed that Presley was blessed with film star good looks. Elvis fixed his top lip into a permanent sneer, greased back his long black hair, grew sideburns down the side of his face, and wore brightly colored clothes that stood out from the traditional dark suits and white shirts worn by most performers. Movie newsreels of Elvis revealed a wild stage show. He virtually made love to the microphone stand as he swiveled his hips in an overtly sexual manner, earning him the nickname Elvis the Pelvis.[14]

"It was Elvis who really got me interested in pop music and started me buying records," said Lennon, who first heard Elvis on the "Jack Johnson Show" on Radio Luxembourg. "I thought that early stuff of his was great. When I heard 'Heartbreak Hotel,' I thought, 'This is it,' and I started trying to grow sideboards, and all that gear."[15]

Paul McCartney thought that "the Messiah has arrived" when he first encountered the King of Rock 'n' Roll.[16] "Before I actually heard an Elvis record, I was aware of him as an image because I'd seen him in an ad for 'Heartbreak Hotel' on the back page of the *NME*," Paul told *Mojo* magazine. "To

This advert in the New Musical Express *of May 6, 1956, convinced Paul McCartney that the messiah had arrived. All four Beatles retained vivid memories of first hearing "Heartbreak Hotel," and Elvis, more than anyone else, inspired them to become musicians.*

hear 'Heartbreak Hotel,' I had to go into a record shop in Liverpool and listen to it through headphones in one of those booths. It was a magical moment, the beginning of an era."[17]

Ringo, too, became besotted by the Memphis God. "Elvis changed my head around. He was the first teenager in my life. Johnnie Ray, Frankie Laine, and Bill Haley were my early heroes, around '54. But they were always a bit like me dad. Elvis was the first *lad* who came out. He totally blew me away. I loved him so."[18]

George Harrison retained a vivid memory of first hearing "Heartbreak Hotel," he told an interviewer in 1999. "One of the biggest things in my life, for rock 'n' roll, was riding along on my bicycle probably '57 or something like that, I was 14 or thereabouts, and I heard 'Heartbreak Hotel' coming out of somebody's house on the radio and it is one of those things I'll never forget. It changed the course of my life, what a sound, what a record!"[19]

Introducing the Beatles

Many of those aroused by the skiffle craze soon lost interest in pursuing a musical career, including some of the members of the Quarrymen, leaving the dedicated few like John, Paul, and George to soldier on. Inspired by the energy of skiffle and the exotic wildness of rock 'n' roll, the three became part of an indigenous music scene that emerged around so-called beat music in the late '50s. Skiffle musicians discarded their tea chests, broomsticks, washboards, and acoustic guitars and replaced them with drums and electric guitars. Beat music emphasized energetic vocals, an attention-grabbing drum beat, and a strong pulsating electric bass; all played loud and fast for an eager dance crowd. The beat groups varied their repertoire by performing chart hits, show tunes, and slow numbers; but all with the same simple beat and insistent guitar sound. The Quarrymen was reborn in 1960 as a beat band with electric guitars and a changed name, the Beatles. The new name derived from their admiration for Buddy Holly and the Crickets, hence the insect beetle, but they changed the spelling of the word to playfully signify their allegiance to beat music. Drummer Pete Best and John's art school friend, bassist Stuart Sutcliffe, joined John, Paul, and George in the new band. Sutcliffe left the group in the summer of 1961 and tragically died from a brain aneurysm the following April. In the summer of 1962, just as they were making their first record, the group fired Pete Best and replaced him with Ringo Starr, the final piece in the Beatles jigsaw.

The four youngsters were all musically gifted, confident, and ambitious, but the group comprised four distinct personalities. Many who met John Lennon as a young man commented on his brashness. Roy Carr, then of the group the Executives and later a music journalist, first met Lennon and the Beatles in Liverpool. "At the bar of the Cavern, where we speak for the first time, he strikes me as a typically mouthy Scouser, incredibly self-confident. If there's a girl he fancies he just starts chatting her up, whispers something in her ear that either makes her laugh or flounce off in a huff."[20]

Frank Allen, who played in Hamburg with his band Cliff Bennett and the Rebel Rousers alongside the Beatles in 1962, was left bewildered when he first met Lennon. "I wandered into the club in the afternoon and ran into John Lennon who was coming out of the dressing rooms. I introduced myself, said I had really enjoyed their set and wished him all the best for their new record. He looked at me suspiciously I thought and said, 'Yes. It's Frank, isn't it? I enjoyed you guys as well. I've been talking to people in the club, and it seems that next to Cliff in the band you're the most popular member. I don't know why. Your harmonies are fucking ridiculous.' I was a bit dumbstruck. I wasn't sure if I had been insulted or missed a joke, so I just wished him well again. He replied in the same way, and we went on our separate ways."[21] Lennon could be humorous and charming, and talk thoughtfully and intelligently on a range of subjects, but he could also be contrary and mean-spirited.

If John was the most outspoken and complicated of the four, Paul was the most confident and the foremost musical talent. His choirboy good looks, charm, and willingness to spend time conversing with fans soon made him a favorite. His musicianship impressed Lennon from the start, and McCartney went on to play not only bass on the Beatles' records but, occasionally, lead guitar, piano, and drums. Many observers portray Lennon as the radical restrained by McCartney's mainstream instincts, but this is far from the truth. Lennon could write a sentimental ballad to match McCartney, and McCartney could be just as outspoken and acidic in his wit as Lennon. Where they differed was in temperament.

Lennon remained more absorbed with his personal demons while McCartney stayed less troubled and more optimistic. Lennon lived the life of the tortured artist who looked inside for inspiration while McCartney showed a more profound empathy and respect for others. Paul often wrote songs about fictional characters or about people and events he had observed: lonely people, struggling mothers, teenage runaways, working girls, and ambitious writers. He was more calculating and careful in his words and actions, while John was more impulsive and reckless, often exaggerating and looking to shock. Lennon's thoughts spilled out, often radically changing his mind on issues and contradicting himself from interview to interview, while McCartney tended to tell the same neat anecdotal stories in every interview over the years. Paul was the consummate entertainer who craved the applause of the live crowd and sought the affirmation of bestselling records. Out of all four Beatles, Paul relished fame the most.

George, the only Beatle not touched by either the death of a mother or the divorce of parents at a young age, seemed the most serene of the four. Dubbed "the quiet Beatle," he was not as dominant as John or Paul but could be equally forthright in his comments. Cynthia Lennon, John's first wife, called Harrison "the most tactless, blunt and often pig-headed of the four Beatles."[22] With his slow, languid style of talking, George often seemed the most thoughtful and taciturn Beatle. To the world, the group emphasized an egalitarian spirit, but, behind the scenes, a strict hierarchy prevailed with Lennon the founder and leader, Paul his co-equal as a songwriting partner, and George the youngest who deferred to the other two. George never really desired the limelight either on stage, where he allowed Lennon and McCartney to take the spotlight, or off stage, where he grew tired of the clawing fans and never satisfied media. The grumpiest of the four, George was the one who least liked acting in the films and disliked the showbiz part of the job, preferring to be a musician perfecting his guitar playing. In 1992, *Rock Compact Disc* magazine asked several people who had known the Beatles, including deejays Kenny Everett, Annie Nightingale, and Alan Freeman, former Beatle Pete Best, and entertainers Kenny Lynch and Screaming Lord Sutch, to name their favorite Beatle. Maybe as a reflection of his withdrawn demeanor and his unwillingness to cozy up to the media, most picked either John or Paul, while no one chose George.[23]

Ringo, not George, was the true quiet Beatle and the least confident of the four. He was the last to join the group, becoming a Beatle when they had already earned a recording contract and were on the verge of stardom. Ringo was unsure of his place in the quartet, believing the others could fire him as quickly as they had Pete Best. He was less formally schooled than the other three grammar-educated Beatles, and he never developed their songwriting talents. As an only child, Ringo was exceedingly happy to be part of a brotherhood. His character, just like his drumming, complemented rather than dominated proceedings: reliable, restrained, and unselfish. There were strains and rivalries among the other three but Ringo, the most affable and least combative of the four, was crucial in easing tensions. Ringo could be outspoken, sullen, and forthright with reporters and fans when annoyed, but his protruding nose, droll humor, and easy-going nature made him a firm favorite with the fans and the media.

The Beat Boom

Many who saw the Beatles play at the tiny Cavern Club in Liverpool thought that they were an exceptional band who stood out from the thousands of other beat groups who played up and down the length of the country. The Beatles made their first appearance at the Cavern in February 1961 and went on to perform nearly three hundred times, at what became their subterranean home. One Cavern regular was Ray O'Brien, who attended the same secondary school as Paul McCartney and George Harrison, and went on to work for a shipping firm in Liverpool. "I was friendly with a guy there, and one day he said to me at lunchtime, 'Do you fancy coming down to the Cavern,' which I vaguely heard about. So off I tottled, and the Beatles were playing. So I became a regular going at lunchtime, and the Beatles used to play; I think on Mondays, Wednesdays, and Fridays with Gerry and the Pacemakers, who were second only to the Beatles at that time. I was going there for most of 1962 when I worked for the shipping company." Ray was mesmerized by what he saw. "Well, they left an incredible impression, because in Britain at that time, it was like Cliff Richard and the Shadows, Mark Wynter and John Leyton who had this clean-cut image. And suddenly in this dingy old cellar in Liverpool, were four guys. Wow it doesn't seem that long now, but it was what seemed to us in those days long hair, black turtleneck sweaters, and black leather trousers. Looking quite outrageous and the sound, the sound was just so loud and magnetic. It was just so different from the pop music of the early '60s in England. I mean in Liverpool at that time, they stood out."[24]

Ray found that each of the Beatles had distinct personalities on stage. "The drummer at that time was a quiet sort of fella, Pete Best. He was the most popular with the girls. Not Paul McCartney, it was Pete Best they were screaming for. He hardly ever said anything, and he had this sort of moody sort of James Dean look in the background. Paul McCartney did most of the talking, and you would have thought he was the leader of the band. George Harrison hardly said a word. He was a very, very quiet chap, very quiet. John Lennon would occasionally just come out with sort of off-the-cuff jokes or sort of thing or shouting at somebody in the audience. But Paul McCartney was the main man sort of 'we are now going to play,' introducing the numbers." Screaming, which became a feature of Beatles' concerts at the height of their fame, was seldom heard at the hot, sweaty, and noisy Cavern. Instead, those in attendance danced to the music, stared at the groups on stage, and shouted out song requests. Many of the boys in the crowd, like Ray, stood near the back of the small cellar, eyeing both the Beatles on stage and the girls near the front and under the arches at the side. The "steaming walls and smell of disinfectant" provided a romantic backdrop to proceedings.[25]

Ray witnessed the infancy of the most popular group in music history, but his friend cemented his place in the story when he became a Beatle for a day. "I worked with a chap, and he used to go at lunchtime, but he was a drummer in a band. I don't know what had happened, but I think Pete Best hadn't turned up on this particular day. They knew this guy, and they said, 'Oh, will you come back with us and play drums?' A guy called Marcus Andrew actually his name was, and he got back, but he could only play three numbers. 'I'm sorry I've got to go. My lunch hour is nearly up.' You got an hour for your lunch, and that was it." So Marcus stepped off the Cavern stage, straightened his tie, walked through the crowd, and disappeared out the door, ending his short career as a Beatle.[26]

Journalist Chris Hutchins saw the Beatles play in Hamburg in November 1962 and was equally impressed. "Music agent and manager Don Arden asked me to set up a rival music paper to the *NME*. I was planning that, and *NME* owner Maurice Kinn got wind of it and fired me on the spot. I phoned Don Arden and said, 'Can we start that new music paper now, because I've lost my job over it?' And he said, 'Well, I can't raise the money. I haven't been able to raise the money. But if you're free, if you've got a couple of weeks free, you can take Little Richard to Hamburg for me because he hates flying and he wants to go on the train, and he needs somebody to be with him.' Well, you know, I had nothing else to do, so with a few possessions in my bag I set off with Little Richard for Hamburg. And we were at the Star Club on Little Richard's opening night, and he went out to the stage while I stayed in the dressing room. He went out to the stage to see what was happening and he came back in and said, 'You've got to see these kids on stage. They are fantastic. This is the best thing I've seen in years.' I went out with Little Richard and saw the Beatles, and like Little Richard, I was bowled over. They were fantastic and they had such incredible energy. Although I learned later of course that a lot of that came from pills." The Beatles had little in the way of a stage act. "I don't remember them doing repartee in Hamburg because of course a lot of the audience was predominantly German. I don't think they bothered talking. They might have made a few remarks to themselves, which would be overheard by the audience. There was no such thing as an act."[27]

Maybe the four lads would have remained in the bars and clubs of Liverpool and Hamburg if it wasn't for Brian Epstein, who helped them gain national and international fame ahead of the other beat groups. Twenty-seven-year-old Epstein, who ran the North End Music Stores (NEMS), a shop in Liverpool, became the Beatles' manager after he saw them perform at the Cavern in November 1961. The music business was based in London, and few of the other beat groups in the North were fortunate enough to have a manager, never mind one with the honesty and artistic flair of Epstein, a businessman and trained actor. While many managers who sought short-term financial gain exploited or mishandled their young charges, Epstein placed the careers of the Beatles above his short-term monetary gains. Less than two months after meeting the group, Epstein secured his boys an audition at Decca records, but the label decided not to offer them a contract. Epstein persisted. He brought the Decca demo to other record companies, who also turned him down; but in the spring of 1962, the Beatles signed to Parlophone, a division of EMI.[28]

The Appeal of the Beatles: Music

EMI provided their new recruits with access to their state-of-the-art recording facilities, the EMI Recording Studios on Abbey Road in London, and, more importantly, a seasoned record producer to nurture their talent. George Martin, a thirty-six-year-old working-class Londoner, adopted a clipped upper-class accent that, combined with his tall frame, made him look and sound like a high-end dentist. Martin's remit was to control the recording session, deciding what to record and how to record it. "In the early days, when they had a new song, they stood around me with their guitars while I sat on a high stool and they sang the song to me," Martin explained. "Then I would suggest some things in the arrangement: what to do for the beginning, the middle and the ending, the solos, you know, and I would always try to demonstrate what I meant at the piano."[29] After much prodding from the Beatles, Martin picked the Lennon and McCartney song "Love Me Do" as their first 45. For their next release, he chose "Please Please Me" but only after they changed the arrangements to suit his specifications. "If you speeded that up, probably doubled the speed of it and made a little hook at the beginning we might have something, maybe put on the harmonica," he told the group when he first heard the song. They went away and returned with "this version which had been changed according to my suggestions."[30]

Over time, the Beatles seized more control of the recording process but still turned to George Martin for advice. "Later on it became a question of orchestration and my injecting instruments that they couldn't cope with themselves. It was the knowledge of that and what one could do with it, and also recording techniques. The addition of things they hadn't thought of—all the backward guitar stuff and that kind of thing."[31] George Martin's jazz and classical background allowed him to recommend instruments, outside musicians, and sound effects that were not traditionally part of the rock 'n' roll pantheon to augment the Beatles' sound. Martin suggested that Paul use strings on his song "Yesterday," which then inspired the Beatles to employ a classical string ensemble on "Eleanor Rigby," the Baroque-sounding piano on "In My Life," and the sitar on "Norwegian Wood."

"The fact that we did that opened up the way for the world being our oyster," Martin reflected, "and it turned the boys on to realizing that they weren't limited to three guitars and a drum kit and that they could pluck from the palette of colors anyone they wanted."[32]

Most performers depended on professional songwriters for songs, but the Beatles wrote their own material. From "Love Me Do" onwards they composed all their own singles and most of the tracks on their albums. The Beatles became so prolific that they provided songs for other artists. Kenny Lynch became the first artist to cover a Beatles song when he issued "Misery" in March 1963. Others soon followed. Billy J. Kramer, Duffy Power, the Kestrels, Tommy Quickly, the Fourmost, Cilla Black, and the Rolling Stones all recorded Lennon and McCartney songs in 1963. Lennon and McCartney became so quickly recognized as groundbreaking songwriters that BBC television featured them on *Songwriters* in July 1965, and Granada broadcast *The Music of Lennon and McCartney* in December 1965.

With the help of George Martin, the Beatles turned elementary compositions into outstanding recordings. Beatles songs employed excellent arrangements, strong melody, and inventive harmonies. They avoided complexity; there was no need for repeated listens to enjoy their fruits; they wrote short and catchy compositions. Their early numbers, which often employed an energy that surged upwards and built to a crescendo, produced in the listener a euphoric adrenaline rush. Uncomplicated lyrics and clear vocals encouraged the sing-a-long nature of the songs. On the early numbers, Lennon and McCartney portrayed themselves as sensitive, intelligent young men who cared deeply about the feelings of young women. Many lyrics portrayed them crying ("Ask Me Why," "It Won't Be Long," "Not a Second Time," and "I'll Cry Instead") and exhibiting an appreciation for the female side in a relationship ("She Loves You" and "Thank You Girl"). While many rock 'n' roll songs celebrated the male pursuits of cars and chasing girls, the Beatles' songs dealt with universal themes of interconnection and romantic relationships.

John, Paul, George, and Ringo fashioned a unique sound that blended a variety of genres that they were exposed to as they grew up in Liverpool. The musicals they watched in the movie theaters provided an early source of inspiration as did BBC radio, which aired a variety of musical forms from classical to big band. Sing-alongs at house parties introduced them to pop standards of the day, music hall tunes, and traditional British and Irish music. Paul McCartney was particularly taken with the American songs from the pre-rock 'n' roll era first introduced to him by his father, Jim McCartney, who had played trumpet and piano as the leader of Jim Mac's Jazz Band. In the '50s, Jim entertained relatives at family gatherings by playing American jazz standards, show tunes, and pop ballads on his piano. "What would happen would be, us kids would arrive at the do, the carpets would get rolled back, all the women would sit around on chairs with their little drinks of rum-and-black, gin-and-it, Babycham and all that," Paul McCartney reminisced about his youth. "Someone would play the piano and it was normally my dad. They would play all these old songs: 'When the red, red robin...', 'Caroline Moon', 'Bye Bye Blackbird.' They'd sing these all night, that was the party."[33]

Rock 'n' roll, of course, stirred the Beatles the most. The driving riffs of Chuck Berry, the powerful vocal style of Little Richard, and the dreamy harmonies of the Everly Brothers fascinated them; but Buddy Holly and the Crickets were especially important. "Buddy Holly was a very big influence because he wrote and sang his own stuff, which is what we were doing," said Paul McCartney. "And he played his own solos. So it gave us clues. When we do it, we'll play a guitar ourselves, not have a guitarist, and we'll stand with a mic-stand. We'll do the solos, we'll sing the songs and we'll write them. When you think about it, that's all The Beatles did. That was the revolution. Even the Stones and those guys didn't do that. We took all that from Buddy, really."[34] The Beatles managed, for the first time, to combine the raw energy of rock 'n' roll with the sweet harmonies found on softer sounding records. "We were mashing Buddy Holly's voice and guitar playing with The Everly Brothers—we loved the harmonies," Paul said later. "Me and John thought we were Don and Phil."[35]

Coming from the city nicknamed "Nashville of the North," it was no surprise to see American country and western music permeate the Beatles' sound. "I listen to country music," Lennon revealed of his influences. "I started imitating Hank Williams when I was fifteen, before I could play the guitar." When Lennon started playing in the clubs, Williams' "Honky Tonk Blues" became one of his favorite songs to perform.[36]

"We went after a real Country and Western flavor when we wrote this one," Paul told *Disc* magazine in November 1964 referring to the song "I Don't Want to Spoil the Party" featured on the new *Beatles for Sale* album. "John and I do the singing in that style, and George takes a real country solo on guitar."[37] John Lennon recognized the country influence in "I Feel Fine" and in some of his other compositions. "I suppose it has a bit of a country-and-western feel about it, but then so have a lot of our songs."[38]

"The first guitarist I actually heard was Jimmie Rodgers, 'the Singing Brakeman,'" reminisced Harrison about the music that inspired him to pick up the guitar. He referenced Chet Atkins' fingerpicking style as a significant influence on his guitar playing.[39]

Ringo particularly loved country music. He sang lead on the Beatles' remake of the Buck Owens song, "Act Naturally," included on their 1965 album *Help!* Indeed, Ringo's first forays into songwriting, such as "What Goes On" on *Rubber Soul,* which he co-wrote with Lennon and McCartney, and his first solo credit "Don't Pass Me By" on the *White Album,* have a distinct country and western sound. When they auditioned for BBC radio in 1962, producer Peter Pilbeam found that the Beatles were "an unusual group not as 'rocky' as most, more country and western with a tendency to play music."[40]

The Beatles fused rock 'n' roll and country, and paid attention to classic songwriting, but their primary love became contemporary African-American music. Like many working-class youths growing up in Britain, the four Beatles wanted something different from the staid and dreary, and admired a music that featured exotic slang and strong sexual innuendo. The smooth vocal harmonies, passionate singing, and strong rhythmic beats ideal for entertaining a live dance audience further drew the Beatles to black music. The Beatles covered a total of twelve songs on their first two albums, eleven of them recorded by African-American artists. The girl-group sound of the Crystals, the Chiffons, the Shirelles, and the Ronettes inspired their harmonies and lyrics. The handclaps and harmonica on their early records derived from African-American traditions. They enthusiastically embraced the music of Detroit's Motown label, and included three covers of Motown songs on their second album. James Jamerson, the bassist on most classic Motown recordings of the '60s, inspired McCartney's style of bass playing. "Oh yes, he was a major influence all around; he was certainly where I picked up a lot of my style. I simply loved all of his bass lines—each one was a gem in itself."[41]

"If the Beatles ever wanted a sound it was R&B," McCartney summed up. "That's what we used to listen to, what we used to like and what we wanted to be like. Black, that was basically it."[42]

The Beatles' music stood out from other contemporary recordings because of the mixing of styles, but there was no doubt about the major source of their inspiration. "Where did the Beatles get the vocabulary of their songs from (all those 'yeahs' and 'babies' and 'twists')?" *Record Mirror* journalist David Griffiths asked in February 1964. "Where did they get the inspiration for their rhythm-and-blues and ballad melodies and chord sequences from? Where did they get their drum kits and electrified guitars from? The answer of course is America. Without the influence of American pop music the Beatles would simply be four haircuts and four unusual jackets."[43] In recognition of this unique mix of American styles, when Vee-Jay Records released the first Beatles single in the US, "Please Please Me," they seemed unsure how to describe the sound of the Beatles and settled for advertising them as "R&B, C&W and Pop."[44]

With each successive record, it became clear that the Beatles considered themselves artists rather than entertainers. John, Paul, and George all passed the eleven-plus examination, earning them entry to the best secondary schools in Liverpool. From an early age, John showed an aptitude for art and literature, often drawing and writing poetry. He attended art college after leaving school and published a book of writings *In His Own Write* in March 1964.

Paul studied Art and English literature at A Level and, even when their music careers took off, the Beatles' bassist still held artistic ambitions. "I decided I'd like to enter art college if we flopped in show business," Paul told the *NME* in August 1963. "I got my GCE in art, and I'm still very interested in the subject. I often sketch when we're on tour."[45]

George performed less well at the Liverpool Institute, but significantly, art was the only subject he passed in his last school exams. "While most of the other lads spent their Wednesday afternoons panting round the school running track I would be content to take a notebook and dream up some new sketches," he told Tony Barrow in 1963. "I was fond of sport—specially swimming and athletics—in the early years but I was fonder still of art."[46] Ringo missed much schooling because of illness, but he became a gifted photographer and, later in life, a painter who exhibited his work. Once the budding artists formed a musical group, the Beatles mixed with poets and artists in Liverpool and in the German seaport of Hamburg. As artists, they were inquiring, intellectually curious, and open to new ideas. They wanted to experiment and expand their horizons, to be creative, and to make each record different from the previous one. Their artistic flair and outlook led them to dabble in more poetic lyrics, avant-garde ideas, and psychedelic sounds.

The Appeal of the Beatles: Appearance

The Beatles' initial appeal was as much visual as musical, and their strong group identity separated them from a music scene ruled by solo artists. The reigning kings of popular music, Bing Crosby, Perry Como, Frank Sinatra, Chuck Berry, Elvis Presley, and in England, Cliff Richard, were all solo acts. Previously, anonymous musicians stayed in the background behind the good-looking front man, but all four Beatles sang and played instruments, and there was no set lead vocalist. Even other groups that emerged contemporarily with the Beatles like the Animals, the Rolling Stones, the Who, Herman's Hermits, the Hollies, and the Yardbirds all employed lead singers. "It was something new," stated George Martin. "When I first listened to them, I tried each voice in turn, wondering which one was going to be my Cliff Richard. Paul was the prettiest, John the most off-beat, and I didn't think George's voice was as good as those two. It wasn't until they started together that I suddenly realized they should be recognized as a group."[47] They were not named Something and the Others, as was usual at the time, but the singular name the Beatles, and they all dressed alike, adding to the image of four equal members.

Brian Epstein alone had the vision to realize that if appropriately marketed, this scruffy bunch of Northerners possessed the talent and the personalities to appeal to a mass audience. When Epstein first saw the group, they dressed in leather and smoked, ate, and fooled around on stage. To sell them to TV and radio executives and, eventually, to a mainstream audience, Epstein had to change their look and curtail their stage antics. He persuaded them to ditch their leathers for European-influenced Mod clothes, forbade them to swear or smoke on stage, and insisted that they bow at the end of their performance. They wore Italian-style tightly-fitted dark mohair suits, shirts with button-down collars, slim ties, and ankle-high boots with thick and slightly tapered Cuban heels. At other times, they dressed in French-style black polo neck sweaters or gray, collarless suits modeled on Parisian designer Pierre Cardin's ideas.

More than anything else, their hair gained the most media attention and added a joie de vivre to their visual appeal. Astrid Kirchherr, a German art student they befriended in Hamburg, first styled Stuart Sutcliffe and George Harrison's hair into the so-called French look: hair combed forward over the forehead, not, as was customary at the time, slicked back over the ears with the aid of grease. Another German friend, Jurgen Vollmer, cut Paul and John's hair into the French style when they visited him in Paris in October 1961. The French haircut was not new to England when the Beatles adopted it, and some expressed anger that these shabby Northerners obtained credit for originating the haircut. "Art students have had this sort of haircut for years—even when the Beatles were using hair cream!" scoffed Mick Jagger when asked if the Beatles inspired his hairstyle.[48] The Beatles let their hair grow long, emphasizing their artistic side, and cementing their zany look. The Beatles' long hair, and their falsetto-backing vocals, added to their somewhat effeminate and non-threatening appeal, especially important for gaining a young female audience.

The Appeal of the Beatles: Personalities

Their stylish look, and especially the haircuts, provided a marketing gimmick for Brian Epstein and played a significant part in the Beatles gaining media coverage, but so too did their charismatic personalities. Some credit Liverpool as the roots of their sense of humor, but working-class boys and girls all over Britain, not just in the Beatles' hometown, developed a dry, irreverent, and rather aggressive humor as a defense mechanism against the travails of the school and the street. The Beatles demonstrated a dislike of authority and middle-class stuffiness in their humor, but also an unpretentiousness and self-deprecating wit that endeared them to their fans. They mixed this with a sense of the absurd and manic, much of it learned from the anarchic humor seen on their favorite radio series, *The Goon Show*.

They would display all of their comedic qualities and impishness when talking to unsuspecting interviewers. In February 1964, American deejay James Carroll became a victim of their surreal humor when he asked the Beatles whether they ever visited a barber, a question they had by now tired of hearing.

"Yeah. Just to keep it trimmed. But sometimes we do it ourselves, you know," replied Paul.

"With our feet," added John.

"The other thing is, it's really only our eyebrows that are growing upwards," Paul added, taking his cue from his band mate.

Moving on to safer ground, Carroll asked Ringo to name his favorite drummer. "What about Big Deaf Arthur?" the by now giddy John prodded Ringo.

"Oh yeah, Big Deaf Arthur. He's good." Lennon turned to Carroll: "You know Big Deaf Arthur?"

A perplexed and nervous Carroll stuttered, "No, I don't."

John quickly added, "He's with Small Blond Johnnie."

Trying to change the subject yet again, and with sweat now visible on his forehead, Carroll asked if any of them spoke a foreign language.

"Oh, we all speak fluent Shoe," John replied.

"They call you the chief Beatle," a worried Carroll said to John, trying to change topics.

"Look, I don't call you names. Why do you have to call me names?" John shot back to the by now totally bewildered interviewer.[49]

Their willingness to joke with each other appealed to young people who wanted to replicate the strong friendships they saw among the Beatles. They were four extremely close friends who looked like they were having such an enjoyable time in each other's company. They answered questions in unison, used the personal pronoun "we" instead of "I" when interviewed, socialized together in the evenings, lived near each other, and even vacationed together, which appealed to teenagers who often struggled to cement close friendships, and especially to girls who put more emphasis on friendships than boys.

The Beatles appeared more honest and authentic than previous pop stars who seemed manufactured and distant, which further emotionally connected them to their fans. While singer Billy Fury, who came from Liverpool, suppressed his Scouse intonations, and other pop stars like Tommy Steele and Cliff Richard and the Shadows hid their working-class roots by adopting clearer pronunciations, the Beatles refused to temper their Scouse brogue and spoke proudly of their working-class backgrounds. Fans felt that they knew the Beatles and invested in them as people not just in their songs. "Why the Beatles?" *The Beatles Book* magazine asked in March 1964. "The great stage, screen and disc stars of yesteryear have been remote, far-off creatures perched upon high pedestals of pop glory," the magazine answered. The Beatles are "as close to our own ideals as our brothers or our youth club mates down the street. They're natural in the things they say and do and they tell reporters the things we've always longed to put into newsprint ourselves. They speak as they think—as they feel—with a bluntness or a friendliness which is so typically Northern. They've never played up to anyone else's ideas of how top-flight top-money entertainers ought to conduct themselves. They've remained, John, Paul, George and Ringo—four intense yet simple Beatle People."[50] The Beatles, more than most, broke down the barriers between star and fans. In 1963, the Beatles answered their own fan mail, even supplying personal information including their home addresses to the respondents. It was not uncommon for young female admirers to be let in to see them backstage after a show. Karen Blyth from Kent wrote to *The Beatles Book* telling fans to approach George Harrison and the others in a less silly way because the Beatles "were normal (though very wonderful) human beings. You know, if I saw you in the street, I don't think I would scream or faint or anything like that, but I'd shout out 'Hello George!' as if you were some old friend of mine."[51]

The Rolling Stones may have cornered the market in generational rebellion, but the Beatles exhibited a more subtle and joyous antipathy to authority figures and to convention. The Beatles were confident, free-spirited, brash, sarcastic, dry, and manic, unwilling to provide serious answers to what they considered journalists' silly questions. With impudent wit and a flippant and anti-intellectual demeanor, they personified a rejection of cloth-cap deference as they demonstrated a contempt for the snobbery of the class system. Parents, teachers, and other authority figures told teenagers to be sensible, to sit still and to obey rules, but the Beatles encouraged their audiences to indulge in mild misbehavior, to scream when they felt happy, to take pleasure in mocking figures of authority, to laugh at the absurdities of life, and to embrace silliness. The Beatles told boys that they could wear longer hair and experiment with their clothing, and girls that they could act outside the boundaries of accepted female behavior. They told their audience to live for pleasure while parents insisted that their children forego immediate gratification and embrace hard work and security. In an era of staid conformity, when parents, teachers, and the media instructed youngsters to reign in their juvenile behavior, and when marriage and "settling down" seemed only a short step away, the Beatles provided a model of free-spirited youth and an exuberant rejection of the mundane, the conventional, the rigid, and the constraining.

The Beatles' appearance at the Royal Variety Performance at London's Prince of Wales Theatre in November 1963 illustrated their mocking attitude towards the upper classes. "I saw them on television on Sunday and really it was difficult to distinguish what they were saying as the Queen's English," Ted Heath (who was then Lord Privy Seal, but later Prime Minister) told a meeting of teachers in his constituency of Bexley in London on October 14 about his views of the Beatles.[52]

Two days later, in the light of Heath's remarks, a TV interviewer asked Paul if they would change their accents for the Royal Variety

Performance. "No, are you kidding?" an indignant Paul answered. "No, we wouldn't bother doing that."

George added, "We just won't vote for him," referring to Heath.

Mimicking an upper-class accent, Paul said, "We don't all speak like them BBC posh fellas, you know?" All four Beatles then erupted into mock laughter. "Jolly good, jolly good," John and Paul said as the interview ended.[53]

Two weeks later, an interviewer asked them about Heath again. Lennon first lampooned "Teddy's" upper-crust accent. "I can't understand Teddy! I can't understand Teddy saying that at all, really." He then added in a severe tone, "I'm not going to vote for Ted."[54] During the Variety performance, it soon became apparent that they had had enough of the pomposity. "Will the people in the cheaper seats clap your hands?" Lennon asked the audience between songs. "And the rest of you, if you'll just rattle your jewelry." The unrepentant Beatle later claimed that they were asked to perform "every year after that—but we always said, 'Stuff it.'"[55]

While the fans in the clubs were mostly teenagers, their records and television appearances attracted a wider audience. Their carefree manner, silly, almost childish humor, and simple two-minute songs appealed to a generation of children. Even the name turned out to be an inspired choice. When the media derided them as "bugs" and worried about an "infestation," youngsters loved the silly name even more. The screwball haircuts and the infectious refrain of "yeah, yeah, yeah" from "She Loves You," the number one single during the summer of 1963, added to the children's pleasure. Adults were generally dismissive of rock 'n' roll, but the less threatening charm of the Beatles won them over. They played rock 'n' roll with a driving rhythm, but there was none of the snarling defiance, overt sexuality, or wild stage shows of Elvis Presley, Little Richard, or Jerry Lee Lewis. They were well dressed, funny and smiling, and some of their songs were rather slow and melodic, appealing to parents. It was the sullen Rolling Stones, who released their first record in June 1963, who became symbols of generational rebellion, not the sunny, exuberant Beatles.

With their intoxicating mix of energetic music, zany appearances, and effervescent personalities, Brian Epstein and the Beatles had managed to package unbridled joy and sell it to the British public. While the stars of so-called Angry Young Men movies such as *Look Back in Anger* (1959) and *Saturday Night and Sunday Morning* (1960) offered a bleak picture of trapped male working-class characters, angry and dissatisfied with their lot, the Beatles personified the working-class confidence and optimism of a time of growing affluence and greater societal freedoms. The smiles on the faces of each Beatle reflected how the audience felt as did the picture sleeve of their "Twist and Shout" EP released in the UK in July 1963, which showed the four Beatles joyously jumping in the air, a feeling most British teenagers could understand.

Beatlemania

The Beatles undertook a series of national tours in 1963 that increasingly brought wild audience responses. Fifteen-year-old Christine Paine from Poole, Dorset, witnessed the Beatles perform on three occasions in 1963. She first saw them when they supported British singer Helen Shapiro early in the year when the response to the group was rather muted. "Reception was warm, fairly enthusiastic, but nothing like the screaming and hysteria that came later." She attended another Beatles show during the summer and once more toward the end of the year. "In November 1963, the Beatles came to Bournemouth again, they had also been there in August 1963 at the Gaumont Cinema. That one wasn't too hard to get tickets for as they were there for six days, but by the time the November date was announced, Beatlemania had hit a peak. The tickets were due to go on sale two days after the schools broke for the summer holidays. The queue started that night." Christine and her three friends ran home from school, quickly changed out of their school uniforms, and traveled to Bournemouth to land their tickets. Lining up to buy the tickets was almost as much fun as the concert itself. "We camped on the pavement for two nights. There were hundreds of us. Loads of portable record players, radios, parents coming and going to check on us and bring food. There was a Fortes café just down the road, and they stayed open twenty-four hours a day going up and down the queue selling sausage rolls, soup, sandwiches, that sort of thing. There was a bus station opposite for loos. We were right in the town center, so it was perfectly safe. I don't think anyone slept the entire time. The tickets went on sale on the Saturday morning 10 a.m., and the queue just got longer and longer. By about 5 a.m. on the Saturday, it went best part of half a mile. Fortunately, the weather stayed dry." When the box office opened, the four excited girls finally got their hands on their treasured tickets.[56]

"We all bought a new mini dress for the occasion, had our hair done, generally dressed up" and then journeyed to Bournemouth on the day of the concert. Paine found the reception the Beatles received in the Winter Gardens in November to be far more boisterous than in the earlier shows she attended. "The concert was manic. The expectation was massive, I can't recall now who the supporting acts were, but they barely got listened to. After the interval, the Beatles came on, and from the second they hit the stage, the noise level was unbelievable. Everyone was dancing in the aisles, on the seats, singing, screaming. The amplifiers were turned up as far as they would go to be heard over the audience noise. I think most of us could hardly speak and were pretty deaf for about two days afterward. The screaming and hysteria was no myth, it happened, and yes I screamed along with everyone else. Looking back, I think it was possibly a sort of mass hysteria thing. People fainted, tried to invade the stage, everything you have heard about Beatlemania is true, but it doesn't go far enough. It was crazy, and we were having the time of our lives."[57]

"I never thought a British audience could or would react this way for anyone," said Josh Darsa, a correspondent at the American CBS network who attended the same concert as Christine in Bournemouth. "Of course, we've read about this sort of thing—we wouldn't be here if we hadn't—but it's still unbelievable and un-British."[58]

Before the end of the year, the Beatles were a sensation. Newspapers coined the term "Beatlemania" to describe the uproar that greeted the group's public appearances. From June to September 1963 they hosted their own BBC radio series, *Pop Goes the Beatles,* and became a regular feature on the leading light entertainment TV shows. Tribute records appeared on the market including The Vernons Girls' "We Love the Beatles," Bill Clifton's "Beatle Crazy," and Dora Bryan's "All I Want for Christmas is a Beatle." On their birthdays and at Christmas, each member received sacks of cards and presents, many of them lovingly homemade. "I just couldn't believe the amount of presents that came in. There'd be enough in a single week to fill a house," remarked Bill Harry, a friend of the Beatles, who worked for a short while in the same office as the Liverpool branch of the Beatles' fan club, "and these were just the ones coming into Liverpool. The headquarters of the fan club in London was probably being inundated by even more stuff."[59]

Most Britons, young and old, had succumbed to the charms of the four callow Scousers, as they had become, quite simply, the most beloved foursome in the country. "It doesn't do to knock the Beatles," warned the left-leaning highbrow newspaper *The Observer* in November 1963, "dissenting voices are few and nervous….[E]ven the grown-ups who reacted with sharp distaste to the Elvis Presley cult a few years back now speak about the Beatles with real affection."[60] Under the front-page headline, "1963…the year of the Beatles," the Conservative-leaning London newspaper, the *Evening Standard,* admitted that they had, "captured the public fancy. I have never seen it so captured by anybody. The British baby's first words are now a standardized Yea Yea. I have seen a certain countess shoving her way to the front and saying with all the determination of her rank: 'I *must* get to Ringo.' They have a following in Balliol College, Oxford, and King's College, Cambridge, and the Inns of Court."[61]

As the British media championed the Beatles and stories of the fan hysteria drifted across the Atlantic, Beatlemania began to stir in the US. Within weeks, the land that had fired the imaginations of John, Paul, George, and Ringo would embrace them with a fervor unmatched even in their homeland.

CHAPTER 2

"The Screams Are Screams of Joy"

Beatlemania

Tommy Roe, an American singer who toured with the Beatles in the UK, returned home with a copy of the *Please Please Me* LP in April 1963, hoping to ignite Beatlemania in the US by enticing his record label, ABC-Paramount, to release Beatles' material. Roe excitedly handed the precious piece of vinyl to the president of the company, Samuel Clark, who placed the disc on the record player, dropped the needle on to the first track, and settled back on his comfy chair surrounded by other record executives to listen to the latest sensations from the UK. After a few bars of "I Saw Her Standing There," the disgruntled Clark had had enough and picked up the needle and fizzed the album into the trash can. "Gentlemen, that was crap!" he exclaimed. "Now, Tommy, you just get on with touring, writing and singing your songs and leave all the business decisions to us. Nice to see you, son. Have a nice day."[1]

The chances of the Beatles gaining traction in America seemed as likely as Samuel Clark becoming record executive of the year. The United States was the center of the music world, home to most of the popular music of the twentieth century, and record label executives like Clark demonstrated little interest in British music. Even Americans living in the UK, appreciative of the Beatles' music, were skeptical about their chances of success in the United States. "The Beatles should be heard and not seen," opined Chicagoan Donald Williams, stationed at an American Air

Force base in Gloucestershire. "Their sound is good but facing an American audience I'd reckon their chances of success at 70-30—against!"[2]

Within a few short weeks, however, the Beatles had seized control of the American imagination. Their appearance on *The Ed Sullivan Show* in February 1964 attracted the largest television audience in US history, newspapers filled their columns with Beatles trivia, and every major store overflowed with Beatles-related merchandise. By April, they claimed all top five positions on the *Billboard Hot 100*. "You know, Sid, the fever in the United States for the Beatles even exceeds England," Brian Epstein told concert promoter Sid Bernstein upon arriving in the US in February 1964. "It's just unbelievable."[3] While the Beatles slowly washed up on the shores of the UK, the Beatles arrived like a tsunami in the US, sending shockwaves across the nation, submerging all before them, and leaving a completely altered landscape in their wake.

The Beatles Come Ashore

In the fall of 1962, EMI sent a carton of records to their US subsidiary Capitol Records in Los Angeles. Included in the package was the Beatles' first 45, "Love Me Do." Artist and Repertoire representative Dave Dexter Jr. listened to the single but found nothing to change his opinion that British acts had little chance of commercial success in the US, and he refused to issue the record. Subsequent Beatles singles, "Please Please Me" and "From Me to You," brought a similar response from Dexter, even though they topped the charts in the UK. Capitol's head of A&R in Canada, Paul White, an ex-pat who had only arrived in Canada in 1957, took a more favorable view of the Beatles, deciding to release "Love Me Do" in February 1963, and following it up with the release of all their other UK 45s. The Canadian releases only sold a couple of hundred copies, which convinced Dexter of the correctness of his stance.[4]

Capitol Records passed on the Beatles, but, due to a fortuitous set of circumstances, an independent label, Vee-Jay Records, ended up releasing the first Beatles record in the US. With Capitol uninterested, EMI tried to sell their records to another American label, and, through Paul Marshall, a lawyer in New York who worked for both EMI and Vee-Jay, they offered the Beatles to the Chicago label. Vee-Jay had enjoyed previous success with Frank Ifield's single, "I Remember You," also after Capitol

Chicago-based Vee-Jay Records, who released
the first Beatles single in the US, had little
knowledge of the group they had signed, evident
by the spelling of their name on the label.

had declined to issue the song in the US. Vee-Jay took a chance on the unknown English group and released "Please Please Me" on February 7, 1963, exactly a year before the Beatles set foot in the United States. Indicative of the company's lack of interest in the music, the name of the group was misspelled "Beattles" on the record label.[5]

Local radio, so crucial for breaking new releases, was reluctant to take a chance on an unknown British group. "So they came to us, and they said, 'Look, we've got this record, and it's a British group, and we'd like you to play it,'" remembered Clark Weber at WLS. "Well we did not want to play it because Cliff Richard had had a shot at American music, and we played his records and had been burned by them. They just didn't happen. So, we were very reluctant to pick up this new foursome. Well Vee-Jay owner James Bracken pleaded with us, and we said, 'OK, we'll play it on weekends for a couple of weeks.'" Thus, Dick Biondi, whose program aired between 9 p.m. and midnight, became the first deejay to play the Beatles in the US, when he played "Please Please Me," on Friday, February 8, 1963. "So, we played it for a couple of weeks on weekends, and it didn't do anything," Weber recalled. "We took it off. Bracken came back to us, and he said, 'Would you put it on for two more weeks, please?' So, as a favor to him we played it for two more weekends. It was no great shakes; as a matter of fact, it was patently bad as far as music was concerned. But we played it. It was something new."[6] On the eighth day of March 1963, "Please Please Me" debuted on the WLS chart at number 40, peaked at number 35 the following week, and then disappeared from the survey.[7] By the summer of 1963, the single had sold only 5,650 copies.[8]

Vee-Jay released a second Beatles 45, "From Me to You," in May 1963. Unluckily for the Beatles, Del Shannon, who toured England with the Beatles in spring 1963 and who had enjoyed a series of hit records in the US, released his own version of "From Me To You" and most major radio stations, including WLS, played his cover of the song. Local African-American radio stations, however, picked up on the Beatles' recording. Bob Wilson was sixteen in the summer of 1963 when he first heard the Beatles on WVON (Voice of the Negro), owned by Leonard and Phil Chess of Chess Records. "They played 'From Me to You.' This was before I heard the Del Shannon version. I didn't think they sounded black, but WVON was an R&B station. It was the summer of '63. Looking back, I think the station thought they were black because they were on Vee-Jay Records, which was primarily an R&B label."[9]

The Beatles made their first appearance on a US radio survey on WLS in March 1963. Dick Biondi was the first DJ to play them. The single peaked at number 35 on its second of two weeks on the survey.

Others had similar experiences. "I started hearing the Beatles on black radio in Gary and the South Side of Chicago in '63," Henry Farag, a singer and promoter from Gary, Indiana, the hometown of the owners of Vee-Jay, claimed. "I could tell the difference, that they were white."[10] WYNR (Winner), which started in Chicago in the early '20s as WGES, employing black deejays and broadcasting a healthy dose of R&B music, also played the Beatles' records. Vee-Jay owner Vivian Carter worked as a deejay at WGES before it relaunched as WYNR in 1962. In July 1963, the Beatles' "From Me to You" reached number 32

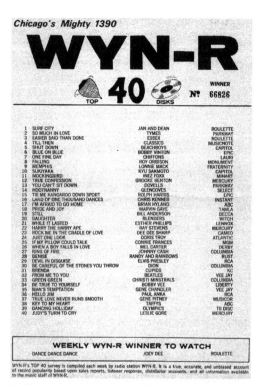

Radio stations with a large African-American audience in the Chicago area played the Beatles in the summer of 1963. WYNR Top 40 Disk Survey, July 19, 1963.

on the WYNR Top 40 survey but failed to chart on WLS or *Billboard*, selling less than 13,000 copies by the end of September.[11]

Swan Records of Philadelphia became the next US label to try to find success with the Beatles when they released "She Loves You" in September 1963. Swan, like Vee-Jay, provided only modest distribution and promotion, and, unsurprisingly, the single flopped. After Shannon's "From Me to You" became the first Lennon-McCartney composition to become a hit in the US, English actor and singer Anthony Newley released "I Saw Her Standing There" stateside in October 1963. The label credited the song to "Lenin" and McCartney! The record failed to start a revolution and charted neither locally nor nationally.

George's older sister, Louise, who had immigrated to the United States and settled in Benton, Illinois, tried her best to publicize her brother's band. She prodded local disc jockeys to play their records, but Louise and the radio stations found it difficult to obtain copies from Vee-Jay or Swan. Dick James, the London-based publisher of Beatles' songs, had to send their records to Louise, who then distributed them to the local deejays. "I was in Illinois, and that's when I started going around to all the radio stations that I could reach and, you know, telling them, hey, this is my kid brother's band," Louise recalled. "They're number one in England, and you should be playing them." None of the stations were impressed. "There was a big, big struggle. I started writing to Brian Epstein and getting *Cash Box* and *Billboard* and the like to kind of educate them about how the music business was over here. Because in England, all you have to do is to get in with the BBC and you're covered. Whereas in this country, there were, at that time, about 6,000 independent radio stations; and in order to get national play, it was very, very different. You almost had to have somebody handing the program directors a Porsche or something. I let them know over in England that they weren't going to get anywhere unless they got some clout behind them in one of the major record companies. Those were the things that I researched that I was telling them all about what they needed to know as far as getting some coverage in this country. I had started watching *The Ed Sullivan Show* on Sunday night, and I would put a p.s. on all of the letters. I used to write a letter every week to Brian, and it was about sixteen pages handwritten. I wish I'd kept copies of them. But anyway, I was telling him in my p.s. get them on *The Ed Sullivan Show*."[12]

The Tide Turns

With radio play at a premium, it was not the brilliance of their music but the wild behavior of their British fans that alerted the American media to the Beatles. On October 14, 1963, several regional newspapers published a United Press International story on how "500 stampeding teenage girls mobbed the rock 'n' roll Beatles quartet after a performance at London Palladium."[13] The *Los Angeles Times*, the *Washington Post*, and the *Detroit Free Press* printed their first stories on the phenomenon in the same month.[14] On November 15, *Time* published an article on the Beatles entitled "The New Madness," and *Newsweek* followed three days later with "Beatlemania."[15] After the publicity generated by the Beatles' Royal Variety performance on November 4, the major US television networks,

ABC, CBS, and NBC, dispatched crews to film a Beatles concert in Bournemouth on Saturday, November 16. NBC's *The Huntley-Brinkley Report,* a popular evening news program, became the first to broadcast Beatles footage on Monday, November 18. With the growing interest in the group, Brian Epstein visited New York City and brokered a deal with the popular TV variety series *The Ed Sullivan Show* for the Beatles to make their first live appearance on American television the following February. At the end of the month, Epstein finally persuaded Alan Livingston, president of Capitol Records, to release the Beatles' records in the US. Capitol scheduled January 13, 1964, as the release date for "I Want to Hold Your Hand," but because of heavy radio play of imported copies of the record, Capitol pushed up the release date of the Beatles' 45 to December 26, 1963, and set the release of their album *Meet the Beatles* for January 20, 1964.[16]

"I remember clearly it was a Friday and a 45 coming, just one in a package," Val Camilletti, who worked at the Chicago branch of Capitol Records, reflected on the day when "I Want to Hold Your Hand" arrived in the office. The staff gathered around the record player to listen. "The needle came down on the record, and everybody loved it. This Beatles thing was a completely different sound. It wasn't that the songs on those very early records were so different than anything else, although they were pretty different. But it was just the sound that happened when you heard that harmony, especially when they hit the 'I want to hold your hand' line. That was not like any other. But at this point, we just had one single. So, the idea that anybody would have even suggested that this was going to be a musical revolution was unheard of..." The record company launched an expensive promotion campaign to propel the Beatles into the public consciousness and to publicize their impending arrival in the US.

The atmosphere in Capitol's Chicago headquarters reached fever pitch as the release of the album *Meet the Beatles* and the Beatles' debut on *The Ed Sullivan Show* on February 9 approached. Capitol instructed their Chicago office staff to wear wigs and to answer phones by announcing "The Beatles are Coming."

"I mean, watching the numbers guy walking around with a Beatle wig in the office is certainly a sign that this was something different than anything that had happened before," said Val Camilletti, describing the scene. "I remember our sales manager and our sales office secretary sat in a seat right in front of me. The phones were ringing like six at a time. And we'd pick up the phone 'the Beatles are coming, the Beatles are coming, the Beatles are coming,' and finally it got to be toward the end of the day Rose Records called, and Pat picked up the phone and then said 'sales department.' The owner of Rose Records says, 'What's the matter, Pat, aren't the Beatles coming anymore?' She said, 'I don't care.' I mean it was just like, oh my god leave us alone, you know."[17]

Capitol's marketing campaign and TV exposure, especially a Beatles segment aired on NBC's *The Jack Paar Program* on Friday January 3, 1964, paid dividends as the Beatles' records started to appear on the local and national charts. "I Want to Hold Your Hand" debuted on the WLS survey on January 17, with Beatles misspelled as "Beattles," and topped the chart on January 31. "She Loves You," one of the songs featured on *The Jack Paar Program*, entered the WLS survey on January 31, and "Please Please Me," rereleased by Vee-Jay, debuted on February 21.[18] On January 18, "I Want to Hold Your Hand" entered the *Billboard Hot 100*, and on February 1, it reached number one.[19] Vee-Jay released the first Beatles LP in the US, *Introducing the Beatles,* on January 10, quickly followed by Capitol's *Meet the Beatles.*

The Ed Sullivan Show

On the morning of Friday, February 7, 1964, the four nervous but excited Beatles arrived at London Airport. As they walked to the jet bound for New York City, hundreds of fans who had gathered in the spectator gallery bombarded them with letters, badges, photographs, and jelly babies. They waved to the crowd, entered the plane, and set off for New York, unsure about the greeting that awaited them. Less than one month before the Beatles reached the States, they told fifteen-year-old Lynn Monahan, who interviewed the group backstage at the Astoria Theatre in Finsbury Park, London, that they doubted that they would succeed in the home of popular music. Lynn asked if the girls in the US would scream at them. "No, of course not," John replied. "They don't know us, do they?"

George expressed pessimism regarding the appeal of Beatles' music outside Britain. "It won't mean a thing anywhere else—in any other country. It's Britain…I don't think we stand a chance in hell in the States."

Even if they flopped, George saw a positive aspect to the trip. "We're just going to go over there and do three shows, but we hope to be good. If not, at least we'll have seen America."[20]

The Beatles landed at the newly renamed John F. Kennedy airport in New York City at 1:20 p.m., and as they descended the steps of the plane, they received a rapturous welcome from over three thousand teenagers standing four deep on the upper level of the International Arrivals Building. The Beatles then held a press conference where they sparred with reporters and displayed their impudent wit. "We knew that unless we attracted their attention with something completely new and different, we didn't stand a chance," Lennon dramatically claimed about their preparation for the US media. "So we relied on our humor even more than usual." Having heard the same questions from reporters at home, the Beatles had their witty answers down pat. "We'd heard them all before but they hadn't."[21]

The Beatles made their first live TV appearance on CBS's *The Ed Sullivan Show* on Sunday, February 9, 1964, at 7 p.m. Central Time. Many young, and not so young, Chicagoans were eager to see what all the fuss was about and wanted to be in front of a TV at the appointed time. Popular local deejay Jim Lounsbury held a Beatles Dance in the suburb of Elgin and placed television sets around the dance hall so that the crowd could watch.[22] Fourteen-year-old Donna Dickinson, who was skating at Chicago's crowded Rainbo Arena, seemed unaware of the fuss. Then "all of a sudden, everybody is leaving the ice." Curious, she followed the crowd to a room used for birthday parties. "It was not just kids. It was adults and everybody," she recounted. "There was a small TV on the shelf. I happened to walk in as Paul McCartney was singing, 'Till There was You.'"[23]

In the living rooms of America, anticipation reached fever pitch. Twelve-year-old Bill Ehm, who had only recently moved from Chicago to the southern suburbs, seemed to have completely missed the hype. "I sat on the floor in my front room with an old Muntz TV... and I really didn't know what a Beatle was, and I go, 'What the heck is a Beatle?' I didn't know what to expect. A magician? But then a music group went on and I said, 'Wow! This is neat!' In fact, when they first came on... just as a joke, I went into the bathroom and combed my hair down over my face!"[24]

"Now tonight, you're gonna twice be entertained by them. Right now, and again in the second half of our show," Ed Sullivan told the studio audience and the watching millions at home. "Ladies and gentlemen, the Beatles..." the rest of his introduction drowned out by the screaming of the studio audience. The Beatles played two spots: three songs at the beginning of the show and two songs to close the show, including their number one hit "I Want to Hold Your Hand."

The sound and the look of the Beatles' performance stunned the viewers at home. To ensure that the three guitars and the solid drumming of Ringo Starr were up front in the sound, the Beatles insisted that the studio technicians mix their vocals and instruments on the same level. "In the years we'd had the Sullivan show, every group we ever did always wanted the vocals [mixed higher than] the backing," Vince Calandra, a production assistant on *The Ed Sullivan Show*, noted. "So that was a first."[25]

The music was important, but it was the look of the group and the response of the studio audience that captivated most viewers. The prominence of a smiling Ringo Starr sitting behind a relatively small drum kit, high on a drum riser, immediately disorientated those accustomed to seeing the drummer hidden at the back of the stage. There was no lead singer out front and no synchronized dancing. Just as importantly, their Mod-influenced skinny black ties, white shirts, and slim-fitting dark suits stood out spectacularly on the small black and white screens. The four English men were evidently enjoying themselves on stage, smiling and glancing at each other, a joyousness that they transmitted to the viewers at home. They shook their heads to emphasize their long hair, adding to the shock experienced by the television audience. The reaction of the girls in the television studio, which the camera panned to regularly, astounded those too young to have seen a similar response to Elvis Presley. The studio audience screamed, jumped, squirmed, and stared in disbelief, as did many of those at home, enthralled by the fun and craziness they witnessed. The national mourning, prompted by the assassination of President Kennedy less than twelve weeks earlier, seemed to lift immediately as the joyous sound filled the living rooms of America.

Eleven-year-old Katie Jones loved "I Want to Hold Your Hand" when she first heard the song on WLS and sat down with her mother and father in her Chicago suburb impatient to see the group's debut appearance on

Ed Sullivan. "I remember the Beatles hitting us as a total package, all at one time. So, it wasn't just the songs. It was the haircuts; it was the suits. They were as cute as hell. We fell in love. We fell in love with them, absolutely, the girls and some of the boys too." Like most girls, she first noticed the look of the group as much, if not more than, their music. "I liked the way they moved, and they moved in unison, and it was very clear that they were all together. The suits were really appealing. The haircuts. I mean that made a huge splash at the time. And they looked happy, happy-go-lucky. They were kind of like the boy next door. I've often told people it was almost like instant puppy love. You know, you get a crush on somebody, and it was like that. It was really intense."[26]

Some teenage girls who watched the show immediately switched their allegiance from reigning teen idols to the Beatles. Hillary Rodham, aged sixteen from the affluent Chicago suburb of Park Ridge, was president of the local Fabian fan club when she saw the Beatles on the night of February 9 with a group of friends including her best friend, Betsy. "We watched *The Ed Sullivan Show* every Sunday night with our families, except the night he showcased the Beatles on February 9, 1964, which had to be a group experience. Paul McCartney was my favorite Beatle, which led to debates about each one's respective merits, especially with Betsy, who always championed George Harrison."[27] Hillary remained a Beatles fan throughout her life and talked of what she experienced that February night when she served as US Secretary of State over forty years later. "I have to confess that the hand-clapping mode was what I first was captured by. 'I Want to Hold Your Hand' was an anthem."[28]

The shock of the new spread rapidly across the Windy City. "I remember thinking that it was amazing! I had never heard anything like that band before, and the high energy that they brought to the show was nothing I had ever seen before," said seventeen-year-old Terry Cessna who watched the program at a friend's house. While girls who watched the show recall how they felt first seeing rather than hearing the group, boys like Terry had clearer recollections of first hearing the Beatles' music and only secondly noting their appearance. "I remember thinking they were an amazing band. We had rock 'n' roll but not to that kind of sound." Once enthralled by the music, he then noticed their look. "Their appearance was different than mainstream America at the time. They dressed conservatively, but their hair was long in a style that we did not wear, so I remember that their appearance was weird, but their music was great."[29]

"Other music that's been around awhile gets to be a drag," a boy from Morgan Park High School told a *Chicago Tribune* journalist. "But the real kilowatt power is in those three electric guitars. It's like four Elvis Presley's.... When you go to a dance and there are these electric guitars, it's a lot of amplified noise. It reverberates and it's like you feel the beat right thru the soles of your feet. Now you combine that with the wild looks of the Beatles and that Ringo on the drums and well, that's it."[30]

Two days after their debut on US television, the Beatles played their first US concert at Washington Coliseum, a sports arena in Washington, DC. The following day, the Beatles performed two shows at Carnegie Hall in New York City. They appeared again on *The Ed Sullivan Show* live from Florida on February 16 and for a third time a week later in an appearance taped two weeks earlier in New York. The Florida performance attracted a TV audience of over seventy million, a little less than watched their first appearance on the show a week earlier, and the third and last show garnered an audience of sixty million.[31] On February 22, the group returned to the UK as conquering heroes.

Beatlemania hardly subsided after the Beatles returned home. On April 4, the Beatles captured the top five positions on the *Billboard* singles chart and boasted an unprecedented twelve entries in the Top 100. The Beatles placed thirty-one singles on the *Billboard* chart in 1964, by far the most of any artist that year with the next closest, Elvis Presley and the Beach Boys, gaining only nine entries each.[32] To cash in on the Beatles phenomenon, record labels rush-released singles that responded to "I Want to Hold Your Hand," such as "Yes, You Can Hold My Hand" by the Teen Bugs and "I'll Let You Hold My Hand" by the Bootles. Beatles tribute records including "We Love You Beatles" by the Carefrees, "A Letter to The Beatles" by the Four Preps, and "A Beatle I Want to Be" by Sonny Curtis soon followed. Some major, and future, stars of the recording industry sought to cash in on the Beatles' popularity. Cher, as Bonnie Jo Mason, with Phil Spector as producer, recorded "Ringo, I Love You;" Ella Fitzgerald released "Ringo Beat;" and Kenneth Gamble, who later with Leon Huff created the "Philly Sound," co-wrote the Swans single, "The Boy With The Beatle Hair."

It was not just teenagers who were caught up in Beatlemania, as this photo of people modeling Beatles wigs at the Loop department store, Wieboldts, illustrates.

"The usually staid and conservative Midwest has virtually flipped its wig over the mop-headed Beatles from Liverpool," *Billboard* reported in its February 15 issue.[33] Chicago's main downtown business and shopping area, the Loop, so called because of the streetcar lines which originally circled the area and the elevated train tracks that later bounded it, became Beatleland. To boost business, some retailers offered free Beatles photos, some with autograph reproductions, with every purchase. Beatles wallpaper, guitars, games, pillows, dolls, lunch boxes, hats, boots, jackets, t-shirts, underpants, stockings, sweaters, wigs, badges, plates, key chains, wallets, pencil cases, toilet paper, and bubble gum cards filled the shelves of the major department stores. Beatle magazines, aimed at the teen market, filled the racks. "Patio Television in Chicago has literally turned its store into a Beatle house and the practice has been followed to a more or less degree by virtually every promotion minded dealer in the city," *Billboard* reported. "Most stores were moving Beatle merchandise but little else."[34]

The Green Duck metal stamping company of Chicago went from making pins of Harry, Dwight, Jack, and Lyndon to making ones of John, Paul, George and Ringo.

"Wiggery waggery reached new heights Tuesday as Loop shoppers began snatching Beatles' wigs from department store counters," the *Chicago Daily News* observed of the furor two days after the Beatles' appearance on Ed Sullivan. "They are selling like hot cakes," one female salesclerk marveled. "The man who manufactures the wig is turning them out at the rate of 20,000 a day with orders for more than 300,000," said an elated Louis Barak, Goldblatt's general sales manager.[35]

Many Chicago-based businesses saw an opportunity to cash in. The Green Duck Metal Stamping Company, who had made its name producing political campaign pins since 1906, entered into an agreement with Seltaeb, the official US manufacturer of Beatles merchandise, to issue Beatles pins. Davidson's Authentic Documents sold reproductions of Beatles birth certificates; the Exhibit Card Company, manufacturer of arcade sports and movie cards, fashioned Beatles cards; and Arrco Playing Card Company produced sets of Beatles playing cards. Hair products proved extremely popular. Bronson produced Beatles hair spray and shampoo to supplement the Beatles combs, brushes, and headbands. Other local manufacturers produced Beatles towels and dolls.[36]

Local entrepreneurs, even those with no previous business experience, found it astonishingly easy to become the official producer of Beatles merchandise. When eleven-year-old Emily Thornton pestered her father Greg Thornton, an artist from suburban Niles North, to draw portraits of each of the four

Bronson was one of many Chicago companies that jumped on the Beatles' bandwagon.

Terry Crain

After some pestering from his eleven-year-old daughter Emily, artist Greg Thornton ended up becoming a producer of official Beatles merchandise.

Beatles for her, Thornton realized that he could reproduce the drawings on postcards and sell them to Beatles-obsessed fans. He wrote to Brian Epstein's business company NEMS to ask for copyright. Thornton and his daughter were surprised to receive a response, never mind one that gave him sole copyright to draw any Beatles portrait postcard in the entire Western hemisphere. Thornton then contacted Curt Teich & Company of Chicago, one of the world's largest printers of postcards. They, too, quickly obtained permission from NEMS to print any Beatles postcard, picture, or portrait. Emily sent a set of the finished postcards to NEMS, who duly returned them with each card autographed by the four Beatles.[37]

The Beatles inspired others to pursue their dreams and desires. "I saw a photo of The Beatles in a newspaper before they played Ed Sullivan or anybody in America had heard of them," South Side Catholic teenager Cynthia Albritton recalled. "I didn't even know they were a rock 'n' roll band. I thought they were a comedy troupe. They were gorgeous-looking with their long, straight bangs, their tight pants.... I was starting to develop a fascination for cocks, even though I'd never seen one before, just by seeing those bulges in the tight pants of The Beatles."[38]

"Dear Beatles, If your rigs [penises] get nervous from being cramped up and need a little exercise when you're in Chicago, we are the girls for you," the ever-helpful Cynthia wrote to the group on behalf of herself and her friend after the Beatles announced a tour of the US in the summer of 1964. "We're two barclays bankers [wankers], our bank has convenient night hours and you can make all the deposits you like." Cynthia received no reply from the busy Mop Tops, but she could not stop thinking about the Fab Four's crown jewels. In 1966, as a nineteen-year-old art major at the University of Illinois, Chicago Circle Campus, her teacher gave the class an assignment "to make a plaster cast of anything that was solid enough to retain its shape." The thoughts of Cynthia returned to those bulges in the Beatles' trousers and she formulated the unique idea of making a plaster cast of a man's erect penis. Cynthia reconsidered, believing the sculptures may not by fully accepted by the professor, but returned to the idea after she left college. Armed with a bag of plaster, Cynthia and a female assistant first tried out their scheme on a couple of willing friends. One of the girls prepared the plaster while the other pleasured the model until he hopefully obtained an erection.[39]

Spurred on by their initial success, the two girls adopted the name The Plaster Casters of Chicago, tracked down visiting rock stars, and enticed them with business cards advertising that they made "Life-like Models of Hampton Wicks" (cockney rhyming slang for pricks). Jimi Hendrix became the first rock star to be so honored in Room 1628 of the Hilton Hotel on Michigan Avenue in February 1968.[40] "One of them looks like a dentist's receptionist," said Led Zeppelin's Jimmy Page, a comment either unkind to the Plaster Casters or to dentists' receptionists.

"They're such grim, sick people," stated a hostile Steve Miller who refused the girl's request to join the collection. "They look like medieval mental cases."[41] Miller aside, the two girls found plenty of rock stars willing to stick their erect penises into a plaster mix assisted by two complete strangers.

Alas, none of the Beatles made it into their prized collection, but the two girls left an impression, if not one made of plaster, on Paul McCartney who penned "Famous Groupies" for the 1978 Wings album *London Town*. "There was a famous pair of groupies years ago called the Plaster Casters," Paul told the *Daily Mirror*. The "song isn't actually modelled on them, but it is based on the same idea."[42]

WLS may have been reluctant to play Beatles' records in 1963, but that all changed in the new year as Beatlemania transformed local radio. The deejays interviewed their counterparts, reporters, and fans from the UK and aired biographies of the four Beatles to familiarize the listeners with the new sensations. The station supplied the latest tidbit of Beatles

KEEP YOUR DIAL SET ON RADIO 890 AND HEAR
THE "NEW" BEATLES

CLARK "BEATLE" WEBER 6-9 AM · "RINGO" TAYLOR 10-12 NOON · "BEATLE BERNIE" ALLEN 12:30 PM-3:00 PM · "BOB THE BEATLE" HALE 3:00-6:30 PM · "RINGO RON" RILEY 7:30-9:00 PM · ART "THE EXCELSIOR BEATLE" ROBERTS 9:00-12 MIDNIGHT · DON "BEATLE ALL-NIGHT" PHILLIPS MIDNIGHT-5:00 AM

WLS deejays, including Clark Weber, were caught up in Beatlemainia.

news and organized all manner of Beatles-related contests. Deejay Art Roberts, for example, told listeners to his show that he would get a Beatles-style haircut if ten thousand of them mailed him cards. The panicked Roberts closed the contest after he received 9,112.[43]

One person they turned to for help was George's sister, Louise, who became a regular guest on the station. At the request of KXOK in St. Louis, Louise began to record sixtysecond reports on the latest Beatles news, "The Daily Beatles Reports," which were then taken up by radio stations across the country. "They were giving, like, thirty dollars a week for ten sixtysecond reports," she remembered. Ron Riley of WLS regularly spoke to Harrison by phone live on air. "WLS would just call me up and ask me what's going on. They never, ever, you know, put out any money for them. Cheapskates."[44] Because of the unprecedented number of Beatle records played on WLS, in the week of February 21, they renamed their survey "Silver Beatle Survey." On the reverse side of the listing, all the deejays wore Beatle wigs and adopted Beatlefied names: Clark "Beatle" Weber, "Ringo" Taylor, "Beatle Bernie" Allen, "Bob the Beatle" Hale, "Ringo Ron" Riley, Art "The Excelsior Beatle" Roberts, and Don "Beatle All-Night" Phillips.[45] "They owned Chicago radio," stated Clark Weber. "I mean everything and anything that was of Beatles nature was talked about and played because, of course, these listeners wanted to hear every little nuance about the Beatles. The disc jockeys were smart enough to recognize it. They could hold that captive audience by just parceling out little bits of information."[46]

A Hard Day's Night

The release of "I Want to Hold Your Hand" introduced the American public to the sound of the Beatles, their appearance on *The Ed Sullivan Show* familiarized them with their exotic look, but it took the release of the Beatles' first feature film, *A Hard Day's Night,* in August 1964 to really acquaint them with the four distinct personalities in the group: the cheerful Paul, the clever John, the quiet George, and the good-natured Ringo. The film, produced in a quasi-documentary style, followed the group as they journeyed from Liverpool to London to appear on a television show. The movie perfectly captured the joyousness of Beatlemania as they ran from screaming fans, used humor to send up the shallowness of show business, and showed a willingness to defy convention. Along the way, they come into conflict with several older authority figures, including a bowler-hatted, *Financial Times*-reading commuter on a train. To add to their image as representatives of a less-deferential generation, the Beatles' manager and their TV director fail to control their exuberant youthful behavior. Using British idioms such as "gear," "grotty," "fab," "jam butty," and "sod off," the novelty of the Beatles' language and accents struck a chord with American youngsters.

On Friday, August 28, 1964, *A Hard Day's Night* opened at Woods Theatre in the downtown Loop district. As morning broke, "several thousand screaming, squealing, giggling and sometimes pushing boys and girls [mostly girls] lined up to get Chicago's first look at the Beatles' first movie," the *Chicago Tribune* reported. When the doors to the theater opened at 8 a.m., two thirteen-year-old girls suffered injuries as the surging crowd pushed them through the theater's glass door.[47] The theater staged seven showings of the movie each day, and teenagers lined up for two blocks before each performance. Some youngsters collected signatures for a "Beatles for President" petition outside the theater, a magazine seller sold Beatles books on the street, and the local parking attendant wore a Beatles wig.[48]

A confirmed Beatles fanatic at the age of twelve, Cynthia Dagnal, her friend Felicia, and their obliging mothers journeyed from the South Side to see the premiere at Woods Theatre. "I was there for the first one with the big funny tickets. It was pandemonium. They didn't really know what was going to happen. So kids were pushing and shoving, and there was finally a window broken as I recall. I don't think that most people understood the hysteria that well. For *A Hard Day's Night*, I don't think the theater people understood what that was going to be like." United Artists had released the *A Hard Day's Night* soundtrack in June, heightening expectation for the movie's release and allowing moviegoers to sing-a-long with the songs as they watched the film. Once inside the theater, however, seeing their heroes close up on the big screen in the company of other Beatles fanatics was too much for the crowds of girls who started screaming as the movie began and kept up the din throughout the showing, often making it difficult to hear the dialogue or even the songs. "There's the big bong from the guitar, and then they start running. All we heard was the bong. The first chord, that's it. After that, what movie? You know, it was just like ridiculous. It was a wonderful movie. I know that now!"[49]

Similar scenes occurred throughout the Chicago metropolitan area as youngsters flocked to the movie. Twelve-year-old Kathy Holden saw *A Hard Day's Night* when it premiered in suburban Joliet. "It was really fun. To get the tickets to see the movie, my dad dropped a group of us off at a music store in downtown Joliet at 4:00 a.m. to wait in line to buy tickets—just for the movie." It did not disappoint. "It can only be described as hysteria. Just imagine about 300 teenage girls screaming at the top of their lungs for no legitimate reason. It was a movie, so the Beatles couldn't hear us. Looking back, I'm not sure where the screaming and fainting even came from. I never actually heard anything in the theater when watching the movie. I first heard the actual dialogue or the storyline when the movie came out on TV!"[50]

If children saw the movie multiple times, so did many of their parents. Lina Schneider of Bloomington, Illinois, fell asleep in the back seat of her car as she was watching *A Hard Day's Night* with her teenage daughter, Michelle, at a drive-in movie theater. "I'd already seen it seven or eight times," she wearily told the local newspaper.[51]

Young Beatles fans loved the movie but, rather surprisingly, critics also acclaimed the film and the comedic qualities of the four stars. "Even if you don't care for their music, you'll find them entertaining and full of a kind of irrepressible humor and exuberance and a refusal to take anything seriously, especially themselves," the *Chicago Tribune* film critic wrote. She praised the film for its ability to poke fun at the trappings of stardom. "The action is chaos from start to finish and really pretty good fun."[52] Richard Christiansen in the *Chicago Daily News* called it "without question, the most entertaining motion picture yet to be released this year."[53] Eleanor Kenn of the *Chicago Sun-Times* described it as "one of the most sophisticated pictures that I've seen in a long time." It was "a wonderfully freewheeling film, fresh, unexpected and hilarious."[54]

College students at first ignored the Beatles but began to heap praise on them when *A Hard Day's Night* hit the theaters. Reviewer Ron Fridell of the Northwestern University student newspaper the *Daily Northwestern* praised the "Beatleness" of the movie. "And what is Beatleness? If there were one word, it would have to be joy. The Beatles are being themselves, and they love it. That they release screams from their fans is no surprise. The screams are screams of joy."[55]

Beatlemania

The sense of sheer joy that the Beatles embodied in their music, look, and personalities translated easily from Britain to America. Mary Merryfield of the *Tribune* received mail from teenagers telling her that they loved the Beatles because "teens are sick and tired of sad, sad songs and like the way the Beatles 'blast off,' 'blow off the lid,' 'make happy sounds.'" A teenage girl from Elmhurst wrote to Merryfield explaining her happiness. "You can call me 'yo-yo' when the Beatles sing and play because I bounce—I bounce all over the place. It's the fast, happy rhythm. It makes me want to dance, sing, smile, bounce, or do most anything but sit still."

A Chicago housewife expressed a similar view. "They're spontaneous and natural—happy. I don't pay any attention to their offbeat looks. It's the happy beat I like."

"Whatever you call it," Merryfield summed up, "let-out,' 'let go' or 'bounce around,' the idea of happy instead of sad music permeates most of my Beatemania mail."[56]

"Have you ever looked at one of those game television shows which give presents away to winning contestants?" one reader wrote to local newspaper columnist Muriel Lawrence who had asked her readers to explain Beatlemania. "If you haven't, Mrs. Lawrence, you'd better do it. You'd better do it, so you can look at and listen to the middle-aged ladies wriggle and jump, squeal and scream when they win mink coats, diamond rings and washing machines. Then you'd know why we Beatlemaniacs wriggle and jump, squeal and scream when we see our dearest Beatles. If the middle-aged ladies can wiggle and squeal with pleasure in winning these presents, I don't see why we teenagers can't do it, too, when we feel pleasure in our Beatles."

At a time when girls were marrying young, and the single independent life was relatively short, girls saw a small window of opportunity for fun before they settled down to adult life. "We know what the years are going to do to us because we have seen what they do to grownups. My love for my darling Beatles is, I know, a 'never-again-thing,' I know how little time I really have for my wild, wondrous, explosive feelings," one girl told Lawrence. Another reader also wrote about the sensations the Beatles evoked in her. "Many people of your generation are not alive but half dead. We know that the Beatles' wild, darling, different, beautiful beat is telling us that our own wild, darling, different and beautiful feelings about things are OK even if they are not like our parents' feelings."[57]

Adulation of pop stars was nothing new, as Frank Sinatra and Elvis Presley faced similar screaming crowds, but the sheer scale of the phenomenon certainly was. The number of young people was historically high because of a baby boom after World War II. In 1965, 41 percent of all Americans were under the age of twenty, thirty million more than there were in 1947.[58] More than previous generations of youngsters, baby boomers, or at least their parents, could afford the records, the merchandise, and the concert tickets, and virtually every home had a television set, a radio, and a record player. While World War II devastated the economies of Asia and Europe, the US emerged from the war as the world's economic and military superpower. Most Americans shared in this wealth. Median family income adjusted for inflation nearly doubled between 1946 and 1960.[59] Chicago, the capital of the Midwest, prospered. Home ownership soared, and nearly every one of these households possessed an array of the most up-to-date consumer products. In the mid-1960s, a study by the Chicago Association of Commerce estimated "the average family income of metropolitan Chicago to be $11,400. This is 30 per cent more than the national average and $1,000 more than New York City."[60]

The Beatles could not have succeeded had not parents, who had survived economic depression and war and lived in an era that lionized the family and children, indulged their offspring's infatuation. Many adults believed that the Beatles were different, strange, and quirky, but no threat to the morals of their children. Mothers and fathers looked at their youngsters with amusement and bemusement, but still provided them with the necessary money to purchase records and merchandise. Linda Milan's father, a chef at the Palmer House hotel in Chicago, for example, used to bring home Beatle magazines and cards for Linda and her sister. When a WLS deejay interviewed the Beatles, her dad "recorded it on his reel to reel device and we used to listen to it over and over again."[61] Some parents joined their children at Beatle-themed parties. "In Chicago's Old Town, Beatle parties were being organized by parents in a number of blocks," *Chicago's American* found when they investigated the reaction to the Beatles in the Chicago area. "Fathers comb their hair into bangs, mothers serve 'jelly babies,' the Beatles favorite candy, the youngsters play the record—and the whole family gyrates with the Beatles."[62]

If four black men had exited the plane from London on the afternoon of February 7, 1964, the reception they would have received from the American media and public would have been altogether different. Black music may have found an appreciative white audience, but not black people. A national poll undertaken in 1966 found that 6 percent of white Northerners objected to their children going to schools with even a "few" black children, 32 percent objected to integration in a school with "half" black students, and 60 percent objected where there was a "majority" of black students.[63] Chicago was even more segregationist. In March 1967, a survey found that 16.7 percent of white Chicagoans thought that blacks and whites should go to different schools and 60 percent thought that whites have the right to keep blacks out of their neighborhoods.[64] In this climate of racial animosity, the Beatles' race helped them win the approval of their white fans and their parents. When *Time* magazine first featured the group in its pages, they told its readers that they would find the Beatles "achingly familiar," but they may not have been just referring to their Americanized music.[65] The race of the four Beatles meant that young white Americans could relate to them on a visual level, and white girls, who would not or could not swoon over black artists, could idolize the Beatles with parental approval. "Up till then the Negroes had cornered the market on music," a young Beatles fan told author Julius Fast. "They were on top of the heap. We all knew they were best. Now here were four white boys who had them licked. I think that meant something to us."[66]

Their skin color helped the Beatles to succeed in the US but so, too, did their British origins. English was an international language, which made the humor and the personalities of the Beatles, so crucial to their success, understandable to an American audience. Other countries produced pop stars, but their language limited their reach and ambition. Not many British performers enjoyed chart success in the US before the Beatles, but more chart toppers came from Britain than from any other country, partly because of the common language and partly because Britain built a thriving music industry with access to the American market. Between January 1940 and December 1963, no less than fifty British acts (forty-three English and seven Scottish) chartered on *Billboard*, with Canada in second place with sixteen, Germany and Italy with eleven apiece, and France in fifth place with only eight acts making the *Billboard* charts. Because of the Americanization of the UK in the postwar years, the Beatles' musical sound was especially familiar to an American audience.[67]

In all areas of entertainment, being British was a plus. In 1963, nearly a third of Broadway hits were British in origin.[68] In February 1963, the theater critic in the *Chicago Tribune* announced a "British Invasion" of Broadway, but far from condemning it, he wrote, "we welcome it."[69] *Lawrence of Arabia* won seven Oscars in 1963 including best picture and best director. The following year *Tom Jones* took home the award for best picture, best screenplay, and best director; and seven of the ten top grossing movies in the US were either made in Britain or starred British actors.[70] *Dr. No*, released in the US in 1963, the first in a series of James Bond movies, perfected the fantasy Britain of bowler hats and Aston Martin sports cars. In a nationwide survey undertaken in 1966, *Newsweek* found that Sean Connery was the most popular personality among teenagers. In the same article, Beverly Goerke, who ordered books for the Chicago public library, reported that Ian Fleming's Bond books were "the big craze now."[71]

African Americans

The lovable Mop Tops appealed across racial lines as many African Americans in Chicago were just as impressed by the British imports as their white counterparts. The Beatles played music with a strong African-American influenced sound and they looked and sounded different from white American acts. "They're absolutely cool! There has never been anything this great since Rudy Vallee," wrote Elaine Munson in the leading black-owned daily newspaper the *Chicago Defender*. "I think they are great-mainly because they're different than any other vocal group," another reader, Helen Econimos, insisted. Michele Taradash agreed: "I think the Beatles are fabulous and should take over the entire Ed Sullivan Show."[72]

As happened in white households, the Beatles caused some intergenerational conflict in black families. "Now it's no longer the bird-brained idiots who astound me, but the Beatle brain-washed, intelligentsia who go for hysterical kind of entertainment, as well," Doris Raynes Johnson forlornly noted. "My youngster of course, says they are the 'last word.' I must be getting old, or I could agree with him. If he meant by this brash delivery of words and music, that harmony has just died."[73]

In February 1966, one mom wrote for advice to Arletta Claire in the *Chicago Defender* complaining that her daughter was infatuated with the Beatles. "She mopes around the house—especially on Saturday nights, when she sits in her room playing her Beatles records so loud even the dog howls."[74]

Cynthia Dagnal's experience of watching the Beatles on *The Ed Sullivan Show* was typical of what was happening in most American homes that February evening. An only child just short of her twelfth birthday, she watched the program with her parents on the South Side of Chicago. "I was on the floor and my parents were sitting somewhere behind me. I think my dad was actually in the dining room kind of away from it. I did not scream. I was not a screamer. I didn't do any of that stuff. I sang. That's probably the only time I ever saw them live where you could actually hear them. I just enjoyed it. I was very smitten because they didn't look like any of the white guys I knew. I was taking piano lessons downtown, so I knew some white guys. I knew the son of the conductor of the Chicago Symphony by then in fact. And the hair. It was just, what was that? You know, is that a British thing? What is going on? I thought they were absolutely beautiful. My father wanted to kill them. My father just wanted them gone. Well, you know, I was really young. There's a sexual aspect to that, that my dad would never have mentioned, but he knew it was there. This is something you don't talk about with your daughter at that age, especially if you're African American and male. Then there's the whole racial thing, these are white boys, what the hell, you know, it was that kind of thing. My mother was indifferent sort of. She just didn't get it. She didn't understand what's going on here. She was from Mississippi, the Mississippi Delta, very simple sweet woman, grew up picking cotton. I have lost my mind, as far as she was concerned."[75]

Stores in the South Side black neighborhoods stocked massive displays of Beatles merchandise. "A lot of the places where black people shopped, which tended to be Woolworth's and some of the dime stores and things like that, were full of Beatles stuff," Cynthia Dagnal recalled. "And you couldn't go anywhere without Beatles stuff being all over, and it was cheap. They knew what they were doing. They put it right up front and kids who had a little leftover lunch money or whatever, you could buy at least the bubblegum and they knew that."[76]

The *Chicago Defender* jumped on the Beatles bandwagon. In the days leading up to the premier of *A Hard Day's Night*, the self-styled "cheery chaps at the *Chicago Daily Defender*" ran a contest offering tickets for a sneak preview at the Metropolitan Theatre on Chicago's South Side. "Carry on, toodle-oo, pip-pip, and of course—yeah, yeah, yeah!" the paper cringingly suggested.[77] The *Defender* printed a photo of the one hundred winners, an ecstatic crowd of African-American children.[78] Under the headline "The Beatles Hit the Jack Pot" the newspaper's reviewer, Judith Smith, called their first movie "the most wonderful laugh a minute movie ever, *Hard Day's Night* is a happy, wild woolly hour and half spent in Beatledom."[79]

It probably helped their cause among young African Americans that the Beatles publicly expressed their disdain for racism. When Chicago's *Photoplay* magazine asked the four Beatles if they would marry a black girl, they all voiced liberal views on race. "I tell you, if I loved a Negro dwarf I'd marry her," replied George. "Same here," said Paul. "I'd marry anyone if I truly loved them. Of any race, or religion." Paul gave credit to his father for bringing him up not "to be bigoted about anything." John, the married Beatle, said that if his son brought "home a colored girl-friend, that'll be all right with me." Leaving Ringo to sum up: "me and the boys will do our part to prove that people are people to us: not Jews, not Catholics, not Negroes, not Chinese or anything else. Does that answer your question?"[80]

When it came to racial matters, the Beatles not only talked the talk, they walked the walk. On each of their tours of North America, they included black artists as support acts and insisted that their contracts contained the rider that they "will not be required to perform before a segregated audience." When the Beatles were told that blacks would be confined to the upper tiers when they played in the Gator Bowl in Jacksonville, Florida, on the 1964 tour, they took a stand. "We've all talked about this and we all agree that we would refuse to play," McCartney told British journalist Ivor Davis. "We're going to watch things closely. We know they sometimes try the trick of saying that the crowd is integrated—all they do is put a few Negroes in one corner of the stadium. We all feel strongly about civil rights and the segregation issue." John Lennon agreed: "We never play to segregated audiences and we're not going to start now," he explained to Davis. "I'd rather lose our appearance money. We understand that in Florida they only allow for Negroes to sit in the balconies at performances, but we will not appear unless Negroes are allowed to sit anywhere they like."[81] The promoter convinced the group that they would play in front of an integrated audience and the concert went ahead.

The Beatles gained almost universal admiration and respect from African-American musicians, which probably also aided their popularity among the wider black population. "I like 75% of the British groups today," Marvin Gaye told Soul magazine in April 1966. "I think that the Beatles are great. Not because they are said to be great, but because of their musicianship, writing ability, and because of their subtle originality."[82] The careers of many African-American musicians benefited from the Beatles recording their songs or from the Beatles providing them with effusive public acclaim. "The Beatles were huge," Smokey Robinson spoke of his admiration. "The first thing they said when you interviewed them was 'we grew up on Motown'.... They were the first huge white act to admit, 'Hey we grew up with some black music. We love this,'" Robinson noted. "I must give credit to the Beatles," the Temptations' Otis Williams agreed. "It seemed like at that point in time white America said, 'OK if the Beatles are checking them out, let us check them out.'"[83]

Many black artists, including rock 'n' roll greats like Little Richard and Fats Domino, jazz stars Ella Fitzgerald, Count Basie, and Duke Ellington, soul legends Otis Redding and Aretha Franklin, and many of the stars of Motown recorded versions of Beatles songs. Black Chicago musicians who recorded Beatles' music included Lou Rawls, who sang "Yesterday" on his 1966 album *Carryin' On!*; Gene Chandler, who included "Eleanor Rigby" on his 1969 long player *The Two Sides of Gene Chandler*; and Jerry Butler, who recorded "Something" for his album *You and Me* released in 1970.[84]

The Beatles, along with the more blues-influenced bands from Britain, brought increased interest to the blues musicians heard in clubs on the South Side of Chicago. Some whites, such as guitarist Mike Bloomfield and singer Paul Butterfield, already played the music prior to the Beatles' arrival in the US, but others began to take an interest in South Side blues thanks to the Beatles. "It may seem corny to you, but this is true: the groups from England really started the blues rolling and getting bigger among the kids—the white kids," John Lee Hooker told *Blues* magazine about the debt blues music owed Britain. "At one time…the blues was just among the blacks—the old black people. And this uprise started in England by The Beatles, Animals, Rolling Stones, it started *everybody* to digging the blues."[85] Muddy Waters believed that "it took the people from England to hip my people—my white people—to what they had in their own backyard. That sounds funny, but it's the truth. It was the Beatles and the Rolling Stones: The Beatles did a lot of Chuck Berry; the Rolling Stones did some of my stuff. That's what it took to wake up the people in my own country, in my own state where I was born, that a black man's music is not a crime to bring in the house."[86]

Fan Clubs and Teen Magazines

The Beatles not only brought immense joy to their young fans, they also inspired like-minded girls across Chicago and America to forge lasting friendships over their love of the group. While the male encounter with the Beatles only went as far as listening to the music, sometimes with friends but more often alone, the female experience was far more deep-rooted and communal. Fan clubs offered girls, many isolated in the newly built suburbs, the chance to enjoy a collective experience and to bond with friends as they listened to their music together, shared stories from teen magazines, and discussed their favorite Beatle. Lining up to buy concert tickets, attending the shows, and hanging around hotels and airports to catch a glimpse of their heroes added to the excitement and adventure of being a female Beatles fan and left memories that would last a lifetime.

The burgeoning fan clubs provided an avenue for girls to keep in contact with Beatles news and to feel part of a wider community. WLS deejay Art Roberts, who took over Dick Biondi's late-night slot after WLS had fired Biondi in May 1963, claimed that he started the first Beatles fan club in America. Roberts maintained that he launched the club after reading about the reaction to the Beatles in England. "I started Beatles Fan Club Number One and we had maybe a hundred and fifty members; not a lot of kids responded to it," Roberts maintained.[87] Brian Epstein launched the Official National Beatles Fan Club or Beatles USA Ltd. fan club in April 1964. The fan club, headquartered in New York City, supplied members who paid their two dollar annual dues with a membership card, a newsletter to keep members abreast of the latest Beatles news, and special offers on Beatles merchandise. The club also began sending members the annual Christmas records, which the British fan club had first given to its members in 1963.[88]

The need for girls to go beyond impersonal correspondence with a distant fan club and to share their love of the Beatles with other fans on a day-to-day basis was evident in the huge number of fan clubs that girls organized across the Chicago area independent of the radio stations and the Official Beatles Fan Club. Some of the clubs were school-based or neighborhood-based while others organized on a citywide basis. The "Chicago Area Continental Beatles Society," "Wheaton Community Beatle Society," "Chicago Beatle Fan Society," "Beatlemaniacs of Chicago," "Beatle Boosters of Chicago," the "Johgeorinpau Beatle Fan Club," "Do Anything for the Beatles Club," and the hard to digest "Official International Midnight Basement Nursery School Beatle Forever United Beatles and Only Beatles Fan Club of Highland Park and Deerfield" were among the many fan clubs to emerge in the Chicago metropolitan area. These clubs elected officers, issued membership cards, established club rules, collected dues, produced fanzines, and communicated by telephone and through regular club meetings. Some clubs raised money for charities, baked cakes for orphanages, gifted toys to children in hospitals, and visited the infirm.[89] One fan club of about two hundred and fifty members collected $1,000 for a leukemia drive.[90] The "National Association for the Advancement of Beatle People" (NAABP) found that record store counters and magazine racks were the best places to recruit new members. They corresponded with fans in Liverpool and with George's sister, Louise, in Illinois. NAABP wrote to *Chicago's American* columnist Jack Mabley asking for publicity because "we don't have many members and we have so much planned," which included an upcoming picnic to celebrate Paul's birthday.[91] Some of the clubs found it easy to attract members. Thirteen-year-old Linda Zimmerman boasted to the *Tribune* that her club, "The World Wide Beatle Fan Club," had two hundred adherents.[92] In Woodstock, Illinois, "The Beatle Fan Club What Ain't Got No Name" published its own paper, *Beatle Beat*, and accrued over three hundred members in the space of a few months.[93]

The "Chicagoland Beatle People," started by six girls at Rich East High School in the suburb of Park Forest, became one of the largest Beatles fan clubs in the Chicago area. Fifteen-year-old Marti Whitman, president of the club, obtained a post office box to receive mail, corresponded with Louise Harrison, who agreed to sponsor the club, and baked cakes and brownies, which the club donated to orphanages and senior homes. The club would meet at a restaurant in the local shopping center and discuss the latest Beatles news found in the teen magazines. They visited the WLS studios in downtown Chicago, where they recruited new members among the girls who gathered to watch the live broadcasts, and secured free publicity from the deejays who discussed their activities on air. In August 1964, Marti appeared on *The Lee Phillip Show*, a popular Chicago television talk show, to discuss the Beatles, and local newspapers devoted space to the club's activities. Soon membership of the "Chicagoland Beatle People" reached more than 1,200.[94]

In addition to fan clubs, teen magazines were critical in sustaining the community of female Beatles fans. The magazines encouraged hero worship, with content concentrating on pictures, gossip, and trite stories, and claimed to reveal personal secrets of the stars. *Teen World* invited girls to enter a "Beatles Kissing Contest" by putting on their lipstick, leaving their kiss-print on a piece of paper and then sending the imprint to the magazine. "The girl whose kiss-print most closely resembles the kiss-print of The Beatles' dream girl" would be the winner and "the prize in this contest will be received by the winner the next time the boys are in the states."[95] Other teen magazines organized contests with the winner meeting the Beatles at one of their concerts or receiving a phone call from the group. Contestants simply had to write to the magazine and state why they wanted to talk to their favorite Beatle. *Teen Life* magazine asked its readers to dream. "Close your eyes. Take a deep breath. Now picture a telephone. Now picture it ringing. The voice at the other end is faint. Now it's getting louder. Now you can hear it! It's the voice of your fave Beatle calling you!"[96]

For some girls, the dream came true. Pat Meyers, aged fourteen from Joliet, entered as many contests as she could, hoping to meet or at least talk to the Beatles and especially to George Harrison. In August 1965, Pat was sitting in her bedroom with two friends. "We were listening to Beatles records, looking at Beatles books and, of course, talking about the Beatles. I received a phone call telling me that I had won a contest to talk to the Beatles long distance from London, England. I would receive this call at 3 p.m. So at 3 p.m. my friends and I, along with my mother and grandmother, were eagerly awaiting this call. And sure enough there they were. I remember speaking to Ringo first. Unfortunately, I don't remember what was said. Each of the other girls took turns talking to the Beatles. Paul wasn't there for the first part of the conversation. John kept joking around. Being silly. I remember this very clearly because I was a George Harrison fan. At the time I had a Siamese cat I named George. I told George Harrison that I loved my cat as if I was loving him. I don't remember his response but I'm sure he thought I was crazy. We were on the phone for forty minutes." The phone call brought Pat some local fame. "When my father got home from work, we told him about it. He arranged for us to go to our local radio station (WJOL) to be interviewed by one of the deejays. At the end of the interview, the deejay told us to 'scream for the Beatles.' And we did."[97]

Teen magazines proved particularly important in disseminating British fashions and changing the look of American girls. Before the Beatles arrived in the US, some girls clung to the '50s bouffant hairstyle while others followed the trends set by actress Audrey Hepburn and First Lady Jackie Kennedy by adopting shoulder length hair flipped at the end. Invariably, young women wore sweaters, matching skirts, fixed stubbornly at or below the knee, and nylon stockings or knee socks; clothes similar to what their mothers wore. While European tourists and travelers regularly visited New York or California, fewer stopped in the flyover city of Chicago, and the influence of European fashion and ideas were even less apparent in the Midwest. When the Beatles landed in the US, girls immediately wanted to emulate the Beatles' haircut. For thirty-five cents, *Beatle Hairdos & Setting Patterns* offered help to girls who wanted to attain the "Beatle Dip," "Beatle Bob," and "Beatle Swirl."[98] Soon, however, the Beatles' wives and girlfriends became fixtures in the teen magazines and inspired many female fans to imitate their style. "She is today's girl," *16 Spec* magazine wrote of Pattie Boyd, who appeared in *A Hard Day's Night* and became the girlfriend and then wife of George Harrison. "She is the girl most girls want to look like. She is the beguiling, old-young mixture that most of today's girls are—sweet and swinging, shy and sophisticated. And her big china-blue eyes, beneath a fine flaxen fringe, reflect today's outlook—a 'hip' innocence."[99] Teen magazines regularly featured pictures of John's wife, Cynthia, and Paul's girlfriend, Jane Asher, both of whom helped to popularize the mini skirt and the long straight hair look in the US. "From model Jean Shrimpton and from fresh young designers like Mary Quant and Jean Muir, London has exported the 'total look,' the boots or little-girl shoes, white stockings, thigh high skirts, long straight hair and Liverpool cap now seen in nearly every US city," *Newsweek* noted in March 1966.[100]

Some girls began to shorten their skirts, but many found it rather difficult to attain the long straight hair, so important to the British look. Claudia Chalden from suburban Evergreen Park, who was eleven years old when *A Hard Day's Night* was released, revealed that "my sister ironed her hair because Jane Asher, Paul's girlfriend, and Pattie Boyd, George's girlfriend, both had long hair that they straightened by ironing it. And when it didn't work out for her, she eventually went out and bought what we called a fall, which was a headband that had long hair attached to it and you would just put your headband on and all of a sudden you have long straight hair."[101]

Debbi Puntini of the northern suburb of Arlington Heights informed the readers of *Datebook* magazine that she had the perfect solution for those unwilling to buy hair extensions. "[A]fter washing your hair, make a bowl of jello and pour it over your head; when it begins to harden, start brushing your hair vigorously. Soon it will be soft, shiny and straight!"[102]

The Beatles also influenced the sartorial style of African-American girls on the South Side of the city. In February 1965, Chicago-based *Ebony* magazine featured an article entitled "Bouffants Are Out, Beatles

Cuts Are In" and illustrated the story with two African-American female models. "The era of the bouffant has ended, and that scintillating boyish haircut is back. In essence, the 'new' styles in the worlds of coifdom are drawn along the lines introduced by those mop-topped madcaps of rock 'n' roll the Beatles."[103] The *Chicago Defender* noted that the Beatles-influenced mod look was evident "in discotheques from the Sunset Strip to Park Avenue; going to school in Chicago and Minneapolis; weekending in or out of town in Cleveland and San Francisco."[104]

"We all tried to look like Pattie Boyd," said Cynthia Dagnal. "Yeah, we did all the hair. I had a flip with a bump in the back…. We tried as hard as we could to have that London look."[105]

"We cut each other's hair short like Twiggy," the English model, African-American Bonnie Greer recounted of her teen years in Chicago. "We bought Mary Quant eyelashes and dreamed we were in Carnaby Street, three black girls, for a moment, in another place…. We loved Yardley cosmetics; even The Beatles, who it was OK to like in the black community by then. We especially liked the Beatles' wives and girlfriends, particularly Patti(e) Boyd."[106]

If miniskirts were the most visible sign of British influence on girls, undoubtedly for boys the major innovation was in the style and length of hair. When the Beatles arrived in the US, crew cuts and flat tops dominated the mainstream, but '50s style greasers, young men with greased back hair and leather jackets, were still a common sight in early '60s Chicago. Under the influence of the Beatles, boys stopped greasing their hair, started to comb it forward, and then let it grow long. Some boys simply grew their hair to look like their heroes. Others saw the haircuts as a symbol of individuality and rebellion, a way to cast off the old and embrace the new. For the first time in generations, boys could now revel in a variety of hair styles and lengths, and each boy had the opportunity to fashion their own unique look. Boys began to voice the idea that they had a right to wear their hair however they wanted. "Part of our American way is the free expression of individuality," wrote a "crew-cut veteran" to the *Tribune*. "Along with free speech and freedom to pay one's income tax, we males enjoy also the privilege to wear long hair if we so desire. The idea of forcing a boy to get an alleged 'all-American haircut'… is most reactionary and un-American."[107]

Others hoped that long hair would make them more appealing to girls. "I myself started imitating their style because the women and girls really found their appearance attractive so I wanted them to find my appearance attractive as well," noted Beatles fan Terry Cessna, for example.[108] Gary Gold of the local musical group the Cave Dwellers said that the success of the Beatles forced them to grow their hair long. "You gotta do it. Ever since the Beatles, the kids expect it. A new rock n roll group with crewcuts couldn't get off the ground."[109]

The Beatles Change the American View of Britain

When the Beatles arrived in the US, Americans had no great understanding of the UK. "There is a standardized mythology about England and the English way of life," English agriculturalist Hugh Willoughby found when he visited the US in the mid-'50s. "The essentials are warm beer, cold rooms, a completely incomprehensible coinage, fog, a constant consumption of crumpets and cabbage."[110] BBC broadcaster Edward Ward and his wife, Marjorie Banks, who arrived in the US in the early '50s found similar negative assessments of the UK. "Do they have electricity in England?" a Midwestern boy asked them. Americans seemed incredulous when the two visitors said they were returning home rather than staying in the US. "They feel on the one hand pity for us, and on the other hand are disgusted with this lot of 'moth-eaten, mildewed, out of date, old European dumps.'"[111] Some Beatles fans seemed equally confused about Britain. "I want to see you in London," Claudine from Cleveland, Ohio, wrote to the Beatles. "Please tell me, what is the quickest way from Cleveland by bike?"[112]

"I love to hear you say 'rubbish,'" Lois from Hollywood, California, wrote to her idols. "I don't know why. Rubbish just sounds great with your Oxford accent."[113]

Thanks to the Beatles, many youngsters became besotted with Britain and wanted to find out more about the country. Teenagers tried to locate the city of Liverpool on atlases and inundated teen magazines with pleas for British pen pals. "Before the Beatles, England was just any other country," Chicagoan Linda Milan recalled. "And after the Beatles everything about England was special. In fact, I had a neighbor who was from England and we would always go over and talk to her and ask her English things. And we loved her English accent."[114] Tutored by *Datebook, Teen*

Screen, and *16 Magazine,* young Americans cultivated a vocabulary of British slang expressions such as "fab" and "gear" (both synonymous with "terrific"). "Teenage America has really gone British," *Datebook* noted in its winter 1965 issue. "Ever since the Beatles invasion, interest in things English has grown steadily until now we are at the peak of our Anglophilia."[115]

Those unable to visit the birthplace of their idols tried to live like the British. "I became a UK fanatic," revealed Ginny Venson Greninger, who was sixteen in the summer of 1964. "I loved everything British. I asked for a bottle of ale (empty of course because I was just a teenager), ate with utensils in the British style, using both fork and knife at the same time pushing food into the fork with the knife. A friend of my mother's had a trip to England planned and I asked if he would bring me some British soil. He did, in a test tube. Not sure what happened to that souvenir. I sent away for tourist information on Liverpool, and even explored going to college in the UK."[116] Meredith Feltmeyer of Pekin High School in central Illinois wrote to *Datebook* to tell them about the English infatuation of her and her friends. "We hold English teas at about 3:00 PM, serve tea and crumpets and wear dainty dresses."[117]

Jeanne Yorke from the Chicago suburb of Naperville, who turned sixteen in the summer of 1964, was typical of many girls who became interested in Britain because of the Beatles. "It was a British revolution, anything British was awesome. So, reading up on things in Britain and styles in Britain. I had an English pen pal for a while. We talked to each other about what it's like in America and she would talk about what it was like in England. But then the reason I started talking about that is looking at the way the girls in England dressed and styled their hair and everything. I kind of took that on. But then I think a lot of other American girls did, too. Yes, the British revolution, for a while, it took over a large section of America." Spurred on by her love of the Beatles, Jeanne developed a positive view of Britain. "It seemed to me, what I've read about and then started seeing on the news or reading in magazines, it seemed that the European people and British people were more sophisticated. Maybe it was just the enigma of them." She also credited the Beatles with sparking an interest in the world beyond the borders of the US. "I never thought about people in other countries before the Beatles kind of drew our continents together a little bit. I think that was what happened. So that the culture of Europe became something that I additionally thought that wouldn't it be cool to live there. You know, those kinds of things."[118]

Because of the Beatles, Britain became much more visible in American popular culture. McGregor-Doniger, one of the biggest American manufacturers of clothes for men, started an English style line for older males called Brolly Male.[119] *Hullabaloo* magazine, which began publication in October 1966, adopted English terms like "Beatle Bird" when referring to the Beatles' girlfriends or wives. In an advertisement promoting the magazine, a girl in a mini dress stood next to a boy in a Union Jack shirt.[120] US television companies broadcast more British shows. *Secret Agent*, known in Britain as *Danger Man*, starred Patrick McGoohan as NATO special investigator John Drake and ran on CBS from April 1965 to September 1966. ABC broadcast *The Avengers* from 1965 to 1968, while NBC went with *The Saint* starring Roger Moore from 1967 to 1969. American-based programs added a British flavor. The spy show *The Man from U.N.C.L.E.* starred Scottish actor David McCallum, and the two secret agents reported to British organization head, Alexander Waverly.[121] For the first time, American viewers saw the FIFA World Cup when NBC televised the final of the 1966 tournament held in London. Shown at 11 a.m. Central Time, nine million watched England beat West Germany and win the tournament for the first, and alas, the only time in their history.[122]

Some individuals saw their career trajectory soar simply because they were British. "The British are Coming," announced Chicago radio station WCFL in September 1965. "First James Bond. Then, The Beatles made our scene...Now, one of Britain's top disc jockeys, Paul Michael joins WCFL...Blimey, ain't he a beautiful bloke? And, he's from Liverpool, luv!"[123] Michael, who actually came from Cardiff, Wales, migrated to America where he began to work as a deejay in St. Louis. WCFL program director Ken Draper recruited him to present the "British Countdown" show where he played music from the British charts. With his Beatles haircut and his claims that he worked with the Fab Four, Michael was a big hit in the British-crazy city.[124]

The Beatles' success paved the way for other British artists to come to the US, heralding a period of unparalleled British dominance of popular music. In 1962-63, only two British acts had number one records in America. In 1964-65, British acts held the top spot on the *Billboard* chart for an astonishing fifty-two weeks. British bands such as the Dave Clark Five, the Zombies and Herman's Hermits became more popular in the US than they were at home. The Dave Clark Five recorded seven Top 20 singles in the US in 1964 and four more the following year.[125] Bands like the Rolling Stones, the Yardbirds, and the Animals played their own version of Chicago blues while the Kinks and the Who celebrated England in their lyrics and in their style. It was not just musical groups who became popular in the US. Duos like Peter and Gordon, and Chad and Jeremy, who enjoyed little success in the UK, and solo artists like Petula Clark and Lulu, followed the Beatles into the American charts.

With the post-Beatles' British Invasion in full swing, it seemed that any musical group with British connections could become stars in Chicago, as the story of the Robin Hoods illustrates. Pete Shelton, a bass player for several bands in the Manchester area in the early '60s, including Marty Wilde's backing band, and Bern Elliott and the Fenmen, saw his life change when he returned home to Blackpool for the Christmas holidays in 1964. "I bumped into some old friends of mine. They were in an Irish showband, and they were preparing to go to America to play for two years on the Irish ballroom circuit. They asked me if I'd join them as a bass player because their bass player quit. I told them no, no, I can't, I'm busy, I'm with a band, and we've got two hit records, and we're touring well. So, anyway, we carried on that night drinking and celebrating. It was Christmas and everything. And the next thing I remember is waking up in Belfast Harbor. They shanghaied me. I woke up on a ferry in Belfast Harbor, and I became a member of an Irish showband due to play in America." Shelton found himself traveling to America as part of Paddy McGuigan and the Big Four, but in actuality, there were only four of them in total, as Paddy McGuigan decided not to travel. By the time they arrived in the US, audiences wanted British rock acts not Irish show bands. "So we were rehearsing our act to go and do this circuit when a guy came in and said 'you should be playing at the Whiskey a Go Go' [a club on Rush Street, the nightclub capital of Chicago] and we got a gig playing, and we did two nights. Then they offered us a contract for sixteen weeks. So we gave up the Irish showband and became an English rock 'n' roll band." Finding an appropriate name for the group proved problematic. "We were actually called the Clan, but our American manager thought it was a bad idea because of the KKK. We were going to be the Flock, but the manager of the Whiskey a Go Go wanted an English name. So, they called us the Robin Hoods."[126]

When the band opened at the Whiskey a Go Go in February 1965, the marquee declared: "England's newest sensations: The Robin Hoods." Lines formed "down Chestnut Street down to Michigan Avenue because we were English. There was a table charge of five dollars per table, and they broke the house record for takings over the bar, $30,000." The Robin Hoods topped the bill at McCormick Place convention center, with Herman's Hermits as support, recorded two singles, won a Battle of the Bands contest against local group the Cryan' Shames at the Aragon Ballroom, and filmed a television commercial for the Three Musketeers candy bar, in which the group's image appeared on the wrapper. Yet, Shelton was brutally honest about the limitations of the group. "Awful name. No, we weren't a good band, and we had no real singer. I was the only singer, and I wasn't much cop. Actually, there was only two of us in the band that were English. The others were Irish and Scottish. I was twenty-eight. I mean, the young kids that used to come and hang around didn't hang around for long because we had no attraction to them. We were old men, weren't we?" He was less than complimentary about their debut single, "Wait for the Dawn," cut at Universal Studios and released on Mercury records. "I almost threw up every time I heard it. It didn't represent the group at all." [127] The disc failed to chart locally or nationally but touched a chord in Singapore where it reached number six in the best-seller lists in September 1965.[128]

Englishness could only take the Robin Hoods so far. "We were booked for sixteen weeks to play at the Whiskey a Go Go. After about six or seven weeks, come 11 o'clock the place was empty because they didn't like the music. The attraction was listening to us talk. They'd ask us to come and sit down at the table, just talk to them at the table. Elvis came in one night with a lot of people. He only stayed about thirty seconds. He just came up to the stage, shook our sax player's hand, and then turned around and they all walked out." The band had broken up by the close of 1965.[129]

The Robin Hoods may have found it difficult to prosper in the US, but the Beatles had no such problems. In the end, the Beatles became popular in the US for the same reasons they did in the UK: they offered young people a new joyous sound, look, and demeanor and an escape from the dull and the staid. But while the British audience was relatively familiar with long hair and the irreverent wit of the Beatles, and the group only gradually rose to fame in their homeland, the Beatles' hair and blunt flippant humor was more of a shock to Americans, as was their sudden appearance in their midst. For many, this was a shock of joy, but not everyone was so enthralled with the Fab Four or the happiness and elation they inspired. Many decried their music, their look, and their influence on young people and saw them not as a benign influence on American youth but as an unwelcome threat to the fabric of American society.

CHAPTER 3

"Delinquent Robin Hoods"

Beatlephobia

A month before the Beatles appeared on *The Ed Sullivan Show*, the *Chicago Tribune* issued a "Beatle warning" to the American public. The British people have lost their minds over a musical group bizarrely named the Beatles, the self-styled "World's Greatest Newspaper" informed its startled readers. The group plays loud guitar-based music, "if you can call it that," the editorial wryly noted. The once staid, reserved, sophisticated Britishers have resorted to wearing "Beatle wigs," imitating the long hair of this ridiculous musical group. "The Beatle wig is a shaggy, shapeless mop, hiding whatever brains and forehead one has under a disheveled mass," the paper helpfully explained. The *Tribune* told its by now extremely alarmed readership that this "Beatle menace" has infiltrated all areas of British society. "And if, until now, you had not yet heard of the Beatles, should America be so unfortunate as to afford this combo further fields to conquer, remember that you got your first warning in our austere columns."[1]

The Beatles brought much happiness to so many young Americans but, as the *Tribune* editorial elucidates, not everyone was so enraptured by the sensations from Britain. In the years following their debut in the US, many Beatles fans found their joyous music an inspiring call for freedom, but others saw the music as disconcerting and the whole phenomenon as a distressing indictment of the modern world. Following their historic US debut, the *Tribune* escalated its criticisms of the

Beatles and Beatlemania and played a leading part in a vociferous anti-Beatles campaign.

Indifference and Dismay

As Val Camilletti at Capitol Records in Chicago found out, people in their twenties and thirties were not as keen to see the Beatles as teens and preteens. "I was at a bar on the Northwest end of Chicago. I said to the bartender when we walked in, 'Seven o'clock, you got to put it on Channel 2.' He said, 'Why?' I said, 'You have to put it on Channel 2.' And he said 'Why?' I said, 'You just do, you have to put it on Channel 2, it's a really big deal.' My friends were just a few years older than me, and some were substantially, but they were in their early thirties, I was twenty-three. So, at seven o'clock he turned it on to Channel 2, and that was the Sullivan show, and all of my friends turned to me and said, 'Ah is that those kids now? That's those kids from England, the kids you like so much. Yeah, the kids with the long hair.' They were totally unfazed."[2]

Many parents just seemed bewildered by what they witnessed on *The Ed Sullivan Show*. The length of the Beatles' hair, which was longer in 1964 than it was when most Britons first encountered the group, was particularly startling to an American audience. "My parents always watched the Sullivan show on Sunday nights," recalled Leann Julian from suburban Joliet, who was nine years old at the time. "I was in my bedroom, and I heard my dad yelling for me to 'come quick and look at these guys.' I ran out to the living room and watched them, and from that moment on, I was a fan! The screaming girls and the cute guys like I'd never seen before, just hooked me." Her parents, however, viewed the Beatles through a different lens. "My dad thought they were 'a bunch of long-haired hooligans, and my mom thought they were just a fad.'"[3]

Kathy Mangan, who lived on a farm in rural Illinois, was fourteen when she watched the show with her mother, father, and two siblings. "I sang 'I Want to Hold Your Hand' to my Dad while they were singing it on Ed Sullivan. I said, 'Well, do you like them?' and Dad's comment was 'Sounds like the thresher machine needs oil,' ... My Mom wasn't thrilled with them. But they did sing a song later on in the program. I don't remember it, but it was a slower song, and Dad liked that one. But, otherwise, threshing machine. Mom would put up with them. But I think she would rather go out and milk the cows than listen to our music."[4]

As Leann and Kathy allude to, opposition to the Beatles not only revealed a generation gap but also a gender one. Many mothers watching the show had the same reaction to Frank Sinatra or Elvis Presley as their daughters did to the Beatles and could at least understand their enthusiasm. Fathers and brothers, however, had no such empathy. In a nationwide survey of 1,375 teenagers undertaken in April 1964, 83 percent of girls but only 58 percent of boys claimed to be Beatles fans. While sixty-five percent of the girls liked the Beatles' hair, only 43 percent of the boys felt the same way.[5] Listening and dancing to pop music was a female interest, which meant that many American boys, besotted with sports, astronauts, and superheroes, maintained their male identity by ignoring or belittling the Beatles and pop music in general. "In the beginning, guys did not like the Beatles, girls liked the Beatles," recalled Bob Smith, born in Chicago in 1950 and raised in the Northwest suburbs from the age of three. He cared little about the Beatles and refused to watch their appearance on *Ed Sullivan*. When Bob became acquainted with the group and their fans, he was not impressed. "It was ridiculous. People were literally passing out. Music wasn't that important to guys. It was important to girls…. It was just something you didn't really do as a guy."[6]

"I never was a huge fan of the Beatles," admitted Tom Ruddy from suburban Plainfield. "The ladies all seemed to swoon over them but never me. Sure, did I go out dancing with their tunes? Of course, that's where the ladies were. They weren't my idols or anything. Neil Armstrong was my idol."[7]

Those boys that admired the Beatles were generally less enthusiastic than girl fans, and many were too scared to publicize their allegiance. "Even though I never told anyone because I was too embarrassed to do so, I flat out worshipped the Beatles," Tom McCabe, a 1960s graduate from West Aurora Senior High School, revealed years later to the *Chicago Tribune*.[8]

Bernie Biernacki, the student at the all-boys Catholic high school on Chicago's Southwest Side who had commented on the divisions the Beatles created in his school, found that sports lovers particularly disliked the Beatles and their effete fans. "There were cliques at the school; there were the sports guys. They played football, basketball, baseball. Those guys were the jocks. The guys who really liked the Beatles, they weren't jocks. They might have started as greasers, but all of a sudden, their clothes got a little bit sharper…they tried to mimic the Beatles talk." The jocks hurled abuse at the Beatles fans, often questioning their manliness. "They would call them names and that riled them up. That's when the shoving would start, just to show their masculinity." Bernie, like many boys across the United States, was neither an avid fan nor a detractor and kept his distance from the fray. "I was just middle of the road and observing everything."[9]

Cultural Traditionalists

Many remained indifferent to the Beatles, but cultural traditionalists, young and old, male and female, voiced utter contempt for the British imports and the joyousness they inspired in their fans. Cultural conservatives, who espoused traditional values such as conventional gender relations, the sanctity of marriage, a diligent work ethic, respect for authority figures, and self-restraint, viewed the Fab Four as upending accepted codes of behavior and as a symbol of the moral decay inflicting the nation. They recoiled at the unbridled consumerism that had exploited the base instincts of young people for naked greed. Some believed that the joyful feelings the Beatles transmitted to their audience could be uncontrollable once set in motion, threatening and disrupting law and order.

Religious groups of all denominations and from all parts of the country expressed unease from the beginning. Many worried that the Beatles encouraged teenagers to be more interested in sensual pleasures than spiritual matters. Christians may have initially voiced concern about the pelvic gyrations of Elvis Presley, but he was a southerner and a Christian who sang hymns. The Beatles were neither. Within a week of their appearance on *The Ed Sullivan Show*, Rabbi Shlomoh Fineberg gave a talk entitled "Beatniks, Beatles, Ed Sullivan—American Neurosis" in the Austin neighborhood in Chicago.[10] In July 1964, Chicago-based *Photoplay* magazine asked: "Do the Beatles believe in God?" In the ensuing interview, the Beatles put the magazine and its readers at ease by professing a belief in God if not adherence to any particular denomination.[11] "Throw your Beatle and rock and roll records in the city dump," recommended Reverend David A. Noebel from Wisconsin. "We have been unashamed of being labeled a Christian nation; let's make sure four

Photoplay *July 1964* *worriedly asked the* *question on the minds* *of many, "Do the* *Beatles believe in God?"*

mop-headed anti-Christ beatniks don't destroy our children's emotional and mental stability and ultimately destroy our nation as Plato warned in his Republic."[12]

In his local newspaper column, Reverend Clarence Brissette of Our Lady of Sorrows Catholic Basilica in Chicago regularly cited the Beatles, and the adulation they engendered, as an example of the declining morals of the young. In May 1964, he decried the deteriorating behavior of young people including "the stomach upsetting sight of teenage girls screaming in ecstasy over the ludicrous 'beatles'—boys, beatnicks with high voices and swinging hips trying to act like girls."[13] The indecent attire of young American women was a sign of a return to "the primitive found in the African jungle," he pronounced in July of the same year. "Young girls as well as old dowagers let skin turn black under the sun and some smear red goo to thicken lips, and give the appearance of painted masks," he added. "For teenagers, the painted medicine men become English Beatles driving hysterical mobs into a frenzy of swooning emotion and just listen to the music…yes listen, the steady rhythm of the tom-tom, the foolish repetition of the same words, such as 'I hold your hand.'"[14] Three months later, he devoted his column to "the mentality of present day teenagers going into hysterics at the sight of the sexless Beatles." The group "look and act plain stupid… the words sound as if they were put together by a ten-year-old child and for the life of me I can't come up with one good reason why young girls should be in the least interested in them." He ended on a note of optimism, however, believing that if parents "create a wholesome family environment seasoned with plenty of discipline" their children "will turn out to be solid citizens."[15]

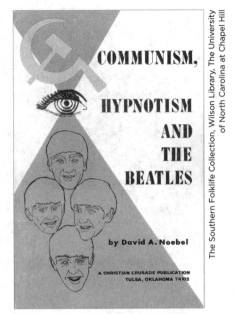

The Rev. David A. Noebel explains the enduring success of the Beatles.

Conservatives feared that the arrival of the Beatles in the US was the latest wave in a rising tide of liberalism. American youth, like their British counterparts, had not only become more affluent but also more assertive and intellectually curious by the early '60s. With McCarthyism in the rearview mirror, comedians like Lenny Bruce, musicians of the folk revival, the Beat Generation of writers, and satirical magazines *Mad* (launched in 1952) and *The Realist* (first published in 1958) expressed dissatisfaction with the inequality and conservatism of American society. The *Students for a Democratic Society* (SDS), formed at the University of Michigan in 1960, criticized the Cold War and called for universities to become centers of freedom of speech and political activism. The air of disobedience and dissent was evident in the modern civil rights movement that inspired so many to question not only racial but also other forms of discrimination.

The sight of thousands of young girls screaming at the shaggy-haired foursome confirmed to the conservatives that the traditional role of American women was changing fast. Congress passed the Equal

Chicago Austin News, July 22, 1964, page 18

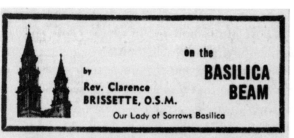

on the

by
**Rev. Clarence
BRISSETTE, O.S.M.**

**BASILICA
BEAM**

Our Lady of Sorrows Basilica

INDECENT EXPOSURE . . . IN ART AND NATURE
WITH ALL the talk of topless swimming suits, reports from Paris, fashion will soon decree bald heads for women . . . no one seems to see a return to the primitive as found in the African jungle. There, unembarrassed women wear nothing above the hips and the ladies of some tribes shave off all the

Fr. Brissette

hair on their heads. For teenagers, the painted medicine men become English Beatles driving hysterical mobs into a frenzy of swooning emotion and just listen to the music . . . yes listen, the steady rhythm of the tom-tom, the foolish repetition of the same words, such as "I hold your hand." Young girls as well as old dowagers let skin turn black under the sun and some smear red goo to thicken lips and give the appearance of painted masks. Take a look at the bearded beatniks, skin-fitting pants and then . . . the swagger and loin cloth of the jungle. For fear you think I am exaggerating, the first Lady of the land retains the nickname "Lady Bird" (given her by her hired mammy) and fondly hands the same on to her daughter "Lynda Bird." Birds are beautiful but human beings rate a higher beauty and no compliment to a man or woman to be named after the lower order of God's creation. In all this I am not moralizing, just calling attention to our new culture.

* * *

In his columns published in the local Chicago newspapers, the very holy Reverend Clarence Brissette condemned the Obscene Four.

Pay Act in 1963, which directed employers to pay men and women the same wages for performing the same job. More married women were going out to work, and divorce rates were rising. Betty Friedan's *The Feminine Mystique,* which questioned the contentment of homemakers, quickly became a landmark book in the women's movement when published in 1963. The pop charts reflected this change. The Exciters' 1962 top ten hit, "Tell Him," which suggested that a girl should go and get her man, and Leslie Gore's "You Don't Own Me," which peaked at number two in December 1963, signaled a growing female assertiveness. The silver screen also began featuring independent young women. The film *Breakfast at Tiffany's* (1961), the story of a young free-spirited New York socialite played by Audrey Hepburn, was indicative of the change. "People don't belong to people," she told her incredulous suitor played by George Peppard, "I'm not going to let anyone put me in a cage."

Changing attitudes to sexual relations worried conservatives too. The Shirelles' "Will You Love Me Tomorrow," in which a girl considers spending the night with her boyfriend, reached number one in December 1960. Helen Gurley Brown's *Sex and the Single Girl*, published in 1962, revealed the unsavory fact that unmarried women had sex and enjoyed it, shocking reviewers but selling millions. Gael Greene followed the trend when she published *Sex and the College Girl* in 1964, and *Time* published an article on "The Second Sexual Revolution" in January 1964. The birth control pill came on the market in 1961, and on June 7, 1965, the Supreme Court announced in *Griswold v. Connecticut* that married couples had a right to use contraceptives. In 1953, Gallup found that 53 percent of Catholics believed that birth control information should be freely available. In 1965, the figure had increased to 78 percent.[16] In 1964, the cultural climate seemed ripe for designer Rudi Gernreich to introduce the topless swimsuit for women, where two thin straps around the neck held up tight-fitting trunks. Most women thought Rudi had gone too far, but bikinis became a common sight on the beaches of America.[17]

Chicago reflected some of these cultural changes. Hugh Hefner, a Chicago native, launched *Playboy* in 1953, a magazine that hit on the winning formula of gravity-defying breasts, cellulite-free thighs, and liberal intellectualism. In 1959, WBKB, an ABC affiliate in Chicago, launched the television series *Playboy Penthouse*. Hefner, overseeing his growing empire from his Playboy Mansion on Chicago's Gold Coast, opened his first Playboy club in downtown Chicago the following year. Attracted by the anonymity of urban life, gay men and women flocked to Chicago, where they could blend into the population and mix with other like-minded people in clubs and bars, if not openly on the streets. Suffering from police harassment, gays in the city began to organize for equal rights. In 1965, activists established the first successful gay rights organization in the city, Mattachine Midwest, named after medieval masked performers to signify that gays had to similarly mask their true identity.[18]

In Chicago, the staunch upholders of traditional values, the *Chicago Tribune* and the paper's editor, W. D. Maxwell, led the way in condemning the Beatles and the changes they symbolized. Born in 1900, in the town of Greencastle, Indiana, to a Methodist revival singer and a schoolteacher, Maxwell joined the *Tribune* as a reporter in 1920, worked his way up through the organization, and became the designated successor to the former owner and editor, Robert R. "Colonel" McCormick, who died in 1955. Maxwell went on to serve as editor of the *Chicago Tribune* until his retirement in 1969. The *Tribune*, the city's leading newspaper and the one with the most national influence, displayed an unabashedly Republican orientated editorial stance while its city rivals, the *Sun-Times* and the *Daily News*, and the major newspapers on the East and West Coasts, the *New York Times*, the *Washington Post,* and the *Los Angeles Times*, held a more liberal or centrist position. The *Tribune* and its sister afternoon paper, *Chicago's Ameri-can*, recommended that their readers vote for firebrand Republican Barry Goldwater for president in 1964.[19] A believer in hard work, unyielding respect from subordinates, and a stickler for quality, Maxwell sat at the *Tribune*'s center desk and reviewed every news article before deeming them fit to be sent to the composing room. A staunch believer in both the free-market economy and a conservative brand of Christianity, he described himself as a "religious capitalist."[20] Reverend Harold Walker, a Methodist pastor from Maxwell's hometown of Evanston, believed that Maxwell's "integrity stemmed from a deep belief in God. His high ethical standards were not optional, they were imperative."[21]

Beatlephobe W. D. Maxwell, editor of the Chicago Tribune.

DePauw University Archives and Special Collections

Across America, the media was underwhelmed by what they saw on *The Ed Sullivan Show* on the night of February 9, but, while other newspapers of note gently mocked the Beatles or their fans, the *Chicago Tribune*'s coverage adopted a more vicious tone. The *Los Angeles Times* concentrated on the gyrations of the studio audience with the head-line "Girls go bug-eyed as Beatles perform" as did the *New York Times:* "Quartet continues to agitate the faithful." Neither insulted the group. The former seemed rather surprised that they "provided their own musi-cal background with string and percussion instruments" while the latter called their performance "businesslike."[22] The *Tribune* editorial, however, led with the headline, "Human Sheep Dogs," and suggested that the

Beatles made "enough noise to bring the plaster down from the ceiling, but the teen-agers respond by howling in ecstasy." More insults followed. "These boys wear their hair like an English sheep dog. They sing—if singing it is—thru bangs that resemble an old-fashioned beaded portiere."[23]

"They look like four of the Three Stooges with a hairy measure of Ish Kabibble," *Tribune* journalist Donald Freeman wrote after seeing them perform on Sullivan's show. "They put you in mind of delinquent Robin Hoods. And if they ever submitted to a barber who loves music—snip, snip!—that would be the end of the act....The Beatles must be a huge joke, a wacky gag, a gigantic put-on." Freeman wondered: "Are those Beatles hairdos reflective of society's de-masculination? Or do they represent a subtle English slap at us for inflicting rock 'n' roll on their shores?"[24] On February 23, the *Tribune* chose to print a guest editorial from the *Hartford Courant*. The paper called the Beatles "the bushy-haired boys whose sex is not immediately apparent," and blamed the "hysterical younger set" of girls for the Beatles' popularity. "Teetering somewhere between childhood and womanhood, they seize on the boy-girl type of crooner who, while undoubtedly masculine, has much of the same appearance as the adolescent girl."[25]

The Great Hair Wars

Long hair on young men, visible in Britain but virtually unheard of in the US when the Beatles arrived, became the most shocking and the most often condemned aspect of the new phenomenon by cultural traditionalists. Their haircuts suggested more than fun. They alluded to rebellion against societal norms. A boy sporting a long mane overturned conventions of male appearance and symbolized a lack of responsibility and a desire for hedonistic leisure pursuits. Hair that touched the forehead or flowed over the ears questioned existing gender roles for men and suggested feminization of the male, or even worse, homosexuality. Many of those watching the Beatles' debut on *Ed Sullivan* literally could not believe what they were seeing. The *Chicago Garfieldian* asked high school students their opinions, and some obviously remained convinced that what the Beatles had on their heads was not their own hair. Junior Phillip Law of suburban Cicero told the newspaper that he liked their music but "I don't care for their wigs." Others who admired the new look also believed that the Beatles wore hair pieces. "[T]here's nothing wrong with the wigs," Junior John Tyler told the reporter while Sophomore Maggie Palli said, "to me, the wigs are kinda cute. They wear them to be a little different, that's all."[26]

The incredulity continued as America became obsessed with the Beatles' hair. Record labels released several singles that highlighted the novelty. The Swans' "The Boy With the Beatle Hair," Donna Lynn's "My Boyfriend Got a Beatle Haircut," The Bagles' "I Wanna Hold Your Hair," The Outsiders' "The Guy With the Long Liverpool Haircut," and Scott Douglas' "The Beatles' Barber," may have lacked musical ability but not chutzpah or humor.[27] Academia turned their scholarly attention to the problem of long hair on boys. In October 1965, Linda G. Allen, research associate for the American Medical Association, spoke at the Chicago Museum of Science and Industry and told her rapt audience that there was a growth in skin ailments like acne since teenagers adopted Beatle-style haircuts. "Unless the teenager keeps his hair off his face, he may end up with what could well be termed 'Beatle skin,'" she warned the audience and the nation. Allen neglected to say whether the same skin complaint would afflict girls with long hair.[28]

The experiences of musician John Sebastian, who attended a private prep school on the East Coast, illustrates the hostility to long hair in the US. "I had been brought up for five years in Europe. I was living in Italy and so my hair was long. It was different. People related to it differently. When I got to prep school, I actually got forcibly taken by students to a dorm room and had my head shaved." Sebastian graduated in 1962 and grew his hair longer again, but it was still a shock to him when he first met Canadian musician Zal Yanovsky in 1964. "Zal really had long hair. That was something very noticeable about him was that this wasn't just a casual let my bangs grow out or something. His hair had been long for several years. He'd been living almost on the streets in Toronto."[29]

Long hair on boys elicited even more bewilderment in Chicago and the Midwest where, as Louise Harrison noted, boys traditionally wore their hair very short. "In England when somebody was a criminal and they were put in jail, they used to shave their head. But in this country, just about everybody had those crewcuts. Back in England, they had the normal length of hair, which, of course, to the Americans with the Beatle head, it was considered long hair. When I came over here to begin with, I thought, *Oh gosh, there are an awful lot of criminals in this country.*"[30]

"Your paper on Feb. 7 carried one of the most revolting pictures I have ever seen—and right on the front page," seventeen-year-old Bernard Phelan from Chicago wrote to the *Chicago Daily News*. "It was a picture of the Beatles. I feel that this was in very poor taste and with very little consideration for the majority of people in Chicago who are sensible."[31] Others wrote to their local papers expressing a similar response. High school teacher A. A. O'Keefe believed that "the Beatles' appearance and antics undermine and destroy all civilized aspects and conduct in Young America."[32] Jeffrey Barron wrote to *Chicago's American* telling readers that his girlfriend seemed enraptured by the Beatles but, secure in his manhood, he was far from jealous of the long-haired ruffians. "I know that I can always let my hair grow, have my vocal chords run over by a lawn mower, have Sonny Liston punch me in the face 47 times, and presto: Ringo Starr."[33] Jeffrey wrote to the newspaper again a few days later saying that he now regretted sending the previous letter. "Since then, my home has been picketed by mobs of 10-year-olds singing 'Ringo for President' and 'Down with Barron.'" His two sisters added to the misery by playing Beatles records "24 hours a day!"[34]

"I don't know if it's just me, but I think long haired male singers look awful," a seventeen-year-old girl wrote to Mary Merryfield in the *Tribune* in September 1966. "Let me put it this way—there is nothing that turns me on faster than a neat looking guy with a good hair cut." To illustrate her preference for short-haired boys, the teenager told Mary about a shorn boy that she had recently befriended. "Every time he had his hair cut, I sat there quivering. He really looked *neat*." Merryfield told the girl that she was not alone in her assessment. "I'm beginning to get a bubbling up of hostility against long hair on males. I'm printing your letter as a representative sample."[35]

Long-haired British bands that started to arrive in Chicago in the wake of the Beatles' success caused quite a stir in this culturally conservative city. On their first US tour in June 1964, the Rolling Stones made a pilgrimage to Chess Records on South Michigan Avenue where they met Phil and Leonard Chess. "I had just acquired a brand-new Porsche convertible and one night gave Brian Jones a lift back to the hotel the band were staying in," Leonard's son, Marshall, recalled. "Brian had shoulder length hair, longer than anyone else in the band, and we had the Porsche's top down. At one intersection we stopped for a red light, and a bunch of Midwesterners took great delight in shouting, 'Homo, homo!' That was the Mid-West in 1964. We didn't have people in Chicago who looked like the Stones."[36]

Sometimes their long hair landed young British musicians in trouble. "I'd met a singer, a girl singer, and I took her out to dinner. We went to Mister Kelly's on Rush Street," the English musician Pete Shelton, who came to Chicago with the Robin Hoods in February 1965, recalled. "I had a guy come over to the table, and he said to me, 'Are you a boy or a girl?' I just said to him, 'Kiss me and see.' He went berserk. I thought he was going to

Pete Shelton

Pete Shelton of the Robin Hoods, second from right, caused a bar fight in Chicago because of the length of his hair.

trash the place. He turned tables over and he went bananas. Everywhere we went, we used to get into trouble because of the hair."[37] Chicago's reputation as a bastion of short hair reached across the Atlantic to the musical fraternity in the UK. "We'd like to tour the States sometime, but not Chicago," Mike Wilshaw of the English group the Four Pennies told a music paper in 1965. "Any male with hair over an inch long doesn't come out of Chicago alive.... If you go to Chicago, buy a one-way ticket."[38]

Most boys who tried to grow their hair, it seems, found it difficult to escape parental disapproval and school codes. "We went to an annual family reunion last week," a teenager wrote to the agony aunt of the *Chicago Tribune* in February 1965. "My two younger brothers and I have long-ish hair, not as long as the Beatles' haircuts, but like theirs and we like it that way. When we got home from the party my father issued an ultimatum: either we get our hair cut like 'gentlemen' or we don't get our allowances. He said he was embarrassed when he saw our cousins with what he calls decent haircuts. They were practically bald!"[39] Long hair on men became fashionable in bohemian, artistic, and student circles but still provoked hostility on Main Street. When the *Chicago Sun-Times* photographed local music group the Cave Dwellers on Michigan Avenue in August 1965, they attracted an angry crowd. "You could hear expressions of disgust from the spectators. They were outraged by the long hair worn by the boys, particularly one whose hairdo a girl might have selected for herself," the reporter observed. "If I had a kid like that I'd shave him bald," a spectator murmured. "If a boy looking like that came calling on my daughter I'd kick him out of the house," a passing woman cried out to anyone who would listen.[40]

The Beatles' stylish clothes added to the accusations that they, and those boys who dressed like them, were unmanly. The sight of tight pants and Cuban-heeled boots on their rather pale, scrawny English bodies seemed to worry many. The Catholic South Side St. Willibrord High School newspaper, *The Spire*, criticized an article in the *Tribune* for calling English male fashions "sexy" because the tight-fitting clothes revealed men's muscles. "What muscles? It doesn't go on to talk about long hair, make-up, hairspray, etc. but that is enough to bring out the point I'm trying to make, and that is—our generation is turning into an entirely new race of peoples—a unisex. This is a race of boys trying to outdo their mothers and girls borrowing their father's clothes. The result is a neuter-looking individual with dubious outlooks."[41]

"What's happening in England to make the boys dress like girls and the girls like boys?" Helen Culhane, columnist at *Berwyn Life* newspaper, asked in August 1965. "And what's worse, this peculiar ideal of the effete, frail and pale young male is gaining momentum in the country." Helen worried about the decline of the traditional American male. "O, woe to women the demise of the days when knighthood was in flower. When men were men and looked like it. And a hero did heroic things."[42] *Datebook's* London correspondent, fifteen-year-old Dominica Hamilton, tried to allay the fears of American readers. "I detect a little worry among some of you over there about the supposed effeminacy of members of our English groups, especially the Beatles, the Rolling Stones and the Kinks. Long hair is considered here as one of the most masculine attributes possible. So stop worrying about the English groups, kids, you got your own problems."[43]

It was not only the long hair and stylish clothes on boys that worried many Chicagoans; it was also the other major British import: short skirts on girls. In April 1966, the Catholic DePaul University student newspaper, *The DePaulia*, asked students about the Mod look, a term in America that simply meant English fashions. "Minny [sic] skirts are the greatest innovation from England since long hair," student Gil Baker told the reporter. "Mod fashions are fabulous," said fellow student Ellen Riley. "The shorter the better, the lower cut the better."

Many DePaul students, however, were not so impressed with the new styles. "The short skirts are horrible," said Maryanne Davis. Rather surprisingly, boys also voiced their disapproval of skirts that offered them their first public view of the female thigh. Norm Bennett and Rich Ross told the paper that they would not go out with a girl who wore a mini skirt. Many thought that the more revealing clothes only looked good on models and were not appropriate wear for college students. Lynn Stack thought they were only suitable for "swingers" not students, while Mike Eichberger felt that "teenage fads should not be exhibited in college by mature adults."[44]

Because of the opposition and cultural traditionalism, the British influence on Chicagoland fashion moved slowly. In November 1964, nine months after the Beatles arrived in the US, *The Spire* featured an article on Nancy Dailey, the "best-dressed Senior girl." Looking like Jackie Kennedy in her coiffured hair and skirt worn well below the knee, *The Spire* insisted that Nancy "is fashion personified," in a "blue plaid, lightweight wool skirt and jacket a stylish combo for crisp fall days." The best-dressed male, Dennis Morales, "definitely dislikes the high 'Beatle' boots," *The Spire* reported, and he continued to adopt 1950s style greased back hair with a "sharp black suede 'shirt-jac'" and slacks.[45] In the spring of 1965, Judy Innes, an English student from Cambridge University, attended a dance at suburban Northwestern University and found little evidence of British fashions. The girls "all seemed to look alike, a feeling intensified by the fact that they all wear madras bermudas or cream coloured jeans hacked off above the knee, plus a shirt, sandals and a minute triangular head handkerchief."[46]

The Fans

The younger generation kept their eyes sharply focused on their TV screens, enjoying every second of the Beatles' startling performance on *The Ed Sullivan Show*, but those few youngsters who shifted their gaze around the living room noticed a rather concerned look on the faces of their parents. "An almost inhuman wail emitted from the TV set and my four-year-old rushed in to the kitchen. 'Mama, the haircuts are on,'" newspaper columnist Patsy Grawey Raab in Peoria, Illinois, wrote. "At first I thought the speaker had finally blown its top but after a few minutes I realized it wasn't our well-worn set, though I'm not sure it will ever recover, but a mob of squealing hair-pulling teenagers."[47] Cultural traditionalists became even more worried as the screaming, first viewed in the Ed Sullivan theater, exploded into more unruly behavior on the streets, in concert halls, and in movie theaters as teenage girls threw away their inhibitions and engaged in unladylike behavior. Parents, police, and government seemingly could not control this generation of young women. They worried that their public displays of lustful emotion, unruly behavior, and lack of respect for authority signaled a new female unconcerned with traditional mores.

"Are the Beatles a menace to our kids?" the Hollywood gossip magazine *The Lowdown* asked in July 1964, answering in the affirmative. Teenagers injured themselves and others as the long-haired musicians brought their fans into a state of hypnotic frenzy, the magazine informed its astonished readers. Even worse, Beatlemania was a sickness that had affected the morals of the young. One policeman told the magazine that they raided a club house and found teenagers "wearing Beatle wigs and nothing else" and indulging in the Beatlenut, "a dance too disgusting to describe." Psychiatrist Max Elber noted the female reaction to Bing Crosby, Frank Sinatra, and Elvis Presley, but believed that this was something different, and Beatle adulation was more disturbing. "All of these men, girls and young boys worshipped, were real men. They looked like men. They were masculine.... I am fearful of what is happening to young girls who, instead of worshipping male looking men, prefer ones with feminine looking hairdos. Are we turning into an Isle of Lesbos?" he worryingly asked.[48]

The assertiveness and lustfulness of young female fans concerned many others. "Watching those young girls—and many not so young— jumping up, screaming, panting with hysteria when the Beatles appeared, sort of nauseated me," newspaper columnist Mary Stuart commented in the *Chicago Garfieldian*. "The boys—with girl's faces—haven't even the talent of ELVIS—with the pelvis trouble. I found them boring."[49] Under the headline, "Beatles incite orgy of teen madness," the *Tribune* was happy to print the views of Dr. Bernard Saibel, a child guidance expert who provided his opinions of Beatlemania after attending a Beatles concert.

"Many of those present became frantic, hostile, uncontrolled, screaming, unrecognizable beings," the doctor wrote. He condemned the children's behavior and the negligence of the adults for "allowing the children a mad, erotic world of their own without the reassuring safeguards of protection from themselves."[50]

The opponents of Beatlemania not only questioned the open display of sexuality among the young fans but also their common sense and intelligence. "[T]he ecstatic reception accorded the Beatles bears a rather appalling witness to the emptiness of youthful heads and hearts," *Christianity Today*, the leading evangelical periodical based in the Chicago suburb of Carol Stream, suggested in February 1964.[51] The *Tribune* believed that the fans were unsophisticated, unschooled, and easily led astray by those like Epstein and the Beatles, who exploited the youngsters for monetary gain. In March, the *Tribune* printed a rather poorly written letter from one "loyal Beatle fan," which they then smugly ridiculed. The paper declared that if they had to say one good thing about the Beatles it was that "they are more intelligent, and almost certainly more literate, than some of their American fans."[52]

The pushing, shoving, Beatles fans seen inside and outside the concert halls, hotels, and movie theaters reminded many of the civil rights demonstrators in the southern states or the urban riots in the North and added to the fear of a growing breakdown of law and order in the country. *Variety* magazine suggested that Beatlemania was "a phenomenon closely linked to the current wave of racial rioting."[53] Inez Robb, writing in the *Chicago Daily News*, saw the behavior as evidence of the decline in orderly behavior in the nation. The "elders have thrown in the sponge of discipline and responsibility," she wrote. "Hundreds of the squealing little monsters I saw on teevee were in the 12-to-15 year-old bracket—far, far too young to be permitted to roam city streets unchaperoned and far, far too old to be permitted to behave like squalling infants." Society "needs parents in it who are willing to maintain family law and order, and rear their young in a civilized mold."[54]

The Music

The loud beats, the handclaps, and the hollering vocal intonations in the Beatles' music, so different from the smooth, refined sounds of classical music, became another target of the cultural traditionalists. They saw

pop and rock 'n' roll as the music of the uneducated and unsophisticated, with lyrics that were inane at best, obscene at worst, and music
that was overly loud and repetitive. Rock 'n' roll was often condemned
as "jungle music" for its rhythmic beat, but the Beatles added even more
African-American derived vocal inflections of oohs and aahs, yeahs and
babies that, to many ears, made the music sound even more moronic.

"I am tolerant beyond recognition where modern music is concerned,"
William F. Buckley Jr., founder of the conservative journal the *National
Review,* misleadingly informed the readers of the *Boston Globe* in 1964.
Buckley, then in his late thirties, claimed that he found Elvis Presley
"worth listening to" but drew the line at the Beatles. "The Beatles are not
merely awful, I would consider it sacrilegious to say anything less than
that they are godawful. They are so unbelievably horrible, so appallingly
unmusical, so dogmatically insensitive to the magic of the art, that they
qualify as crowned heads of anti-music."[55]

Many Chicagoans were equally dismissive. "George, who has a sore
throat, did not sing. From the sound of what came out, John and Paul
had sore throats too, but they sang anyway," Terry Turner, television
critic at the *Chicago Daily News,* drolly noted of their Sullivan appearance. "The musical beat is strong and has been known to bring rain from
cloudless skies. Or those, perhaps, were tears from musicians. Other
variations of the form have been used with fertility dances in the South
Seas. In the studio audience a sizeable group of teenage females reacted
Sunday night with the primitive rituals of their appreciation." A group
of teenagers waited for the Beatles outside the television studio but "the
Beatles escaped the mob. Maybe next time?" Turner hopefully opined.[56]
Bill Irvin, TV critic of *Chicago's American,* mocked the "quartet of young
men with mixed-up haircuts and eyebrow-length bangs" when he first
saw them on Jack Paar's show. He simply could not get past the fact that
when they sang, they "shrieked with the noise intensity of a ward full of
pain-wracked calves."[57] *The Ed Sullivan Show* hardly improved his mood.
"Sullivan's teen-age audience screeched and shrieked and yelled themselves silly every time the Beatles bleated," Irvin stated. "And then, after
the Beatles' first appearance, came another commercial—fittingly, this
time, for a headache remedy."[58] Some seven months later, *Chicago's American* complained about "yowling voices, a throbbing drum beat, a 'Yeah,

yeah, yeah' and the screams of teenagers.... If the Beatle industry comes up with some effective ear plugs, they might well clean up in America."[59]

Music lovers inundated the letters sections of the *Tribune* and *Chicago's American* with condemnations of the Beatles' singing and songwriting abilities. They produced "all-but-artless nonsensical noise," opined Donald Duclow of Chicago, which, when played, "my head begins to thump, my stomach to upheave."[60]

"What really scares me is that today's classical greats were scorned in their time. If I live to see the Beatles considered great music—but no, the thought is too terrible," Susan Ostberg from Lincolnwood wrote.[61] "After hearing the British Beatles, seven year locusts don't sound so bad," wrote Arnold Glasow, an alleged humorist that the *Chicago Tribune* often relied on for lighter moments.[62] Readers of the *Tribune,* both young and old, were incensed when a letter to the paper compared the Beatles to classical composers. Teenager Dana Webb called the Beatles "screaming savages" who could not be compared to those who performed and wrote classical music. Sixteen-year-old Frederick Majer suggested that the Beatles "will be forgotten in three or four years but in a hundred years from now the music of great men such as Beethoven and Schubert will still be heard."[63]

"The Beatles are a curse to humanity," Walt Sands wrote to the *Tribune.* "They have no talent. They cannot sing. They cannot play music. They have absolutely no showmanship. They do have queer hair-dos and no doubt an efficient promoter. The world is disintegrating into a bedlam of chaos."[64]

Anti-British

There had been waves of nativism in US history, and the Beatles' arrival in the US coincided with a renewed nationalistic fear of outside influences. In the mid-1850s, the anti-immigrant American Party, more commonly known as the Know-Nothings, elected eight governors, more than one hundred congressional representatives, and mayors of Boston, Philadelphia, and Chicago as anxiety over Irish Catholic immigration gripped the nation. Later in the century, anti-Chinese feeling led to the passage of Chinese exclusion acts. The years before and after World War I saw a virulent Americanization campaign directed at new immigrants from Southern and Eastern Europe and the rise of the so-called second

Ku Klux Klan, who turned their ire against Catholics and Jews as much as African Americans. During the height of the Cold War, anticommunists decried communism as an un-American foreign influence. Nativist sentiment appeared again as the 1965 Immigration and Nationality Act, which opened the United States to non-westerners by abolishing the national quota system that favored European immigration, stoked nationalist ire. The *Chicago Tribune* opposed the legislation, stating it would put Americans out of work. "Greater immigration isn't going to make everybody happy," the editorial suggested, and "it certainly isn't in the interest of the United States, which is what should count."[65] Letters supporting the *Tribune's* position poured into the paper. "We can't even deport the gangsters now, let alone encouraging more to come here," one reader wrote. "The sooner immigration is cut in half, the better. Let's take care of our own, those who believe in America first."[66] A Harris poll released in May 1965 showed that the public opposed the new immigration law by 58 percent to 24 percent.[67]

Confronted with the influx of British entertainers, many wanted to put America first. In April 1963, Angus Duncan, president of the Actors' Equity Association, wrote to the US Secretary of Labor, Willard Wirtz, to complain about the number of British actors coming to the US in search of work. Similarly, some worried about the British domination of the music charts and the seemingly endless number of British bands heading across the Atlantic. The American Federation of Musicians, concerned that the Beatles and other British groups were taking their members' jobs, lobbied Willard Wirtz to stop the upcoming 1964 Beatles tour and to limit the number of British groups coming into the country. Their efforts failed.[68]

Brought up on lurid stories of oppressive redcoats during the War of Independence and of the British burning down Washington, DC, during the War of 1812, many Americans held some negative impressions of the old motherland that were used against the Beatles. Americans imbued with the principles of republicanism saw the British Empire as antithetical to the ideals of liberty. Britain seemed autocratic and class ridden as the monarchy and the House of Lords played a major role in governing the nation. Some believed Britain could not be trusted because they had tricked the United States into World War I, and Americans were reluctant to join them in another conflict in the fall of 1939. At the end of the war, "The image of the Englishman as class-conscious snob and imperialist…was as deeply rooted in the American imagination as Huck Finn," suggested historian Cushing Strout.[69] Popular anti-British feeling continued during the Cold War helped by the image of Britain portrayed in Hollywood movies. British actors invariably played haughty autocratic rulers in historical epics, such as Laurence Olivier as the ruthless Crassus in *Spartacus* and Peter Ustinov as the insane Emperor Nero in *Quo Vadis,* while American actors invariably played oppressed slaves and persecuted Christians, replaying in symbolic form the stereotype of the evil colonizers and the brave patriots found in American history textbooks.[70]

Some used the language of the American Revolution to demonize the Beatles and other British groups. The "British Invasion," a term that alluded to an unwelcome menace, became a ubiquitous expression to describe the success of British groups in the US. *Billboard* used the even more incendiary expression "Redcoat invasion."[71] *Variety*, too, adopted the redcoat tag, calling British bands "rocking Redcoats" and describing the influx of touring British groups as the "Redcoat's US invasion."[72] *Billboard* and other newspapers and magazines gleefully reported the failure of any British group in the US, hyped any emerging American alternative, and often eagerly, and prematurely, suggested that the Beatles' fad was over. "The Yankee rock 'n' rollers whipped the British Redcoats in the Brooklyn-Manhattan battle for teenage attendance between Murray the K's show at the Brooklyn Fox and the first U. S. appearance of the Animals at the New York Paramount," *Billboard* reported in September 1964.[73] The poor attendance at some Dave Clark Five and Rolling Stones concerts in 1964 led *Billboard* to announce, "Redcoats Wane in US."[74]

Chicago, dominated by Irish politicians and geographically removed from the English influence evident on the East Coast, historically held a particular distaste for Perfidious Albion, and the perceived deceitfulness and treachery of British monarchs and politicians. In 1920, when King George V was visiting the US, Mayor Bill Thompson told the British King to stay out of his city. When a reporter asked him what he would do if George V decided to visit Chicago anyway, the rambunctious mayor replied, "If George comes to Chicago, I'll punch him in the snoot."[75] The *Chicago Tribune's* owner Robert R. "Colonel" McCormick espoused isolationism and American nationalism. The paper's masthead carried an American flag above the slogan, "The American paper for Americans." A virulent Anglophobe, McCormick equated British imperialism with the Nazi takeover of Europe and opposed American entry into World War II because he worried that a US victory would rescue the British Empire.[76] In the postwar years, the paper condemned so-called "pro-British" teaching in the schools and campaigned, often successfully, for the removal of "pro-British" textbooks from the Chicago public schools.[77] The paper worried that Americans attending British universities as Rhodes scholars had been indoctrinated into pro-British views and, aping a Red Scare, expressed concern over "the state department's strong pro-British slant."[78]

Anti-British feeling bubbled up again in the Midwest as some felt threatened by the Beatles and the seemingly never-ending influx of British groups. The Beatles "who specialize in a weird sort of tribal chant set to music (music?)" will "bring a dose of modern English culture and couth to our simple shores," the *Chicago Sun-Times* editorial of February 10, 1964, feared. "We trust that this country, strong and confident in its nuclear strength, dedicated to freedom everywhere to all men, will survive this cultural onslaught," they continued with maybe a hint of irony.[79] In December 1964, some five hundred students attended the Loyola University Debate Society meeting on the topic, "That the Beatles are un-American."[80]

"I'm so tired of reading about British groups," a reader complained to *TeenSet* magazine. "Isn't anyone ever going to wake up and see the great American groups? I have nothing against England, but they really aren't the only ones playing rock and roll. Let's see more about our performers."[81] D.W. of Joliet was so concerned about the hate directed at English groups that she wrote to *Tiger Beat* magazine expressing her disgust. "I'm all for American entertainers," she wrote, "but why can't we like the English ones too?"[82]

Chicagoans, too, evoked the language of the American Revolution to voice their resentment. To celebrate George Washington's birthday in February 1964, *Bridgeport News* drew on revolutionary traditions to ridicule the Beatles. "Almost 200 years later, four English boys invade this country and with the aid of rock and roll and four Beatle wigs remove more money from this beloved land than the cost of the whole

Revolutionary War, which was the cause of so much discomfort to the father of our country."[83]

Popular music also summoned the Spirit of '76 to condemn the Beatles. In their song "Declaration of Independence '65," the Chicagoland group the Exterminators described themselves as minutemen who would save the country from the tyranny of the Beatles and other British Invasion groups. Chicagoan Allan Sherman, who won a Grammy for his number two *Billboard* hit "Hello Muddah, Hello Fadduh!" in 1963, rallied parents behind the Red, White, and Blue. Sung to the tune of "Pop Goes the Weasel," Sherman's song "Pop Hates the Beatles" contrasted Sherman's views of the Beatles with those of his daughter. He sings of his hatred of the Beatles as his daughter persuades him to attend one of their concerts. She screams in delight during the show while he derides the Beatles' lack of musical skills. The song ends with Sherman suggesting that the Beatles' hair should be shorn and they should be thrown into Boston Harbor.

The Left and the Folk World

In contrast to the traditionalists who raged over the influence of the Beatles, the American Left generally ignored the phenomenon. Most had little time for pop music, which they saw as shallow at best, indicative of bourgeois decadence at worst, or for pop stars, who they believed were manufactured by large corporations to exploit and manipulate gullible teenagers. *Pravda*, the official newspaper of the Communist Party of the Soviet Union, believed that the Beatles represented "a plot by the ruling classes to distract…youngsters from politics and bitter pondering over disgraced and shattered hopes."[84] Soviet propaganda suggested that Beatles fans suffered from a "psychosis." In this state, they "forget the world's troubles," "don't want to know what's happening" in society, and "don't care about anyone else."[85]

"It's unfortunate that today's teen-agers aren't as informed and interested in politics and government as they are in the Beatles," John Tierney wrote to *Chicago's American,* voicing the concerns of the Left. "Beatlemania serves only as another escape from problems facing us."[86]

The folk community seemed more dismissive of the Beatles than the political Left. Alan Rinzler, a folk singer and editor at Simon & Schuster, reviewed the Beatles' first concert in Carnegie Hall, New York, for

The Nation magazine. Like the cultural conservatives, Rinzler looked contemptuously at the young audience. He suggested that great public relations and the help of the press, radio, and TV "contributed to a triumphant exploitation of the affluent teen-ager." He compared the crowd at Carnegie Hall unfavorably with the ones found at civil rights events. "There was mayhem and clapping of hands, but no sense of a shared experience, none of the exultation felt at a spontaneous gathering of good folk musicians, or, more important, at a civil rights rally where freedom songs are sung. The spectacle of all those anguished young girls at Carnegie Hall, trying to follow 'I Want to Hold Your Hand,' seems awfully vapid compared to the young men and women who sing 'I Woke Up This Mornin' With My Mind' (...Stayed on Freedom)." Rinzler summed up that "Beatlemania as a phenomenon is manna for dull minds."[87]

Chicago native Jim McGuinn, later Roger McGuinn of the Byrds, was one of the few playing in the folk clubs who loved rock 'n' roll. A huge admirer of Elvis Presley, his parents bought him a guitar for his fourteenth birthday. His musical allegiance changed when folk musician Bob Gibson visited his school. "When I was, I think, 15 years old, I was at the Latin School of Chicago—it's a private school in Chicago—and the music teacher invited Bob Gibson to do a 45-minute set for us. And I loved it so much that she told me about the Old Town School of Folk Music, and I went over there. And I'd go down to the Gate of Horn. On weekends, they'd have open mike and hootenanny."[88] The Gate of Horn was the city's preeminent folk club, and the young folk enthusiast eventually became a member of the club's house band, the Frets. McGuinn liked the Beatles immediately. "I might have been one of the first people to dig what the Beatles were into musically," he said. Fired with enthusiasm, McGuinn started to perform some Beatles songs in the folk clubs. "I was really getting a terrible audience reaction, the total cold shoulder. The folk purists absolutely hated what I was doing. It was blasphemy. They wanted to stone me or burn me at the stake."[89]

African Americans

Just as the Beatles divided opinion in the white community, they also split opinion on the black side of town. "When the Beatles came out, I had almost exclusively black friends," remembered Cynthia Dagnal, then an eleven-year-old student at a segregated public school on Chicago's

South Side. "There was a schism. It was a real problem there. It was 'white kid stuff, why are you doing this?' Motown versus this invasion of Brits. We used to fight about this. I mean, literally, fistfight about this stuff on the playground. I remember that very vividly because I was a 'white girl' after that. It was about the Four Tops then, all of those guys, the Miracles, Smokey, and it was very, very difficult for you if you didn't go along with that. I had been introduced to so much music by my father that I didn't do that. I couldn't be either this or that way." Peer pressure forced some black kids in Cynthia's school to hide their admiration for the Beatles. "I had one girlfriend who went along with me. She rode it out with me. There were some others who couldn't say it. They would sneak by and look at magazines with us on occasion. But we were also on the cusp of the civil rights movement. We were on the cusp of a lot of things. There was a racial thing going on underneath all of that, so it was kind of tough."[90]

Overall, African Americans were more dismissive of the Beatles and their music than their white counterparts. Black-owned radio station WVON may have played the Beatles in the summer of 1963 when Vee-Jay released their records, but when they became a media phenomenon in early 1964, WVON prided themselves on ignoring the British imports. "We've already got enough of menagerie," Gwen McDonough of WVON contemptuously told *Billboard*.[91] The *Chicago Defender* was full of dismissive comments. "Even though they look like morons with that wild Beatles' haircut, Beatlemania is sweeping England," music columnist Pamela Drake incredulously noted in February 1964.[92]

An editorial in the *Defender* expressed relief that the Beatles had returned home after their first visit to the US. "Now that the Beatles, that strange breed of British entertainers, are back in England, America may have peace and return to normalcy." One consequence of their visit was "that it has projected an entirely novel conception of the American estimate of Great Britain as an Old World culture. It's no use now for British publications with headquarters in the Rockefeller Center to flood us with magazine articles and display pictures about Old World charm and 400 years of Shakespeare. The Beatles have spoiled that image."[93]

Some readers calling themselves "Theophilus and Associates," wrote a "Ban the Beatles" article in the *Chicago Defender* in June 1964 in which they suggested that the Beatles had a "degrading influence on" young

Americans. They believed that "vast sums of public revenue have reck-lessly been thrown into the pockets of these alien invaders, while our youth has been brainwashed and our pockets emptied."

"Don't even let them into the United States. Shoot on Sight! Demol-ish the plague to a growing civilization," they wrote, hopefully jokingly, and urged readers to write to the president to "Ban the Beatles" from the US.[94] Judith Smith, a student at Loop Junior College, was in the minority among her friends. "I wonder why everybody hates the Beat-les?" she asked. "Most people think they look like women.... Everyone readily admits that they like the 'Liverpool Sound' or the 'Mersey Beat,' but they don't like the long-haired source of the sound." Judith was proud to proclaim her allegiance. "So, I take my life in my hands and stand on my own private soapbox and duck as my fellow reporters throw things and I say, BEATLES FOREVER."[95]

Black Chicagoans mostly grew up in segregated neighborhoods on the South or West Side, which fostered a strong black identity and an inability or unwillingness to embrace white culture. Blacks frequented their own establishments, created their own entertainment, and adopted their own cultural heroes. Those African Americans who watched the Beatles and the exclusively white studio audience on *Ed Sullivan* instinc-tively knew that this was not their music. "We weren't that much into Ed Sullivan and what have you," Chicago musician Chuck Colbert said. "We had our own artists that can sing better than them." There were few headlines about the Beatles in black newspapers, he said. "If they did, it would say 'white group trying to steal black ideas.' If they wanted to hear Motown, they would go to Motown. That's why actually when they first came out and when a lot of groups first came out there weren't a lot of black people in the audiences. The reason why I didn't want to go to see them is if you can't sing better than me then I don't need to go see you."[96]

"I remember *The Ed Sullivan Show*, but for African Americans, the Beatles really weren't exactly our kind of music," Sylvester Cottrell, born in Joliet in 1950, suggested. "They had a beat. They had a sort of a rhythm. I liked the way they dressed. The music they played was obviously very influenced by African American music.... they just weren't that popular among us. My parents didn't think anything of them at all. My parents were more or less into church music. People saw them as copycats, you know, imitators. Because again they came about at a time when you had the hot black groups, the Temptations and the Four Tops, and Martha and the Vandellas and Gladys Knight and the Pips, Smokey Robinson and the Miracles. The Beatles were accepted and appreciated, but I don't think it dominated our culture the way it did white American culture."[97]

As the views of Sylvester Cottrell demonstrate, not everyone was so enamored with the Fab Four. The Beatles' core audience in the US comprised chiefly of white teenage girls, but they enjoyed less praise from adults, boys, and African Americans. The political Left and the folk world tried to ignore the latest pop fad, but cultural traditionalists decried their loud music, their feminine look, and the behavior of their fans and viewed them as an unwelcome foreign influence on the young. Anti-Beatles sentiment may not have led to street demonstrations or the development of anti-Beatles organizations, but this fear and loathing would not be silenced. Indeed, hostility would come to the surface when the Beatles finally arrived in Chicago in the summer of 1964 as part of their first groundbreaking tour of North America. Welcomed with open arms by many city officials elsewhere, they received a frosty reception from the administration of Mayor Richard J. Daley and from the local press as fear of the mop-headed menace gripped the city.

CHAPTER 4

"Raging Mass Dementia"

The Beatles' First Appearance in Chicago, 1964

Richard J. Daley, mayor of Chicago, exerted almost paternalistic control over his domain. As soon as Beatlemania swept the Chicagoland area, letters and petitions poured into the mayor's office from excited teenagers urging him to stage a Beatles concert in the city.[1] "The next time you take dictation for the mayor could you please sit on his lap a little while longer and tell him that you have been requested to ask him to bring the Beatles to Chicago," Joan Marek wrote to the mayor's secretary.[2] It is highly unlikely that his secretary pleaded Joan's case from the comfort of Daley's lap and even more unlikely that Daley played any part in persuading the British sensations to tour the US. Indeed, more than most, Daley looked on with dread and foreboding as the Beatles fulfilled the dreams of Beatlemaniacs and announced that they would tour North America in the summer of 1964. Their first concert in the Windy City would take place at the International Amphitheatre on Saturday evening, September 5, 1964.[3]

A Tour Unlike Any Other

Brian Epstein chose New York-based General Artists Corporation (GAC) to organize the Beatles' first tour of North America, and they, in turn, picked Triangle Productions to take care of arrangements for the stop in Chicago. Triangle owners, Frank Fried and Chad Mitchell, seemed the unlikeliest of promoters of a Beatles concert. Fried, born in March 1927 on the North Side of Chicago, served in the Navy during World War II and then became a steelworker in his native city. At the age of seventeen, Fried joined the Trotskyist Socialist Workers Party (SWP) and devoted himself to fermenting a socialist revolution in the US. In 1954, the SWP expelled Fried because of political differences with the leadership, but he remained a committed Trotskyist, active in socialist politics for the rest of his life. Laid off from his job as a steelworker in 1956, Fried began organizing benefit concerts for left-wing causes and then became a full-time concert promoter. Fried launched Triangle Productions in the late '50s with fellow socialist Fred Fine and future Bob Dylan manager Albert Grossman. Triangle promoted shows by Frank Sinatra, Johnny Mathis, and Barbara Streisand, but this would be the first time the company had staged a show by a pop group.[4] Fried, like many left-wingers, loved the folk revival but was disdainful of the Beatles and pop music in general. "The Beatles were a terminally cute, clean-cut, clever group with original songs that were not particularly profound—lightweight love songs, bubblegum music. Their dress was unusual but not at all threatening." Fried, who had staged shows by Pete Seeger and Bob Dylan and managed the Chad Mitchell Trio, unfavorably compared the Beatles to his other charges. "In this company, the Beatles seemed lightweight, unconnected to what was going on in America. Maybe they were inspiring the kids, but they weren't inspiring me."[5]

Frank's partner, Chad Mitchell, also inhabited a completely different world from the Beatles. A native of Portland, Oregon, Mitchell became part of the folk singing group the Chad Mitchell Trio in 1959 and met Fried when the group performed in Chicago. "The first time we played Chicago was at the Palmer House, and we shared the bill with Dorothy Loudon. Frank came to see a show and introduced himself." The group liked the genial Fried and accepted his offer to become their manager. Mitchell described himself as "apolitical" when they first met, but this would soon change. "I got very left-oriented just hanging around with Frank."

Subsequently, Mitchell replaced Fred Fine and Albert Grossman as Fried's partner at Triangle. "Whatever the Trio's income was, it went into Triangle Productions," Mitchell explained, but he avoided involvement in the day-to-day running of the business. "He kept calling me the Little Prince because I didn't want to have anything to do with promotion."

Alice Fried

Frank Fried, Trotskyist, civil rights activist, and promoter of Beatles' concerts in Milwaukee and Chicago, with his business partner Chad Mitchell.

Mitchell was as equally dismissive of the Beatles as Fried and others in the folk fraternity. "I didn't pay much attention to their music," he admitted. "I just thought they were a pop phenomenon. They were just a group for teeny-boppers."[6]

Frank Fried was far from the sophisticated businessperson one would expect to see mixing with the rich and famous. "He did such funny things," Mitchell affectionately recalled. "When I met him, he was driving a Chevrolet Corvair. The driver's seat was broken, so it tipped and went back and forward. Frank dealt in his mind almost entirely. So, if he was driving a car, he'd start to pull out and kind of bump the car ahead and then he'd back up and bump the car behind, meanwhile talking to me the whole time. He was just oblivious of his physical surroundings. And he smoked in those days. I had a brand new suit that I'd gotten from the cleaners in the back seat and, he was smoking, and he put the arm over the seat, and burned a hole in my new suit. When Francoise, his wife, came to me when Frank asked her to marry him, she wanted to have me say that Frank was okay, a good guy. It was sometimes hard to figure that out because he just didn't pay attention to the normal social courtesies. You know, manners. I said, 'Frank is a solid soul. The only thing you have to worry about is he may burn you to death!' I remember one time, I was living in the back room of his new office, that was really an old townhouse. I suddenly smelled smoke. He'd set the garbage wastebasket on fire and left the place. He was a true character. And his pants were always falling off!"[7]

GAC and Frank Fried underestimated the popularity of the Beatles. Veteran concert promoter Ed Pazdur offered to put the Beatles on at White Sox Park, home of the Chicago White Sox baseball team, but GAC turned him down in favor of Frank Fried's offer to stage the show at the more modest thirteen thousand capacity International Amphitheatre, believing the smaller venue was a safer bet to sell out.[8] Built adjacent to the sprawling stockyards in 1934, the Amphitheatre was a cavernous shed more accustomed to rodeos and livestock shows than pop concerts, and organizers had to lay out some 5,000 folding chairs on the floor to complement the 8,000 seats in the stands. The tickets cost $2.50, $3.50, $4.50, and $5.50, a relative bargain. The most expensive seat at $5.50 is worth just over forty dollars in today's money.[9] The show sold out immediately, and Triangle sent back $50,000 worth of unfilled applications.[10] Fried admitted that he would have booked Soldier Field if he had known the scale of the demand. Fried asked GAC if he could add a second show at the Amphitheatre, but the over-committed Beatles turned him down.[11]

The Beatles were swept up in a tour the likes of which had never been seen before. Their first concert took place on August 19, 1964, at the Cow Palace in San Francisco. In an exhausting itinerary, the Beatles played an astonishing thirty-two shows in twenty-four cities in thirty-three days. They flew thousands of miles in an American Flyers Airline jet back and forth across the US in a haphazard route, performing in large arenas and sports stadiums rather than in the smaller theaters they played in Europe. Musicians today would have a huge entourage and teams of roadies to assist them on tour, but in 1964 the Beatles had only two old friends from the Cavern days to look after their equipment and their personal needs. Neil Aspinall, dubbed "Nell" by the group, became their most trusted confidante. A small, slender man, he worried and fretted about his charges as he tried his best to take care of their every need. Joining Aspinall was twenty-nine-year-old Mal Evans, a six-foot-three, burly but affable Liverpudlian with thick framed glasses who looked after their instruments, protected the dressing room from intruders, and helped

Aspinall to forge the Beatles' autographs ravenously required by eager fans. Brian Epstein brought along his personal assistant, Wendy Hanson, and his nineteen-year-old secretary, Diana Vero.

In the wake of the Kennedy assassination, those tasked with security were constantly on edge, worried that the group could become a target for some maniac. Bomb threats were a common occurrence requiring strict surveillance of luggage and periodic searches of the plane. "Within the first few days of the tour, before the threats even began, I issued an order that our planes be kept under guard at all times," recalled Ruby Hickman, direc-

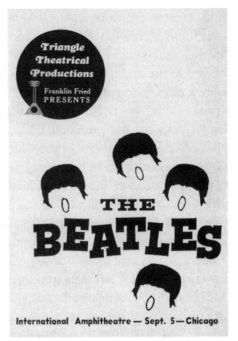

The program for the 1964 stop in Chicago. Chicago was the only city that produced their own free program for each of the three North American tours.

tor of public relations and executive assistant to the president of the airline, who traveled with the Beatles. "Either police or Pinkerton men were engaged well in advance of our arrival, were always waiting when we landed and did not leave until we were airborne. This cost the airline money, but I didn't care. At first, it was to keep souvenir hunters from stripping the plane, later it was from concern for the Beatles."[12] The concern was justified. The "plane at the end of the tour it was full of bullet holes," the pilot of an airplane used on one of the three US tours divulged to George Harrison years later. "Apparently, that's what used to happen," a disbelieving Harrison noted, "jealous boyfriends at the end of the runway with these guns trying to take pot shots at us."[13]

"North America was then a far-off place of which we thought we knew much—hadn't we seen it in the cinemas and read about it in comics from our earliest years?" tour press officer Derek Taylor wrote, expressing the opinion held by most Brits on their first visit to the States. "Yet nothing, but nothing, could have prepared me for our first bewildering collisions with the United States."[14] Confined to their hotel rooms, people constantly knocked on the doors, the telephones in the rooms ceaselessly rang, and hordes of noisy girls kept an around-the-clock vigil outside the hotels. When the Beatles left the safety of their rooms, security bundled them into a car as crowds of delirious girls jumped on the roof and the hood and pushed contorted faces up against the windows. "The crowds seemed intent on getting a chance to touch the performers, and since not everyone could touch one of the musicians, they settled for touching any one of the rest of us who were part of the entourage," wrote reporter Art Schreiber. "During that tour, I had three suits torn to pieces by young, exuberant fans grabbing at me. I also lost two typewriters and three tape recorders. After a crowd encounter in Milwaukee, I discovered that someone had used a pair of scissors to cut off the inside portion of my necktie."[15] Police motorcycles and cars with sirens wailing and lights flashing escorted their limousines from the airport to hotel, from hotel to venue, and back to the airport. The hotels, venues, and airports found it challenging to deal with the hordes of excited fans. "It was berserk," said assistant press officer Bess Coleman. "Horrifying at times, too. There were times when you genuinely feared for your life." At one venue, she opened the backstage door to be met by a horde of fans. "I was knocked unconscious and woke up in an ambulance. That happened more than once."[16] Brian Epstein's secretary, Diana Vero, recalled that when she tried to enter one venue, "Bess Coleman and I were clouted across our stomachs by a policeman who thought we were a couple of gate-crashing fans."[17]

Those in positions of authority acted as badly as the overzealous fans. "Any Mayor or Governor or Police Chief, any promoter or record company executive who believed that the Beatles owed them a debt, presumed they could demand anything," Derek Taylor stated. "It was quite normal for one of these people to say: 'Look John (or Paul, or George or Ringo) we've done a good job for you. Now just sign these pictures.' Or 'Meet my wife' or 'Phone my daughter.'"[18] Local radio stations and TV networks pressured the Beatles for interviews. "Often the Beatles told me that long flights were the best part of the tour," Ruby Hickman suggested. "The flights were, in reality, the only time the Beatles could relax and feel safe—30,000 feet in the air."[19] George Harrison, who was the most scared of flying, recounted it slightly differently. "The only place we ever got any peace was when we got in the suite and locked ourselves in the bathroom," Harrison moaned. "The bathroom was about the only place you could have any peace."[20] Even worse, he claimed in an interview with journalist Art Unger, "the only time we do get to ourselves is actually when we're asleep."[21]

The support acts on the tour found the pandemonium impossible to comprehend. "I had never seen nothing like that in my life," African-American singer Clarence Henry chuckled as he remembered stops on the tour. "I had never seen something like with the Beatles, you know, the crowds. In New Orleans, the kids, they broke the barrier, and the police were attacking them like they were football players. The kids got out, and they were trying to get to the Beatles." The Beatles escaped injury on that occasion but on another stop, fans were not so lucky. "They had nurses, they had ambulances and one little girl in Dallas, Texas, they pushed in that glass and broke the glass, and she was all cut up."[22]

"The fans were something else," marveled Lillian Walker of the New York singing group the Exciters, who experienced Beatlemania up close during their stay in Key West, Florida. "We were in our hotel room just relaxing, and we heard a knock on the door. I don't remember which one of us went to the door. We asked who it was, and it sounded like it was the chambermaid or something like that. So, we opened the door. Oh my God, like I can't even tell you how many there was, but it was like a crowd of teenage girls just rushed into our room. And they're looking everywhere. They're looking in the closet, they're looking in the bathroom, they're looking under the bed, everywhere you could possibly look. We had a big suite. They went in every single room, looked in every nook and corner. We were like, 'The Beatles are not here. They have their own villa.' All the people on the show stayed in the motel and then the Beatles stayed in their own little villa right off from the motel. They said, 'Oh you're lying, you're lying.' It was so crazy. We never saw anything like it before in our lives. Never. It was crazy."[23]

On occasion, the Beatles tried to escape the confinement of their hotel rooms. "Malcolm Evans and I got to be pretty good friends," recounted Bob Tucker of Bill Black's Combo, another support act on the tour. "He called me one night when we were in Atlantic City. It must have been about two or three in the morning, and he said 'Ringo wants to go to a bar. Do you want to go with us?' I said, 'Yeah I'll go.' We went to this little bar and we walked in there, and there's maybe three people. Well, the bartender recognized Ringo. I saw him go to the phone. and in twenty minutes, the place was packed. We had to leave. It was tough. We could go about town, they couldn't." Unable to visit the shops, the shops came to the Beatles. When they were in Dallas, Neiman Marcus sent over a range of expensive women's clothing for the Beatles to buy for their wives, girlfriends, and family. "I had a girlfriend that flew in there to see us and Malcolm called me and said, 'look, they've got a sales lady from Neiman Marcus up here. We need a girl to try on some stuff.' So, we went up with my girlfriend. She got to try on very expensive minks and clothing." In Key West, Florida, Ringo made a simple request. "Ringo came to me and said, 'Look, we got to have some music. Would you go into town and buy some albums?' I went into town with $400 and bought every damn thing I could find I thought they'd like. I brought it back to the hotel, and they would put it on the turntable and listen to a cut or two. They'd just listen, but when they got to the Memphis sounds, Carl Perkins, Jerry Lee Lewis, Roy Orbison, you could tell that that was stuff that really got to them. They really loved it."[24]

Lillian Walker realized that the Beatles were prisoners of their fame when the traveling party arrived in New York City. "We had this friend named Ronnie, and he owned his own record store. It was a big record store. So, they were talking about the blues and all of this, and we were telling them how Ronnie had rare records and old records that most other record stores didn't have. And they probably could get some good stuff. We were going to sneak out and go to the record store and buy records and then meet some of our friends." The mother of the Exciters' Brenda Reid, who chaperoned the girls on tour, got wind of the plan. "They were saying 'No, because if anything happened to the Beatles, oh God, what are you guys going to do? It'd be all your fault.' So, we all chickened out. We said, okay, never mind. Brenda's mother told us it was a hair-brained idea. 'What were you guys thinking? And they are just as stupid as you listening to you all.'"[25]

According to Lillian, there were some lighter moments on the tour. "When we were on the plane, we used to turn the seats over and sit on top of the seats. I used to bring my music everywhere I went. I had my portable record player, my records, and we would jam on the plane." Some of the time, they were able to talk to the Beatles. "They were awesome. First

The Exciters: Herb Rooney, Lillian Walker, Brenda Reid, and Carol Johnson were caught up in a tour the like of which they, and the world, had never seen before.

of all, they were very funny. All of them had a great sense of humor. We were all teenagers then, seventeen, eighteen, and nineteen. As teenagers, even when you're mature, you can be a little silly. We would laugh a lot. Each one had their own little personality. We used to say 'Who's our favorite?' And we'd go this one is our favorite, no he's our favorite, no he's our favorite. But they were all very nice. We got along well. All of us used to hang out together on the plane because we didn't get to see them at the venues. They would come at the last minute and would be in their dressing room. Mainly when we used to hang together would be on the plane. We'd be talking about what's the teenage styles and fads in New York and England and then we mainly talked about music. It was totally awesome."[26]

The touring party had a short break in Key West before the concert in Jacksonville on September 11, and here the Exciters introduced John, Paul, George, and Ringo to the delights of soul food. "One day we were talking to them, and they would say 'Oh, goodness we're so tired of this restaurant food, and we're so tired of the same thing over and over again.' We were about to have a three-day break. Brenda's mom said, 'Well when we get to Florida if we have a stove and kitchen, small little kitchenette in our hotel room I'm going to make you guys a meal.' They said really, really, really, and she made them some food. Oh my God, they went bonkers. They loved her food. They were so happy to eat a home-cooked meal. They started calling her mama. She was really popular with them."[27] Indeed, Ringo complained about the quality of American food to *New York Post* reporter Paul Sann but mentioned one feast he really enjoyed. "He says the only good meal he ever had on these shores was the Southern fried chicken whipped up in Key West by Mrs. Jernice Reid, whose daughter Brenda is in the Rock and Roll singing group traveling as one of the Beatles' warm-up acts and named, needlessly, The Exciters."[28]

Chicago Prepares

Excitement rose among fans in Chicago as concert day approached. Some teenagers passed the time making gifts to present to the Beatles. Five students at suburban New Trier High School expended five months of their time making a rug to present to their idols, while the Wheaton Community Beatles Society baked a huge cake. Some Beatlemaniacs made reservations in all the top hotels in Chicago hoping that they would be able to stay in the same lodgings as the Beatles.[29] Four days before the concert, a teenage girl was found hiding in the Amphitheatre press box with enough food to last until show time. Police put barbed wire around the entrances and greased the pipe poles to stop others from sneaking into the building. In the days leading up to the concert, teenagers and parents inundated promoter Frank Fried with requests for tickets. Fried took to answering the telephone by saying, "Mass hysteria department."[30] Some offered to perform with the Beatles, to usher at the concert, or "do anything" to obtain entry to the show. Ticket holders wanted to know if they could throw jelly beans on stage during the performance. "Is there any way I can get some of the old jellybeans that will be thrown at them?" one fan asked Fried. "There's a chance that one of the Beatles will have stepped on them."[31]

Mayor Richard J. Daley was also preparing for the visit. The grandson of Irish immigrants, Daley was born in 1902 and raised in the working-class neighborhood of Bridgeport on the South Side of the city. Daley spent his youth brawling in the streets and his adult years fighting his way to the top of the tough world of Chicago politics. The people of Chicago elected him mayor in 1955 and then reelected him five more times, serving until his death in December 1976. Daley was blessed with neither film star good looks nor the Irish gift of the gab. When chastised for providing his son John with a lucrative job working for the city, Daley told his critics, "If I can't help my sons, then they can kiss my ass." As both chair of the Cook County Democratic Party and mayor of Chicago, he accrued enormous power in his hands, gaining the nickname "The Boss." During his reign, Daley reignited a political machine that had lost influence under previous mayors. He gained popular support by administering political patronage, guaranteeing efficient municipal services, and

Mayor Richard J. Daley worried about the impending visit of the Mop Tops to his beloved city.

Mayor Daley collection, University of Illinois at Chicago

attracting new investment and jobs to the city. His domination of the Democratic Party in Illinois guaranteed influence in the legislature in Springfield and in Washington, DC, where Illinois' congressional representatives bowed to Daley's wishes.[32]

Mayor Daley was no fan of the Beatles or the progressive cultural values they symbolized. In his victorious 1955 election campaign, he ran as "A Family Man for a Family City." In Daley's world of traditional morals, men should be hard-working breadwinners, women tenders of the home, and sexual relations confined to heterosexual acts between married couples. He appealed not to the intellectuals or the sophisticated media but to the "good family man," a phrase he used often. A dedicated husband and father, he woke early and ate breakfast with his seven children and his stay-at-home wife, Eleanor "Sis" Daley. A devout Catholic, the portly Daley, always neatly resplendent in his smartly tailored suits, shirt, and tie, then left his rather modest brick bungalow in the Irish-American neighborhood of Bridgeport to attend mass in the local parish church. After taking communion, Daley headed to the downtown office where he did his best to maintain the racial segregation that prevailed in the city, including in his own South Side neighborhood. Daley preached respect for those in authority including the Church, the police, and parents, and feared feminism, declining deference, and the civil rights campaigners that threatened his family's time-honored way of life.

While the mayor stayed in the background, Colonel John "Jack" Reilly became the official spokesperson regarding the Beatles' visit. Born on January 9, 1899, in Ossining, New York, the grandson of Irish immigrants, Reilly left home to enlist in World War I at the age of seventeen and went on to earn the rank of sergeant. He also served in World War II becoming a lieutenant

Jack Reilly wanted the Beatles out of Chicago as quickly as possible.

colonel. After the war, Reilly began working for the local government in Chicago and became a loyal follower of Mayor Daley, who appointed him Director of Special Events for the City. Reilly organized parades, formal dinners for distinguished visitors, and ceremonial events; but he also became an important advisor to the mayor. The colonel began wearing eyeglasses with a dark lens over his left eye after surgery in 1955, making him look even more formidable. Even in his sixties, Reilly would leap out of bed at 5:30 a.m., jog to Lake Michigan and back, and then drive downtown to City Hall from his North Side home. There he would climb, two steps at a time, to the mayor's office on the fifth floor where he would receive his orders for the day. Married to a ballet dancer, Reilly, like Daley, was no fan of pop music or the fan worship it engendered among the young. As an Irish nationalist who started the practice of dyeing the Chicago River green for St. Patrick's Day, he expressed even less enthusiasm for a group of musicians from the old enemy of England.[33]

Many teenagers wrote to Mayor Daley hoping he could arrange for them to meet the Beatles, pass messages to the group, or provide tickets for the concert.[34] Marilyn Everhart wrote to the mayor asking him to buy a subscription to the *Chicago Sun-Times* from her, and to find her other subscribers so that she could win two tickets in the *Sun-Times* Beatles' Battle contest.[35] Marilyn received a disappointing response. "His duties as Mayor of the second largest city in the United States do not allow the time for him to solicit newspaper subscriptions," Jack Reilly replied on the mayor's behalf.[36] Ruth Tully and Annette Moody tried to appeal to the Mayor's compassionate side to solicit *Sun-Times* subscriptions. The two girls forlornly revealed that "out of the thousands of people we've asked, we've only sold one subscription. If we don't get to go, we'll jump in the Chicago River!! And that's a promise!! Thanks."[37]

Other teenagers asked the mayor to grant their idols an official welcome to Chicago. One girl wanted to present the Beatles with the keys to the city and threatened, "to get my 500 fellow Beatlemaniacs together for our demonstration in Buckingham Fountain. If we still receive no answer to my plea, we will sign petitions and stage a lay-in at City Hall. If that doesn't work, we'll change the recent song by the Young World Singers, Ringo for President, to Ringo for Mayor."[38] Over six hundred "Beatlemaniacs of Chicago" signed a petition urging Mayor Daley to declare September 5, the day of the concert, "National Beatles' Day in Chicago."[39] Two girls wrote asking the mayor to present a bouquet of flowers to each Beatle. "In the United States it is not customary to present bouquets to men," Jack Reilly matter-of-factly responded to the girls' request.[40] "The teens of Chicago think you should have let the Beatles have a parade down Michigan Avenue," wrote eighteen-year-old Chicagoan Fran Sanocki to Jack Reilly. "You gave Queen Elizabeth a royal welcome and the Queen enjoyed the Beatles at the Royal Command Performance in England and we think they could have the same privilege," she indignantly exclaimed. "My parents are voting for the Republican nominee for mayor in the next election, they also love the Beatles."[41] Chicago Beatle Fan Society co-presidents, fifteen-year-old twins Cindy and Cathy Strohacker, wrote to the mayor asking if they could represent the city of Chicago and present the Beatles with a symbolic key to the city at a welcoming ceremony. "We have no knowledge of the Beatles other than what we have read in the papers," Jack Reilly replied in the negative to the girls' pleas. "The Beatles will be one more group of entertainers coming to Chicago and their status will be that of all entertainers who are interested in nothing more than that they will have a bunch of customers at the box office."[42]

When the Beatles touched down at other stops on the tour, local politicians greeted the visiting musicians, delighted to see them in their hometown. The wife of New York governor Nelson Rockefeller took her two children to see the Beatles at Carnegie Hall on their first visit to the US. Margaretta Rockefeller, appropriately nicknamed Happy, pronounced the concert "one of the most extraordinary things I've ever seen. I loved it," she gushed, "it was marvelous. They have a lot of talent."[43] On their first stop of the 1964 tour, city officials in San Francisco planned a ticker-tape parade through the downtown area to welcome them to the US. Because of security concerns, the Beatles declined the offer. The wife of Wisconsin governor John Reynolds attended the Beatles' press conference in Milwaukee with her two daughters.[44] When the Beatles arrived in New Orleans, Mayor Victor Schiro attended the Beatles' press conference where he presented the group with the keys to the city and proclaimed September16, 1964, "Beatles Day."[45] In Los Angeles, Mayor Sam Yorty found time out of his busy schedule to welcome the Beatles at a charity event. "I'm anxious to meet these young men," he told the media.[46]

Mayor Daley, in contrast, was unwilling to greet the Beatles or even to let them stay in his city, as he feared that their presence would lead to a breakdown in law and order. Chicago had recently seen two public school boycotts by black students calling for the removal of public school superintendent Benjamin Willis. The first, on October 22, 1963, saw nearly two hundred and twenty-five thousand public school students, virtually every black student in the city, stay away from school and one hundred and seventy-two thousand supported the second boycott on February 25, 1964.[47] On August 15, racially tinged violence broke out in Dixmoor, a south suburb of Chicago, leaving over thirty people injured. Newspapers carried headlines of disorder on previous stops of the tour, adding to the sense of foreboding. "It's almost like Miami during the hurricane season," wrote *Chicago's American* on the day of the concert. "You know the big blow is coming, but you can't get away from it. The only thing to do is sit tight and hope there isn't too much damage. After the storm, you clean up the mess."[48] Some were not taking any chances. GAC wanted the Beatles to stay at the plush Astor Tower Hotel on the Gold Coast, but executives turned them down. "They feared the ornate trappings would be wrecked by the nervous teens," noted *Chicago Tribune* columnist Herb Lyon.[49] "We don't want them here," an assistant to Mayor Daley, probably Colonel Reilly, bluntly told GAC. Unwanted by the city's fathers, the

Beatles had little choice but to fly into Chicago the day of the show and leave for Detroit immediately after their performance.[50]

The day before the concert, the mayor called representatives of the police, fire, traffic, and health departments into his office to finalize their plans to save their cherished city from the threat of Beatlemania. Now, more than ever, the city had to live up to its reputation as the City of the Big Shoulders. "Don't worry, Mr. Mayor," said Lt. Robert Lynskey, commander of the Chicago police department's task force, trying to soothe the anxieties of the increasingly worried looking mayor. "We've been in tight spots before. We'll handle the Beatles just like every other big emergency. It calls for tight security and a stiff upper lip." Jack Reilly was next up to allay the fears of his boss. "We know they've caused trouble everywhere else they've been but we think we're prepared for anything," commented an outwardly confident Reilly, who had survived the trenches of World War I and the storm troopers of Nazi Germany, and felt he could deal with four long-haired pop stars. He refused to divulge the city's intricate plans to deal with the mop-headed menace from Liverpool. "We're going to try to sneak them in and sneak them out," was all he would say. Lt. Lynskey, tugging at his shirt collar on a warm summer day, warned the press that "there are thousands more Beatle fans who will try to get in" to the concert, but he would post three hundred police officers around the Amphitheatre to handle the invasion. "Good luck to you both," said Fire Commissioner Robert J. Quinn to Lt. Lynskey and Colonel Reilly, as if preparing to leap the trenches at the Battle of the Somme, "I hope we all get thru this thing unscathed."[51] Reilly and Quinn, two of the "Irish Neanderthals," as Daley's press secretary, Earl Bush, called Daley's inner circle, swept out of the room and set to work, protecting their beloved city from the Fab Four.[52] The city battened down their hatches, and the local newspapers tried to settle nerves further but without minimizing the gravity of the situation. "In the 127 years since it was incorporated as a city Chicago has survived many a vicissitude and met many a challenge," an editorial on the day of the concert in the *Chicago Sun-Times* stated. "Nothing has been able to shake Chicago. Now comes the acid test. The Beatles arrive today for a performance of their art."[53]

Publicly, the mayor and local officials voiced indifference or even hostility to the Beatles, but behind the scenes, their families and friends pressured them to use their influence to obtain tickets to the show. Mayor

Daley, who spent his spare time at the Chicago White Sox ballpark rather than the concert hall and whose musical tastes ran to a rousing Irish tune like "Danny Boy" or "Garryowen," exhibited no interest in popular culture and certainly not in the Beatles. He had, however, three daughters and four sons, three of whom were teenagers caught up in Beatlemania, and Daley requested twenty-five tickets for the concert.[54] Two of the mayor's sons, John, who was seventeen, and the youngest, Bill, who had just turned sixteen, attended the show.[55] Illinois Attorney General William Clark, also no fan of the Beatles, asked for fifteen tickets to the performance.[56] Clark's oldest daughter, Merrilee, attended the concert with three friends on her sixteenth birthday.[57]

The Beatles were due to arrive in Chicago from Milwaukee on the day of the concert, but fearing a riot if thousands of teenagers gathered to greet the group upon their arrival, Reilly wanted to keep the time and location of the Beatles' landing a secret. Unfortunately, Frank Fried's press officer in Chicago, Alan Edelson, phoned the newspapers and radio stations to inform them that the Beatles would arrive at O'Hare airport on the North Side of the city at 4:30 p.m. "I just wanted to save the fans the trouble of looking around," he explained. Reilly quickly called the Beatles in Milwaukee, informing them that Chicago officials had changed the landing site to the smaller Midway airport on the Southwest Side of the city. Authorities wanted to keep the new location a secret too, but Edelson again leaked the switch to the media. Reilly was outraged. "This has been the cheapest publicity stunt in the history of the United States," he fumed. "There is no purpose served in announcing their arrival point." An irate Reilly phoned Edelson. He "was so mad that he didn't care if the kids tore the Beatles apart," the chastised press officer revealed.[58] Hundreds of disappointed teenagers waited for the Beatles at O'Hare airport, learning too late of the switch.

The city informed the Beatles that for their protection and to avoid a potential riot, they would have to land not at the main passenger terminal at Midway but at a remote airfield, and that they would not be allowed to greet their fans. "I can't understand it," a frustrated Paul McCartney told reporters in Milwaukee before they departed. "They tell me that in Chicago in 1959 there were 4,000,000 people who turned out to see Queen Elizabeth and they handled the crowd without any trouble. We aren't royalty. We won't have anything like 4,000,000 but they won't let us get out and see anything." Colonel Jack Reilly saw it differently. "The city of Chicago is not going to spend thousands of dollars protecting them.... Our sole interest is that Chicago kids in their enthusiasm for the Beatles, do not get hurt."[59]

On the evening of September 5, the Beatles took a short twenty-minute flight from Milwaukee. The plane touched down at Midway Airport at 4:40 p.m. to be greeted by five thousand ecstatic fans that had patiently waited for hours to catch a glimpse of their favorites. The plane glistened in the late summer sun, the door opened, and the Fab Four led by Paul McCartney walked down the steps through a barrage of reporters, television crews, and photographers. They waved to the distant crowd, but security ushered them quickly into their limousines, where Paul signed autographs out of the window for the few fans who managed to escape the clutches of the police. "Do you like the welcome?" a reporter asked Paul.

"Yes, it's marvelous," he replied.

"Why is it different from anywhere else?" the reporter asked.

"It's good, it doesn't have to be different," an irritated McCartney replied, setting the tone for the rest of the visit.[60] Many fans tried to

Crowds greeting the Beatles at Chicago's Midway Airport as they arrive for their first performance in the city on September 5, 1964.

scale the fences as the police strained to keep order. Some youngsters succeeded and chased after the disappearing car.[61]

The Beatles were driven for twenty minutes to the Stock Yard Inn, a lavish Tudor-style hotel and restaurant adjacent to the International Amphitheatre. The Inn served the hungry musicians prime rib of beef sandwiches, mashed potatoes, and coffee in a private dining area.[62] After their meal, the exhausted Liverpudlians held a press conference in the Saddle and Sirloin Club on the second floor, a place accustomed to hosting US presidents and other dignitaries. The room was full of seasoned reporters but also young teenage girls, some of whom were fan club members, some who had won journalist passes given away as prizes by teen magazines, and some who were daughters of the press, management, and politicians. Among those in attendance was Louise Harrison, who had journeyed from her home in southern Illinois at the behest of local radio stations. "Many of the cities where I was doing my reports, the radio stations, wanted me to come on in and be at the radio station and do a call-in program the night before the concert and then another one the day after. I didn't realize it at the time, but it was a way for some of the deejays to get to talk to the Beatles by being with me. I didn't realize the reason why I was being courted so heavily by all these people was because, if they were with me, they had a chance to actually talk to the Beatles."[63] Louise tried to enter the press conference by telling a police officer that she was George Harrison's sister. "Didja hear that?" the police officer shouted to nobody in particular. "Why lady, you're too old for that stuff. We've had 5,000 teen girls trying to get in with that sister stuff tonight." When WLS disc jockey Ron Riley assured the police that she was indeed a sister of one of the Beatles, the officer finally let her in.[64]

The press conference started with a presentation to Ringo Starr undertaken by the Chicago-based Ludwig drum company. Ludwig, begun by brothers William and Theobald Ludwig who opened a drum shop in Chicago in 1909, hit the jackpot when Ringo, who had previously played British-made Premier drums, purchased a Ludwig drum set in a shop in England. In the shop, "the guy wanted to take the sign out, but I love everything American, the music and the instruments. So I made him leave the sign on."[65] Hence, when the Beatles appeared on *The Ed Sullivan Show,* the Ludwig logo was prominently displayed at the top of the bass drumhead above the words "The Beatles." Following the Sullivan appearance, the demand for Ludwig drums increased so dramatically that the company had to add a night shift at their factory and then build an extension to the plant. President and owner of the company, William F. Ludwig II, referred to his luxurious home as "the house that Ringo built."[66] At the press conference, William F. Ludwig II and his sixteen-year-old daughter, Brooke, stepped forward and presented Starr with a one-of-a-kind, 14-karat gold-plated snare drum as a token of their appreciation.[67]

William Ludwig was not the only one who wanted to meet the Beatles and present them with a gift as a gesture of gratitude. Eight members of the Chicagoland Beatle People fan club from the suburb of Park Forest and three adult escorts drove into the city the morning of the press conference determined to present the Beatles with a plaque. The girls slipped into the Stock Yard Inn where, as luck would have it, they ran into the always-amenable Derek Taylor. Taylor handed three of the girls passes to attend the conference: Marti Whitman, president of the fan club, vice president Jan McFadden, and publicity officer Linda Macht. Taylor allowed the three excited girls to approach the stage where they handed the plaque to a bemused looking Lennon. "I must have gone into some kind of shock," Marti said. "I didn't scream or jump up and down but I don't remember anything that happened." Jan claimed that she was so numb with excitement that she could feel nothing. Lennon slapped her lightly on the arm and asked, "You feel that, don't you?" She was hoping that her arm would turn blue, but it stubbornly remained a pasty color. When the girls returned to school on Monday, their fellow students had elevated them to the level of celebrities and asked if they could touch the hands that had shaken hands with the Beatles.[68]

Once the question and answer session got underway, there was little of the jovial repartee seen at the Beatles' first press conference in New York City the previous February. All four had contracted sore throats before the show in Milwaukee. "A local doctor with a rare sense of humour marched into the Beatles' room, ordered them to drop their pants and fired generous needlefuls of penicillin into the four simultaneously proffered Beatles bottoms," witnessed Iain Smith of the *Daily Mail*. "He pronounced them badly run down and in need of a rest."[69] No rest was forthcoming. Now, the four Beatles seemed tired from the touring and from the constant questions about what they were going to do after the bubble burst, what kind of girls they preferred, and how they managed their long hair. They were easily irritated and exasperated with the questions, barely bothering to reply with jokes or quips that had made them so appealing at earlier news conferences. "George looked like Count Dracula—pale, gaunt, his eyes burrowed deep into sockets surrounded by black circles," journalist Larry Kane noted. "The other three, stymied by severe sore throats, looked awful too. The ravages of sleeplessness were starting to show."[70] On top of this, the Liverpudlians were annoyed at reports that blamed them for ignoring the fans at the airport. "We definitely asked to meet them or at least drive past 'em, and they told us, 'No,'" said McCartney. In turn, the seasoned, male, Midwest reporters, unimpressed with the four cocky upstarts and less enamored of their fame than the celebrity loving New York and Californian reporters, were clearly hostile to the Beatles. "What was your impression of the Chicago skyline?" one reporter, who was particularly proud of his city that was etched onto the magnificent Lake Michigan, asked.

"Oh, yeah. Good," John nonchalantly replied.

"That's it?" asked a startled journalist expecting a more impressive answer.

"Well, it looks like any other, you know," insisted an annoyed John.

"We thought it was rather distinctive" the indignant reporter responded.

"Oh, well. Everybody likes their own hometown, don't they?" an exasperated John replied.[71]

Their replies to the reporters also belied a rather different view of America than the one they had held before arriving in the country. "We felt it was a little bit backward," McCartney averred. "It hadn't kind of had the sort of youth revolution that we'd had in the UK and in Europe. So I remember talking to fans and things and sort of asking them questions, you know. 'What about your boyfriend?' and stuff and he'd be the guy with the flat top, the football playing guy, you know, with those kind of very old fashioned values. It was like 'Oh he's still like that is he. Oh ok.' You know, we didn't mind it, it just seemed a bit old fashioned, they had a bit of catching up to do.… We were some exotic beast to them. Nobody had ever seen people with their hair all sort of down like that and all the gear and the clothes, the mod look. They were a little bit in the dark ages about all that."[72]

"The Americans were years ahead with teeth," stated George Harrison, comparing dental care in the US with the UK, but then concurred with Paul's impressions about the cultural backwardness of America. "The first thing we noticed when we went to America was that they all had their hair in curlers and their teeth in wires, all getting ready for the great day."[73]

Lennon was characteristically more forthright. "And when we got here, you were all walking around in fuckin' bermuda shorts, with Boston crew cuts and stuff on your teeth," he opined. "The chicks looked like fuckin' 1940s horses. There was no conception of dress or any of that jazz. We just thought 'what an ugly race,' it looked just disgusting.… You tend to get nationalistic, and we would really laugh at America, except for its music. It was the black music we dug."[74]

It was not just the outlook or the dress sense of Americans that the Beatles complained about. John Lennon told journalist Art Unger in the summer of 1966 that he was shocked at how Americans are "always eating. All the food over here just seems like (there's) more of it. Everything is twice as heavy, twice as big. Even the candies or sweets are ten times bigger than any other countries, it seems. So, everything you sort of pick up over here has twice as much weight from the kick-off. Everybody eats more food than anywhere else than I've ever seen in my life over here. You know, that's what it is. That's what it is. That's what's giving them all acne and fat."[75]

Years later, Paul voiced his amazement at "the size of the steaks" he found on their first visit to America. "You know, we could all have eaten from the one steak that hung over your plate. Then it was kind of over the top, was all we thought. The Americans do it bigger than we do."[76]

Ringo, probably the most chauvinistic of the four, complained about American women. "They have too much to say here," he moaned to Paul Sann of the New York Post. "They boss a man around. I'll have no woman bossing me around."[77]

John, Paul, George, and Ringo had never been to Chicago before, but movies, television, music, and the British press had created a vivid picture of the Windy City in their imaginations. For Paul, the city was closely associated with music from his youth. "People from Liverpool have a very close connection to Chicago," Paul told an excited crowd many years later when he took the stage at the United Center in Chicago.

"You know, for us in Liverpool, Chicago was magical, very glamorous place. The whole idea of Chicago, like wow Chicago. My dad used to play piano and he would play and sing the standard 'Chicago' in his jazz band."[78] The song Paul was referring to was "Chicago (That Toddlin' Town)," a tune made famous by Paul Whiteman and His Orchestra and that celebrated the popular dance of the day, the toddle.

The other Beatles also knew about the city's musical heritage. Chicago big band drummer Gene Krupa inspired Ringo Starr. "He had a great smile and was as mad as a hatter," Ringo recalled. "I only saw him in movies, never saw him live."[79] They were all acquainted with the legendary Chess record label because of the music of Chuck Berry and Bo Diddley. They enjoyed contemporary Chicago soul music including the work of Sam Cooke, Major Lance, and the Impressions. Sam Cooke's "Bring It On Home To Me," released in 1962, "is one of my all-time favorite songs," Lennon revealed in 1975. "I love it man."[80] Lennon covered the song on his Rock 'n' Roll album while Paul McCartney recorded the number on his 1988 collection of oldies, Choba B CCCP. When they returned from their first trip to the US in February, Paul descended the steps of the plane at London Airport with a copy of Um, Um, Um, Um, Um, Um: The Best of Major Lance under his arm.[81] "I think he's marvelous," Ringo said of Major Lance in June 1964 when he included records by Lance and the Impressions on his list of favorites.

"Anything by Major Lance is OK by me," added John Lennon, who also picked a Lance record, "Hey Little Girl," on his list.[82] George also expressed a liking for the Impressions, but he seemed to think they were a Motown act. When interviewed on the British TV program Ready Steady Go in 1964, George told the interviewer that he admired "all the Motown, Tamla records, Mary Wells, Miracles, Marvin Gaye, Impressions, all that crowd."[83]

Chicago may have been a city with a great musical heritage, but for the Beatles and other visitors, the Windy City was most known for gangland violence and the legendary figure of Al Capone. As the four Beatles grew up in England, they could not avoid seeing newspaper headlines about violence in Chicago. "Chicago Gun-Battle in London" the Daily Mail front page lead headline screamed in October 1955 when unarmed police confronted "a Chicago-style gang who tried to gun their way out of a police net."[84] In June 1959, the Daily Mirror back page caption read:

"Chicago comes to Theobald's-road" as a "nineteen-year-old youth was shot down Chicago gangster style in the doorway of a London restaurant last night."[85] In May 1961, after a man was shot dead in a South London street, the *Daily Express* called it "a Chicago-style gang raid."[86] It wasn't just newspaper editors who used Chicago as another word for violence. One mother who lived on a violent council estate where her son had been shot in September 1962 called the area "little Chicago."[87]

"Injustice has been done to a great city," barked Mayor Daley in April 1964 when he heard that the city of Reading in England had changed the name of one of its streets from Chicago Road to Sandcroft Road. "Residents of the street have nothing against the city of Chicago," explained Reading's Mayor J.C.H. Butcher. "They say they just got tired of being asked by visitors where they could check their guns."[88]

"We've all heard a lot about Chicago," the ever-agreeable Paul answered when asked at the 1964 news conference what he was looking forward to seeing in the capital of the Midwest. "And I want to see all your gangsters with their big hats and their guns."[89] Probably not the impression Mayor Daley was hoping to convey of his beloved city.

The Beatles declared themselves uninterested in politics while in England, but Paul, at least, seemed much more willing to express his political views in the US and to plant his mast on the liberal side. They had seen the candidates for the upcoming presidential election on TV back in the UK, but now they had time to watch American television, listen to the radio, and read newspapers in their hotel rooms where they learned more about the nominees. On August 23, 1964, a reporter in Los Angeles asked them what they thought of the conservative Republican Barry Goldwater. "Boo!" said Paul, giving thumbs down to the Senator from Arizona. "I don't like him...I don't like him."[90] Five days later in New York, a reporter inquired as to who they would like to see as president. "Ringo, and Johnson's second choice," replied Paul.[91]

"Who do you support for president?" one reporter in Chicago asked the group.

"From what I've heard Goldwater say, I think Johnson should be president," Paul swiftly replied.[92]

One of those working at the Chicago press conference was Lily Venson, a reporter from a suburban newspaper and the mother of a sixteen-year-old Beatlemaniac. Lily's daughter Ginny, who had seen *A*

Hard Day's Night dozens of times, woke up that morning excited to be going to the concert with two of her friends. "I made my parents put the concert ticket in their bank safety deposit box for safe-keeping. I made a large poster with 'countdown to concert' and every day I crossed off the calendar, which put the concert date a day closer. I had this poster on my bedroom wall."[93]

The morning of the concert, Lily awoke at 5 a.m. to find Ginny and her friend, who had slept over, in the kitchen ironing their hair. "What are you doing?" the astonished mom asked.

"Oh, we read that the Beatles like girls with long straight hair," Ginny replied nonplussed. Worried that they would lose their tickets if they kept them in a purse, the girls disappeared "behind a closed bathroom door and they emerged minutes later wearing pleased smiles," Lily observed. "I knew better than to ask where they had put the tickets, but I could venture a very good guess."

The girls, sporting their "Ringo for President" buttons, ran out of the house to catch the bus from their home on the North Side of the city to Midway Airport where they waited to greet the Beatles. Shortly after, Mom left the house armed with her tape recorder and press credentials and headed to the Stock Yard Inn. She passed the milling teenagers and entered the press conference, taking a front row seat. Even though the four Beatles were not at their scintillating best, they captivated Lily and the other female journalists. "I spoke with some of my fellow scribes and we agreed that maybe the fans were right after all—these are four very likable fellows and we were beginning to understand the infectiousness of Beatle madness."[94]

Other, male, journalists present at the press briefing were more skeptical than Lily regarding the mop-topped quartet. *Chicago's American* sports reporter Bill Gleason referred to the Beatles as "four medium-sized creatures" when he saw them enter the news conference. "They could have been unshorn sheep," he quipped. "One of them looked like Rocky Graziano after the Rock's third fight with Tony Zale. Another one looked like Jim Landis during a barbers' strike. The third one looked like the late Gorgeous George, who might have come back to haunt the place. The fourth one looked like Bo Belinsky in one of Mamie Van Doren's black wigs." When the three fan club members stepped up to present the Beatles with the plaque, Gleason was happy that he "was able to sort out the three girls from the four Beatles. The girls were the ones with the short hair and the low-cut shoes." He may not have been impressed with their look, but after listening to the witty and forthright Beatles, Gleason reluctantly concluded, "I like the bums."[95]

After the press conference, the Beatles returned to their hotel rooms, changed into their stage clothes, and readied themselves for the concert. Epstein asked one of the ushers if he could go and find a hairdryer for one of the Beatles. The chief usher, Jack Gallagher, found this particularly amusing because "men didn't use them at the time."[96] Louise Harrison chatted with her brother and the rest of the group. "When it was time for them to be on stage, a man appeared on the fire escape at the window to lead them safely into the auditorium out of sight of the crowds."[97]

The concert attracted teenagers from all over the Midwest. Some arrived in specially chartered buses, some by train, and others drove with family or friends. Mary Mack Conger was fourteen when she traveled from Iowa to see the Beatles. On April 17, she sent the money she had earned from babysitting to Triangle Productions to purchase three $3.50 tickets for herself, her friend Sue, and Sue's older sister, Mary Beth. The ecstatic girls received their tickets on June 7. The day before the concert, the three girls drove to Chicago, staying two nights at the Lake Shore Drive Motel. Even though the show began at 8:30 p.m., Mary Mack, Sue, and Mary Beth joined the line outside the Amphitheatre at noon, clutching their cameras and binoculars and trying to ignore the smell of rotting meat that wafted over from the Stockyards next door. Crowds of girls camped along the side of the building eating their lunches, reading their teen magazines, and singing Beatles songs. On a regular basis, someone would shout that they saw a Beatle and screaming would break out along the line. "Some girls had regular dress-up clothes, like Sue and me. Others had cut-offs, Beatle buttons and ragged gym shoes. There were girls who had on a lot of leather or suede, Beatle hats, dark eyes and black socks." The doors opened at six, and the girls took their seats in row 48 of the huge auditorium.[98] More than thirteen thousand eager fans, 95 percent female and most young teenagers, packed the Amphitheatre as show time approached.

Even though many African Americans liked the Beatles, few attended their concerts. Many felt unwelcome among a predominantly white crowd. Even worse, many blacks had been physically attacked in the neighborhood surrounding the Amphitheatre on the Southwest Side of Chicago. Some African Americans, such as twelve-year-old Cynthia Dagnal and her friend Felicia, overcame their fears and bought tickets for the show. Their parents reluctantly allowed the girls to attend the concert, "but they made sure that they took us because that was a bad neighborhood." As they neared the stadium, Cynthia's mother grew more fearful as they noticed they were the only black people in the crowd. "That doesn't mean there weren't any, but I don't remember any at all. I remember my mom sort of being perturbed by that because of my mother, I don't like to say she was a reverse racist, but she had a thing about white people from her childhood because she'd been through some awful stuff in the South; and she used to take me there every summer so I could experience that. We would do the summer tour. My fifth-grade teacher was Emmett Till's mom. [Till, a 14-year-old African American from Chicago whose lynching in Mississippi in 1955 gave momentum to the modern civil rights movement]. And so, I remember her being a little bit shaken up by the fact that we were like the only black kids that she saw anywhere." As the mothers left the two girls to enter the Amphitheatre and walk to their fifth-row seats, Cynthia, too, began to worry. "I remember thinking, for like a split second, *Wow, this isn't for me. This is not my place.* I didn't worry about it for too long. I didn't get upset. I just thought, *Ooh, all white people and these lines of white cops.* It was a clear message to me. Then they started throwing white kids around to get them away from the stage, and I thought, *Oh but they're going to kill us all.* It was the Beatles, and it was solidarity. You know, if you were into the Beatles it's all good."[99]

The first person to address the expectant crowd was Chicago Police Commander Robert Lynskey. He strode on stage at precisely 8:30 p.m., grabbed the microphone, and instructed the young audience to stay seated during the performances and not to venture into the aisles. To help them maintain order, Chicago authorities employed one hundred and fifty firefighters, forty private detectives from the William J. Burns Detective Agency, and three hundred police, a number of whom stood directly in front of the stage wearing earplugs. Triangle also employed one hundred and sixty Andy Frain ushers to help control the crowd. The ushers pointed a flashlight into the face of anyone who stood or moved out of their seat. Chicago firefighters walked the aisles with small bottles of ammonia and wads of cotton and placed the ammonia-soaked cotton under the nose of a girl who looked like she was going to pass out. The emergency services readied two ambulances outside the Amphitheatre and stocked a first aid station inside.[100]

Promoters in other cities had picked local deejays to MC the shows, but betraying his inexperience at staging pop concerts, Frank Fried had chosen the middle-aged local newspaper columnist, Jack Mabley. "The Beatle cacophony is anti-music," Mabley wrote in his column in *Chicago's American,* just four days before he introduced them at the concert. "Give the Beatles a haircut and what would you have?" he dismissively asked his readers.[101] Mabley first introduced Bill Black's Combo, who played a short set of instrumentals and then provided musical backing for the other support acts: the Exciters, Clarence "Frogman" Henry, and Jackie DeShannon. Several times during DeShannon's performance, a wag backstage thrust a mop through the stage door, sending the crowd into a frenzy.[102] When DeShannon finished her short set and departed the stage, "We want the Beatles" echoed around the Amphitheatre. Jack Mabley once again approached the microphone. "I have been instructed not to mention a certain seven-letter word or everybody will start screaming." He shouted above the screams: "Here are the Beatles."[103] Dressed in dark blue suits with velvet collars, white shirts, black ties, and black boots, the Beatles "ambled on to the stage through a back door, looked around, found their instruments, tinkered with them a minute or so, and started playing," stated the ever-cynical Mabley. Their "entrance had been as sloppy as I had ever seen in a theater."[104] At precisely 9:50 p.m., "a noise never to be duplicated, vibrated, pierced and tore through the Amphitheatre," Walter Johnson, who worked at the concert for WGN television, declared. "The Beatles had come on stage. The noise was louder than the combined noise of 25 jet planes, Niagara Falls, 100 4th of July fireworks celebrations, 100 ambulance sirens and the Comiskey Park scoreboard. If you asked someone who was there, they may consider the previous description to be an understatement."[105] Hundreds of camera flashes filled the darkness and continued flaring throughout the show.

There were no elaborate stage sets, no sophisticated light shows, no dry ice or special effects, just the four musicians who cajoled the audience that hardly needed cajoling. The Beatles refused to gyrate like Elvis or cavort like Little Richard or Jerry Lee Lewis. Paul stood stage right,

Chicago History Museum

The Beatles performing at the Chicago International Amphitheatre, September 5, 1964.

John stage left, and George positioned himself in the middle just in front of Ringo. John and Paul were the most exuberant, George held back, hunched over and concentrating on his guitar playing. "John told the crowd to clap their hands instead of screaming," fourteen-year-old Mary Mack Conger wrote in her diary. "Of course, that didn't work. It just made us scream louder."[106]

"Why don't you join in?" Paul screamed above the noise. "Clap your hands, stomp your feet, maybe even shout."[107] Lennon could not sing all his vocals because of a bad throat, and Paul took over more of the singing duties.[108] Lennon was "leering slightly and licking his lips with foxy guile whenever the screaming rose to a new high, or stamping his feet and clawing the air with his hands when Paul asked the audience to join them by clapping hands," referring to Lennon's cringeworthy habit of mocking the disabled. George was "smiling confidentially at every freak display of frenzy, and shouting over to John and Paul between songs." Paul was "the most animated of them all, asking the audience if they had enjoyed the show, shaking his mop of hair so that the fans could hardly stand it, smiling at the girls with the look of a fallen choir boy and nodding in approval when his fellow Beatles came up for their solos." The smiling

Ringo's hair flopped around as he continued to "thump away with deep intensity at the drums."[109]

Fans had only seen the Beatles infrequently on black and white television sets, but here they were live and in color, which led to an explosion of emotion in the cavernous arena. Many were simply happy to share the same space as the Beatles or to participate in a communal experience with other like-minded fans and cared little about hearing the music. Others, deep in their impure thoughts, wriggled and writhed. Some girls leaned over balconies shouting out the names of their favorite Beatle; others just sat and cried while most screamed. "When we squeal," said thirteen-year-old Linda Zimmerman, "we get all our problems out of us. It takes all the badness out of you. And it shows the Beatles we care about them." She entered another world. "I can't remember a thing," Linda said. "You're in a kind of a trance. I screamed and I couldn't hear myself screaming. All I got was a headache."[110]

"There had never been anything in the US entertainment world to that time remotely resembling it," Jack Mabley wrote. "The wildest demonstrations for Frank Sinatra of earlier generations paled into tea party dimensions compared with the frenzy of the Beatle pandemonium. It was thirty minutes of raging mass dementia." Larry Kane, who had witnessed every show on the tour, described the concert as "the loudest reaction yet to the Beatles. The Amphitheatre was small, and the screaming seemed to resonate as it were projected into a canyon."[111]

"I saw rows and rows of faces with tears pouring forth. Some of the more hysterical girls clutched shocks of their hair in their fists and all but pulled them out by the roots," journalist Lily Venson noted. "[W]hat we had witnessed there was not likely ever to be repeated in the history of Chicago entertainment."[112] One of those screaming was her daughter Ginny, who was in "frenzied ecstasy. The extreme energy, no one sat still for two hours. Screaming, arms wailing about, heads tossing, it was quite the experience, and I remember this vividly fifty years later. There was surprisingly little security, compared to concerts today. There was so much screaming that I never heard the music after the first few minutes. My hearing was diminished for about two weeks or more afterward. My mother was totally convinced that I had permanently lost my hearing!"[113]

Journalists, photographers, and TV cameras zoomed in on the most emotional members of the audience, but very few girls were actually out of control, exhibiting symptoms such as fainting, crying uncontrollably, or pulling their hair. First aid stations reported that only twenty-six girls fainted or injured themselves while just two ended up in the hospital.[114] For most of the girls, screaming was less an emotional reaction and more a calculated response. It was a way to show appreciation, just like adults would applaud or a sports crowd would cheer. If they wanted, most girls could have kept their feelings and emotions in greater check, but a Beatles concert provided them with the opportunity to throw off cultural restrictions and to let themselves go. Teenagers knew that screaming was accepted and even expected behavior at a Beatles concert because of the images they saw on TV and in the movie *A Hard Day's Night,* and because the Beatles publicly stated that they were happy to hear the fans scream.

This freedom to behave in an uninhibited manner, to act in an unladylike fashion, and to exhibit such desire in public was eagerly grasped upon by young women, who faced many more restrictions and constraints on their behavior than did young boys. Teen magazines were full of letters from anxious girls asking for advice on how to attract boys without appearing too forward and how to behave appropriately on a date. "Where do you sit in the car?" one girl from Chicago asked *Datebook* columnist Mike Brian in his "Ask the Boy" column. "Do you sit over by the window, or in the middle, or right smack-dab by the boy? Where's a nice girl supposed to sit anyway?" she anxiously asked. "Anywhere, as long as the boy's hands remain on the wheel," Mike helpfully advised.[115] In September 1964, "Behind the Times" wrote to advice columnist Ann Landers in the *Chicago Sun-Times* asking for counsel about her scandalous twenty-year-old daughter, Doreen, who went out at night with her girlfriend. "Am I old-fashioned because I believe it is improper for young women to go unescorted to bars or cocktail lounges and become friendly with men they never saw before?" No, she was not old-fashioned, Ann Landers responded. "It is NOT respectable" for Doreen to go out at night without a man. "A girl who values her reputation doesn't rattle around town unescorted, or with another female."[116]

Some girls were annoyed at the screaming, including teenager Andee Levin, who attended the show with her older sister. "We were maybe fourth-row center. I was so close to them I just felt like I could reach out and touch them, but I couldn't hear a damn thing, and I was so frustrated. I just wanted all these screaming girls to just shut up so we can hear them." The crowd may have disappointed Andee, but the Beatles did not. "They were just wonderful. They just looked like they were having fun. They'd shake every time they'd sing their oohhhs, the famous head shake. They were just terrific. The Beatles had stage makeup on and everything. You could see the pancake makeup on their skin." Andee must be one of the very few people who saw both Elvis Presley and the Beatles perform in the same venue. At the age of five, Andee's parents took her to see Elvis' 1957 show at the International Amphitheatre, but she was less than enthused by the King. "I think I fell asleep halfway through, but I do remember it." She stayed awake for the duration of the Beatles' concert.[117]

In addition to screaming, the audience chucked a variety of items at the Beatles. Girls near the front wrote their phone numbers on bits of paper, rolled them into balls and threw them on stage. Others hurled objects hoping to hit a Beatle, the nearest they would get to touching their idols. In Britain, fans threw soft jelly babies, but here they launched the much harder jelly beans at the group. Louise Harrison, who positioned herself behind the line of police in front of the stage, cowered as George kicked the candy onto her head, chuckling and smiling as he did.[118] Not just jelly beans, but stuffed animals and flashcubes from instant cameras landed on stage. "Maybe it was the location," Art Schreiber from KYW Radio in Cleveland wrote, referring to the Stockyards next door to the Amphitheatre, "maybe the Beatles just look undernourished…but whatever the reason…a big juicy steak landed with a thud at the feet of George Harrison while he was on stage with the other Beatles in Chicago last nite. What's more—a big, plaster hand came crashing near John Lennon. The steak…and replica of a human hand…were among the assortment of items thrown at the Beatles by Chicagoans."[119]

One of the one hundred and sixty Andy Frain ushers who worked at the concert was Jim O'Boye, from the South Side of Chicago. Frain ushers wearing their distinctive blue and gold uniforms were a regular fixture at sporting and other events in Chicago since the 1920s. O'Boye became an Andy Frain usher in the summer of 1963 when he was a sophomore at Mount Carmel High School, an all-boys Catholic school in Chicago. The company kept a rigorous check on their employees, forcing male ushers to keep their hair short and faces clean-shaven, and female ushers to use "soap and water, not paint and powder." In August, the head office informed Jim that he would work at the Beatles' show. "I liked their music," O'Boye affirmed. "I liked their songs. I wasn't wild and fanatic like most kids were. I was thinking *Yeah, this is pretty cool that I'm going to be able to work the Beatles' concert.* I didn't think a whole lot of it except, *I wish I could bring a date. I could get a girl to go with me to the Beatles' concert.*" When O'Boye arrived at the Amphitheatre, his supervisor positioned him in the mezzanine stage right. Those around him paid scant attention to the support acts but exploded when the Beatles appeared on stage. "I was at the front of my section. Once everybody was in their seats, everybody stood up and sang at the top of their lungs. I remember thinking, *Well, why did you come to this concert? You can't hear a word that the Beatles are singing because all I can hear is the person next to me singing at the top of their lungs.* Then all the other mass noise of all the people singing and everything. When they'd stop, and they would introduce the next song, it's about the only time you'd hear the Beatles."[120]

The Beatles found it difficult to hear themselves on stage, which, as Ringo bluntly stated, affected the quality of their performance. "After the count-in I would be watching John, George, or Paul's feet, or even their bottoms—I'd be watching their asses for which way they were shaking. It was like I was playing by body language mainly. And I couldn't do any fills because if I got off the snare it just went into silence."[121] The setlist in Chicago consisted of "Twist and Shout," "You Can't Do That," "All My Loving," "She Loves You," "Things We Said Today," "Roll over Beethoven," (the only song sung by George), "Can't Buy Me Love," "If I Fell," "I Want to Hold Your Hand," "Boys," (sung by Ringo), "A Hard Day's Night," and "Long Tall Sally."[122] Sooner than the audience wanted, Paul pointed to his watch miming "This will have to be our last," and they concluded their thirty-five-minute set with a rousing version of "Long Tall Sally." They then walked up the stairs and through a door in the rear of the stage, waving to the crowd. There were no encores, the house lights came on, and the crowd was left stunned. "Presley, and Presidents, Capone and Conventions. There's never been anything like this," a Chicago police officer cried as he leaned on the Beatles, getaway car. The tired foursome ducked inside, and the chauffeur whisked them away from the Amphitheatre and straight to the airport.[123] "Hope I never see this place again. It's too hot and sticky," Derek Taylor moaned as he exited the venue.[124]

One last surprise awaited the exhausted Beatles. Waiting outside the venue were the Plaster Casters of Chicago. They had sat in their third-row seats, with Cynthia dressed in her "dark lowcut dress, black lace nylons and big round glasses," trying to attract the attention of the boys on stage. The two girls left early and waited with other fans near the Beatles' limousine for the group to emerge. Realizing that their heroes would not notice them among such a large crowd, the girls set off down the road. As the limo approached, they held up a sign to the astonished Fab Four. "McCartney just kept staring and staring at us—he couldn't believe his eyes." On the sign, they had simply written "Charva," a word that they had been told meant "fuck" in England.[125] When the Beatles arrived at the airport, hundreds of fans were waiting for them, some there since the group arrived earlier in the day. The plane left for Detroit at 11:30 p.m. They had barely spent seven hours in Chicago.

The concert may have been short, but the audience was undoubtedly satisfied. "Well, it's over and I could just cry," Mary Mack Conger wrote in her dairy two days later. "This is something I will never forget for the rest of my life."[126]

"When The Beatles were in Chicago, I took my daughter and her younger brother, as a birthday gift, to see them," a parent of a fourteen-year-old girl wrote. "I was first of all tremendously impressed to see the thousands of young people, all beautifully dressed and clean, so admiring, so respectful.... I was also very impressed by the showmanship, presence of The Beatles, and their respect and appreciation of the love the audience had for them."[127] Doris Fine, who worked for Triangle Productions and was the wife of the previous Triangle shareholder Fred Fine, gave a couple of tickets to her young niece. "Well, did you enjoy yourself?" she asked. "Oh yes," said the girl. "Did you hear anything?" Doris inquired. "No, not a note," her niece replied. "But just being there was enough."[128]

The audience might have been thrilled, but the local media displayed a more mixed reaction to the concert. In the *Chicago Sun-Times*, reporter Leighton McLaughlin was extremely contemptuous of the Beatles' performance, highlighting the amount of money the group was earning for their appearance, their "curious haircuts," and the screaming that "filled the huge hall with a sound that was wordless, wild, and to all appearances witless."[129] Thomas Fitzpatrick in the *Chicago Tribune* was equally dismissive. "Everything you've heard about the effect the Beatles have on teenagers is true. Confusion reigns when they appear. Teenagers, and even adults, reach an uncontrollable state.... It was impossible to find out if they had any talent because no one in the Amphitheatre was able to hear a note."[130] Others were more appreciative. Another *Chicago Tribune* reporter, William Leonard, wrote that it was "a performance that impressed amazed adults as well as screaming young ladies.... They have an infectious quality of insouciance...they radiated good spirits, and they had workmanship as well as showmanship....Yes, it was a good show!"[131]

At the end of the 1964 tour, which finished in New York on September 20, the Beatles and the rest of the touring party were exhausted. "The Beatles and the few Pressmen who are flying, driving, eating, sleeping, playing poker with and often protecting them are a battered and battle-weary crew," Iain Smith of the *Daily Mail* wrote. "The Beatles themselves no longer look the fresh-faced boys portrayed on record album covers. In fact, they are haggard and grey skinned.... Certainly, no one who has taken part in this hilarious adventure will ever be the same again."[132] Lennon agreed. "We'd never go for as long as five weeks again. That was just bloody hell, what with all the rubbish that went on over there."[133] The "rubbish" included acting as healers for the infirm. "On our American tour, theatre managers kept bringing blind crippled and deformed children into our dressing room and this boy's mother would say to us: 'Go on kiss him—maybe you'll bring him back his sight. We've got as much compassion as the next feller and we'd give anything to help the poor kids. But we're entertainers, not faith healers."[134]

George, who exuded a greater anti-authority stance than the other three, particularly resented being ordered around by managers, promoters, press officers, and police. "I'm a bit fed up with touring," George told Ray Coleman of *Melody Maker* in November 1964. "Not so much in England but particularly in America, for instance. I feel sure we wouldn't do another tour of the States for as long as five weeks ever again. It's so exhausting and not really that satisfying for us like that."[135]

"The strain for all of us had been enormous," Derek Taylor complained. "The pressure of press, public, and police on the Beatles and those around them was unbelievable and relentless. The Beatles, because they are the Beatles, had borne up pretty well. But our patience was almost at an end and little things were annoying all of us."[136] By the end of the tour, Taylor had lost twenty pounds from his already slim 150-pound frame.[137] When the trip was over, he resigned his post after a row with Brian Epstein. He and his family moved to California and worked for several American musicians including the Byrds. Taylor would return to the Beatles' inner circle in 1968 when he came back to London to work as the press officer for the newly launched Apple Corps. Epstein's secretary, Diana Vero, left the employ of the Beatles; and in 1965, she moved to Los Angeles to work for Taylor.

Taylor's assistant, Bess Coleman, found the trip equally stressful. The "Beatles could be charming—but they could also be extremely uncooperative, cutting, insulting and arrogant. John might be rude to an important reporter. George might refuse to get out of bed for a photo call. Paul might show up late for a press conference. In fact, they were not the easiest people in the world to work with—or for!"[138] Coleman found that "me and my colleague, Derek Taylor, were quite frequently treated like the enemy: we were the ones who'd get them out of bed and make them do photo shoots and press conferences. It was a nightmare. I had to be very tough skinned and learn how to yell back." Coleman's overall view of John, Paul, George, and to a lesser degree, Ringo was not exactly complimentary: "Arrogant, very amusing, extremely difficult and highly intelligent," were her comments on Lennon. "Great command of expletives; could annihilate or humiliate anybody with his acid tongue, which was an all-too frequent occurrence. No respect whatsoever for authority." Paul fared little better: "Self-appointed PR for the group when things got out of hand at press conferences, which was on a daily basis. Nauseatingly, charming arrogant. Great sense of humour. Extremely self-centred." George was, "Very quiet. Infuriating, obstinate. Deep thinker. Did not tolerate fools gladly. Polite—sometimes. Sensitive. Hated flying. Warped sense of humour. Would not do anything he did not want to—especially getting out of bed for press conferences." Ringo came off the best: "Usually thought of as the thick one, but was very knowledgeable. Co-operative—sometimes. Keen photographer. Brunt of many jokes, which he took in his stride."[139] Bess Coleman returned to London to work for Brian Epstein after the tour but soon quit and joined Island Records.

Frank Fried put the profits from the Beatles' concert to good use. At the same time as promoting the Beatles, Fried was participating in the civil rights movement. He subsequently walked with Martin Luther King in the heroic march from Selma to Montgomery, Alabama, in March 1965, helped King stage the Chicago Freedom Festival at the International Amphitheatre in March 1966, and promoted a series of benefits for King in 1967. Fried then became active in the movement to end the Vietnam War, raising money for the cause and marching against the war. Much of the rest of the profits from the Beatles' concerts ended up supporting various Trotskyist causes.[140]

While some city politicians pleaded with the Beatles to stage another show in their city to appease the thousands of disappointed fans unable to purchase tickets, Chicago was glad to see the back of the Beatles. Indeed, Jack Reilly thought he would never see the Beatles again. "Please believe me," he replied to one teenager who had the temerity to write to the mayor asking for concert tickets, "the Beatles will come to Chicago, and the Beatles will leave the next day. The world will not change one bit because of their appearance here and their departure. A year from now some other entertainer will occupy the spot light and you will be wondering 'Who were the Beatles?' faintly remembering you had heard that name somewhere."[141]

CHAPTER 5

"Lolitaville"

The Beatles' Second Appearance in Chicago, 1965

Much to the chagrin of Jack Reilly, America had not forgotten about the Beatles as they set out on another successful tour of North America in the summer of 1965 with Chicago again included on their itinerary. Having learned from the problems experienced on their previous visit, GAC had prepared a less demanding schedule. The length of the tour was much shorter, with concerts at only ten cities spread over seventeen days, and travel arrangements were better planned, with the expedition starting in New York and taking a westward direction until it ended in California. The arenas were larger, more often outdoors, and the Beatles invariably played two shows at the same venue on the same day. City officials, including Mayor Daley and Jack Reilly, were more prepared and less fearful of Beatlemania. "It was much better than last time," stated George Harrison. "Last year they weren't quite sure what was going to happen. This year, they knew exactly and so the security was very much better. Travel arrangements were better and we didn't fly so much."[1] This time, the Beatles stayed overnight in Chicago, spending two nights at the O'Hare Sahara Inn Hotel, allowing the fans the opportunity to get up close and personal with their idols and leading to one of the most enjoyable stops on the tour.

A More Modern and Professional Tour

Frank Fried and Triangle Productions, who were once again the promoters in Chicago, realized that they needed a larger venue to accommodate

The cover of the program for the 1965 Beatles concerts in Chicago illustrates the number of world-class performers promoted by Frank Fried and Triangle Productions.

the huge numbers who wanted to see the four most famous musicians in the world. Hence, on Friday, August 20, 1965, the Beatles headlined two shows beginning at 3 p.m. and 8 p.m. at White Sox Park baseball stadium on the fifth leg of the tour. Tickets cost $2.50, $3.50, $4.50, and $5.50; and the Beatles earned over $150,000 for the two shows compared to only $30,000 for their 1964 appearance.[2]

Chicago and Minnesota were the only Midwestern stops on the tour, and Triangle expected large numbers of fans to attend from the surrounding states. There were no shows in Cincinnati, Cleveland, Detroit, Kansas City, Indianapolis, or Milwaukee, and the Beatles snubbed St. Louis again. In 1964, there was no need to place advertisements in local newspapers, but with the considerable number of seats to be filled this year, Triangle paid for ads in local papers and employed a series of promotional tie-ins to sell tickets. 7 Up ran a contest where two thousand winners of a sweepstakes won tickets to the 3 p.m. show. Some sixty carriers who sold a minimum of four subscriptions to *Berwyn Life* newspaper earned tickets, spending money, and transportation on a chartered bus to White Sox

Park.[3] Local savings and loans societies offered free tickets to those who opened new accounts or added money to existing ones.[4] "The evening performance is a sell out, and we have only some cheaper seats for the afternoon," Fried announced on June 5. "All the kids want the most expensive seats. If I had it to do over again, I'd price 'em all at $5.50."[5] In the end, twenty-five thousand attended the first show and thirty-seven thousand the second.[6] The combined attendance of sixty-two thousand meant that more people saw the Beatles in Chicago on August 20, 1965, than on any other stop on any of their North American tours.

Although some hotels "nixed the unnerving idea" of accommodating the Beatles, according to *Tribune* columnist Herb Lyon, a full four weeks before the concert, the O'Hare Sahara Inn announced that they had agreed to host the Beatles.[7] The Sahara, a modern upscale club/motel adjacent to O'Hare Airport, was previously known as the Sahara Inn when local mobster Manny Skar built the hotel in June 1962 at a cost of $10.5 million. With a huge swimming pool, fine dining restaurant, and the best in musical entertainment, Skar aimed to create a "Little Las Vegas" in the Midwest. Under Skar's ownership, leading gangsters became frequent guests attracted by the plush surroundings and the major singing stars that performed at the hotel. Skar owned the Sahara until July 1963, when Ringo Starr's childhood hero, the singing cowboy Gene Autry, bought the hotel.[8] In December 1964, Isabelle and Carl Berg, who owned a restaurant in south suburban Thornton, took over the Sahara.[9] By accommodating the Beatles, the new owners hoped to leave behind the hotel's gangland past and create a fresh modern image for the establishment. The Beatles booked two suites and fifteen double rooms for two nights to accommodate themselves, their entourage, and the journalists who traveled with them on the touring plane.[10]

Indicative of the greater professionalism evident on this tour, instead of picking a middle-aged newspaper columnist to MC the shows, as he had in 1964, Fried chose WLS, the big success of Top 40 radio in Chicago. As the official radio station for the Chicago leg of the 1965 tour, their deejays received exclusive interviews with the Beatles when they arrived in the city, acted as masters of ceremonies at the two concerts, and organized contests in which they awarded tickets to the winners. This gave WLS a vital victory in the radio wars between WLS and their new rival,

Park Forest Star, August 1, 1965, page 4.

SEE THE BEATLES FREE!

Open a new $300 account* (or add $300 to an existing account) and receive I FREE ticket to the BEATLES CONCERT, Friday, August 20, 8 P.M. at White Sox Park!

HURRY! TICKET SUPPLY LIMITED!

$4\frac{1}{2}$% Earnings on all Accounts Current Rate.

Next Dividend Date August 31, 1965

Park Forest Savings and Loan association

140 PLAZA • PARK FOREST, ILL. • TELEPHONE 747-2400

With so many tickets to sell in 1965, companies across the Midwest gave tickets away with the purchase of their products.

the Chicago Federation of Labor-owned WCFL, who dropped its labor programming to play Top 40 records in 1965.[11]

The rivalry between the two radio stations was intense. Program directors at WLS and WCFL would phone Capitol in Chicago haranguing the staff for new Beatles material, wanting a copy of their latest single before their competitors. Capitol, however, had to make sure that they did not favor one station over the other. "Those two guys would split up. One would go to the lobby of the building that hosted WLS, and the other went to the lobby at WCFL," Val Camilletti at Capitol in Chicago explained. "They would call from a lobby phone; one would call the other and tell him he was going up the elevator to deliver the Beatles' single to the program director at his respective station. Because if one of those program directors got the single, one minute before the other one, we would have been destroyed. They would threaten anything, threaten never to play other Capitol records in their lives. Which they couldn't do, of course, because no Top 40 station couldn't play a Beatles record. This was their wedge. So in order for the guys to not show any preference to the program director at WLS over the program director at WCFL, they would time their ride up the elevator so that they would walk into that program directors office at the same time and hand them the new Beatles single."[12]

Although WLS hosted the 1965 concerts, the newly energized WCFL would not take defeat lying down and sought to maintain an active presence around the tour. "Frank Fried liked us and had a sense of where we were going, but WLS had been there for so long and we were still new, so it made sense for him to do the show with WLS. But he had no objection to our doing what we were doing," mused program director Ken Draper, who had previously worked in Cleveland radio. "Because WCFL had one time carried the White Sox baseball games, we had access to the sports booths," Draper continued. "So we put all of our disc jockeys in the booths at night, and they were on the air from the concert, with the noise of the concert in the background, and playing the same records that the Beatles were playing. If you were listening to WCFL, you had the sense that you were at the concert. We did the same thing in Cleveland. When the Beatles came, there was a radio station competing with us that was hosting them. We had a guy on the plane when they came in. We had free tickets to give away. We just played Beatles records and were on as though the event was ours. And if you were listening, there would be no reason to go anywhere else. We had a newsperson in the dressing room, helping when the show was on and talking to people backstage, and to the Beatles. We had a deejay riding with the Beatles and in their hotel rooms. And so we usurped the concert." Deejay Jim Stagg, who worked on the Beatles' summer 1964 tour when employed by KYW in Cleveland, switched to WCFL in Chicago in 1965 and traveled with the Beatles on their plane, much to the annoyance of WLS. Stagg interviewed the group on each stop of the tour and broadcast exclusive updates to a rapt WCFL audience on "your Beatles station."[13]

The Beatles Arrival in Chicago

In the previous stop of Houston, Texas, hundreds of teenagers had greeted the Beatles by running across the runway and jumping on the wings of their plane. Worried about a similar incident in Chicago, the police again refused to allow the Beatles to land at O'Hare and directed them to Midway, where they landed at 3:15 a.m. on Friday morning. A tired Ringo exited the plane followed by George, Paul, and John. Even with a curfew in effect, some 300 teenagers greeted the quartet. The Beatles drove from Midway north to their hotel, the O'Hare Sahara Inn, where they arrived at 4 a.m. with hundreds of fans waiting for them in the parking lot.

Four enterprising girls from Detroit had slept all Thursday night in a hotel bathroom.[14] Many others had simply booked rooms at the Sahara and waited for their heroes to arrive. Escorted through the crowd, the Beatles headed straight to their rooms on the fifth floor. However, the foursome enjoyed little sleep. Art Unger, publisher of the teen magazine *Datebook,* who traveled with the Beatles from the first stop in New York City to Chicago, reported that "the hotel seems to be filled with teenage boys and girls partying and wandering about." He saw "cases of beer and empty cans all over...some of the girls brazenly knocked on doors in middle of night and seductively asked if they could come in and talk awhile about the Beatles...some of the DJ's laughingly referred to the Hotel as Lolitaville." Fans not only coveted anything the Beatles touched, but anything touched by those who encountered the Beatles. Art Unger was smoking in the hallway chatting with a group of fans when one of the girls dashed into her room to retrieve an ashtray for Unger's cigarette. "Thanks," he said to the extremely polite teenager.

"Oh, don't thank me," she replied, "I'm going to keep this."[15]

Four teenage girls from Louisville, Kentucky, arrived at the hotel the night before, determined to meet their idols. The girls spent months planning their trip. They first obtained tickets to both White Sox Park shows, and then before they knew where the Beatles were staying, they wrote to fifteen Chicago hotels for reservations; only two hotels turned them down. When they arrived in Chicago, they headed to the Sahara where the girls waited for the Beatles to arrive. "I touched Paul," an excited sixteen-year-old Carol Francisco exclaimed. "I asked him if I could touch him and he nodded." Her excitement turned to anger when she threw her framed sketches of the four Beatles into the car window onto John's lap. "He just glanced thru them and left them there," a forlorn Carol said. "He didn't care; they don't care, and they didn't nod at us or even look at us. They ignored everyone." The girls spent all weekend trying to get onto the fifth floor but to no avail. "The whole hotel was like a dormitory," said Carol. "But the Beatles' press agents and the hotel managers were as mean as ever, yelling at us to stay in our rooms." The girls were unable to fulfill their dreams of meeting the Beatles, but they managed to buy four stained and crumpled napkins from an employee of the hotel who claimed that they had touched the Beatles' lips at breakfast. When she returned home, Carol donated her napkin to a local radio station who gave it away to the winner of a Beatles contest.[16]

Ruth Ann Moore and her sister Judy from Kansas City reached the Sahara the morning of the concert. The alarm woke the girls at 4:30 a.m. They quickly dressed in their white lace stockings, "black mod dress," "gold suede John cap," and "square toed Mr. Beatles." They caught the plane at 6:45. Neither had flown before. They arrived in Chicago at nine o'clock, picked up a morning newspaper that informed them where the Beatles were staying, and took a cab to the Sahara Inn. When they arrived at the hotel, they saw six police officers barring the entrance and a crowd of boys and girls looking up at the building. On the roof was "a tall skinny boy in purple lacy Merseybeat-type shirt" being chased by burly policemen. The crowd swelled to the hundreds. Someone screamed, and the crowd pushed, "as if we were all animals, crying, pushing and screaming," Ruth recalled. "I would have died to see Paul's eyes. The policeman pushed us back, but the crowd was much stronger and we almost smashed through the glass doors."[17]

The boy that Ruth Ann Moore saw on the roof of the hotel was Albert Hernandez, a sixteen-year-old Cuban immigrant who attended high school in Chicago. That morning, he had received a phone call from a friend whose aunt worked at the Sahara telling him that the Beatles were staying there. Albert and a companion dashed to the hotel arriving at noon to find "500 frenzied teenagers in the parking lot screaming at the top of their lungs. A hundred police and security guards firmly stood between the crowd and the entrance. It was absolute pandemonium." The two boys forced their way through a service entrance at the side of the building and climbed up a staircase to the top floor where two security guards chased them up onto the roof. The crowd below cheered and waved at the boys before they disappeared through an opening. They emerged through a hallway where they claimed they spotted George

Fans took over the O'Hare Sahara Inn Hotel when the Beatles played in Chicago on August 20, 1965.

Harrison. There the adventure ended, alas, as security guards escorted Albert and his friend out of the building.[18]

To avoid the crowds, the Beatles escaped out of the back of the hotel the afternoon of the concert in a Sahara-owned vehicle. According to WLS deejay Clark Weber, they headed for a luncheon hosted by Capitol Records and WLS at the Saddle and Cycle Club on North Lake Shore Drive.[19] Chicago PR man Jim Feeley asked Weber if his girlfriend, WLS weather presenter Edwina "Winky the Weather Bunny" Rast, could meet the Beatles. "So, I said, 'Yes, sure. Send her over.' So, he sent Winky over, and she was a tall leggy blonde and a very attractive young woman. She showed up wearing a two-piece white outfit. The guys went absolutely bonkers when this big-titted blonde walked in. Harrison took one look at her, and his eyes went tilt. So, she sat down with Harrison, and he talked to her for, I don't know, maybe twenty minutes or so, and she said, 'Well it was nice meeting you, but I have to leave.' Harrison said, 'You can't go.' So, she said, 'What do you mean I can't go?' She had a modeling audition, and she said, 'Watch me.' So she got up and left.

Well, Harrison was upset with me, and he figured I was just jerking his chain, trying to tee him off a little bit with a tease. I said, 'No, that wasn't the case at all.' So, he left." Winky the Weather Bunny attended the White Sox Park concert that evening. In a tight-fitting black cocktail dress, she stood to the side of the stage next to Clark Weber, an obvious distraction for the smitten Harrison.[20]

Clark Weber's opinion of the Beatles was hardly complimentary. "Initially, I thought they were four hyperactive eighteen-year-old high school students. They were really wound up pretty tight. I understood why; they were suddenly cast into the role of stars and they really were ill-equipped to move into that area so rapidly. Some kids move up slowly. You know, they struggle in little bars for years, and then they get a medium-size hit and then another and another. Gradually they become stars. But these four kids were just railroaded right into stardom, and it was pretty hard on them. Lennon was the more boisterous of the four. He was full of himself. I think he was the one that already was into drugs about then. But he was a studious kid. Ringo was like a puppy. He sort of followed around the other three. Harrison, of course, was honked off at me. McCartney was the one I liked the most."[21]

The Beatles arrived at the stadium at 2 p.m. and headed to the clubhouse, which they used as a dressing room. Today's pop stars are known for writing ostentatious lists of personal demands, or riders, into their tour contracts. On their 1982 tour, Van Halen produced a fifty-three-page long rider that included a request for M&Ms, but with all the brown ones taken out. Mariah Carey insisted that promoters supplied bottles of water to bathe her dogs in and an aide to dispose of her used chewing gum.[22] In much simpler times, the Beatles asked for four cots, an ice cooler, a portable television, mirrors, and "clean," as opposed to dirty, towels.[23]

Outside, the sky was blue and the temperature, in the mid-seventies, was unseasonably cool, which made for a perfect day for an outdoor show. The atmosphere surrounding the concert matched the pleasant weather; it was much less tense than the previous year. Mayor Daley and Jack Reilly stayed in the background, delighted that the Beatles had sneaked into the city at the dead of night and, with four hundred Andy Frain ushers, one hundred firefighters, and 150 police officers ready to control the crowd, confident that the concerts would be incident-free.[24]

As the clock struck 3 p.m., Police Commander William McKeon walked up the steps onto the plywood stage erected at second base and instructed the excited teenagers to stay in their seats during the show, warning the youngsters that security would eject them if they disregarded directions. WLS deejays Ron Riley, Art Roberts, and Don Phillips meandered up the steps and onto the stage to introduce the support acts.[25]

The King Curtis Band and the Discotheque Dancers were the first acts to emerge out of the dugout. Born Curtis Ousley in Fort Worth, Texas, in 1934, Curtis was an African-American saxophonist who had recorded with both Buddy Holly and the Coasters, and he played on the Shirelles' "Boys," a song the Beatles covered on their debut album and played on their 1964 tour. Curtis then branched out on his own and enjoyed several hits in the '60s including "Soul Twist," which reached number seventeen on the *Billboard* charts in 1962. On the Beatles' tour, the King Curtis Band added musical backing to the gyrations of the Discotheque Dancers, a dance troupe comprising one boy and five girls. One of the dancers, seventeen-year-old Denise Mourges, was a big fan of the Beatles and had seen them perform at Carnegie Hall in her hometown of New York City on their first visit to the US in February 1964. "I had watched on TV with the girls screaming at the Beatles at the airport, and I didn't get it. When the Beatles come out at Carnegie, the girls start screaming and almost running down the aisles. I suddenly felt it inside me. I felt this energy. I understood why those girls had been drawn. I could actually feel something overtaking my body. It surprised me. It was something I had never experienced before."[26]

Denise found work as a dancer after she left high school and became a "Murray the K Girl," one of New York deejay Murray the K's dancers who opened for the Rolling Stones on their first visit to the Big Apple in June 1964. The following year, Denise passed an audition for the Discotheque Dancers, who were formed to tour with the singer Tony Martin. "We're there on the first day of rehearsals, and there's a phone call. Our choreographer gets off the phone, and he looks at us and says 'we've just been booked on tour with the Beatles.' We looked at each other like *Oh my God.* I remember going home and walking in my house where there was my sister and my friend Susan, and I said, 'We're opening for the Beatles.' I remember hands around my throat; they were just on me. Not really killing me, but they wanted to. Of all the people in the damn city, and in the world, us five girls and one boy were picked. We got like $125 a week, which was standard for the contract," Mourges added. "If we knew we were going to be with the Beatles, we would have probably paid them."[27] Dressed in boots, shorts, and glittery tops, the Discotheque Dancers opened the show performing their routines accompanied by the King Curtis Band, who played instrumental versions of popular songs, including some Beatles tunes to keep the crowd happy.

According to Denise, Paul and Ringo mixed much more freely than the other two during the tour. John and George were rather distant and serious, spending most of their time at the back of the plane playing cards with Mal Evans, Neil Aspinall, and Alf Bicknell, the Beatles' chauffeur who joined Mal and Neil as part of the road crew. "Paul and Ringo were charmers. They were normal, very normal. Very friendly, fun. They would come and hang out with us." Denise remembers one particular act of kindness from Paul. "It was really shocking; I mean his goodness. I was not well. The tour was super tiring. I fainted coming off stage in Portland. So they brought me back to where they set up a nurse's station, which was way back in the bowels of this stadium, and I was just on a little stretcher kind of thing. I had my eyes closed, and I heard something. I opened my eyes and there's Paul McCartney sitting in a chair next to me. He says, 'How are you? How are you feeling? Are you okay?' I was shocked." Because of sickness, Denise ended up missing the last show of the tour.[28]

Once the dancers left the stage, King Curtis performed their own short set and then backed the vocal group Cannibal and the Headhunters. Inspired by doo-wop, Motown, and other black sounds, four teenage Mexican Americans from Los Angeles, Frankie "Cannibal" Garcia, Richard "Scar" Lopez, Robert "Rabbit" Jaramillo, and his brother Joe "YoYo" Jaramillo, formed the group in 1963. Their first single, "Land of a Thousand Dances," reached number thirty on the *Billboard Hot 100* in April 1965. Allegedly, Paul McCartney was impressed with the "Na, Na, Na" refrain featured on the song, wanted them on the tour, and later used a similar refrain in one of his most popular songs, "Hey Jude."[29] The young Californians proved to be the crowd favorite as they performed energetic dance routines to James Brown's "Out of Sight," The Temptations' "The Way You Do the Things You Do," their latest single "Nau Ninny Nau," and the crowd-pleasing "Land of a Thousand Dances."[30]

After Cannibal and the Headhunters, the King Curtis Band stayed on stage to back Brenda Holloway, a nineteen-year-old African-American singer from California who became the first West Coast artist to sign to Motown. She recorded not in Detroit but in California and, without the backing of the legendary house band the Funk Brothers, produced a softer, lusher sound than was traditionally heard on a Motown record. "Every Little Bit Hurts" was her biggest hit, peaking at number thirteen on *Billboard's Hot 100* in the summer of 1964. Holloway claimed that Berry Gordy sent Brian Epstein some of her records, in the hope that he would include her on the tour. Epstein and the Beatles, already familiar with her song, "You Can Cry on My Shoulder," a big hit in the UK, agreed to include her on the bill. "I'll never be able to tell you how wonderful it was, how really nice the Beatles are," Holloway told a Detroit reporter at the end of the tour. "Ringo is my favorite. He's so friendly. On the plane he talked and joked all the time, even with the dancers. He didn't have to; he just likes people." George was the Beatle that least impressed her. "He always looks messy. His hair is the problem. He doesn't even comb it. He's rich and he acts it—not mean, just careless and cold. I don't think he'll even get married with that terrible hair and that terrible attitude." Brenda suffered from nerves before stepping on stage. "I prayed before every show. Nobody had come to see me they all wanted to see the Beatles. Cannibal and the Headhunters would have the crowd up—you know, excited. Then I would come on and sing mostly slow songs, like 'Satisfaction' and 'You Can Cry on My Shoulder.' I was afraid they wouldn't like it."[31]

Brenda Holloway and the King Curtis Band vacated the stage, and the six-member Sounds Incorporated, formed in the county of Kent in the south of England in 1961, took their place to perform saxophone-heavy instrumentals. Sounds Incorporated had begun their career in the UK by backing visiting American rock 'n' roll acts including Gene Vincent, Jerry Lee Lewis, and Little Richard. "They're the best backing group in England," said the very impressed Little Richard. "I'd go as far as to say they're the best backing group in the world."[32] They first met the Beatles when they performed at the Star Club in Hamburg, Germany, but the Merseysiders failed to excite Sounds Incorporated saxophonist Alan "Boots" Holmes. "I didn't think they had something special; they were just another band from Liverpool. There was Kingsize Taylor and the

Dominoes there, there was Billy J. Kramer, and they were just really rough and ready rock 'n' roll bands. The Beatles were held back by the drummer Pete Best who missed his beat. Every time he was on a fill, he would come in on a different beat. Apparently, he was very popular with the females, but he couldn't keep a proper beat." Brian Epstein admired Sounds Incorporated and signed them to his management company, decked them out in smart suits made by the Beatles' tailor, Dougie Millings, and used them as a backing band for another one of his stable of acts, the singer Cilla Black. The four Beatles got on well with the members of the band, and Epstein took them as a support act on the Beatles' tour of Australia in 1964.[33]

For Alan "Boots" Holmes the 1965 North American tour seemed more of a chore than a joy. Many American performers, including Discotheque Dancer Denise Mourges, saw the baseball stadiums as special places: "I remember feeling that I was standing on hallowed baseball ground," she said.[34] For a seasoned British musician like Holmes, however, the whole experience of performing on a baseball diamond was slightly less reverential. "We were playing on a boxing ring basically that was on the place where the bloke would bat a baseball. All the grass, of course, had to be left. No one was allowed on the grass. The crowd was about 400 yards away, and the P.A. was just a load of 100-watt columns. There was no way anyone could hear anything. They were very accommodating, these baseball people, but it was just weird. The whole thing about America was just the strangeness to us. They had gigantic dressing rooms. I don't know how many people they have in a baseball team, but there was actually a few of us. It was extraordinary, but it was just a weird, weird, weird experience." Holmes also found life on the road less than enjoyable. "We would all just be bored in the hotel," he groaned. "No one was allowed up to our floor because you'd be harassed. It was all a bit boring, really. It's a very weird life because every day, you get on the plane, and then you get in a car, and then you go to your hotel, if you're lucky, or you go straight to the gig and set everything up, and eventually you get to go out and go mad for an hour and then you have to pack it all up and do the same thing the next day."[35]

Even though the Beatles were surrounded by grinning, ingratiating faces, their every joke laughed at louder and longer, their every whim pandered to, their every word treated like tablets delivered from on high,

Holmes was impressed by how the four Liverpudlians remained unaffected by the adulation. "They tried really hard and succeeded mainly in staying exactly as they were. They tried not to be influenced and get what we call 'big time.' John had these ups and downs where he would come out with stuff and be very sarcastic, and that was kind of how he was. Paul was the show business one. He was always trying to put on an act for people, be the cheery chappy, and be the face of it all. They were struggling to maintain their

Saxophonist Alan "Boots" Holmes of Sounds Incorporated was less than impressed with the 1965 tour of North America.

identity. They made a conscious decision to remain as they had been. If you start to believe your own publicity, you'll go mad. A lot of people did go mad."[36]

After the support acts finished their short sets, three WLS deejays, Art Roberts, Don Phillips, and Ron Riley, climbed on stage and Riley simply announced, "Here they are…the Beatles."[37] The grinning Beatles, wearing black suits with velvet collars, black ties, and the famous Beatle boots, and with John sporting a cap, walked calmly from the home dugout holding their guitars. They stepped onto the plywood bandstand erected over second base as the sun beat down from a picture-perfect blue sky. Triangle only sold seats from third base through first, and the bleachers behind the group were left eerily empty. The Beatles plugged in their instruments, Paul greeted the crowd, and they launched into "Twist and Shout." The Beatles' setlist continued with "She's A Woman," "I Feel Fine," "Dizzy Miss Lizzy," "Ticket To Ride," "Can't Buy Me Love," "Everybody's Trying To Be My Baby," "Baby's In Black," "I Wanna Be Your Man," which replaced "Boys" from the previous tour as Ringo's solo spot, "A Hard Day's Night," "Help," and "I'm Down."[38] Like in 1964, they omitted "Please Please Me" from the set, but even more surprisingly, they also opted not to play "She Loves You" and "I Want to Hold Your Hand," their iconic early hits that they had performed on their first appearance on *The Ed Sullivan Show* and during the 1964 tour.

White Sox Park, "which has been the soundbox for millions of baseball fan cheers over the years, never heard anything like this," Glenna Syse of the *Chicago Sun-Times* remarked. "It was pure frenzy, the howling of thousands of banshees."[39] Tony Barrow, who had replaced Derek Taylor as the Beatles' press officer for the tour, had seen the Beatles play in Europe on many occasions, but this was the first time he'd seen them perform in the US. He found that "audiences in continental European territories tended to shriek and scream less than the Americans and would listen more attentively to the music. European audiences had more boys in them, American audiences had more young girls, many only just into their teens."[40]

Aside from the screaming of the fans and the acoustics of a big open-air stadium, which on their own made it difficult to hear the group, the Beatles performed without the aid of stage monitors and used a rudimentary sound system. "A 100-watt amp, you've probably got that in your motor car these days," George Harrison derisively said of the sound equipment they used. "And the P.A. system, the microphone system, is probably just two microphones on the stage, and they're probably the same mikes that were used to announce the oncoming baseball players. Any sound that comes across from any guitars or drums is purely coming from those two vocal mikes. Nothing else is miked. Nowadays you'd have the whole drumkit with five or six mikes on it and have its own mixing system being pumped back out through the P.A. system. So it's a miracle, really, that anything comes across."[41] It was not just the sound system and the size of the stadium that weakened the aural experience, it was also the Beatles' performance. "The thing about the Beatles is they never rehearsed. Never, ever," an incredulous Alan Holmes of Sounds Incorporated noted. "Ringo said to us he never rehearsed with this lot. He was right. He never had a rehearsal with the Beatles. So he just went up and played. That's what they did. At Shea Stadium with 56,000 people they were peeing themselves, and they came and asked us. They said, 'Do you know the words to this song? We've forgot the words of our songs.' So, they were crapping themselves. They hadn't played for about three months, you know. So, they went on, and they were dreadful actually, really bad. You couldn't hear anything because of the screaming, and it was the same kind of noise as an airplane taking off."[42]

David Kell Blanchard

The view from the stands as the Beatles played in White Sox Park.

The band seemed to enjoy the novelty of playing in a baseball stadium in front of such a large crowd and eschewed the restrained stage manner seen in 1964. Emulating the Chicago gangsters that they had heard so much about, John and Paul used their guitars as machine guns to shoot down the crowd.[43] "Between songs, they talked to the audience, explaining various facts about the songs, thanking the kids for their great behavior, and joking among themselves," wrote teenager Sharon Simons, who traveled from Green Bay, Wisconsin, for the show. The band was all smiles as John and Paul waved to sections of the audience that then rose as one to wave back.[44] "John walked to the edge of the platform and assumed a diving pose as if he would dive off," noted Jan Tekampe, who also journeyed from Wisconsin for the afternoon show. "He cracked jokes, played his rhythm guitar, sang duets with Paul and just generally clowned. Paul made faces of pretended innocence and at one point got down on his knees during a song. He jumped around, made the girls scream and played his bass guitar. He and John sang and clowned through the majority of the songs."[45] For the last number, "I'm Down," Lennon put his leg on the piano imitating Jerry Lee Lewis. "We died a little when Paul announced the last song, which meant the end of something we wished could go on forever," wrote Sharon Simons. At the end of the show, the four Beatles walked back to the dugout as fireworks erupted into the blue sky.[46]

Some, such as Cynthia Dagnal and her friend Felicia, who had seen the Beatles in Chicago in 1964, were unenthusiastic about the concert. "I didn't like it because you couldn't see them. They were too far away. It was not as personal. We had fifth row seats the first time even though it was scary in front of the cops. We were really close. The second time it was like they were little ants out there. I know they had to do that. I understood it but it didn't feel the same, which is probably why I didn't go back for the third time in 1966."[47]

The Beatles enjoyed little peace and quiet between shows as a stream of visitors descended on the locker room. An Irish priest, a familiar sight in Catholic-dominated Chicago, walked around the dressing room. "This guy had a huge repertoire of blue jokes that I don't think I've heard before or since," Alf Bicknell wrote in his memoir. "He kept the band enthralled with his salty humor."[48] Paul claimed that a police officer came to the locker room and asked the GAC representative to "make out the check to me," a blatant demand for a payoff. When asked if they would pay, Paul responded: "Sure we will. After all, we want to come back to Chicago some time, don't we?"[49] Lennon was less pleased. "We already paid 150 dollars for police protection in Chicago. But here was a bobby who wanted more. It's shocking."[50] The Beatles provided interviews to touring reporters. Lennon complained that the concert was too early and he was sleepy. Ringo said he didn't like the outdoor concerts as much "as indoor with the people a bit closer, you know. 'Cuz they're too far away, really."[51] The Beatles posed for a photo with reporter Larry Kane, as Lennon held up a copy of the Chicago-based *Ebony* magazine with the front-page headline: "The White Problem in America."[52] The Beatles had asked Sherman Wolf, the Chicago public relations man, if he could find them some American comics, something they had loved since their days as children. Wolf turned to his five-year-old son, Stuart, for help. Stuart promptly arrived in the dressing room with the precious treasures and presented them to the delighted Fab Four. The disgruntled Stuart is still waiting for the return of his comics.[53]

As the evening show approached, the Beatles held a press conference in the Bard's Room of the stadium, a place where reporters and guests usually met for food, drink, and conversation after a baseball game. Among those in attendance was P.W.R.C. Haley, British deputy consul general in Chicago. "Do you think you're doing a good job for your country?" he stuffily asked.

"Yes, do you?" Lennon shot back.

One reporter asked about their song writing plans. "People will like us a lot more when we're older, you just watch," McCartney prophetically predicted.[54] Overall, the reporters acted less aggressively than they had the previous year, and even though they were tired from their earlier performance, the Beatles seemed more relaxed than they had been at the 1964 press conference. A teenage girl asked about their haircuts and what shampoo they used, but the questions failed to annoy because they came from a young girl rather than a middle-aged reporter. John, whose voice was hoarse from the first performance, respectfully answered that his hair had always been long, and he showed no preference for a particular type of shampoo.[55]

Sitting near the back of the room among the seasoned reporters was the small figure of Katie Davidson. At the tender age of thirteen, the ever-adventurous Katie traveled with two friends by Greyhound bus from her hometown of St. Louis to see the Beatles in Kansas City. That concert and the film *A Hard Day's Night* inspired her to set out on a mission: to meet the Beatles. When GAC announced the 1965 tour schedule, she phoned long distance information in Chicago to see if they could tell her who was promoting the show. They gave Katie the number of Triangle, who told her that there would be a press conference, but only representatives of the media would be allowed to attend. Katie called all the major newspapers, television networks, and radio stations in her hometown to ask if she could represent them in Chicago, but they all turned her down. Even though she had never met him, in desperation she phoned her Uncle Andy, who worked for *Seventeen* magazine in New York City. The lovable uncle wrote to Triangle Productions and asked for press credentials for his niece and friends to represent the magazine at the press conference. Due to demand, Triangle could not guarantee the request but would let Katie know if her appeal was successful when she reached Chicago on the day of the concert.

With $200 in her pocket and concert tickets in hand, Katie and her friend Madeline set out on a Greyhound and met six other friends at the Sherman Hotel in downtown Chicago, where they stayed for three nights. On the day of the concert, Katie phoned Triangle to see if the press credentials had come through and was delighted to hear that they were waiting for her at their headquarters on the nearby Gold Coast. When Katie and Madeline arrived, Triangle could only supply one pass. "It was the most thrilling piece of paper I ever had in my life," Katie exclaimed, but her friend was less pleased. "Madeline started crying on the walk back and sobbing and tears like Niagara Falls were coming out of her eyes. For a moment I thought, should I give this pass to her? But I could not give it up. I worked too hard for this piece of paper." Katie arrived back at the hotel and had to give the bad news to her crestfallen friends. She turned to walk away and felt a kick on her backside.[56]

Smartly dressed in a two-piece corduroy skirt and jacket, stockings, and Mary Jane shoes, and armed with a tape recorder borrowed from a friend, a camera, a sharpened pencil, and a notepad, the excited Katie took her seat at the press conference. "I suddenly grew up ten years. Instead of a little screaming teenybopper, I became a reporter on check. My focus was on those microphones. I acted mature on the outside. When they walked in, it was other worldly. I could not believe this was happening. It was heaven. They were four Gods walking in the room. They looked exactly as I thought but smaller." As the press conference continued, Katie waited for a lull in the proceedings before bravely putting her hand up and asking George her prepared question. "I hear you have a nightclub in London with Sybil Burton," Katie said in her most grown-up voice. "Could you tell us about that?"

"It's not my nightclub really, I just invested some money in it," he replied. She took several photos, but only five came out, and the tape recorder failed to work. Once the press conference finished, she met her jealous friends outside. "I started turning into this 14-year-old Beatlemaniac again instead of this calm cool collected reporter. 'I just met the Beatles. I just met the Beatles!'"[57]

Another teenager, Kathie McKinnon, aged sixteen from Oak Creek, Wisconsin, and her friend Lynda met the Beatles at the press conference thanks to *Datebook* magazine. *Datebook* gave away press passes to their readers, which enabled them to attend Beatles' press conferences and obtain interviews with the group. To become a *Datebook* Stringer, a reader simply had to send an application form and a stamped self-addressed envelope and, in return, they received a press card.[58] Paul evidently took a special liking to Kathie. "All through the interview he kept stroking my hair, which is very long (26 inches). And whenever I asked a question he'd touch my hand while answering which I found to be a very sweet habit." When she announced that they had to leave to return home, Paul said "It's a pity, we've needed someone to have a rave with."[59]

Katie MacLeod Davidson

Thirteen-year-old Katie Davidson attended the 1965 Chicago press conference and tried her best to photograph her heroes.

The doors reopened at 6:30 p.m. for the evening show, and the fans poured into the stadium. The floodlights came on at 7 p.m. to be met by screams from the gathered crowd. Darkness began to fall, and a cooling breeze blew in from Lake Michigan.[60] At 8 p.m., WLS deejays Clark Weber, Bernie Allen, and Dex Card introduced the support acts and then, when they had completed their sets, the deejays ran onto the stage to present the headliners. "I do recall them asking us not to stir the kids up to a fever pitch because they were already well stirred," claimed Clark Weber, who spoke to security before they introduced the Beatles. "Our introduction was rather short because the kids were screaming even when we stepped out onto the stage. And the noise was so intense that you could hold your fingers up and you could feel the sound. I'll never forget this, *feel the sound.*"[61] At precisely 9:23 p.m., the Beatles ran out of the dugout carrying their guitars, this time wearing light tan jackets, black pants, white shirts, and black ties. For the evening performance, the Beatles sang "Twist And Shout," "She's A Woman," "I Feel Fine," "Dizzy Miss Lizzy," "Ticket To Ride," "Everybody's Trying To Be My Baby," "Can't Buy Me Love," "Baby's In Black," "I Wanna Be Your Man," "A Hard Day's Night," "Help!," and "I'm Down."[62]

The group seemed energized by the lateness of the hour. "Paul rocks back and forth, brisk and steady, then switches to a knees-up-and-down movement," the Chicago *Daily News* reported. "Suddenly, he lifts the end of his guitar twice, quickly into the air." John, wearing his Bob Dylan style cap, seems to be the most energetic of the four as he "takes his guitar and gingerly takes a step down the stage. The scream volume rises. Two steps, three. Now four," according to the *Daily News*. "Then he runs quickly up the steps and turns to Section 16 and waves."[63]

Fifteen-year-old Jamie Barnhart from Bloomington, Illinois, who journeyed to Chicago with four friends, was mesmerized by what she saw. "Paul shook his hair and the girls screamed. George waved and they screamed again. John went down on his knees to sing and the crowd went wild. When Ringo waves his drum sticks the noise was tremendous."[64] John was jokingly interjecting over Paul's introductions to the songs. The two playfully hit each other before the group launched into "Baby's in Black." Throughout the show, they went to the front of the stage waving to the crowd. At one point, Paul descended to his knees and asked, "Which side loves me better?"[65] Unlike the fans, WLS deejay Clark Weber was less than enthused about the performance. "I was quite bored. I had my hands behind my back. Because standing next to the stage, I couldn't hear the music. I just wanted to get the hell out of there."[66]

Two fans, Bonny Kaske and Linda Myers, seemed more interested in those around them than in what was taking place on the distant stage. The girls were particularly annoyed with the WLS "Don't Scream" campaign that encouraged the audience to sing not scream. "The Beatles themselves seemed cheerful, pleasant and eager to please, although it was quite difficult to hear anything that was said in spite of the many amplifiers and microphones. There were the usual screamers, but they weren't half as annoying as a movement of teens with the slogan 'Sing... Don't Scream.' Anyone that wanted at all to hear the Beatles' own voices must have been lucky enough not to get seated near a group of these singing girls. Perhaps if the Beatles will be back in Chicago next year these girls can schedule their own concert miles away from the place where the four Liverpool boys are going to perform."[67]

Throughout the show, ushers and a line of police who sat facing the stands fought a constant battle with overzealous teenagers who tried to run onto the field. At one stage, scores of fans "jumped railings, knocked

Headaches, tears, and laughter. The three faces of Beatlemania at White Sox Park, August 20, 1965.

over saw horses, pushed around 200-pound policemen and guards, and streaked toward the singers," *Chicago's American* reported.[68] Larry Kane claimed he saw a naked woman run across the field before security tackled her to the ground.[69] "I don't recall that at all," said Andy Frain usher Bob Mitchell. "Even if I didn't see it at that time, you know, definitely I would have heard of it."[70] Chuck Dingée, who was a month short of his twelfth birthday, sat with his friend next to the dugout where the Beatles came out for the evening show and disappointingly only saw a fully clothed girl run on to the field. "The girl crawled underneath, got through, and started running toward the stage while the Beatles were up there. She almost made it. I remember John Lennon was kind of reaching out a hand to bring her up on the stage, and the police tackled her and brought her back."[71]

Among the crowd was twelve-year-old Ruby Wax from suburban Evanston, who was taken to both shows by her doting Austrian-born mother. Besotted with Paul McCartney, she tried to model herself on his girlfriend, Jane Asher, but finding a mini skirt proved difficult because they "did not exist in Chicago at the time." At the end of the afternoon performance, Ruby saw the Beatles exit through the dugout and hatched a brilliant plan. "When the evening show started, I stayed for the first song, then cleverly sneaked off to the dugout to wait for my betrothed, Paul. Annoyingly, I found myself followed by four other fat, sad, hairless, girdled girls and we all hid in the shower together. Before getting into the shower stall, I went around touching the toilet lids because I believed they had Beatle germs on them." Ruby and her new friends excitedly awaited the arrival of the Fab Four. "Gradually we realized the screaming had stopped, so we hesitantly emerged wondering where our dream boys were. The stadium was empty and dark, there was silence only broken by my mother's voice shouting, 'Vooby vooby ver are you?'"[72] The Beatles had finished their set, jumped into golf carts that organizers had hidden below the stage, and exited through the outfield gates to their waiting limousines, chased by scores of fans.

As a treat for the Beatles, brought up on American films with images of ice cream parlors, the driver took them to Margie's Candies, which had been in business since 1921 and was one of gangster Al Capone's favorite haunts. According to owner Margie Poulos, a big limousine pulled up outside and deposited the group and five girls at the door. They ordered "Atomic Sundaes," which consisted of six scoops of ice cream, topped with a sprinkling of nuts, whipped cream, a cherry, and fudge with sugar wafers served on the side. John, she said, "was the only one who talked to me."[73] A small crowd started to gather outside staring through the window at the four Beatles devouring their enormous ice creams. "We got wind of that from one of our friends whose dad was a cop in that district and got about a hundred feet from the front door before we got rousted," insists David Cacioppo, who was fourteen years old at the time. "Got to see 'em diggin' in and when they left. I don't think any of the boys had ever seen a banana split much less one as big as Margie's did. They had these eyes as big as saucers just looking at all that ice cream!"[74]

The band then headed back to the O'Hare Sahara Inn where Beth-joy, the Beatle-crazed thirteen-year-old daughter of Leonard Borris, one of the hotel's general managers, was waiting for them. Bethjoy and four friends had organized their own Beatles fan club after seeing them on *The Ed Sullivan Show*. She then convinced her doting parents to act as chaperones and take the lucky girls to see the Beatles at the Amphitheatre in 1964. In the Spring of 1965, her life took an even more exciting turn. "We were at a picnic at the Forest Preserves near Winnetka, and my father turned to me and said, 'The Beatles are coming to stay at our hotel.' I couldn't believe it. It was like insane! He said, 'You cannot tell anybody.' I'm like, 'Oh, don't do that. Are you kidding me?' I'm a good secret keeper, so I didn't tell anybody," she claims. The family lived in Glencoe, a North Shore suburb of Chicago, but Bethjoy pestered her parents into letting her stay in the hotel while the Beatles were in town. "The exits were all blocked, and there was security at every exit and entrance. I didn't leave the building the whole time I was there. There were phone calls coming into our room for the Beatles because the phones were all locked. Some people were just dialing numbers and there were phones ringing, and we're going, 'Sorry, we're not the Beatles.'"[75]

"I stayed in the room right across the hall from their room. They had two rooms. My mom was there almost the whole time until she went home to get my brothers. Then they wouldn't let her back in the building. She had to get back in the car and drive home to call my dad, and Dad had to go and pick them up." When her mother returned, there was a knock on their door. "My mom opens the door, and it's John Lennon standing there, saying, 'I can't get in me room.' Because he didn't have a key to his room, and he was up ahead of the security. My mom is like, whoa! John Lennon! My father had to let him in his room. Later I saw Brian Epstein racing up and down the hall half-dressed, screaming about his suit. The restaurant made beautiful chocolate chip cookies. I peeked my face out of the door, and I asked Ringo if he wanted a chocolate chip cookie, and he said, 'Little girl, it's very late. You should go back in your room.'" Bethjoy only briefly met the Beatles to shake their hands but spent some time with Neil Aspinall and Mal Evans. "They came in the room and chatted with us. They were really such nice guys." She gave them her *Help!* album for the Beatles to autograph, and they returned it to her signed "to Beth." However, it was not what it seemed. "My brothers and I, maybe six years ago, finally decided we weren't really attached to the thing, and so we wanted to auction it off. We've had it analyzed by three different auction houses and all three told us the same thing: that during that period of time, the Beatles did not sign their own autographs." Neil Aspinall or Mal Evans, not the Beatles, had signed her precious album cover.[76]

Also present at the hotel that night were Louise Harrison and her friends from Benton who had befriended George when he visited Illinois in September 1963. Among the Benton contingent was Gerald "Gabe" McCarty, bass player with the Four Vests, who George had joined on stage when he saw them play at the Eldorado VFW dance hall, and Jim Chady and his wife, Daryl, friends of Louise's who had seen George play in Eldorado. The Benton contingent, who had witnessed the concerts from the comfort of the dugout, seemed overwhelmed by the experience.[77] "There were people standing in the aisles," an incredulous Jim Chady later said. "It was thunderous. People wouldn't have done that for Elvis or Pat Boone."[78] At the end of the concert, they drove to the Sahara Inn to meet George and the other Beatles. Gabe McCarty complimented Harrison on his iconic Beatle boots. Harrison took them off and gave them to his "American friend," as he called McCarty when he introduced him to the rest of the band. The next morning, however, Brian Epstein told Harrison they had no more Beatle boots in his size and an embarrassed Harrison had to ask McCarty to return his pair.[79]

Bethjoy kept a close watch on the goings-on. She peeked through her bedroom door to see girls coming and going to the Beatles' rooms late into the night. "There were girls running up and down to their rooms. I'm sure they made sure they were old enough," she said hopefully.[80] The four horny Beatles certainly enjoyed the pleasures of the flesh on tour. "The Beatles tours were like the Fellini film *Satyricon*," Lennon remarked in 1970, likening the tours to a movie that focused on the sexual exploits of Ancient Rome. "We had that image. Man, our tours were like something else, if you could get on our tours, you were in. They were *Satyricon*, all right."[81] McCartney refused to admit to such debauched behavior. "I mean, it's a bit of an exaggeration. It was definitely quite decadent. The whole thing about getting into a band was to get girls, basically. Money and girls. Probably girls first. So when you are on the road, and there was time for a party, we had a bunch of those. There was an element of *Satyricon*, although that overstates the case a bit. But there were certainly some elements that you wouldn't talk about in the newspapers. Privately, I could tell a tale or two."[82] In 2018, he was a little more forthcoming. "There weren't really orgies, to my knowledge," he told *GQ* magazine.

"There were sexual encounters of the celestial kind, and there were groupies." On the 1964 tour stop in Las Vegas, the promoters offered the group the services of some prostitutes, an offer too good to turn down: "I requested two. And I had them, and it was a *wonderful* experience."[83]

Whatever happened behind closed doors the night before, the Fab Four were feeling less than fab in the morning. "My dad actually had breakfast with them both mornings that they were there," Bethjoy jealously recalled. "I so wanted to have breakfast with them. They said to my dad, 'You don't want your daughter to see us like this.'"[84] After breakfast, two black limousines turned up at the front of the hotel, acting as decoys as the Beatles escaped out the back and headed to Midway Airport. The Beatles departed for Minneapolis, seen off by hundreds of adoring fans.[85]

Once the Beatles had left for the airport, the staff began to clean the Beatles' rooms, as Bethjoy recounts. "They had housekeeping go into their rooms and started to take the sheets off their beds and started to cut them up. She went downstairs and started to sell them on the street. And my father, I think he fired her. He just went, 'This is unacceptable! You cannot do that!' Then I took the sheets. I asked my dad, if I could have the sheets. My mom goes, 'Absolutely not, we're washing those sheets.' I go, 'You can't wash those sheets!'" Her benevolent father collected the sixteen sheets the four Beatles had slept on over the two nights and cut them into 960 pieces, stamped each remnant with the name of the hotel, and then handed them out free to the hundreds of fans waiting outside. Bethjoy collected some other souvenirs from the Beatles' suite, including pillowcases, photos, a bubble gum wrapper chain, and racy fan mail from girls. "My mother's like, 'You're not reading those.'"[86]

The Beatles' tour provided mixed results for the support acts. Brenda Holloway continued to have some chart success with Motown, but in 1968 she quit the music business, married a minister, and spent the next twenty years raising her children. King Curtis went on to enjoy a more successful career, reaching a height with the 1967 recording of the proto funk classic, "Memphis Soul Stew." He continued working as a session musician and played saxophone on John Lennon's album *Imagine*. Unfortunately, Curtis' life was cut short in August 1971 when he was stabbed to death after an argument in New York City. For Denise Mourges, the experience widened her horizons and gave her the confidence to move to Los Angeles to pursue a career in dancing. "I got to experience things that if I hadn't gone out to LA with the Beatles, I don't know when I would have gone out there or if I would have gone out there. It altered the trajectory of my life."[87] Cannibal and the Headhunters never again matched the success of "Land of a Thousand Dances" and broke up within a couple of years.

When the US tour finished, Sounds Incorporated returned to England and normality. "I think I came home with 500 quid from that tour, which would be equivalent to 5,000 pounds by today's money," Alan Holmes recalled. "We played at the Hollywood Bowl for two nights for four thousand people on each night, and then when we got back, we went and played at the California Ballroom, Dunstable, to about fifty people. You go from Debbie Reynolds coming around asking us for our autographs to playing in this shit hole. You have all these expensive hand-made suits that had cost probably 1,500 quid a pop in today's money, and then you'd be changing in the gent's toilets." Sounds Incorporated staggered on for a few more years but without any great success. Alan Holmes, together with another member of the group, Barrie Cameron, played on the Beatles' *Sgt. Pepper* album and Holmes joined the Kinks in the 1970s.[88]

Among the excited crowd who left White Sox Park that summer night were several young Chicagoans who had been inspired by the Beatles' appearance on *The Ed Sullivan Show* to form their own musical groups. Many of the fledgling musicians exited the stadium as unknowns, but within a matter of months, they, too, would be performing in front of thousands of screaming fans, enjoying local and national chart success and contributing to one of the most fertile periods in Chicago music history.

CHAPTER 6

"The Beatles Put the Guitar in My Hand"

The Chicago Music Scene of the 1960s

"Sampson was a fair man," guitarist Rich Hintz of the local group the Males said of Paul Sampson, the owner of the Cellar, a teen club that had opened in the Chicago suburb of Arlington Heights in the spring of 1965. "Some people thought he was incompetent or pretentiously hip, but I think he proved himself. He was in his thirties. I remember he bought the first pair of bellbottoms and they were a foot too short; that kind of thing interfered with his image." The Cellar hosted all the major local acts to emerge in the wake of the Beatles but also some of the foremost national and international stars of the day including Buffalo Springfield, the Spencer Davis Group, the Who, the Yardbirds, Van Morrison, Cream, Sly and the Family Stone, Three Dog Night, the Steve Miller Band, and Steppenwolf. Sampson could have booked the Rolling Stones to play at the Cellar in the summer of 1965, but the decadent reputation of the English bad boys put him off. "So in order to discourage that type of image, he brought in the Byrds instead of the Stones, thinking their image as folkies was preferable," Hintz recalled. Sampson questioned his decision to choose the Byrds over the Stones when "he walked into the dressing room and found one of the Byrds making it with a girl barely out of junior high on a card table."[1]

Having to choose between the Byrds and the Rolling Stones, rubbing shoulders with Pete Townshend and Eric Clapton, and wearing the latest in British fashions seemed a million miles away for the rather sober Paul Sampson, the owner of a record store in the sleepy Northwestern suburb of Arlington Heights, as he sat down with his young family to watch the Beatles on *The Ed Sullivan Show*. He saw the English group as just another fad that would disappear as quickly as Davy Crockett's coon-skin caps and laughed at the mop-top haircuts and the screaming girls. Within weeks, however, Paul's life would undergo a dramatic transfor-mation as he was caught up in the whirlwind of Beatlemania to become one of the most influential men in one of the most vibrant and creative of music scenes.

The Birth of the Chicago Scene

Sampson may not have been inspired by the Beatles' appearance on Ed Sullivan's show, but young people, many barely out of elementary school, certainly were. Youngsters saw four friends on stage, enjoying each other's company. There was no extravagant horn section, no backing singers, and no elaborate dance routines, just John, Paul, George, and Ringo making it all look deceptively easy. Young Americans, envisaging themselves up on that stage, picked up musical instruments for the first time, formed groups, and began to play in garages, basements, and living rooms across the length and breadth of the country. "I don't know if there would have been a career," surmised Ronnie Rice of the Chicago band the New Colony Six. "I don't think there would have been a band. I don't think there'd be half the bands you see today if it weren't for the Beatles."[2]

At no time in American history were more people participating in a musical movement, and never before was the age of the participants so young. There are "a jillion new amateur rock 'n' roll groups who have taken over the scene in the last few years," the *Chicago Tribune* reported in August 1965. "There was a time when every high school had one combo, a valiant little band whose prize offering was effort; now, any high school is apt to include a half dozen quartets, each with its own outlandish name, all with virtually the same repertoire: neo-Beatlese, set to guitar and drum."[3]

"There was a garage band on every block of every town in the Chicago suburbs and probably in the city too," noted Dean Milano, who arrived in the Chicago area from Milwaukee, Wisconsin, in 1964. "You could ride your bicycle around on a Saturday morning and hear bands on almost every block playing in garages. There were kids forming bands everywhere. You'd probably have fifty kids on their bicycles around the garage watching the band play."[4]

As a direct result of the Beatles' appearance in America, the musical instrument industry experienced a boom in sales. In 1963, Americans bought seven hundred thousand guitars. In 1964, sales of guitars jumped to 1.1 million and to 1.5 million in 1965. The guitar replaced the accordion as the most popular musical instrument in the Midwest. In 1964, Americans spent $27 million on drum kits. In 1965, the figure almost doubled to $50 million. The sales of instruments and accessories topped $955 million in 1966. "This surpassed the dollar volume for record sales," *Billboard* reported. "It was greater than the combined dollar volumes of all spectator sports, still and movie cameras, comic books and playing cards. Instruments also outsold the entire hobby industry."[5]

"[F]ive years ago, we sold two guitars a week," a Chicago suburban music storeowner told WCFL deejay Jim Stagg in early 1966. "Now, we're selling 75 to 100 a day…they're all anxious to have their own electric guitars and professional model amplifiers. Owning this combination is the latest status symbol for these young people."[6] Chicago-based guitar makers Kay doubled the size of its Chicago plant in 1965, increasing output to five hundred guitars a day, while Harmony added an extension to their factory in 1967.[7] Gibson, owned by Chicago Musical Instruments Company, the largest manufacturer and distributor of instruments in the nation, saw production reach a record of over one hundred thousand guitars in 1965.[8] The Gibson guitar factory in Kalamazoo, Michigan, worked on a six-day double shift to keep up with the demand, and the plant workforce increased from 300 in 1960 to 800 in 1965.[9]

Many of these new musical groups emerged out of the city's basements and garages to play at house parties, restaurants, and high school gymnasiums, but the New Colony Six became the first of the new wave of Chicago bands to enjoy chart success. Like so many of the new musical outfits, the members of the New Colony Six began to perform while in high school. In 1964, Ray Graffia was part of the school choir performing at an end-of-year dance held jointly by his all-boys St. Patrick High School on Chicago's West Side and the Notre Dame high school for girls. Some boys wanted to get up on stage and lip-sync to "I Want to Hold Your Hand."

"Why don't you let us do it and we won't lip-sync it? We'll sing it,"
Graffia told the organizers. Graffia and the choir performed the Beatles'
hit and were such a success that Notre Dame invited them to perform at
a dance in the fall. The boys turned up with their musical instruments
and called themselves the Patsmen, in honor of the school they attended.
A raving success, they played at other dances but soon assumed a new
name. "We decided that everyone who was hot in rock 'n' roll at that time
was British, so we would bring rock 'n' roll back to America," stated Ray
Graffia. "Britain called America the 'new colony,' and there were six of
us. Hence the moniker the New Colony Six. We dressed up in red coats
and white slacks."[10] In 1965, the New Colony Six flew to California to see
if they could interest a major record label, but they had a huge surprise
when they auditioned for the television show *Where the Action Is*. "We
ran into Paul Revere and the Raiders doing a showcase," guitarist Bruce
Mattey recalled, referring to the West Coast-based band who had also
hit on the idea of wearing Revolutionary-style clothing. "We didn't know
what they were wearing, and they didn't know what we were wearing, so
as we approached each other, we're like, 'Oh my God, we're wearing the
same outfits. Why didn't somebody say this?'"[11] After criticism that they
had copied the more successful Paul Revere, the New Colony Six ditched
the colonial look.

Gradually, the New Colony Six also changed their sound. Initially,
they employed the harmonies and prominent guitar sound of the Beatles
but, to distinguish themselves from the Fab Four, added hard-driving
organ. This sound gave them their first hit. On their return from California, the band's parents clubbed together to start the Centaur record label
to release their debut single, "I Confess," just before Christmas 1965. "I
Confess" reached number four on the WCFL charts in early 1966 and
number two on the WLS survey.[12] "The early stuff was very garagey and
very raw," remembered Bruce Mattey. "But the later years when we were
writing the ballads and such, we became very polished, and you couldn't
tell it was the same band."[13]

The architect of the new sound was Ronnie Rice, who joined the
New Colony Six in 1966. Born in Haifa, Israel, in 1944 and raised in the
Humboldt Park neighborhood of Chicago, Ronnie had already released
records as a solo artist, some of which had made the WLS Top 40 in
the early '60s. Rice co-wrote with bassist Les Kummel the band's biggest

hits, "I Will Always Think About You," which climbed to number sixteen on the *Billboard Hot 100* in 1968, and "Things I'd Like To Say," which reached number twenty-two in 1969. "I was lucky enough to get my hit record I always wanted in my life with the New Colony Six," Rice recalled. Others were less pleased. "I'd had a couple of people say, 'Hey Ron, the New Colony Six were a garage band until you messed them up and made them a bubblegum or ballad band.'"[14] The group amassed a total of ten records on the *Billboard Hot 100*, more than any other Chicago combo of the era.[15] Members joined and left and, in one form or another, the New Colony Six staggered on until 1974.

The Shadows, Paul Sampson, and the Cellar

The New Colony Six were the first of the new generation of Chicago rock bands to enjoy a local hit, but the Shadows of Knight were the first to dent the top ten of the national charts with their single "Gloria," released in early 1966. Formed in 1964 by five students at Prospect High School in the Northwest suburb of Mount Prospect, the Shadows, as they were then known, became one of the most beloved garage rock bands. The lead singer, Jimy Sohns, was born in Chicago in 1946, but his family moved to the suburbs when he started first grade. "I played saxophone, flute, clarinet, and oboe from first grade through junior year. I was in the choirs and choruses. I had the lead in a musical, *Bye Bye Birdie*, which was to me like being Elvis. I've always been into music." If not for the Beatles, Sohns would have pursued his interest in sport. "I was an all-conference, all Illinois baseball player in high school," he proudly proclaimed, and insists that he could have enjoyed a career as a baseball player. Then he saw *The Ed Sullivan Show* on the night of February 9. "I saw the girls react to them, and I was all into that. I could have gotten a scholarship and played baseball and went to college. I was really good," he said modestly, "but I was very small for my position, which was pitcher. I probably would have had to have gone to the minor league. The Beatles came along, and I was able to make some instant money, which my family needed." Jimy Sohns spelled out what he liked about the Beatles when he first heard their music. "The beat was a lot different. The Beach Boys were almost acapella. There were some guitar breaks and stuff, but there was no drum within their mix. It was mostly guitar with singing. With the Beatles and the Stones, there was a beat, and it made you move."[16]

The Beatles inspired the boys from Prospect High to form a group, but the Fab Four exerted less influence on the musical direction of the Shadows than other British bands. The Beatles' harmonies seemed difficult to emulate, as did their musical ability; so the Shadows looked to the rhythm and blues output of the Kinks, the Rolling Stones, the Animals, and the Yardbirds for inspiration, admiring their surly vocal style, rebellious attitude, and fast, raw guitar-driven sound. The strong Bo Diddley beat of the Stones' "Not Fade Away," which broke the top 20 locally in the spring of 1964, and the distorted guitar sound of the Kinks' "You Really Got Me," which reached number

Jacs Bruscato

Jimy Sohns in Paul Sampson's record store in Arlington Heights. The Beatles dramatically changed the lives of both men.

two in Chicago in the fall of the same year, made a big impression on budding musicians like the Shadows.

Sohns was inspired to become a lead singer after seeing that the blues-orientated British bands, such as the Rolling Stones, the Animals, and the Yardbirds, all employed lead vocalists. "We played probably ten Beatles songs, and we'd play twenty-three Stones songs and some Yardbirds and some Animals. But I didn't sing the Beatles. It's not my style. The other guys sang those. We did the first two Beatles, Stones, Kinks, Animals, and Yardbirds albums. I had heard them sooner than most because I had a cousin who was in the Army stationed in Germany, and he had sent me that stuff well before everybody knew about it." In such a segregated city as Chicago, there was no direct contact between most white suburban musicians and the blues scene on the South Side, so, ironically, British bands introduced the Shadows, and many other youngsters, to the Chicago blues sound.[17]

The Shadows' career may have stalled if not for the intervention of Paul Sampson. Born in Chicago in 1936, Sampson's family moved to the suburb of Arlington Heights where he attended the local high school. Married with young children and sporting short hair and smart suits, he hardly seemed the man to ignite a suburban cultural revolt.[18] Like Brian Epstein, who also worked in his family-owned record store far from the center of the music industry, Sampson had grown bored with simply selling records and was looking for a more exciting, and more financially rewarding, way to earn a living. Noting the complaints of his teenage customers that there was little to do in this quaint suburb, he decided to stage a concert. "I had heard about a relatively local band that was playing up at the VFW Hall in Arlington Heights and apparently attracting some amount of fan allegiance. I do recall that I went by and noted that there were teenage girls googling over them. I thought to myself it would be an excellent thing if I could produce, do something of the same nature." In the fall of 1964, he rented the Mount Prospect Country Club for one hundred dollars and paid the Shadows, the local band that he had seen a few weeks earlier, eighty-five dollars to play for the night. He charged one-dollar admission, and much to his surprise and delight, over six hundred youngsters turned up. "It was more of a business thing at that time. It was associated with trying to run teenage dance functions. The Shadows just happened to be the very first group that I decided to use based on that fact that they had local popularity."[19] Impressed by the band and the size and reaction of the audience, Sampson became their manager.

Buoyed by the success of the concert, Sampson staged other shows at various venues in the area, but his ambition was to open his own club. "I wanted to create a place that looked like The Cavern, the place in England where the Beatles performed," he said.[20] The demand for such an establishment was there. The suburbs had seen a huge growth in the teenage population, and although local high schools put on teen dances, and Sampson and other promoters staged shows at VFW halls, suburban teens wanted their own purpose-built spaces where they could see some exciting rock 'n' roll bands away from the watchful eyes of principals and teachers. Sampson rented an abandoned basement belonging to the former St. Peter Lutheran Church and School in Arlington Heights, and with the help of the Shadows, who were eager to have a place to play on a regular basis, built a stage and installed a sound system. In the spring of 1965, Sampson and his partner, Tom Johnson, opened the first permanent home of the Cellar, but with a capacity of only 200, it quickly outgrew its location due to its popularity. Within a year, Sampson had resettled the club into a larger 700-capacity facility on nearby Davis Street.[21]

The Cellar became the prototype for other suburban teen clubs. Sampson designed the club to have a minimum of furniture, believing that "if a fight were to start, the best weapon in

Paul Sampson, on the right displaying his Beatle boots, and Tom Johnson his business partner.

the world is a chair." The decor consisted of nets hung from the ceiling and graffiti-covered concrete block walls. The music was raw and loud. "I was mortgaged up to the hilt to be doing it, but one of the first things I did was put in a sound system in that small, first club—second, as well— that would blow your socks off," stated Sampson. "I didn't want it where you had to stand up front to hear."[22]

A journalist from *Omnibus* magazine who visited the new Cellar in the spring of 1967 noted the lack of tables and chairs and the constant swinging of bathroom doors. "This is the air conditioning," he sardonically noted. "The Cellar is where it's happening in Arlington Heights, and although at times the old factory building seems about to lose its roof and its cool, and the din causes shudders to the over-thirty crowd who may be passing by, the kids dig it." Security provided by local police was tight. Four or five uniformed police officers mingled with the crowd to disentangle overly passionate couples or discourage fights in the dimly lit club. Sampson refused to allow alcohol on the premises but provided soda pop and snacks. "Drinking of alcoholic beverages is absolutely not tolerated and even a suspicious breath (Sen-Sen is a dead giveaway) is enough to get the suspect firmly evicted and asked not to return."[23] This did not deter the local teenagers, as they created traffic jams in this sedate town and queued around the block to gain entry into the hottest club in the Chicagoland area. "I've found my niche," said a delighted Paul Sampson. "College aptitude tests indicated I should be a social worker. I've taken the best of social work, working with young people, and made it a business."[24]

Dave Grundhoefer, who was the lead singer of the local band the Huns, and a regular Cellar dweller, spoke of Sampson's bond with local teenagers. "My friend Mark and I went over there, and of course we weren't real bad guys. We wrote the name the Huns all over the outside of the Cellar. But we did it in shoe polish because we wanted it to be able to come out. The cops caught us and took us to the police station and gave us a good talking to and called Mark's parents and dialed my parents and my sister. Paul comes in, and he's laughing and giggling. 'It's okay,' he says, 'I don't want to press any charges against Dave. He's one of my favorite guys here. I'm not going to do anything.' The cops are like, 'Well, you can press charges you know and we can get fines against them.' 'No, no,' he says, 'it was all in good fun. If they go back and clean it up, I have no issue with it.' We had to go back and clean it up, which wasn't too hard." Unlike some club owners, Sampson dealt fairly with the bands that appeared at the Cellar, including the Huns. "He wasn't a dirty dealer the way other guys were. All those guys, it seemed like they thought they couldn't succeed unless they stepped all over everybody. Sampson wasn't like that."[25]

Because of the Cellar's success, new clubs opened in old factories, stores, and warehouses across suburban Chicagoland. Exotically named venues like the Pink Panther in Deerfield, the Crimson Cougar in Aurora, the Green Gorilla and the Hut in Des Plaines, the Dark Spot in Roselle, the Pit in Glenview, the Deep End in Park Ridge, the Jaguar in St. Charles, and many others would go on to play significant roles in the lives of local youngsters. In recognition of the burgeoning scene, suburban newspapers started regular columns that listed and commented on club activity in the local area.[26]

The Shadows became a fixture at the Cellar. "It was hugely successful, so much so that we had to do two shows a night on Friday and Saturday.

The Cellar, Arlington Heights' answer to the Cavern, hosts another group heavily influenced by the Beatles, Saturday's Children.

We would start a little earlier and burn the place up, and they'd bring a second crowd in," recalled Sohns with some pride.[27] Other bands wore identical suits on stage, but the Shadows looked rather scruffy and perfected the sullen look in photographs. According to members of the Shadows Fan Club, lead guitarist Warren Rogers was "gay, witty and charming," vocalist Jimy Sohns "likes girls," and bassist Wayne Pursell, the youngest, was quiet, "very serious and probably the most polite of the group." Because of his short hair, rhythm guitarist Norman Gotsch gained the nickname "Collegiate Joe," while drummer Tom Schiffour, the senior member, adopted a wild drumming style, was "very moody and exhibited a quick temper." He charmingly told the fans, "I hate people."[28] The Shadows had a steady turnover of members. Jerry McGeorge replaced Norman Gotsch, who was drafted into the US Army; Wayne Pursell left the group to attend college; Warren Rogers took his place on bass; and Joe Kelley joined on lead guitar. This lineup developed an explosive live act. "What he lacked in musical skills he made up for in understanding crowds and what it took to stir them up," McGeorge later said of Sohns. "A lot of the Shadows' energy came from Tom emulating Keith Moon, and maybe me trying to copy Townshend's guitar clangs and bangs."[29] Kelley, an excellent blues guitarist, added to the ferocious and slightly shambolic sound. "It was like below zero, and we went over there with our equipment, and on stage, there was a group called the Shadows of Knight," recalled local musician Jim Peterik of the Shondels. "And we're seeing these long-haired mutants from Arlington Heights, and we're just like, 'Holy shit, this is what rock 'n' roll is all about.'"[30]

Dunwich Records

The popularity of the Shadows caught the attention of a new locally-based record label, Dunwich, owned by Bill Traut, Eddie Higgins, and George Badonsky. Bill Traut, originally from Wisconsin, played saxophone in Chicago's swanky hotels and worked for the Background Music Department at the Seeburg Corporation, a maker of jukeboxes. In the early '60s, Traut met Massachusetts-born Eddie Higgins, a jazz pianist who gigged in some of the major jazz venues in Chicago at night and worked as a recording engineer at Universal Recording Studios during the day. In 1963, Higgins began working with Traut at Seeburg making background music, but almost immediately, both began plotting their exit strategy. The two men started to produce jazz records, including those of the Eddie Higgins Trio, but quickly realized there was a better route to financial success. "We decided at that point that we needed to get real about rock 'n' roll, or I would never make enough money to get out of Seeburg," Traut said. They met George Badonsky, a sales representative for Atlantic Records, and started Amboy records, quickly renamed Dunwich in honor of H.P. Lovecraft's book *The Dunwich Horror,* which Higgins and Traut both admired. The three men set out to find local acts to record at Universal Recording Studios on Rush Street, the city's state-of-the-art and most popular recording studio for independent record labels.

Badonsky and Traut visited the Cellar to see the Shadows and were suitably impressed. They made plans to go into the studio but discovered that a popular English band was using the same name. "As we were going to record, our management/producers said we had to change our name," said Jimy Sohns. "They said 'You're going to be the Tyme.' I said 'No, we're not. That's stupid. We have this huge following.' He said, 'All right, smart guy, what are you going to be then?' 'We are the Shadows of Knight,' with a K because I thought it sounded English."[31] The name of Prospect High School sports teams was the Knights, which probably influenced Sohns' thinking as well.

The Shadows of Knight's first release on Dunwich Records was a remake of "Gloria," a song previously recorded by the Irish band Them and released in England as the b-side of "Baby Please Don't Go" in November 1964. Sohns first heard the record when his cousin, stationed in the Army in Germany, sent him a copy. The Shadows' recording reached number one on the WCFL and WLS surveys, and number ten on *Billboard* in the spring of 1966.[32] The Shadows of Knight became the first Chicago rock band of the era to record an album, *Gloria*, released on Dunwich in April 1966. In recognition of their popularity, in May 1966, students from three local high schools in Arlington Heights met with village officials urging them to build a memorial fountain in front of the original location of the Cellar, containing busts of Paul Sampson and the Shadows of Knight. The officials, unsurprisingly, rejected the proposal.[33]

While the New Colony Six tried to avoid controversy, "We were basically the Pat Boones of rock music," said lead singer Ronnie Rice, the Shadows of Knight seemed to seek it out.[34] In September 1965, three members of the Shadows, Joe Kelley, Tom Schiffour, and Warren Rogers, were charged with "contributing to the delinquency of a minor" after some fifteen-year-old girls were found to be drinking alcohol at a party they attended. A judge placed them under the supervision of the Circuit Court for one year.[35] The members of the group let their hair grow to a length unseen in Arlington Heights. Soon, their hair copied the sheepdog style of Brian Jones of the Rolling Stones. Stories of excess on the road were many. "They billed themselves as Chicago's Rolling Stones, and they lived that life," Bill Traut remembered. "They were reasonably bad. They always tore places up. Sohns was pretty much devoted to having as many girls as possible in his hotel room the night after the show. Every time they went to a town, I'd get a report from the hotel that they did something, either stole the pillows or turned fire extinguishers on all the cars in the parking lot or dumb things like that."[36]

The heyday of the Shadows of Knight was all too short as they failed to take advantage of the chart success of their first single. They followed up the release of "Gloria" with further covers of material first recorded by British acts. For their second single, they recorded a version of Bo Diddley's "Oh Yeah," based not on the original but on a cover released in October 1964 by the London-based group, the Others. Then they released "Bad Little Woman," previously recorded by the Wheels, from Ireland.

Its misogynistic message added to the Shadows' dangerous and macho image. With its slightly menacing vocal, fantastic Keith Moon-like drums, and searing guitar work, their fourth single, "I'm Gonna Make You Mine," an excellent prototype punk record ten years ahead of its time, was the best of the lot, but it barely scratched the *Billboard Hot 100.*

"I really believe we were grossly mismanaged and that had we been with the right management and agency, things might have been a lot different," moaned Jerry McGeorge. With "Gloria" riding high in the best-seller lists, Sampson made a deal with a booking agency who had little experience with rock bands, and the group continued to play small venues, ignoring major markets like California, the Pacific Northwest, Texas, and Florida, and taking in little money as they toured in an old school bus. "Paul's lack of experience was probably critical here, but he'd been our mentor and had stuck with us, so early on we didn't say much about it."[37]

Sampson himself admitted to "a series of mistakes that were made that I, as a novice, allowed to be made," including setting them up with the wrong booking agency. The other mistake, Sampson confessed, was to allow George Badonsky and especially Bill Traut to soften and commercialize their sound in the studio. "George was a much artier guy," Sampson said of Badonsky. "I think Bill was, oh, I don't know; kinda 'bubblegummy' and maybe that was some of the stuff the guys were upset about in their recording."[38] Dunwich was torn between Badonsky's view of the Shadows of Knight, which was to produce a white urban blues band, and Traut's, which was to create a sunshine pop hits machine. "I was concerned with selling more records because I wanted the company to be successful and continue making a lot of money," stated Traut. "After all, I was in rock 'n' roll for the money, not the glory."[39] The band complained that they received little from record royalties or live appearances and this, together with the volatility of the personalities in the band, caused constant disagreements. The band ousted Sampson as manager in 1967 and then collapsed. "I fired everybody on the 4th of July in 1967," Sohns stated. "I moved on."[40]

Jimy Sohns continued with the name Shadows of Knight and, at the tail end of 1968, the new incarnation of the band scaled the charts with "Shake," which reached number forty-six on the *Billboard Hot 100.*[41] Success with the new line up was short-lived, and the group soon disintegrated. In the '70s, Sohns became road manager for the Chicago punk band Skafish. On tour with the band in 1978, he garnered headlines after a violent altercation with Sid Vicious of the Sex Pistols in a New York City club. In March 1982, federal agents arrested Sohns and nine other men for selling cocaine in a multimillion-dollar operation. According to agents, Sohns was the head of a drug ring that had operated throughout the Northwest suburbs. A judge sentenced him to six years in prison. Forever the rock star, while incarcerated he sang in the group Jimy Sohns and the Cons. When released, he reconstituted the Shadows of Knight, and he still performs under the name today.[42]

The Buckinghams

The Buckinghams went on to even greater national success than the Shadows of Knight and became the most successful group to emerge out of the Chicago area in the '60s. Carl Giammarese, from the North Side of the city, started playing guitar at the age of thirteen in 1960. He joined his cousin's band in the Northwest suburbs, the Kingsmen, who changed their name to the Centuries in December 1963 after a band with the same name from the West Coast entered the charts with "Louie, Louie."[43]

"We were doing a lot of instrumentals and songs like 'I Couldn't Sleep at all Last Night' or 'On Broadway,'" recalled Giammarese. "We were the first band around Chicago to cover Beatles songs and play and sing. Playing instruments and singing at the same time wasn't really the style up until then. Every band around Chicago was a backup band with two or three singers upfront."[44]

Beatles songs required sophisticated musical skills, as Centuries' bassist Curt Bachman explained. "The Kinks and the Stones were easier songs to play than the Beatles, so we did a lot of that stuff. The Beatles were playing chords and melodies that took more of an experienced musician to pull off. I remember the Beatles' song, 'You Can't Do That.' The Centuries worked for weeks trying to figure out the riff. It took us weeks to learn that song. Because all you had was the record to play."[45]

In early 1965, Giammarese and Bachman joined the Pulsations led by not one but two vocalists, Dennis Tufano and George LeGros; the latter soon left the group, a casualty of the draft. The Pulsations won a Battle of the Bands contest to appear as the house band on the thirteen-week *All Time Hits* television show on WGN. The producers of the

series disliked the name the Pulsations, thinking it too suggestive,
and wanted an English-sounding
name. "This was 1965, and they
wanted something that just capi-
talized on the British Invasion,"
recalled Giammarese. "There was
a guy we made friends with who
worked for the TV show. He was
the security guard, John Opager.
John came up with a name. He
says, 'You know, how about The
Buckinghams?' And we were like,
'Wow, that's kind of cool.'" Buckinghams sounded English, and
there was also a famous landmark

THE FABULOUS CENTURIES
CARL, GERRY, NICK, CURT
Handled Through
WM. MORRIS BOOKING AGENCY
CHICAGO — 312-467-1744

The Centuries, with Carl Giammarese on the left and Curt Bachman on the right, displaying the pre-Beatles look.

in Chicago called Buckingham Fountain. "We couldn't believe nobody
was using it, so we started doing the show as the Buckinghams, and it
just stuck." The group sang several Beatles songs on the show and slowly
adopted Beatles-style haircuts and Carnaby Street style attire. "The first
show we had gold lame suits, and our hair was piled on top of our heads;
and then as the show progressed with every week, we had Beatley looking suits on, and then you'd see one or two guys with Beatle haircuts, and
then the next guy and then the next. By the time we had gotten to the end
of that show, we were the Beatles."[46]

"The Beatles had a really big influence on us," Nick Fortuna, who
replaced Curt Bachman on bass, agreed. "The players and musicians
really got touched by the Beatles. And that whole English scene. That
little country really did a lot of damage here and it was a change of life, a
change of thinking, a change of attitude, everything."[47] Because of their
appearances on the show, the Buckinghams landed a recording contract
with Chicago-based USA Records.

Singer and local deejay Carl Bonafede managed the group and
co-produced several of their recordings with swing bandleader Dan
Belloc at Chess studios. In February 1967, the Buckinghams became the
first Chicago group to reach number one on *Billboard* with the single
"Kind of a Drag."[48] Leaving behind their garage roots, the song relied

on restrained singing and jazz-tinged smoothness. The brass arrangements used on the record influenced others to employ horns, which became the signature sound of 1960s Chicago rock. Nevertheless, people so identified the Buckinghams with the British Invasion that when they appeared on *The Smothers Brothers Comedy Hour* in 1967, Union Jack flags surrounded them on stage. "They thought we were a British group," the bemused Carl Giammarese remembered. The Buckinghams finished their contract with USA Records and Carl Bonafede, and they signed with Columbia Records and new manager, Jim Guercio.

After the success of "Kind of a Drag," the Buckinghams saw another lineup change as South Sider Marty Grebb joined the band. Born at the end of World War II, Grebb's father and mother were both musicians and encouraged him to play piano at the age of eight. He joined his first band, the Quintones, at the tender age of twelve. A gifted multi-instrumentalist, Grebb played saxophone, keyboards, and guitar in this mostly instrumental band. In the early '60s, Grebb, his high-school friend Peter Cetera, who played bass, and the singer and guitarist Kal David, formed Kal David and the Exceptions. After David left the group, they carried on as the Exceptions, playing raw rhythm and blues music in clubs across the Chicago area. They developed into one of the most musically accomplished bands in Chicago but achieved little commercial success, even though they released several records on Vee-Jay.

Grebb, initially at least, was no fan of the Beatles. "I didn't like them. I thought, *Oh, man, this has no R&B in it at all. There's no roots in this that I can determine.*" Many of the old groups and solo singers from the early '60s suffered decline because of the Beatles, but the Exceptions decided to adapt to the new look and sound. "We started doing some of their material and, I'm ashamed to admit, putting on Beatle wigs during our shows at clubs. People went crazy. They went out of their minds."[49] The Exceptions broke up in 1967 after Marty Grebb left the group to replace keyboardist Dennis Miccolis in the Buckinghams. Bassist Peter Cetera joined the Big Thing, who went on to become the band Chicago, and drummer Bill Herman joined the New Colony Six.

Going from relative obscurity to a hit-making machine like the Buckinghams proved a difficult transition for Grebb. "I got caught up in a lot of the overwhelming business and celebrity status part of the music which took me back a few steps. Fame was overwhelming. I wasn't prepared for dealing with that. Suddenly I was having people show up at my parents house, and I was getting phone calls in the night, and people wanted to be around me because of who they thought I was, not because of who I was." As Grebb came to compose most of the Buckinghams' material, he felt enormous pressure to write commercial songs that would continue the band's chart success. "Back then you had to come up with hit singles every few months. We sort of got locked into a place that the record label wanted us to stay in. They didn't want us to leave the bubble gum teeny-bopper place. It was making them too much money."[50] They amassed seven *Billboard Hot 100* hits and were the only Chicago rock band of the '60s to appear on *The Ed Sullivan Show*.[51] The Buckinghams are "the biggest group to happen out of the Midwest to date," *Tiger Beat* told their readers in March 1969. "The Buckinghams are one of the mainstays of pop music and are destined to be around for many moons."[52] A few months later, however, a worn out, disillusioned Grebb left the band. The rest of the group found it difficult to fill Grebb's songwriting shoes, and the hits dried up. The Buckinghams disbanded in 1970.

The American Breed

The American Breed, like the Buckinghams, claimed fame as a clean-cut pop band but they too emerged from rhythm and blues roots. Gary Loizzo, from the Southwest Side of Chicago, received a Roy Rodgers guitar as a present at the age of eleven, and learned to play the instrument by strumming along to the records of his rock 'n' roll idols. In 1961, while still a high school student, he started his own band, Gary and the Knight Lites, with Loizzo's father installed as manager. Loizzo admired the harmonies of the Everly Brothers and the beat of rhythm and blues and wanted to meld the two genres together into a pop sound.[53] Gary and his band cut their debut record at a recording studio owned by musician Charles Colbert. Assisting Colbert with production duties was his son Charles "Chuck" Colbert. Born in Argo, Illinois, in August 1939, Chuck started playing drums and bass guitar at the age of six. He played "everything from classical to country to R and B to blues and jazz" and "just thought music at that time was music." He joined a couple of gospel groups and, as a teenager, Chuck became an integral part of the doo-wop quintet the Trinidads. By the time he met Loizzo, Chuck had joined the Daylighters, who had a local hit with "Cool Breeze" in 1962. Chuck played bass with Gary's group on their first session, which produced the Loizzo composition "I'm Glad She's Mine," subsequently released as a single on Charles Colbert senior's Nike label.[54]

Chuck became a permanent part of the group joining Gary Loizzo on vocals and guitar. With the help of Colbert's connections in the entertainment world, the group played in the black clubs on the South Side of the city and, after WLS DJ Ron Riley took a liking to the band, they began to play to white audiences at Riley's record shops in the city and in the suburbs. Gary and the Knight Lites went on to record some rhythm and blues covers and a number of their own songs including the James Brown sounding "One, Two, Boogaloo," which appeared under the name the Light Nites on Dunwich in 1967.

Loizzo and Colbert continued on their path as the Beatles and the British Invasion swirled around them. Loizzo watched the Beatles on *The Ed Sullivan Show* and enjoyed their fresh sound, intriguing but uncomplicated lyrics and their willingness to move into different musical genres. "The Beach Boys were surf songs, the Ventures instrumentals, but the Beatles played a wide range of songs." He declined, however, to grow his hair at the time and the quartet continued with their pop rhythm and blues sound that they had nurtured in the clubs. "The look did not do it for me," Loizzo said of the Beatles' hairstyles.[55] Chuck Colbert was even more adamant that the Beatles had no impact on the group. "No, no, no we were who we were, and we were doing that type of stuff even before they were doing it."[56] Both, however, protest too much as the band started to adopt Beatles-style haircuts and move their sound closer to that of the British Invasion sound.

Gary and the Knight Lites signed to Acta Records and came under the influence of producer Bill Traut. Traut told Gary and Chuck to change the name of the group to the American Breed. "They thought that we should have a more popular name, one more conducive to what the group was all about," Colbert recalled. "And that being the first integrated pop group in the country."[57] American Breed increasingly adopted a slicker, more polished sound. Their biggest success was with the song, "Bend Me, Shape Me," which peaked at number five on the *Billboard Hot 100* in early 1968, and became the first song by a Chicago rock group to chart in the UK where it reached number 24 in February 1968.[58]

"American Breed is certain to have hit after hit," journalist Jacoba Atlas of the *KRLA Beat* wrote in January 1968. "Their sound is the thing that has sold records since the beginning of the rock era. It is slick, interesting, moving, with a terrific beat. As long as there are people who dance and 'dig rock and roll,' there will be a need and an audience for the American Breed."[59] It was not to be. Under pressure from Acta Records and producer Bill Traut, the American Breed, like the New Colony Six, increasingly adopted a commercial pop sound as they searched for greater chart success. Acta and Traut also wanted to make changes to the group. "The record company and Bill thought that Gary would be a good solo artist," Colbert revealed. "And the company was kind of pushing for that because they didn't understand that the reason why we were who we were and the reason for the sound that we got was the people that were in the group. And they kind of broke that up because they didn't understand and all they were looking at was record sales, and they thought that would happen, but it never happened. They were leading us in the wrong direction. They were trying to make us an all pop group, and that's who we were not." By 1970, Chuck Colbert had quit the group and formed a new funk band that eventually adopted the name Rufus. He had gone "back to his roots," Colbert said. The American Breed disintegrated, and Gary Loizzo went on to open his own recording studio and to work closely with the Chicago group Styx until his tragic death in January 2016.[60]

The Western Suburbs

The Cryan' Shames, another Chicagoland band formed in the wake of the British Invasion, wore their Beatle influences proudly on their sleeves. The Shames emerged from the Travelers, founded by high school student Gerry Stone in the suburb of Hinsdale in the early '60s. The Travelers disintegrated after Stone left high school and enrolled at suburban La Grange Township Junior College. In the spring of 1965, Stone set out to reconstitute the Travelers. "Do you know anybody that can sing?" he asked his college friend Tom Doody. "I said, 'Yeah, I can.'" Doody had wanted to be in a band since he had seen the Beatles on *The Ed Sullivan Show* while he was sitting in a crowded lounge in his dorm as a freshman at the University of Illinois. "I was just flabbergasted. Their sense of harmony and the way that they played their guitars was a different voicing than you would hear in old music, doo-wop and stuff like that. It was much more prominent." Tom was inspired. "Everybody that was in a Chicago band at that time that I know of were incredibly influenced and driven to join a band because of the Beatles."[61]

The opportunity that Gerry Stone presented to Tom Doody was too good to pass up. "I didn't have a musical family, and our family really couldn't afford music lessons for me," Doody lamented. "So, I sang in a choir in a Catholic grade school for the Latin masses, and I did that up until eighth grade. That was the last time I sang. He invited me for a tryout. I did three Beatles' tunes, and

Introducing the Cryan' Shames 1966. Tom Doody, with the unfortunate nickname of Toad, sitting in the front.

they said, 'Yeah, you're great, we'll let you in the band.' We rehearsed for about two or three months and then we had our first job at La Grange Township Junior College." The new singer was soon joined by tambourine playing Jim "JC Hooke" Pilster, named because he had a hook rather than a left hand. When they found out that there was another group called the Travelers, they decided to change their name. "We had a meeting in Jim Pilster's basement to decide what new name we were going to come up with, and we came up with like twenty dozen different names, including the Wrath of God. We were taking a break, eating some hamburgers, and Pilster just casually said 'Man, it's a crying shame we can't come up with a name.' We all looked at each other and went, 'That's it.'"[62]

When the new group set out to hone their sound, they looked to Liverpool, England, for inspiration. "The Beatles were our heroes," said Pilster. "We bought the fifteenth row out at the Amphitheatre. We had a date in Rockford, but we were late because we went to see the Beatles."[63] They forged a sound built around strong melodies, sweet harmonies, and jangling guitars primarily inspired by the Beatles. The first song the ensemble recorded was the George Harrison number "If I Needed

Someone," before the Beatles released it in the US, but the Shames' label was unable to obtain permission to issue the recording as a 45.

The suburban club scene was now taking off, and the Cryan' Shames soon attracted huge crowds as the house band at the Blue Village in Westmont. "We used to joke it was so crowded in there, if someone did pass out, at least they wouldn't hit the floor," Jim Pilster chuckled.[64] Sixteen-year-old Jane Quinn first saw them in concert during the summer of 1966. "Never—and I mean NEVER—have I been so excited by a live gig. The combination of musicality to such a high standard and performance energy was second to none. Opening with the fastest-ever version of 'Hey Joe' was a stroke of genius. Toad, the lead singer, bounced the microphone stand off one heel and caught it on the other, while wild man, one-armed percussionist JC Hooke propelled his tambourine high into the rafters, recapturing it with his huge steel pirate's hook where, rumor has it, a left hand might once have been—or not. It was impossible, surreal, chaotic, mesmerizing, exhilarating. Suffice it to say, it was the funniest fun that I have ever funned, or ever will."[65]

Radio, and particularly WLS, played an important part in breaking local artists like the Cryan' Shames. "We were the first one to start playing local bands," Clark Weber bragged. "The fans from these local bands would just go crazy if they heard their own boy-girl, or girl, or boy-boy-boy band. We created that niche that created everything from the Buckinghams to the Cryan' Shames, any one of a number of bands from the Midwest that did reasonably well. Some did quite well. The Cryan' Shames got all the way up into the Top 5."[66] Local radio established contacts with local record companies and played demos and debut singles from unknown acts. "I could record something, go to Chess Records, cut a dub and take that dub—not even a pressing—up to WLS that night to find out if I had a hit," recalled Jim Golden, who worked for USA Records and then ran its subsidiary Destination Records, a label that focused on records by local talent including the Cryan' Shames. "It was a great test station! It was the best. It was almost like taking candy from a kid. That's how important WLS was in those days."[67] With strong signals heard all across the country, WLS and WCFL proved crucial in helping Chicago bands gain national exposure. "Without WLS and WCFL jumping on the local talent team, it would have taken a lot longer to get the Chicago music out there," Jimy Sohns of the Shadows of Knight insisted. "Fortunately for all of us, they jumped on us right away and gave us a shot, and we rewarded them with the fact that all the different cities liked us also."[68]

In return for playing their records, local groups agreed to appear with the radio deejays at their dances. As the groups became more popular and attracted bigger crowds, the hops became extremely lucrative, at least for the deejays. "For the first five or six years, I was on almost every weekend because you were paid anywhere from $250 to $350 for an appearance," remembered Clark Weber. "You could do two or three of those a week, close to $1,000 in side-money. I had my own plane, so I was able to fly all over the Midwest. I could be just about anywhere in the Midwest in a little over an hour. I was quite busy."[69]

The importance of local radio was apparent in the early success of the Cryan' Shames, who attracted the attention of WLS deejay Dex Card. Card introduced the group to Bob Monaco, the promotions manager for Destination Records, who released their debut 45 "Sugar and Spice," a cover of a song by the Searchers from Liverpool. "We did the whole thing in about an hour and fifteen minutes, both sides," remembered Tom Doody. "We were packing up our equipment from Sound Studios and going on our way home. We got in our car and turned on WLS, which is what we always did. Dex Card came on, and he said, 'I have something hot off the presses. This is a brand new song by a brand new group called the Cryan' Shames.' Within twenty minutes of when we had finished recording, we heard it on WLS."[70] Being broadcast to a national audience helped "Sugar and Spice" reach number forty-nine on the *Billboard* charts. The Shames then switched to Columbia, becoming the first Chicago rock group to sign and record with a major label. They scored four more local hits over the next couple of years and released their debut album, *Sugar and Spice,* in October 1966. "It Could Be We're in Love" reached number one on the WCFL and WLS charts in the summer of 1967, but they found it difficult to achieve national success.[71] After the release of their third and final album, *Synthesis*, the Cryan' Shames disbanded at the end of 1969.

Many of the Chicago groups had trouble writing their own material, but the Ides of March faced no such problem, as they were led by Jim Peterik, probably the most successful white songwriter to come out of the Chicago area in the '60s. Born to Czech parents in 1950 in Berwyn, a near western suburb of Chicago, Peterik played in his first band, the Renegades, in eighth grade. He formed his next group, the Shondels, or Shon Dels Unlimited as they appeared on their self-penned debut single "Like It or Lump It." The Shondels was the name of an obscure British band that Peterik had found in a copy of the music paper *Melody Maker* that his sister had brought back from a visit to the UK. The name also acted as a tribute to a local hero, singer Troy Shondell. They played covers of the Ventures, the Beach Boys, the Beatles, and the Crestones, a Chicagoland band who had a couple of local hits in 1964. "We started emulating the Beatles and the Kinks, and suddenly the Zombies and all those British bands became our heroes. 'Like It or Lump It' is nothing more than me channeling the Kinks, even to the pronunciation of the word 'paradise,' which, when I listen to it now, I was really trying to be Ray Davies."[72] In 1966, to avoid confusion with the similar-sounding Tommy James and the Shondells, who had a hit with "Hanky Panky," they changed their name to the Ides of March. Peterik became the singer, lead guitarist, and principal songwriter. His nerdy glasses made him an unlikely rock star, as did his commitment to his Christian faith and to his wife, whom he met in high school. Their debut release, Peterik's "You Wouldn't Listen," scored big in the Chicago area in the spring of 1966.

The Ides may have adopted the British Invasion sound, but as high school students, they found it difficult to adopt the British look. "Morton West High School had a hair policy. Our hair was not long, but, to them, it was long. Every Monday morning we had to go in front of the dean. We would go over to guitarist Larry Millas' house, which was on the way to school. We'd wet our hair down, comb it back and tuck it in our shirt collars, turn our shirt collars up, and parade in front of the dean. We did that for weeks in a row getting away with murder, and the dean would say, 'Oh, you're okay, no problem.' We would towel off our hair and walk around and knew the routes where we would not run into the hall guards or the deans." Peterik and the band finally resorted to wearing wigs on stage to achieve the long-haired look.[73]

The Ides started as a British-style band but, influenced by soul music and probably the success of the Buckinghams, they added a horn section. "Soon we got enchanted by the Memphis sound, and we started adding brass so we could do 'Midnight Hour,' 'Knock on Wood,' 'Soul Man,' and 'Sweet Soul Music.' It kind of morphed into the horn rock thing."[74] The

Ides reached the *Billboard Hot 100* on five occasions, with their biggest success coming with the horn-driven rhythm and blues-influenced rocker "Vehicle" that peaked at number two in 1970.[75] The song also reached thirty-one on the UK hit parade in the summer of 1970, staying on the charts for nine weeks.[76] On the back of the single's success, the Ides released their debut album *Vehicle* in 1970 cut at Columbia Studios in Chicago. The horn sound dominated, but they acknowledged their roots with the song "Symphony for Eleanor (Eleanor Rigby)." The Ides of March disbanded in the fall of 1973 when Jim Peterik left to pursue a solo career. Peterik went on to form the band Survivor and co-write the monster hit "Eye of the Tiger," the theme song of the Sylvester Stallone movie *Rocky III*. Peterik calls his beautiful home "The House Stallone Built" and, in honor of his musical hero, christened his recording studio "Lennon's Den."

The Motor City Madman

The Chicago music scene was energized by migrants from elsewhere, including a shy, retiring youngster who went on to find great success and notoriety as the Motor City Madman. Theodore "Ted" Nugent was born in December 1948 in Michigan and was already playing guitar in a couple of local groups, including the Lourds, before his family moved to the Northwest suburbs of Chicago. "My dad was transferred to Chicago in 1965," Nugent told an interviewer. "After the Lourds went to the moving van company and destroyed all the vans trying to keep me from moving that summer, my dad took me to the barber shop and made me get a G.I. haircut. He threatened to get rid of my guitars, but he knew it was hard on me and let it slide."[77] Nugent attended William Fremd High School in Palatine and then enrolled at Saint Viator High School, a recently opened Catholic boy's school in Arlington Heights. "In the summer of 1965 while standing in line at the Cellar, I met the boys that would become the Amboy Dukes that very first week upon my arrival," Nugent recalled of the origin of his new group. "After our first audition, we literally took over the local scene at the iconoclastic Cellar with Paul Sampson and crew, and played every possible gig within a few hundred miles of Chicago nonstop those two phenomenal dues-paying years."[78] The competition in Chicago failed to impress the bombastic Nugent, who says he favored the louder and wilder Detroit groups. "I saw the Ides of March, the Shadows of Knight—give me a (expletive) break. They were 20 years behind. They were playing 'Gloria' just like it was written. We poured rocket fuel on the (expletive) flames, and we bastardized the whole thing and turned it into this 'In-A-Gadda-Da-Vida' precursor to jam hell."[79]

Once settled in his new home, Nugent started to regrow his hair, catching the attention of Saint Viator's principal who told him, Dave Grund-hoefer, and a couple of other students not to return to school until they pruned their flowing locks. "I came back, and everybody got their hair cut," Grundhoefer groaned, but the principal still complained, scolding him for not cutting his sideburns. "We

Ted Nugent, second from left, with his band the Amboy Dukes, which he formed in Chicago.

got in a big fight about it, and I said 'I'm not cutting it back, I'm not going to this school.' I ended up graduating from Arlington High School. But Ted Nugent, he broke down, and he cut his hair. I was the only one who was defiant enough to say, 'Forget you guys.'"[80] Nugent's decision to cut his Beatles-style hair may have stalled his musical career. When the Amboy Dukes auditioned for Bill Traut at Dunwich Records, Traut was not impressed: "They were awful," he said. "But Nugent played with a lot of determination and desire; and his hair was shorter than mine!" The underwhelmed Traut decided not to offer the Detroit import a recording contract.[81]

In 1966, Ted Nugent joined another local band, the Males. Males bassist, sixteen-year-old Warren Willingham, who had taken guitar lessons from the age of six, watched *The Ed Sullivan Show* at home in the western suburb of Addison with his mother, father, and two younger sisters. "I think seeing the Beatles on Ed Sullivan put the bug in me to be in a band." Willingham had jammed with a few instrumental groups, "but the Beatles sang, so I wanted to be in a band that sang." He joined his first group, the Cyclones, and then moved on to play with the Males. Willingham, who graduated from Willowbrook High School in 1965, remembered the Males first performance at his alma mater. "There was like 800, 900 kids in our graduating class. We started with 'Can't Buy Me Love.' They stood up, threw the chairs back and got up and started screaming and dancing on the cafeteria tables." The Males journeyed to the Cellar in Arlington Heights, hoping to convince Paul Sampson to let them play at the popular teen club. "We stood out there and introduced ourselves to the crowd," Willingham recalled. "The girls just wanted to hear us play." Sampson auditioned the group and said, "'If you can do "Help," I'll give you guys some dates.' Sampson didn't know that we had been out there schmoozing. We practiced it and really did it good. The girls were screaming. 'I don't know what's going on here,' Sampson said. 'The crowd sure was behind you.' We became regulars at the Cellar, and Paul Sampson became our manager." In March 1966, Mercury wanted a band to record the theme song for *Kiddie A-Go-Go*, a local television series, and Sampson used his connections to secure the gig for the Males. The show failed to further their careers or to fill their coffers. "We didn't even get paid for doing it," Willingham laughed.[82]

After the US Army drafted guitarist Rich Hintz in 1966, the Males approached Ted Nugent, whom they had seen play at the Cellar with the Amboy Dukes, to take his place. "There weren't a lot of guitar players to pick from," Willingham recalled. "We went to talk to him, and we jammed some. At that point, he was just kind of learning. We called him the Chicken Picker because he picked fast. He didn't have a lot of soul or thought into it, but he moved really fast. He said he would come with us only if his rhythm guitar player, Gary Hicks, joined with him, so those two came to the Males."[83]

Ted Nugent felt that suburban Chicago failed to appreciate his hard rock sound, and he told Warren Willingham that he had began to think about returning to Detroit. "He'd say, 'Hey, do you want to go to Detroit with me? I know people there, and I'm going to go up there and get famous.' I just looked at him one time and said, 'Your mom won't even let you go out after the gig with us. We have to take you home first. You're going to Detroit?'" When he graduated from high school in 1967, Nugent returned to the Motor City, where he reassembled the Amboy Dukes. Willingham was drafted and had all but forgotten about his old band mate as he served his time in the Army. "I was at Fort Bragg, and this guy comes in dragging this record *Journey to the Center of the Mind*.

'Isn't that the guy that used to play with you?'" The startled Willingham could only respond in the affirmative.[84]

Jeff Boyan, Folk Music, and the Beatles

Many in the folk community disliked the Beatles but, as the story of Jeff Boyan from Hammond, Indiana, illustrates, some folkies immediately switched their allegiance. The folk revival began to fascinate the teenage Boyan, and he was drawn to the booming scene in Chicago. As soon as he was old enough, he traveled on the South Shore Railroad commuter train from Hammond to Chicago to attend the folk clubs of Old Town and Rush Street. Although he was too young to enter establishments with liquor, Boyan would sneak into the Gate of Horn to watch his favorites and play at open mic sessions at It's Here, the Fickle Pickle, and Mother Blues. "I really had no interest in rock 'n' roll," Boyan revealed of his devotion to folk, but that quickly changed when the Beatles arrived. "I bought every album that came out, from *Meet the Beatles* [on], sat in my bedroom and played every one of those songs." Subsequently, Boyan began performing Beatles songs in folk clubs with a Beatles-style haircut and an amplified acoustic guitar.[85]

"When I got into the Beatles, I said, 'I love this group,'" Boyan professed. "'I've got to have one of these. I've got to play in one of these bands.'"[86] He launched the Blackstones, comprised of four youngsters from Northern Indiana who sported Beatle-style haircuts, black suits, pencil ties, and Beatle boots. Boyan, with his warm, soulful voice, became the lead singer and primary songwriter in the group. To sound more English, Boyan changed his name to Geoff Bryan while drummer David Kell Blanchard changed his to Dave Kell and bought a Ludwig drum kit identical to one he saw Ringo Starr use on *The Ed Sullivan Show*.[87] The group adopted the name Dalek/Engam: The Blackstones for their recordings. Dalek because of the Daleks in the British science fiction television show *Doctor Who* and Engam because it stood for English/American. "We were supposed to pretend that two of us were English and two of us were American," remembered Blackstones guitarist Jerry McGeorge, who later went on to join the Shadows of Knight. "I couldn't fake an English accent so I was told to keep quiet." The Beatles influence even extended to songwriting credits. "In the spirit of doing all things in Beatle-esque fashion, Jeff decided that his originals needed a second credit. We did almost

Linda Ulreich

Louise Harrison meets the New Beatles (The Blackstones).

exclusively original material, so I got credit for a lot of his stuff, he got credit for mine." One of the group's first gigs was supporting the Herman's Hermits at Chicago's McCormick Place in June 1965.[88]

The Blackstones quickly gained a reputation as the new Beatles. Louise Harrison read about them in the newspapers and asked to meet the group when she came to Chicago in August 1965 to see her brother perform at White Sox Park. The Blackstones drove up from Indiana, met Harrison, and then caught the Beatles at the afternoon show. With their Beatle haircuts and British-style clothes, some of the crowd mistook the Indiana Four for the Fab Four. "We were almost mobbed in the parking lot because people thought we might have been them," drummer David Kell Blanchard laughed. If the band wanted to pick up any tips from the world's most admired rock musicians, they were disappointed. "We were intrigued just in the excitement of the crowd. Then when the girls started screaming and yelling, you couldn't hear them anyway. But it was a great show. I'm glad I did it, but I can't say I learned anything from it, because I couldn't hear a thing."[89]

Jeff Boyan left a lasting impression on the Chicago music scene. He not only composed songs for the Blackstones but also for other Chicago bands including the Centuries, the Cryan' Shames, and the Shady Daze. "He was a great guy," David Kell Blanchard recalled of his old friend,

David Kell Blanchard

The Blackstones in 1965. Over a year after the Beatles arrived in America, musicians may have grown their hair long but boys in the Midwest audiences still wore short hair.

"and one of the best collaborators as far as music is concerned. He was the backbone of the group. He wrote the songs. He had a great voice. He came up with different ideas."[90] The Blackstones became a crowd favorite in the clubs of Chicago and at the Cellar, and they recorded a number of excellent songs including the classic "Never Feel the Pain," but they disintegrated in the fall of 1965 after David Blanchard and bassist Tom Osborne fell victim to the draft. Curt Bachman, previously of the Centuries and the Buckinghams, briefly replaced Osborne on bass, but the group soon disbanded.

In February 1966, Boyan with the help of Paul Sampson put together a new band called Saturday's Children. The name of the group, derived from an old folk standard "Saturday's Child," and the folk inflections on their songs betrayed Boyan's first love, but there was no mistaking the most significant influence on the project. "I used to pick people according to how they looked on stage," Boyan admitted. He modeled his bass playing on Paul McCartney, Ron Holder played guitar like Lennon, and George Pal (originally George Paluch) "fit the 'Ringo' pattern in the formula." Boyan then "molded Dave Carter in the George Harrison image" and added Rick Goettler on organ. Saturday's Children played

Beatles covers, used Beatles-style harmonies, sported Beatles haircuts, and dressed like 1963/64 era Beatles. In their first publicity photo, Saturday's Children posed in suits with one member hoisting an umbrella, mimicking the cover of the *Beatles '65* album. They even tried to write songs that sounded like recently released Beatles recordings. "Very often Jeff would hear a Beatles' song that he really liked and it would impress him so much that we'd stay up all night writing

Linda Ulreich

It's the Beatles! No hold on, it's Saturday's Children.

a new tune with all the ingredients of that song," Ron Holder remembered. "In personality, appearance and even in the way we walked, we really fell into what the Beatles were doing," Paluch admitted. "I have quite a few newspaper articles written about us where they called us 'the Second Beatles.'" [91]

Saturday's Children, one of the most beloved of Chicago bands because of their dynamic live performances, probably tried too hard to be like the lovable Mop Tops, an image and sound even the Beatles had now left behind. They released three singles on Dunwich but failed to achieve chart success and disbanded in 1968. Boyan joined the Chicago psychedelic band H.P. Lovecraft, and when they split in 1969, he returned to his roots, performing in Chicago coffee houses as a solo artist. "I was soon disgusted with driving up from Hammond to Chicago in freezing winter nights after being in Lovecraft, flying to New York and playing with the Jefferson Airplane. It was frustrating and those were basically the final days that I played music." Boyan disappeared from the music scene in the '70s and sadly passed away at the age of sixty-six in 2013.[92]

Girl Groups

One of the least discussed aspects of the Beatles' legacy was their ability to inspire girls to pick up musical instruments. Girls organized Beatles parties in their homes, in which they mimicked individual Beatles, performing songs with fake drums and guitars; but, for most, that was as far as their dreams would go as tradition declared that males produced rock 'n' roll music and females consumed it. Parents frowned upon the late nights and constant traveling required of musicians, few female role models existed, and prevailing ideas of femininity restrained girls from wild or aggressive stage antics. Yet some girls, inspired by the Beatles' harmonies and melodies, their feminine image, and their girl-centered lyrics, managed to circumvent societal constraints and parental disapproval and turn their dreams into reality. The pioneering all-girl bands that emerged in the '60s refused to simply copy the Beatles but instead forged a new style that combined the harmonies and attitude of sassy girl groups such as the Ronettes, the Chiffons, and the Shirelles, with the guitar-style music of the Beatles.

One of the first and most successful all-female groups, Daughters of Eve, began under the guidance of Buckinghams manager, Carl Bonafede. Carl recruited Judy Johnson on lead guitar and vocals, and Marsha Tomal on organ, rhythm guitar, and vocals, and then embarked on a mission to find a drummer and bass player to complete the lineup. Just before Christmas 1965, a friend told fifteen-year-old Debi Pomeroy from far north Rogers Park that Bonafede was looking for a drummer in an all-girl group. Debi initially played guitar with her brother Justin's band, Dirty Wurds, but soon switched to drums and auditioned for the new band. Bonafede quickly hired her. "I didn't even have a drum set," Debi mused. "I had to borrow my boyfriend's drum set."[93] Her father, a liberal-minded and supportive Lutheran minister, allowed the band to practice in his Church basement, bought his daughter a Ludwig drum set identical to Ringo Starr's oyster pearl kit, and suggested the Biblical name Daughters of Eve for the new group.

"The band is going to be rehearsing at her father's Church on Saturday, and so she told me and my friend Sue we should come and watch them," remembered Debi's friend and guitarist, fourteen-year-old Andee Levin. "We head over to the church, and Debi is there with two other girls, Marsha and Judy, and Carl Bonafede. Carl is this crazy Type A personality and he's pacing back and forth, talking to himself and swearing because the bass player is not showing up. I'm the kind of person that likes to fix problems. So, I said, 'Well, how about before she gets here, I'll play?'" That evening Carl Bonafede phoned Andee's parents and asked their permission for their daughter to join the group. Once on board, things moved quickly. "My dad got me a Fender bass guitar and we got an act together. Carl took us down to Maxwell Street, got us costumes, and then the next thing I know, we're working these gigs, and we're in a recording studio." The Fender proved too cumbersome for the young teenager, so she bought herself a Hofner, Paul McCartney's favored bass, which was much lighter to hang on her young shoulders.[94]

"One of our first shows was at McCormick Place, at the car show there. We attracted all the boys," a delighted Pomeroy exclaimed. "They did not scream; guys are different. They will throw stuff on the stage, phone numbers. It was really something. They all wanted our autographs. We were like the female Beatles. It was just amazing." Subsequently, they performed all over Chicago and the Midwest, driving to gigs in a van with the name of the band on the side. "Iowa, Wichita, Kansas, Nebraska, that whole area of the country. One time we flew to Rapid City, South Dakota, and we had a big show up there; and as we got off the plane and got into the limo, Carl was there, he turned up the radio. They were announcing that we had just landed. And we packed the place. Wherever we went, we packed the place."[95]

Some members of Daughters of Eve even managed to stage an impromptu performance for the Beatles. Debi, Andee, who had seen the Fab Four in Chicago in 1964, and their friend Sue, attended the Beatles' show at the International Amphitheatre in 1966 while Andee's father waited for the girls outside. "You couldn't hear anything, except I noticed that Ringo's bass drum was broken," Debi stated. "He didn't even bother to put another bass drum pedal on his drum."[96] While the girls were enjoying the show, Andee's father was busy outside. "He found out exactly where the Beatles were staying. At the end of the concert,

Daughters of Eve. Notice Debi Pomeroy's Ringo-style Ludwig drums and Andee Levin's Paul-style Hofner bass.

he whisked us over to the hotel and we got out our guitars, and we're all singing our Beatles songs, the three of us outside. We could see the drapes pull back and the Beatles looked out of their window, and they waved. It was very exciting."[97]

Daughters of Eve signed a recording contract with USA Records, and in 1966, they released their first 45, a remake of Debbie Dovale's 1963 hit "Hey Lover." They released two more singles: "Symphony of My Soul" and "Don't Waste My Time." "Hey Lover," in particular, combined to startling effect the sweet harmonies of girl groups and the guitar sound of the British Invasion. "The sound was the two voices of Marsha and Judy, and whether they were individual or together, they had a unique sound," Andee Levin reflected. "When I look back, I'd say the band could have gone someplace. Could have and should have."[98] None of their records entered the charts, but being in a musical group elevated their status among classmates. "I was never real popular in school," recalled Debi. "I was very shy, because I was so short, and school seemed so big to me. All of a sudden, we had kind of a hit record with 'Hey Lover,' and 'Don't Waste My Time.' I'd come to school and the next thing you know they'd say, 'Ooh, I heard your record last night.' All of a sudden, I'm real popular."[99]

Andee quit Daughters of Eve in 1967 and joined another all-female group, the Weaker Six. "That band was musically much better. We were able to have a little more variety, but again, poor management and no recording contract, and that was the end of that." Andee left the Weaker Six at the end of the decade, moved to California, "and lived a normal life."[100] Daughters of Eve broke up in late 1968. Two members married, and Debi Pomeroy joined another all-girl group, the Luv'd Ones, from Michigan, who released three 45s on Dunwich Records. Pomeroy then relocated to California, where she continued to play drums in local bands.[101]

Daughters of Eve was just one of a number of all-girl bands that emerged in the Chicago area inspired by the Beatles and the British Invasion. The Same, five high school girls from the northern suburbs, came together in the fall of 1965. The group comprised two sisters, Judy and Vicki Selman, on lead guitar and bass guitar respectively, Debbie Reiss on rhythm guitar, Donna Smolak on drums, and Vicki Hubly on vocals. The girls performed a couple of their own songs but mostly played cover versions of the Beatles, the Mama and Papas, and other pop groups of the day. "We were the same as the other bands and did the same material they did, and the same bands could cover them as well. So we figured we're the Same," recalled Donna Smolak about the origins of the group's name. They played at park districts, WCFL sponsored hops, and at the Cellar, where they met Paul Sampson. "We wanted Paul Sampson to take a bigger interest in us and manage us, but that didn't happen," Smolak said regretfully. In 1967, the Same released the single "Sunshine, Flowers and Rain," but it failed to chart. When lead singer Vicki Hubly accepted an offer to join another group, and Judy Selman left to attend Northwestern University, the group disintegrated.[102]

"A few years ago, there weren't many all-girl groups, so that if someone dropped out, there wasn't really too much we could have done," Vicki Selman stated in December 1967, recognizing the growth in the number of female musicians. "Today, on the other hand, there are so many other talented girls that it is possible to get a new member if something should happen to one of us."[103] When the Same broke up, Donna Smolak joined the Chips, another female-only group from the Chicago area who had already achieved some success. The Chips had been a part of Dick Clark's Caravan of Stars tours and recorded two 45s, "Break It Gently," released in February 1968, and "When You Hold Me Baby," issued in November of the same year. The Chips performed a tougher rhythm and blues sound in exciting live shows in clubs and bars in Chicago. "We went to one lounge where the owner was having to close down because he had nothing going on. Our manager Dwight booked us there, and he was quite angry when he found out that the Chips was a girl group. By the end of the six-week thing there, his lounge had two shows a night, standing room only. And he paid off his house." They went on to play in Germany and London, but the Chips split in 1970.[104]

The female bands parted for the same reasons as the boy bands: infighting, lack of success, musical differences, members heading off to college or marrying but, unlike the boy bands, those around them provided at best only qualified support for the girls' endeavors, which often caused additional strains. Worried parents disapproved of their daughters taking off into the night and going on tour. Jealous boyfriends and husbands wanted the girls to stay at home. Managers, promoters, fellow musicians, and audiences refused to take girl groups seriously. Debi Pomeroy constantly faced insulting comments about her drumming skills. "They used to tell me, 'Oh, you play pretty good, for a girl.' So many females are out there; that is so amazing as far as drummers and musicians right now, which just blows my mind. I was at the forefront of it."[105] Donna Smolak faced similar insults. "It was kind of like World War II, and the musicians were gone. They filled in when something else was not going on. So they were not taken seriously."[106]

Smolak remembered a bizarre incident that summed up what club managers and audiences wanted from female groups. "I met another girl group when we opened up for Chubby Checker in Detroit. They were a topless band, and I'm like 'you're kidding.' They came to see us. I mean they had clothes on, but they asked us to come and see them. I said 'Let's go check them out.' They couldn't even tune their guitars. I was tuning their guitars for them. Nobody cared what they sounded like." Smolak endured some bitter experiences during her short career but has no regrets. "We needed just some powerful management and great direction. It could have been a great outcome. But it wasn't, and it didn't, but I wouldn't change a minute."[107]

Judy Bloom, second from right, with Marie Antoinette and the Cool Heads, summer of 1967, in front of Chicago's Buckingham Fountain.

Judy Bloom

Like many other boys and girls in the Chicagoland area, the Beatles inspired fifteen-year-old Judy Bloom from the suburb of Berwyn to pick up a musical instrument. "I had an epiphany during the first *Ed Sullivan Show* when we watched the Beatles. I wanted to see if they could play as good as they were on the records, and they were even better. And they were playful. I wanted to play guitar. I had an uncle, Jerry, who was a very gifted jazz guitarist. He gave me an old Silvertone guitar. The Beatles put the guitar in my hand." Judy became lead guitarist with the all-girl Marie Antoinette and the Cool Heads who built up a following playing in suburban teen clubs and in lounges in Chicago.[108]

Judy Bloom's band, who wanted to perform more blues material and some of their own songs, found the attitude of club owners frustrating. "We could play. That was always our beef, that we wanted people to love us for musicians, not because we were a girl band. A club hired us because we were a girl band. But when we tried to do an original tune, we weren't allowed. We were really restricted. They wanted lighter music from the girls than the guys. I remember one time going out there and really letting loose on a lead, and the club owner says, 'You're a girl; act like a girl.' I used to get down on my knees when I was young, I'd go into a trance sometimes, and literally, I didn't know I was on the floor." Eventually, the group tired of the treatment they received. "We did record a demo at Chess Records. I believe that was in 1969. Took it to radio stations. Never got the recording contract. We just played for years every weekend, we traveled, but we just didn't get that big break. We thought, *Oh, we missed our mark with that record.* We'd never had a chance to make it big, and everybody just kind of threw in the towel." Marie Antoinette and the Cool Heads broke up in 1970.

Judy continued to play in the clubs, but parental disapproval stymied her last chance for a career in music. "In July of 1976, we got to play at a club called the Roadhouse in Wheeling, Illinois. Albert King was going to be on the main stage and we were going to be in the side bar," Judy recalled. King watched from the audience and was impressed. "Hi, Miss Judy," King said to her after the show. "I enjoyed your playing and I could use you as second guitarist in my band," and handed her his phone number. Judy stepped outside and saw his huge tour bus. "Oh my God, this is my chance," she said to herself and headed home to tell her parents of her once in a lifetime opportunity to tour with a blues legend. "My mother just said, 'Judy, if you do that and get on that bus, you'll break our heart.' And my dad said, 'Don't come back home.' So, I didn't do it." Judy's dream was over. "I didn't want to play anymore. It just hit me really hard. I went into a real bad depression, sold my amp, and put the guitar under my bed for thirty-one years."[109]

The Decline of the '60s Chicago Rock Scene

The Chicago music scene of the '60s was like a firework that sparkled brightly but quickly faded. Only the New Colony Six and the Ides of March continued to record into the early '70s. The Dunwich record label folded after the Shadows of Knight split in 1967. When Jim Golden and Bob Monaco of Destination Records joined Bill Traut in the production company Dunwich Productions in 1968, Destination virtually ceased operations and USA Records no longer enjoyed much commercial success.[110] Traut continued to produce local bands into the early '70s, but by the middle of the decade, he had relocated to California where he became the manager and legal representative for several well-known acts including the Ohio Players and REO Speedwagon.[111]

In truth, Chicago rock groups always found it difficult to prosper because the recording industry and the national media, based in New

York and California, all but ignored what was happening in the Midwest. "There was an abundance of talent and venues here. It was a great place to be," recalled Carl Giammarese of the Buckinghams. "The industry was not. We weren't getting the attention that a lot of the New York and L.A. groups were getting, like the Mamas and Papas and the Turtles and the pop groups out of the West Coast, and the Doors. The record industry was out there. The same thing with New York. We recorded every one of our hits except for 'Kind of a Drag' in New York City at the CBS Building."[112]

"It was very tough for a Chicago band to get on national TV," said Jim Peterik of the Ides of March rather wistfully. "The Buckinghams did get on *Ed Sullivan*, which we were all jealous of, but never New Colony Six, never us. We got on the *Mama Cass Show*, which was a Dick Clark Production, and we got on the *John Byner Show*, which was national, but we never got to the Big Apple of Sullivan or Johnny Carson or anything like that."[113]

The culture of Chicago as a tough, working-class city failed to encourage innovation and further accounted for the scene's demise. With the ascent of the West Coast groups like the Doors and Jefferson Airplane, artistic ambition, social significance, and pomposity was now required of rock stars, but most Chicago bands were unable to move with the times. The virtuosity, improvisation, and glamorous chic of Cream and Jimi Hendrix were the rage, not the suits and early Beatles sound of Saturday's Children. When the Buckinghams appeared on *The Ed Sullivan Show* in January 1968, the Chicago favorites seemed rather dated compared to the progressive rock bands like the Doors who had appeared on the show a few months earlier with their casual dress, provocative lyrics, and innovative music.

Even those that attempted to innovate found the cultural conservatism of Chicago difficult to overcome. The Big Thing, who incarnated into the group Chicago, started by playing Top 40 cover versions in clubs around town, sporting suits and short hair. Influenced by the musical innovations of the Beatles and the music coming from the West Coast, they introduced jazz influences and improvisation into their repertoire, much to the annoyance of club owners. In the summer of 1968, The Big Thing left their hometown and journeyed to California to find a more accepting environment. "We were more progressive. We weren't Top 40 radio at all," recalled drummer Danny Seraphine. "We were more underground. We felt we had to leave Chicago. There weren't as many clubs, and there wasn't as much opportunity. We were starving, and we were getting fired everywhere because people wanted us to play cover stuff. Club owners wouldn't accept our original material."[114]

Changes in local radio that favored well-known acts over up-and-coming ones halted the emergence of new groups in the area. In November 1967, ABC sent the combative and controlling John Rook, who had been a huge success as program director at KQV in Pittsburgh, to Chicago to take over as program director at WLS. Before Rook arrived, many local bands performed for free at the deejays' record hops and, in return, the deejays played their records on the radio. Some musicians disliked the arrangement and played only reluctantly. "Art Roberts and Ron Riley were real pricks and forced any bands booked on their weekend shows to play without pay," said Jerry McGeorge of the Shadows of Knight. "They knew they had everyone by the throat."[115] Shadows singer Jimy Sohns was a little more accepting. "I don't want to say the payola word, but there were ways that you paid for them to play your record. It's how the business always worked."[116] John Rook set out to undermine the cozy relationship and reduce the power of the deejays. The meticulous Rook insisted that deejays could no longer plug their hops on air and could only play records he endorsed. "Every single recording that was played on WLS I approved, and it didn't matter if they were from Chicago or elsewhere. Would you play a new Glen Campbell record or a Cryan' Shames record?" he bellowed. "I think if I say here's Glen Campbell a lot of people's ears are going to go up. If I say here's the Cryan' Shames back then, most ears would go, the what?"[117] Rook resigned in February 1970, and by then, WLS concentrated on playing the hits and no longer provided Chicago bands with favored exposure.

New groups needed places to play, but the suburban clubs, including the Cellar, started to close as owners faced a moral panic from the local community. "The Cellar had a bad reputation from the start," Sampson admitted. "Surprisingly, a lot of parents viewed me with resentment, and felt that I was responsible for getting their kids drunk. We used to have some fights between the 'greasers' and the 'freaks.'" Local authorities and police were worried about drug-taking inside his establishment. Sampson faced complaints from local residents about damage to local property, fights, noise outside the club, and cars speeding up and down the street. The local high school grumbled that youngsters were going to the Cellar rather than attending school sports events.[118] The injury of an off-duty policeman and the arrest of three youths led to its temporary closure in the summer of 1966. Sampson reopened the club, but he had to introduce a membership policy and tighten security.[119]

His job as a club owner, band manager, promoter, and talent spotter for Dunwich began to take a toll on Sampson. He was the manager of the Shadows of Knight, the Mauds, the Males, and Saturday's Children. Dunwich appointed him as head of its management division, Windy City Artists, later renamed Arkham Artists, where his job was to find new talent. "The phone was constantly ringing," he moaned. "I did not have a spare minute to call my own. There was no way I could raise my family properly and still handle the business affairs. I had to rearrange my priorities."[120]

"He was having a lot of political problems out in Arlington Heights. Combined with some other problems, he pulled out of the business completely," remembered Bill Traut. "He was the guy who discovered all the bands in the first place."[121] At the end of 1969, Sampson retired from Arkham, and in June 1970, he closed the Cellar, left the music business, and concentrated on a career in electrical engineering.[122]

The heyday of the Chicago rock explosion stretched from 1965 to 1967, and although it sputtered on for another couple of years, by the '70s, the leading groups had disbanded, and the teen clubs had closed. There is now no trace left of many of the clubs, some replaced by parking lots and some converted into shopping malls. The building that housed the second incarnation of the Cellar still stands as an auto shop, haunted at night by the sounds of garage bands of the '60s. Some of the musicians found success with other bands or struggled on to eke out a living on the bar circuit. A few groups from the '60s reformed and play in the local area today. Others gave up their musical dreams and entered into other professions only to be surprised some fifty years later when an inquisitive historian from England who was interested in their teenage dreams and aspirations contacted them to speak about their role in one of the most exciting eras in Chicago music history.

CHAPTER 7

"The Beatles' Popularity Had Waned"

The Final Tour, 1966

As the Beatles prepared for their third summer tour of North America, the heyday of Beatlemania appeared to have passed. "The British Boom: Is It Over?" asked the British magazine *Rave* in February 1966, worried about the decline in popularity of the Beatles and other UK acts in the US.[1] In 1964, the Beatles had held the top two places on the *Billboard* end of year list with "I Want to Hold Your Hand" and "She Loves You." In 1965, "Help" was their highest placed 45 reaching number seven; and in 1966, their highest end of the year chart entry, "We Can Work It Out," made it only as far as number sixteen.[2] In March 1966, *Newsweek* asked 775 teenagers what famous people they most admired. John F. Kennedy came top with 47 percent of boys and 50 percent of girls choosing the deceased president. The Beatles finished seventh in the poll, with only 2 percent of boys and 5 percent of girls saying they admired the Fab Four the most. Elvis Presley came eleventh with only 1 percent of boys choosing the King but, rather surprisingly, 5 percent of girls; the same number that had picked the Beatles.[3]

Frank Fried and Triangle productions, once more the promoters of the Beatles' stop in the Windy City, recognized that they could not match the ticket sales of the previous year and therefore wanted Wrigley Field, the home of the Chicago Cubs, to host the Beatles for a single afternoon show. The Wrigley front office, seeking to protect the hallowed turf in the friendly confines, turned Fried down. Fried settled for two performances at the thirteen thousand capacity International Amphitheatre, the same venue the Beatles had played in 1964.[4]

The Beatles had grown up and moved away from the lovable mop-top image, which partly explains the decline in their popularity among teenagers. In September 1965, Ringo became the second Beatle, after John, to become a father when his wife, Maureen, gave birth to a son, Zak. George Harrison married Pattie Boyd in January 1966, leaving Paul the only unmarried Beatle. In a February 1966 article entitled "Why marriage is killing the Beatles," *Teen Circle* magazine suggested that the female reaction to the foursome had "mellowed somewhat by the disappointment many of their fans feel, disappointment over the fact that only one of the Beatles—Paul McCartney—has not yet become involved in matrimony. What happens when he, too, is engaged?"[5]

The Beatles seemed to go out of their way to tarnish their clean-cut image. For the cover of their new American album, *Yesterday and Today,* set to be released by Capitol in June 1966, the Beatles agreed to be photographed dressed in butchers' overalls and covered with raw meat and an array of doll parts. The photo attracted criticism as the record company sent out advance copies. Capitol responded by hastily pasting an alternative photo over the offending one before releasing the album on June 20.

Reflecting their more adult image, the Beatles proved much more willing to comment on world events, particularly on the escalating war in Vietnam. The songs of Bob Dylan and Barry McGuire's "Eve of Destruction" brought political protest into the mainstream, but the climate was still hostile to those who spoke out about the conflict. Opinion polls showed that most Americans supported the war, and no other major pop star, including Dylan, had criticized US involvement in the conflict. Paul McCartney claimed that he became more knowledgeable about events in Vietnam after he spoke to philosopher and peace activist Bertrand Russell and to the American musicians who felt threatened by the draft.[6] McCartney had already said he opposed the draft when asked in Boston in September 1964. "Would you advocate sending all the young boys your age to Vietnam?" the reporter asked the Beatles.

"No. Not unless they wanted to, you know," Paul replied.[7]

When they arrived in New York on August 13 for the 1965 North American tour, a reporter inquired as to whether they would entertain the troops in Vietnam. "I wouldn't go there, no," John replied.[8] Ringo, who said little at the press conferences, conveyed his views to the journalists traveling on the Beatles' plane. Radio reporter Larry Kane asked Ringo if he was angry at the "war drums beating now."

"I think it's unfair that you get a leader of a country—then they force so many people to fight each other, and they don't get touched hardly. It is all the young men of the world who get shot, and bombed, and blown to bits. It's unfair. I know it sounds silly but they should let *them* fight it out, instead of fetching all those innocent bystanders."[9]

By the summer of 1966, the Beatles began to extol strong pacifist views. "This picture is not just important, it's terrifying and urgent," Paul told British music paper *Disc and Music Echo* after seeing *The War Game,* a movie that depicted a nuclear attack on Britain. "*The War Game* should be compulsory viewing, it's so important," he said, and now he saw what the Campaign for Nuclear Disarmament (CND) "were on about after all."[10] In an interview published in March 1966, George Harrison said he thought about the Vietnam War "every day and it's wrong. Anything to do with war is wrong. They're all wrapped up in their Nelsons and their Churchills and their Montys—always talking about war heroes. Look at *All Our Yesterdays* [a British television series on the events leading to World War II]. How we killed a few more Huns here or there. Makes me sick."[11] On June 30, a reporter in Japan asked them what they sought next. "Peace," said John and Paul in unison. "Ban the bomb," they both added. Another reporter asked them how much interest they took in the Vietnam War. "We think about it every day, and we don't agree with it and we think it's wrong," Lennon responded.[12]

In April, their newly acquired outspokenness caused a furor in Pittsburgh after local deejay Steve Rizen aired an interview with Liverpool deejay Bob McGrae who claimed that the Beatles called Barry Sadler's hit single, "Ballad of the Green Berets," "terrible" and "dreadful." "I felt listeners deserved to hear what the Beatles and other singers are saying about a patriotic American song," maintained Rizen.

The "Beatles stand to upset all the good they've done," the *Pittsburgh Press* opined but admitted that there was a possibility that Bob McGrae "is trying to stir up controversy." Nevertheless, the good people of Pittsburgh wrote to their local paper, with only one letter defending the Beatles and more than a dozen criticizing them. "We make them famous and bring them millions of dollars and they have the nerve to insult America's patriotic song," was a typical response. Outraged patriots threatened a boycott of record shops unless they removed Beatles records from the racks, prompting worried shop owners to contact Capitol Records telling them to "have the Beatles cool it with this kind of talk."[13]

More Popular Than Jesus

The events in Pittsburgh proved to be a foretaste of things to come as an even greater outcry erupted over John Lennon's comments on Christianity that first appeared in an interview published in the London newspaper the *Evening Standard* on March 4, 1966. Reflecting their greater willingness to discuss current affairs, Maureen Cleave, a reporter and friend of the group, interviewed each Beatle separately on a wide range of issues. Lennon's thoughts on religion would cause the most controversy. "Christianity will go," he stated. "It will vanish and shrink. I needn't argue about that; I'm right and I will be proved right. We're more popular than Jesus now; I don't know which will go first—rock 'n' roll or Christianity. Jesus was all right but his disciples were thick and ordinary. It's them twisting it that ruins it for me."[14] Lennon did not mean to say that the Beatles were better than Christianity, as many later claimed, but that the religion was in decline in the UK and that young people were more enamored by the Beatles and pop music than by Jesus Christ.

This was not the first time that Lennon, or indeed the rest of the Beatles, had voiced a less than admiring view of Christianity and the Christian Church. "We probably seem antireligious because of the fact that none of us believe in God," Paul declared in an interview with *Playboy* in 1965. John seemed more uncertain about his beliefs. "If you say you don't believe in God, everybody assumes you're antireligious, and you probably think that's what we mean by that. We're not quite sure what we are, but I know that we're more agnostic than atheistic." The Beatles levied the bulk of their criticism against the religious leaders who they believed misrepresented the ideas of Christ. "The only thing we've got against religion is the hypocritical side of it, which I can't stand," said John. "Like the clergy is always moaning about people being poor, while they themselves are all going around with millions of quid worth of robes on. That's the stuff I can't stand," Lennon concluded.

"But believe it or not, we're not anti-Christ," commented Paul.

"Just anti-Pope and anti-Christian," added the ever-helpful Ringo.[15]

George also made disparaging remarks about religious leaders in his interview with Maureen Cleave. "I think religion falls flat on its face. All this love thy neighbor, but none of them are doing it. How can anybody get themselves into the position of being Pope and accept all the glory and the money and the Mercedes-Benz and that? I could never be Pope until I'd sold my rich gates and my posh hat. I couldn't sit there with all that money on me and believe I was religious."[16]

Author Michael Braun reported on a raucous incident with a Roman Catholic priest who visited the Beatles' dressing room in November 1963, just before they went on stage in Sunderland. "Why are there so many big churches in countries where people are starving?" Paul asked the priest, wanting to know how much a member of the clergy was paid. Ringo handed the priest a Scotch and Coke, George asked him if he was allowed to drink, and John made some remark about the English occultist Aleister Crowley and black masses. The Beatles headed for the stage with the priest calling after them: "I wish I had time to convince you fellows about the benefits of religion" adding rather ruefully, "We'd have a real bang-up fight."[17] A local teacher had heard about the incident and told her pupils at St. Hilda's Secondary Modern School to write protest letters to the Beatles. The *Sunday Mirror* led with the headline "Girls Boycott 'Rude' Beatles: Rumpus over a brandy for the priest." The priest, Father Coughlin, threw oil on the fire. "Some loaded wise cracking went on," he told the newspaper, "and there was a pushing incident." The Beatles said it was all a joke and denied that there was any physical confrontation. "We like the padre and were surprised that he's taken it this way," George said. "We would like to tell our fans we were not being rude."[18]

Lennon's comments in the Maureen Cleave interview caused little stir in Britain or even when they first surfaced in the US. On March 21, *Newsweek* published a short article on Cleave's interview with Lennon. Even though the piece included Lennon's quotes on Christianity, the editor buried the story on page 52 of the magazine.[19] Lennon's observations appeared again in *The San Francisco Chronicle* on April 13 under the headline "Do the Beatles top Christ?" but the columnist, Charles McCabe, simply opined that Lennon was wrong to assert that "what he and his mates do is more popular—and ergo more important—than what Jesus Christ did." In the end, McCabe suggested, "Mr. Lennon has every right not to believe in Christianity."[20] Periodicals continued to publish the comments without too much fuss. The *Detroit Free Press* Sunday magazine printed all four Maureen Cleave interviews with the individual Beatles and included the religious quotes in the Lennon interview but deemed them not sensational enough to warrant a headline. The paper led with "John, in His Gorilla Suit seeking…what?" "John Lennon: Shades of Henry VIII," "John Lennon on ugly people," and "Lazy John Lennon obsessed by Celts."[21] Maureen Cleave summarized the four interviews for an article that appeared in *The New York Times* magazine on July 3, and included Lennon's comments on the relative popularity of Jesus. Evidently, the editor saw little controversy in the remarks and headlined the article "Old Beatles: A Study in Paradox."[22]

When Lennon's comments appeared in the teen magazine *Datebook,* the editorial slant was entirely different. Launched by liberal New Yorker Art Unger in September 1957, *Datebook* was aimed at teenage girls but was not afraid to discuss the social issues of the day. When Unger toured with the Beatles in the US in 1965, he struck up a friendship with their management. In March 1966, Beatles press officer Tony Barrow wrote to Unger and suggested that he obtain permission to print the Maureen Cleave articles in *Datebook,* believing the interviews would be a good fit for the magazine and would promote the more mature image the Beatles craved.[23] Unger wrote to Cleave and asked if she would condense the four interviews into a five thousand word article. He refused to believe that other US teen magazines would print the articles because "all of the teen magazines here print only the most superficial and phony material.… They're more likely to steal some quotes and blow them up into hair-raising stories."[24] Cleave refused Unger's request, replying that the $150 he offered was "laughable." So Unger went ahead and bought the four complete articles.[25] In April, Unger wrote to Barrow asking "if you or the boys felt there was any distortion in the material since there is still time to cut or correct in case of factual error."[26] Unger went ahead and published the Ringo and George articles in the August 1966 edition of the magazine, and the Paul and John interviews in the September edition, which appeared on the streets before the start of the 1966 tour.

There is little doubt that Art Unger and especially his new Managing Editor, Danny Fields, believed that the Lennon and McCartney interviews would gain some much-needed publicity for the magazine. Fields,

Datebook, *September
1966, the magazine
that ignited the more
popular than Jesus
controversy. Note that
McCartney and his
comments on race
relations receives pride
of place on the front
cover.*

a twenty-six-year-old New Yorker, was no great fan of the Beatles, preferring Bob Dylan and the Rolling Stones, but he had an eye for publicity
and self-promotion. With the Paul and John interviews at the center,
Unger asked Fields to turn the September issue into a special "Shout-
Out" edition that focused on controversial subjects. Fields perused the
interviews and saw that McCartney had suggested that the US was not a
model of egalitarianism, but a nation ravished by racial inequality: "it's a
lousy country where anyone who is black is made to seem a dirty nigger.
There is a statue of a good Negro doffing his hat and being polite in the
gutter. I saw a picture of it."[27]

"Paul McCartney decried racism in America, saying 'it's a lousy
country.' I thought, 'Whoah! There's a cover line for my teenage magazine! Bet they've never seen anything like that!'" recalled Fields. "And
then John Lennon says, 'I don't know which will go first: Rock n' Roll or

The October 1966 issue of Teen Life *magazine ran the same Lennon interview as* Datebook *but with a completely different tone.*

Christianity?' And I go 'Whoah! There's another one!"[28] Danny Fields thought that McCartney's views on race would provoke a greater reaction than Lennon's comments on religion, so he placed McCartney's words, "It's a lousy country where anyone black is a dirty nigger," at the top of the front page above Lennon's quote: "I don't know which will go first—rocknroll or Christianity." To reinforce the point, he put a photo of McCartney, not Lennon, on the cover of the magazine. Fields "thought the issue would bring attention to the teen magazine but not provoke the controversy it did. Who would have known? I wanted to bring attention to the fact that there was more to the Beatles than hopping up and down, wearing the same clothes, and singing catchy songs. I wanted a conversation on the issues and could not have foreseen the controversy it became."[29]

Teen Life also published the Lennon interview in the October issue of their magazine, but they presented it entirely differently from *Datebook*.

The *Teen Life* article omitted Lennon's comments about the decline of Christianity but it did include the quote: "Jesus was all right. He had the right ideas, but his disciples were thick and ordinary. It's them twisting it that ruins it for me. Jesus never meant it like that." *Teen Life* used a less volatile front-page headline: "Only Pix Ever Taken Inside the John Lennon House. How he lives: Purple walls, Black carpets, Crazy gadgets," and the issue included no mention of his comments on Christianity either in the headline or in the subheading of the article.[30]

Doug Layton and Tommy Charles, who presented a morning talk show on the local radio station WAQY (appropriately pronounced Wacky) in Birmingham, Alabama, obtained a copy of the "Shout-Out" issue of *Datebook* and fumed on-air over Lennon's comments. The two deejays made it seem that he was boasting that the Beatles were more important than the teachings of Jesus Christ. Neither Layton nor Charles were religious fanatics, but they knew that Lennon's views on religion would provoke the most anger among their listeners. "We just felt it was so absurd and sacrilegious that something ought to be done to show them they cannot get away with this sort of thing," Charles stated. John's comment struck a nerve, especially coming a short time after a *Time* cover feature from April 1966 headlined "Is God Dead?" posited an overall decline in Christian beliefs and church attendance in the US. The excited deejays claimed that they polled their audience, and over 90 percent agreed that the station should ban Beatles records. They asked listeners to bring their Beatle records and memorabilia to the station for a bonfire on August 19, the day the Beatles were due to play in Memphis.[31]

How the deejays obtained the issue of *Datebook* is unclear. The September issue was due to hit the newsstands on Thursday, August 4.[32] "I knew that was a controversial one, and I sent advance copies to Bible Belt disc jockeys who started the campaign to ban Beatles records," claimed Art Unger many years later.[33] Danny Fields denies Unger's claim, saying that the issue hit the newsstands earlier than August 4 and that the mother of a teenage girl in Alabama saw the magazine and passed it on to the broadcasters. It does seem unlikely that Unger would have sent an advance copy of the magazine to a radio station described by a book on the history of Birmingham radio as "a paltry low-powered daytime-only station"[34] "No, no, no, inconceivable that he would send a copy to rural Alabama," insisted Fields.[35]

Other radio stations in the South quickly followed the example set by WAQY and announced boycotts of Beatles records. In Texas alone, a reported two hundred radio stations imposed a ban on the Beatles.[36] In Longview, Texas, KLUE conducted a poll to see if listeners wanted to ban the Beatles. Some 1,100 people phoned the station, and 97 percent were in favor. On Friday, August 12, a crowd deposited their Beatles memorabilia near the KLUE transmission tower, and the station owner and staff set the pile on fire. God, it seems, was none too pleased. The following day, a bolt of lightning struck the KLUE tower, knocking the station off the air.[37] Local newspapers reported other bonfires in Florida, Georgia, Louisiana, Mississippi, North Carolina, Oklahoma, and Virginia.[38] Instead of playing Beatles records, the wonderfully named WAKY radio station in Louisville, Kentucky set aside ten seconds of silent air time every hour for prayer.[39] "We have banned the Beatles from our programming and they ought to stay out of the country," Chuck Newton from WGAT radio station in Gate City, Virginia, ominously warned.[40] The Ku Klux Klan, who had seen their profile slipping with the passage of civil rights legislation, saw this as an ideal opportunity to regain relevance and credibility. In Tupelo, Mississippi, Dale Walton, Imperial Wizard of the Knights of the Green Forest, urged teenagers to "cut their locks off" and send them to a Beatle burning organized by the Klan.[41] In Chester, South Carolina, Grand Dragon Bob Scoggins nailed Beatles records to a large wooden cross and set the cross on fire.[42]

The Lennon backlash took hold in the US rather than in Britain because of the deeply held religious convictions in America, particularly in the Deep South. A Gallup poll from 1968 found that 98 percent of Americans believed in God, the most in the 12-nation survey, while only 77 percent of Britons held the same belief, ninth in the survey. Some 73 percent of Americans believed in life after death compared to 38 percent of Britons, and 60 percent believed in the devil compared to only 21 percent of British people.[43] Protestants, who felt that their religious beliefs were under sustained attack, were more upset with Lennon than Catholics, who saw their faith recently gain some long overdue acceptance in America. The nation elected its first Catholic president, John F. Kennedy, in 1960; and while the Supreme Court declared prayers in public schools unconstitutional in 1962, the Elementary and Secondary Education Act passed in 1965 provided federal funding to parochial schools for the first time. In March 1967, Gallup found that 60 percent of Protestants thought religion was losing its influence on American life, while only 48 percent of Catholics felt the same way.[44]

Deeply held religious convictions may have inflamed passions in the Bible Belt, but opposition to Lennon's remarks spread far beyond the South. Pennsylvania State Senator Robert Fleming introduced a resolution in the legislature calling for promoters to cancel the Beatles' appearance in the state on August 16, for radio stations to stop playing their records, and for jukebox operators to remove their singles from their machines.[45] State Representative Charles Iannello of Massachusetts condemned the "four creeps" and tried, unsuccessfully, to revoke the permit for their concert in Boston.[46] "Citizens of the State of Michigan" sent a petition to the Detroit City Council demanding that these "undesirable aliens" be prevented from performing in Detroit. They also petitioned Michigan representatives in Congress, asking them to deny the group their visas to enter the country.[47] Radio stations announced boycotts of Beatles records in Connecticut, Idaho, Indiana, Kentucky, Massachusetts, Michigan, Minnesota, New York, Ohio, Pennsylvania, and Wisconsin.[48] "Parents forced to listen to ear-splitting Beatles records for the past three years can rejoice soon," the local paper in Columbus, Indiana, gleefully reported. "It seems the records now are owned only by the 'out-crowd.'" The Beatles "are strictly from Hicksville these days."[49] *Datebook* received hundreds of letters criticizing Lennon, most from states outside the South.[50] Newspapers reported bonfires of Beatles records and memorabilia in California, Illinois, Indiana, Nevada, and Pennsylvania.[51] "Yellow Submarine" and "Eleanor Rigby," released as a double A-sided single in the midst of the controversy, only reached number 2 on the *Billboard Hot 100*. Singer Maxine Brown blamed Lennon for the failure of her cover of "We Can Work It Out" to chart in the US. "It came out about three weeks before John Lennon's quotes about the Beatles being bigger than Jesus Christ broke," she told an interviewer. "Of course they stopped playing anything connected with the Beatles then. Including my record."[52]

Many of the more clear-thinking conservatives recognized that Lennon was simply declaring that Christianity had declined among young people, and they took this as an opportunity to criticize the Beatles-obsessed youth of America. "Mr. Lennon's rather coarse ejaculation," a rather coarse choice of words itself by conservative author William

F. Buckley, "was to be sure the plain truth, hardly shocking to students of the Bible, who know the relative attractions of mammon over God." The Beatles "prey on the reserve of veneration in young people, which in healthier ages would be directed at objects more venerable than the Beatles." The Beatles, with their "non-music," had manipulated gullible young people into worshiping them, not Christ. "But it is, I judge, not altogether stuffy to observe that someone who remarks on the diminution of Christianity ought probably to go on to elevate the suitability of some of Christianity's successors to fill the void."[53]

"Atheist John Lennon—simply told the TRUTH—as he sees it," Edward R. Sneed, an attorney with a penchant for capital letters, wrote to his local paper in Missouri. "Most people seem more familiar with ROCK AND ROLL JUNGLE music—authored by atheist and Communist BEATLES - than they are with our beloved Jesus Christ."[54] Many men of the cloth agreed with Lennon's comments, even if reluctantly. "Lennon was saying only what I say, almost anything is more popular than Jesus: boats, baseball or the bed on Sunday morning," Leslie G. Warren, the dean of St. Paul's Episcopal Cathedral in Detroit, told his congregation. "Jesus never said he'd get top rating."[55]

A not too dissimilar reaction occurred in Chicago. "I think that the statement reveals the emptiness of many of our youth today," African-American evangelist Reverend Robert Harrison stated. "It is our responsibility to make people like the Beatles and others understand that the gospel will always be powerful." Bishop James A. Forbes said that Lennon's remarks were "in bad taste," and that the Beatles were simply a passing fad while the teachings of Jesus would endure.[56] Teenager Andrew Teton bought two tickets for the 1966 Chicago concert for him and his girlfriend, but his girlfriend's mother was less than pleased. "No daughter of mine will see those godless punks." After much pleading, the mother finally gave her daughter permission to attend.[57] "Lennon's nuts," eighteen-year-old Sue Salatine, ex-president of the Society for the Promotion and Protection of the Beatles, informed *Chicago's American*. The "Beatles ought to be banned from Chicago and everywhere else because success has gone to their heads," another teenager, Olga Regalado, told the newspaper. "He shouldn't have commented on religion." Linda Jamen, seventeen, was equally appalled: "They'll do anything to make money," she said, "I wouldn't spend another quarter on their records."[58]

THE BEATLES BEAT THE CHURCH?

Even some in the evangelical community believed that the Beatles were indeed more popular than Jesus. Christianity Today, *September 2, 1966, page 54.*

"Our advice to Lennon would be shut up and sing," a *Chicago Daily News* editorial bellowed.[59] The *Chicago Tribune*, of course, stoked nationalist fires. "Rich Beatles Think Poorly of Americans: Assert Yanks too Money-Hungry," ran a caption in the *Chicago Tribune*, after Paul had said Americans "believe that money is everything," and George that he was "not looking forward" to the tour of the US.[60] Others seemed resigned to the decline in Christianity. *Christianity Today*, an evangelical journal based in the Chicago suburb of Carol Stream, called the Beatles "a British rock 'n' roll quartet that displays more hair than talent" but noted that "many ministers were willing to admit that Christianity isn't all that popular." Lennon's "latest remark just hit at the wrong time."[61] "The Beatles are more popular than Jesus," a Midwest pastor admitted to Chicago-based *Moody Monthly*. "But so is the golf course."[62]

Anger over Lennon's comments in the Roman Catholic Archdiocese of Chicago, however, was rather muted compared to the Protestant South. A city with towering cathedral-like parish churches, convents, two Catholic Universities, a major seminary, a Catholic-dominated Democratic machine, and the largest parochial school system in the nation exuded strength and buoyancy, not fear of the views of a pop star. Furthermore, many of those in Chicago, including the Catholic Church, were more concerned with the violence leveled at civil rights marchers in the city than with John Lennon's views. In July, the Chicago Freedom Movement marched into all-white neighborhoods on the city's Southwest and Northwest Sides, demanding equal access to housing in the face of a hostile and sometimes violent response from residents. On Friday, August 5, Martin Luther King and about six hundred supporters marched through Southwest Side neighborhoods and were met by an angry white mob carrying confederate flags, shouting racial epithets, and raining rocks and bottles down on the marchers. Summing up the attitude of many, one sign read: "Reds, race mixers, queers, junkies, winoes, muggers, rapists…you are all persona non grata here." One rock struck King. "I've never seen anything like it in my life," he said. "I think the people from Mississippi ought to come to Chicago to learn how to hate."[63] Little wonder, that as Catholic priests and nuns marched to end segregation in Chicago, front-page headlines in the diocese newspaper, the *New World*, focused on the "City's Race Problem" rather than Lennon's religious views.[64]

The Beatles Arrive in Chicago

When the Beatles landed in Chicago, they entered a country and a city where the sweltering heat matched the social climate. In June 1966, tensions between the police and the Puerto Rican community on the Near North Side erupted into four nights of rioting that resulted in millions of dollars of damage and dozens of injuries. In July, rioting on Chicago's West Side began when African-American youngsters, who had turned on fire hydrants to gain relief from the heat, confronted an unforgiving police. In the ensuing disturbances, crowds looted shops, snipers fired from rooftops, two died, more than eighty were injured, and more than 500 arrested. The rioting ended after Mayor Daley sent 1,500 National Guards onto the streets.[65] In early August, the attacks on Martin Luther King and the civil rights marchers gained national and international headlines. "Brick attack by Chicago 'White Power' Mob," Britain's *Daily Telegraph* headlined its front page as it reported on the vicious attack "by an infuriated mob of 3,000 white people chanting 'White Power.'"[66]

Stories of violent crime filled the local newspapers, adding to the tenseness of the long hot summer. "For eight months street-gang fighting has terrorized Chicago's South Side," stated the *Chicago Daily News* on August 5, a few days before the Beatles landed in the city for the start of the tour. "One of the leading combatants has been the Blackstone Rangers—probably the biggest, toughest and best disciplined teen-age gang Chicago has produced in a decade." In the previous three months, the Rangers had been involved in more than forty-five shootings. Judge Saul Epton set a $50,000 bond for a gang leader accused of shooting three other youths. "I'm sick and tired of all this violence," an angry Epton admonished the court. "It seems to be snowballing and it shouldn't be."[67]

"Has our society gone berserk? Violence is the order of the day," noted *Chicago Sun-Times* columnist Irv Kupcinet on August 3. "Veteran newsmen can't remember when so many stories dealing with violence were breaking simultaneously."[68] In 1966, reported crime in Chicago rose 4.9 percent on the previous year, but murders rose 29.3 percent, robbery 12.7 percent, and assault 9.4 percent during the same period.[69] In July, Chicago recorded seventy-two murders, the highest on record for any month in the city's history, exceeding the old record set in August 1965 by twenty-two fatalities. The most notorious of the murders occurred on July 14, 1966, when itinerant Richard Speck brutally murdered eight student nurses after he broke into their dormitory on the South Side. Chicago Police Superintendent O. W. Wilson blamed the hot weather. "I'm hoping for fifteen feet of snow," he said hopefully. "Maybe that will help keep the murders down."[70]

"Will the Beatles be safe in America?" the *New Musical Express* asked. "Demonstrations and protests are expected all along the tour," the worried New York correspondent suggested, "enough for the organizers to be seriously concerned for the Beatles' security." *NME* journalist Chris Hutchins warned that "Americans are demonstrative; their protests can be fanatical. Violence which is unheard of here is going on in some part of the US every day."[71]

"America is not too settled at the moment and I don't think it is any time for the Beatles to be here," cautioned former press officer, Derek Taylor, now living in California. "There is much violence and the sun is burning out of the hard sky. Psycho, schizo, paranoid are words as familiar in the newspapers here as freeze, crisis and rain are in the British press."[72] The Beatles departed London airport to a chant from two thousand fans of "John, not Jesus."

"John, please don't go," one fan yelled at the airport. "They'll kill you."[73]

Beatles manager Brian Epstein flew to New York City to discuss the tour with lawyer and friend Nat Weiss and the General Artists Corporation. On August 6, he held a press conference to explain Lennon's remarks. Epstein claimed that *Datebook* had taken Lennon's comments out of context. Journalist Chris Hutchins, a friend of Elvis Presley's manager, Colonel Parker, alleges that a desperate Epstein contacted Parker to see if Elvis could make a supportive statement on Lennon's behalf.[74] Nothing came of the request, and a fraught Epstein flew to Chicago for the start of the tour. GAC asked a reticent Frank Fried to meet Epstein at O'Hare with a limousine. "In my eight years in the business I had occasionally been forced to hire limos for artists, but I had drawn the line at attending them personally. This time I reluctantly agreed, sure that this was the final step in my career as a sell-out." After a quick handshake, the two men sat in the back of the limousine in silence. Fried was not bothered by what Lennon had to say: "I was much more interested in Vladimir Lenin's views than in John Lennon's."[75]

The Beatles arrived at a remote part of O'Hare Airport at 4:15 p.m. on August 11, avoiding the waiting fans and press. Years later, George Harrison retained a vivid memory of the drive from O'Hare to the Astor Tower Hotel. "I remember going to Chicago," he reminisced. "There had been riots in the black ghettoes, and as we drove through, the cops, tense, trying to be smart, directing the traffic, no hands on the handlebars, were falling off their motorbikes. As we came through in a limousine, one would go ahead to the next junction, stop the traffic, we'd then cross and the other one would go ahead and so on. These guys would be so flash, so 'into the mania.' They drove those big Harleys, holding both hands up, with a loud whistle in their mouths, sun-shades on, braking and skidding off their bikes. They were like madmen."[76]

The Astor Tower Hotel, an upscale modern establishment located in the affluent Gold Coast neighborhood, had turned down the Beatles' request to stay there in 1964, worried about the fan hysteria. As hundreds of waiting fans swarmed the Beatles' limousine, jumped on the hood, and banged on the roof as it sped into the garage, the owners probably had second thoughts about their decision to allow them to stay this year. "Chicago fans surrounded our hotel right round the clock," the

Beatles' press officer Tony Barrow recalled. "Gazing out of the window of his 27th floor suite, Brian Epstein smiled proudly when he saw the size of the crowd: 'No evidence there of any decline in the boys' popularity!'" Epstein triumphantly declared to Barrow, trying to lift his failing spirits.[77] Barrow briefed Lennon before the Beatles met the media to face questions about his comments on Christianity. "Never before or afterwards did I see John in such a distraught state, not because he believed he owed anyone an apology, but because he knew that the tour could be cancelled unless he swung the media over and gained their support at the imminent conference," Tony Barrow wrote some years later. Lennon leaned forward in his chair, his head in his hands, and started sobbing.[78] When Epstein met Art Unger at the hotel, he blamed the American publisher for the controversy and asked him to withdraw from the tour. With the support of Lennon and the other Beatles, Unger refused.

The most important press conference of the Beatles' career took place in Tony Barrow's suite on the 27th floor of the Astor Tower Hotel on the evening of August 11. Surrounded by the three national television networks and the international press, Lennon said that young people in England admired the Beatles more than Christ. "I just said what I said and it was wrong, or was taken wrong." When a reporter asked Lennon if he was sorry, he replied: "I am. Yes, you know. Even though I never meant what people think I meant by it. I'm still sorry I opened my mouth." In a second press conference with local journalists and deejays, a reporter told Lennon that the Alabama deejay Tommy Charles demanded an apology: "He can have it," Lennon shot back. "I apologize to him. If he's upset and he really means it, you know, I'm sorry. I'm sorry I said it really for the mess it's made, but I never meant it as a lousy or anti-religious thing, or anything. You know, I can't say anything more than that. There's nothing else to say, really, no more words. If he wants one he can have it. I apologize to him."[79]

Frank Fried hoped that there would be "some fireworks," but his "hopes were dashed immediately. The whole point of the press conference was to capitulate, to back off, and from their point of view, they handled it well."[80]

"John, Paul, George and Ringo were humbled," said Tony Delano of the *Daily Mirror*. "In fact, their meekness was almost embarrassing."[81] *Moody Monthly*, published by the Moody Bible Institute of Chicago, headlined their story, "Sorry—yeah, yeah, yeah!"[82] Danny Fields became friends with Linda McCartney and many years later met Paul. "Does Paul know that I was the editor of the magazine that caused the whole religious controversy in 1966?" he asked Linda.

"Let's ask him," she said.

When they told Paul, he simply said: "So you're the one," and the three heartily laughed, the episode all but forgotten.[83]

The 1966 Tour Begins

On Friday, August 12, 1966, the Beatles headlined shows at 3 p.m. and 7:30 p.m. at the International Amphitheatre on the first stop of the North American tour. Triangle priced the cheapest tickets at $3.75, 50 percent higher than two years earlier, and the more expensive tickets at $4.75 and $5.75. Triangle chose WLS rival WCFL as the official radio sponsor of the shows.

Triangle announced that both concerts had sold out, but all was not what it seemed.[84] Polk Bros., the home appliance and electronics retailer in Chicago, attained two thousand of the $4.75 tickets, which they sold at a reduced price of $3.75 with every purchase of a Sunbeam shaver.[85] On August 10, just two days before the concert, Frank Fried was running

advertisements in local newspapers informing readers that tickets were still available.[86] The experience of Mike Koldyke is indicative of the difficulty Triangle encountered in selling tickets. A generous benefactor sold Koldyke, a thirty-four-year-old investment banker and budding philanthropist, one thousand tickets for the matinee performance and five hundred tickets for the evening show at face value. Koldyke's wife served on the board of the Children's Memorial Hospital, and the big-hearted husband wanted

The 1966 tour program for Chicago.

to sell the $5.75 tickets for $10 each and donate the profits to the hospital. As the concert approached, Koldyke was left with hundreds of unsold tickets. "It wasn't sold out," he recalled. "The problem was that the Beatles' popularity had waned. I had to go out to McCormick Place and set up a booth. I was selling tickets at face value because I couldn't get rid of them. I just wanted to get my money back. I did sell all the tickets finally. I was selling them to anyone I could find. I was competing with the box office. There were no premiums being paid. I hoped that we would have a killing because of the Beatles' popularity, but we did not."[87]

The Remains, formed in Boston in 1963, became the

Chicago Tribune, August 4, 1966, page 6

Stores were virtually giving away Beatles tickets a week before the 1966 Chicago show.

first support act to take the stage on the Beatles' third North American tour. The Remains' manager, New York-based John Kurland, had secured his charges an appearance on *The Ed Sullivan Show* in December 1965, even though the group had only enjoyed a couple of regional hits. Now he achieved an even bigger coup; he won the Remains the opening slot on the Beatles' tour with the help of Bob Bonis, the Beatles' US tour manager and Kurland's business partner. "Bob Bonis took an interest in the Remains and just came to us one day and said, 'Would you guys like to be the opening act on the Beatles' tour?'" bassist Vern Miller recalled. "I think it took us about two seconds to reply, 'Yes.'"[88] Drummer Chip Damiani, however, was not so enthusiastic. "Chip decided that he didn't want to go on in this direction," keyboardist Bill Briggs stated. "He thought it was going to ruin our intimate communication that we had musically and just felt that it was the wrong thing to do. So, he decided not to do the Beatles' tour, and the band replaced Damiani with Norman Smart."[89]

WCFL deejay Joel Sebastian stepped onto the Amphitheatre stage and introduced the nervous Remains who performed a twenty-minute set of six songs to the largest crowd they had ever played before. It was the first time the Remains had taken the stage with their new drummer and, without a recognizable hit single in their repertoire, they had to win over an audience unfamiliar with their music. "It can be a bit intimidating to be the opening act for the biggest band in the world," Vern Miller remembered. "We didn't know what to expect, but we were able to win all the crowds over."[90] The Remains stayed on to back Bobby Hebb, a twenty-eight-year-old African-American singer from Nashville, Tennessee. Hebb's song "Sunny," which entered the higher reaches of the *Billboard Hot 100* as the tour began, peaking at number two, guaranteed him an excellent reception from the crowd. "Bobby Hebb was a really good showman. It was the first time I've ever seen anybody put stage makeup on," Bill Briggs of the Remains recalled.[91]

Bobby Hebb and the Remains left the stage to be replaced by another act flying high on the charts, the Cyrkle. The Cyrkle started out at Lafayette College in Easton, Pennsylvania, in 1961 as the Rhondells, singing Beach Boys and Four Seasons covers at fraternity parties, high school dances, and college events. When performing in Atlantic City in 1965, their lives changed forever as keyboardist, Earle Pickens, testified. "A man named Nat Weiss, who represented Brian Epstein in the United States, came into our nightclub, and he recognized that we were pretty good. He called Epstein and negotiations began through the fall and into 1966. Epstein signed us to a management contract." After a suggestion from John Lennon, the band changed their name from the Rhondells to the Cyrkle. Epstein made a big impression on Pickens. "I thought he smelled great. He always wore a suit and tie and was immaculately dressed. He was lovely. He was kind, he was nice, he was well-spoken, he was a gentleman; polished."[92] The Cyrkle signed with Columbia Records and, in March 1966, entered a recording studio in New York City. "The biggest thing Columbia had at that time was Simon and Garfunkel. Paul Simon wrote 'Red Rubber Ball.' He had done a demo, but he was not going to record it. So we went in the studio in March and recorded three songs. One of them was 'Red Rubber Ball.'" The group released it as a single in April 1966, and in July it reached number two on *Billboard*.

Earle Pickens, who had just completed his first year as a medical student at the University of Chicago, spent his summer break touring with the Beatles. "I had just finished my Freshman year of medical school and lo and behold, they ended medical school in May, and we didn't start back until October that particular year. In July, Brian says, 'Well, I want you to tour with the Beatles.'

Earle Pickens, medical student at the University of Chicago and keyboardist with the Cyrkle, spent his summer vacation touring with the Beatles.

So, we said, 'Hey, yes. Okay.'" The money came in handy for the cash-strapped student. "I think the entire group got paid $10,000. In those days, Brian Epstein got 25 percent off the top. The booking agent, GAC, got 15 percent. So, there's 40 percent gone. Then you split it four ways. The expenses, taxes, and everything. I was able to buy a new car. But our fee in those days for playing at the University of Florida was $2,500." The Cyrkle, with their short hair and striped blazers, looked slightly out of place next to the more fashionably turned out Remains and Beatles. They played a melody of Beach Boys songs and other hits of the day and their crowd-pleasing chart-topper, "Red Rubber Ball."

"We were very pleased," Pickens said. "We did our little twenty-minute show, and I thought we were very well received. There's no question who they'd come to see, but we got lots of applause."[93]

Once the Cyrkle finished their set, the Remains returned to the stage to back the Ronettes. The Ronettes had no time to rehearse with the Remains, so the girls simply sent them sheet music to learn their songs. According to David Noble, music critic of *Chicago's American,* the Boston-based musicians seemed to have done their homework. "The Remains, a group whose rhythmic execution was not precise (one of the less forgivable sins in this rhythm 'n' blues-descended music) but who proved their professionalism and endurance by providing accompaniment for two long vocal acts without losing vitality," Noble reported. "In the long haul, they were the best of the curtain-raisers."[94] Once the Ronettes vacated the stage, there was an intermission of about fifteen minutes while the roadies prepared the stage for the main act.

The look and character of the four Beatles had changed since the first tour in 1964 and so, too, had that of their audience. "The British influence on fashion is very evident here," WCFL news journalist Carole Simpson, who had covered the Beatles' concert the previous year at White Sox Park, told the radio audience. "There's the miniskirts, the bell bottom trousers, and the bright mod colors, splashes of color. Of course, the hair on both boys and girls is long and straight."

Fellow reporter Howie Roberts interjected: "You do have trouble telling them apart, don't you," he prompted.

"Yes, you do, you certainly do," she replied.[95]

The Beatles built their success on a female fan base, but they were now attracting more boys to their concerts. Judith Sims, editor of *TeenSet,* arrived at the Astor Tower Hotel to see it "surrounded by milling, screaming girls (and boys—they were much more in evidence this year)."[96]

"This year we got more boys in the audience," Ringo agreed. "There's about 30% more boys than we ever had.... I think it's only because they don't really listen when the girls have got a fab rave—they sort of put it down instantly, you know. I used to! I think most boys did—if the girls liked it and you like it, you were a sissy or something, you know."[97]

Every time the curtain at the back of the stage wiggled, huge waves of screams erupted. Finally, Jim Stagg of WCFL stepped forward, introduced the Beatles, and they came running down the stairs at the back and onto the stage. They wore dark green suits, "were tieless and the shirts were lemon plaid, high in the collar and long in the cuff."[98] The group's entrance was met "with a knifing scream which instantly passed the aural threshold of pain," the *Tribune* reported. "Flashbulbs from a thousand cameras stabbed the dark hall with continuous lighting."[99]

"America doesn't like the Beatles anymore? Forget it," wrote a delighted Tony Delano of the *Daily Mirror*, who had previously reported on the 1964 US tour. "At their first concert here today, 13,000 fans gave them a wilder, louder and more joyful reception than on their previous two tours of America. And there was not a single protest."[100] Earle Pickens of the Cyrkle saw the Beatles from the side of the stage. "My heart was jumping up in my throat. It was like an atomic explosion. The venue was totally dark, but all of a sudden, it was light. It was like spotlights everywhere, and there was nothing but flash bulbs. I thought the place was going to explode. It never stopped."[101]

Mal Evans tested all the equipment before the show but "the minute they step on stage, the damn thing goes off," he recalled. "Everything was going crazy and I was on the stage changing amplifiers. I couldn't figure out what was wrong. But luckily, we found it pretty quickly."[102] Their "amplifier, overloaded with screams, gave out, leaving Ringo Starr's drum solo practically unaccompanied," Thomas Miller of the *Chicago Tribune* wrote. "John Lennon flashed his cheesecake smile at a photographer and tried a Hindu neck trick or two. Paul McCartney said it was good to be back and thank you to everyone. George Harrison spent much of the time getting his guitar, at least, turned on."[103] As Lennon, who wore orange-tinted granny glasses, looked across the arena, he noticed the banners proclaiming support for him during his recent troubles: "We love John Lennon and God," "We Luv You More Than Ever," and "Say What You Think, John" hung from the balcony.[104] One section raised an eight-foot long poster saying "We Send All Our Loving To You."[105] Some fans wore "I STILL Love the Beatles" buttons.[106]

Once Evans solved the technical problems, the show restarted. The crowd threw jellybeans, candy, toys, and other gifts on stage, and girls sobbed and screamed, just like they had on previous tours. "In Chicago a purple and yellow stuffed animal, a red rubber ball and a jump rope were plopped up on the stage," marveled McCartney. He "had to kick a carton of Winston cigarettes out of the way" as he played.[107] Bess Coleman, previously the Beatles' assistant press officer on the 1964 tour and now managing editor of *Teen Life*, saw that "one girl in the balcony was showering the platform with stones from a catapult in the hope of getting her favorite, George."[108] They started their set with Chuck Berry's "Rock and Roll Music," the first of two covers. They continued with "She's a

Linda Ulreich

John Lennon on stage at the International Amphitheatre, August 1966.

Woman," "If I Needed Someone," "Day Tripper," "Baby's in Black," "I Feel Fine," "Yesterday," Ringo's contribution "I Wanna Be Your Man," "Nowhere Man," "Paperback Writer," and ended with Little Richard's "Long Tall Sally."[109] Not only did they avoid playing any of the early hits associated with Beatlemania, but they also played nothing from their new album, *Revolver*.

Eighteen-year-old Kathy Whitgrove drove from Joliet with three high school friends to attend the afternoon show. Kathy sat far away from the stage at White Sox Park in 1965 and screamed her lungs out, but this time, she sat near the front. "I did no screaming because I thought if one of them looked at me and saw me acting like a fool, I would die."[110] Fifteen-year-old Pat Meyers, also from Joliet, attended the performance with fellow Beatlemaniacs she had met at a Beatles USA Limited Fan Club meeting held at the Palmer House hotel in Chicago. It was her first pop concert. "There was so much screaming, we couldn't hear a thing. We were told not to bring cardboard posters into the concert so we painted 'WE LOVE YOU' on a sheet so we could bring it in under our clothes. Also, we baked them Snickerdoodle Cookies. We tried to find their room. We must have been close because there were men guarding the stairwell we found."[111]

Allen Shaw, assistant program director at WCFL, enjoyed a unique behind-the-scenes view of the concert. "I remember Brian had just purchased a brand new 35-millimeter camera, one of these really expensive ones with a big lens and everything. And he spent most of the time backstage snapping photographs of anything that he found interesting. He just wanted to use that camera. When the Beatles came on, it was pandemonium with all the young girls screaming at the top of their lungs. I decided to go out to the front of the show after it got started to see what it was like. I remember it was so incredibly loud that you could hardly hear the Beatles play. I was probably twenty feet from the speakers on stage and it was still hard to figure what was going on because the screaming overshadowed everything. I went backstage because it was just hard to take."[112]

Even though the Beatles played in other Midwestern cities in 1966, many still traveled from out of state to the Chicago shows. For his first ever concert, sixteen-year-old John Blocker and three friends boarded the eastbound Illinois Central train in East Dubuque, Iowa, on the morning of the concert. At each stop, more Beatles fans boarded the train, many of them carrying signs declaring their love for an individual Beatle. "There was a frenzy building from anticipation until we got off at Union Station," said Blocker, referring to Chicago's main downtown train station. They took a cab to the Amphitheatre, and after a nearly two-hundred-mile trip, finally glimpsed their holy grail. "A light flashed up above the stage and there they were." John Lennon shouted, "Hello America. It's great to be back." After the concert, the four friends fought their way through the crowds to get back to Union Station, but they missed the last train and spent the night sleeping on the station's wooden benches.[113]

Because of the Lennon controversy, Frank Fried demanded extra security. Some 180 policemen, thoughtfully provided with cotton wool for their ears; a hundred fire fighters; two hundred Andy Frain ushers; and a number of private detectives from the William J. Burns Detective Agency worked to control the crowd. To protect Lennon, more police were positioned in front of the stage than two years earlier.

Maybe the security was not as tight as promoter Fried had hoped, however, as fourteen-year-old Katie Jones found out. Katie, her friend Nancy, and Nancy's "pretty hip dad" sat in the first-row balcony. As the Ronettes performed, the excited Katie visited the bathroom. "I got lost on the way back and wound up backstage. I ran into Mal Evans who was right behind the stage fixing Ringo's drums. They had already cleared the backstage area, and he said if I didn't scream and I behaved myself, I could stay." Katie stood with the technicians, promoters, and deejays, watching the objects of her desire. "I just happened to be in the right place at the right time. I got the view of a lifetime. I was about eight feet behind to the left of Ringo. I had a Beatle-eye view." Katie stood mesmerized for about ten minutes. "I was thrilled to my toes. It was one of the most incredible experiences of my life. Getting backstage made a big difference. It was an absolutely electric thing. You could feel it in every nerve of your body." Alas, the police arrived and awoke Katie from her trance-like state, telling her to return to her seat.[114]

Katie spent the rest of the show rather grumpily complaining about the experience in the balcony compared to the one backstage. "I really wished that everybody would just shut up so I could hear what was going on." The whole experience left Katie slightly concerned about the Beatles' safety. "It would have taken very little for that stage to get rushed. It was bedlam. But back then, us kids obeyed authority, especially in the Midwest. Midwest people tend to be rather reserved and polite, and we would listen to the security."[115] The performance lasted twenty-seven minutes. As they came off stage, John grinning broadly said to Tony Delano of the *Daily Mirror*, "Just like old times. What a relief."[116]

"We've always had a great time in Chicago," Ringo told a reporter after the show. "The people have always been great. So Chicago wasn't worrying us."[117]

Jerry G. Bishop of WCFL introduced the Beatles for the evening show. They strolled down the steps, this time dressed in dark green suits and red shirts, and proceeded to play the same set that they had played during the afternoon show.[118] "From a seat in the second row, I could barely hear the amplified voices," David Noble wrote. "Inexcusably poor performance from the sound equipment," meant he had to concentrate on the look of the band. "John Lennon radiated patience and serenity. Song-writer Paul McCartney labored to keep the excitement up, while George Harrison and Ringo Starr, more or less, kept the group mood of relaxed outgoingness."[119]

Barb Fenick, aged fifteen from Minnesota, caught the overnight train to Chicago to attend the concert with three girls from the local Beatles fan club and one of their mothers. They hung out at the Astor Tower Hotel in the afternoon hoping for a glimpse of their idols. "In this throng of fans you felt that kindred spirit we wouldn't feel again until the Beatles conventions of the '70s." The girls attended both shows. In the evening, Barb sat in Row 12 in the balcony behind the stage. "I could see them relatively close up and screamed my pitiful brains out that night. And felt good about it, too! I was screaming for John.... I for one wanted him to know that I was on his side!"[120]

When the concert ended, the tired Beatles returned to their hotel. The Beatles enjoyed their reputation as partiers but, on this night, the wholesome Beach Boys outdid them. At the same time that the Beatles played in Chicago, California's finest were performing at the Illinois State Fair in the state capital of Springfield. After their concert, Mike Love and Bruce Johnston flew to Chicago on a charter plane to renew acquaintances with John, Paul, George, and Ringo, whom Love had previously met in August 1965 when the Beatles performed in Portland, Oregon. Arriving at Midway at 1 a.m. Saturday morning, the two headed to the Astor Tower Hotel ready to party. "[T]he Beatles were a drag," they later told Debbie Hutson, a reporter for *The State Journal Register,* who had helped them organize the trip. "They were ASLEEP when we got there," complained the incredulous Beach Boys, not too sympathetic to their evident jet lag. Love and Johnston eventually managed to raise the reluctant Mop Tops from their slumbers.[121]

Bruce played the Beatles the unreleased "Good Vibrations" on the piano in the hotel room, but even that did not energize them.[122] "They don't know how to party at all. It must have been the seventh day for them, all they wanted to do was rest." The meeting petered out, and the energetic Beach Boys flew back to Springfield and on to Duluth, Minnesota, for another concert that night.[123]

On Saturday morning, George Spink, later a jazz critic for various Chicago publications, claims that he was standing in front of the Catholic Archbishop's Residence in Chicago's Gold Coast district when a limousine pulled up, and the driver asked him for directions to the legendary Big John's blues club. It just so happened that Spink was working as a bartender at Big John's, and so he hopped in the front seat and directed the chauffeur to the blues landmark. The youngster turned around to look at the passengers in the back seat and was stunned to see the four tired Beatles staring back at him. "I couldn't have said anything, anyway," Spink stated, "I was too dumbstruck." When they reached their destination, Spink jumped out of the car. The Beatles briefly looked at the club and then the limousine sped off to O'Hare.[124] The visit to Big John's seems to have left a mark on the Fab Four, as they subsequently referenced blues greats in some of their new songs: BB King in "Dig It," Muddy Waters in "Come Together," and Elmore James in "For You Blue."

Their last visit to Chicago left a mixed impression on the Beatles and their entourage. "All I remember about the last time we played Chicago was seeing the stockyards," Paul McCartney said when he returned to the city with his group Wings in 1976.[125] "It's a shame that you weren't able to get out in Chicago because you was right in the midst of really the most interesting section of Chicago," Art Unger of *Datebook* told George Harrison. "It looked great, Chicago," Harrison replied, even though he saw most of the city out of a hotel window or from the back seat of a limousine.[126] Years later, Harrison would have darker memories of his visit, highlighting the trip to the city as a significant part of the dangerous 1966 World Tour. They barely escaped with their lives from the Philippines after failing to turn up at a reception for first lady Imelda Marcos, and they caused controversy among Japanese nationalists for playing at the sacred Nippon Budokan Hall, but Chicago still received a dishonorable mention from Harrison as one of the worst stops on the tour. "I was talking about not touring at least a year before saying, 'I can't stand this.' It was just so dangerous, like The Philippines and Japan and Chicago and all these riots."[127] In October 1987, Harrison again mentioned the city when he drudged up memories of the US tours. "That last year, when we toured America, there was like race riots going on in Chicago, and we'd arrive in the middle of that."[128]

The tour failed to provide a boost for the careers of the support acts. The Ronettes' popularity peaked before 1966, and the Beatles' tour did nothing to revive their fortunes. The group broke up in 1967. Some of Bobby Hebb's material became popular on the Northern Soul scene in the UK, but "Sunny" remained by far his biggest hit. Hebb died from cancer in 2010. At the end of the tour, the Remains' leader, Barry Tashian, quit the band, and the group disbanded a few months later.

The Cyrkle, too, were unable to build on the publicity they had gained from being on the tour. "We played in a barroom in Indiana for forty people after the last stop on the Beatles' tour in San Francisco. The last show we ever played was Colby College in Maine. I left the band at that time." Earle Pickens returned to the University of Chicago Medical School to complete his studies and went on to enjoy an illustrious career as a surgeon in Florida. Pickens still retains fond memories of his time with the Beatles. "It was just incredible. We did all of the Beatles' songs, even crazy songs because we love them so much, and then we got to see them and spend this time with them. We'd look back there, and there's Ringo in a striped shirt, and I'm saying, 'Good Lord, I can't believe this.' It was just overwhelming. We thought with Brian Epstein that we were going to be successful. It didn't take long for that to evaporate. I tell people we were very famous for about three weeks."[129]

The extent of the outrage over Lennon's comments was evident as the tour progressed. Many concerts failed to sell out, including their return to New York's Shea Stadium on August 23, which saw over ten thousand of more than fifty-five thousand tickets left unsold. *Billboard* noted the decline in attendances and the reduced enthusiasm of fans in an article entitled "Beatlemania Turns To 'Beatle-waneia.'" The Beatles, the paper gleefully reported, "have begun the long, slow downward journey."[130] The Ku Klux Klan picketed their concert in Washington, DC, and, in Memphis, someone tossed a firecracker on stage and, for a moment, the group feared that one of them had been shot. The fallout from Lennon's remarks continued after the tour had ended. The Beatles "are not getting anything like the air play they had a year ago, and the hangover—(continually and malevolently revived)—from John's unpopular 'Jesus' quotes persists," wrote Derek Taylor, over a month after the tour had finished. "There's still a nasty smell isn't there?" one major TV executive gossiped to Taylor.[131]

The 1966 North American tour was the last time the Beatles appeared together in front of a paying audience. "With the concerts and the Beatlemania, after a while the novelty wore off and then it was very boring," Harrison stated some thirty years later. "It wasn't just the noise on stage, not hearing the music and playing the same old songs; it was too much everywhere we went. Even when we got away from the screaming fans, there were all the screaming policemen and the Lord Mayors and their wives and the hotel managers and their entourages."[132] Ringo, too, recognized the futility of touring. "I couldn't go through the turmoil all over again," he said in 1969. "We had five years of Beatlemania and it was enough. No sleep, no proper meals, living out of a suitcase, being torn to bits mentally and physically...Oh, never again!"[133] John Lennon, understandably, referred directly to the Jesus controversy when discussing the end of touring. "I didn't want to tour again, especially after having been accused of crucifying Jesus when all I'd made was a flippant remark, and...with the Klan outside and firecrackers going on inside. I couldn't take any more."[134]

Seventeen-year-old Gerald Langford from Chicago followed the Beatles on the whole of the 1966 tour with five of his friends. The six Beatlemaniacs all worked part-time jobs during the school year to fund the adventure. Then they bought tickets for every evening performance, which cost them $75.50 each, and paid $110 to rent a bus for the three weeks they were on the road. In Memphis they sneaked into a Beatles press conference, they rated the New York concert the group's best performance, and they particularly enjoyed their stay with friends in Los Angeles. As soon as the tour ended, they returned home and resumed work, saving up for the next Beatles tour.[135] Little did Langford know that they would never perform again, and that he and his friends were probably the last Chicagoans to see the Beatles in concert.

CHAPTER 8

"Acid on Vinyl"

The Beatles and the Counterculture, 1967–70

The Beatles ceased touring in the summer of 1966 and never again performed in Chicago, but they continued to exert a strong influence on the life of the city. Through records, radio, TV, newspapers, and magazines the Beatles continued to inspire people to emulate their musical and nonmusical pursuits. The release of *Sgt. Pepper's Lonely Hearts Club Band* in the summer of 1967 signaled a profound realignment in the interests of the group and in their desire to influence their audience. While the 1966 tour had seen the Beatles distance themselves from their mop-top image of fun and frivolity, they now adopted an even more serious demeanor as they became strongly associated with the hippie phenomenon and countercultural ideas. "Except for a few spiritual gurus and swamis, the hippie movement is leaderless and loose," *Time* asserted in a cover story that introduced hippies to mainstream America in the summer of 1967. "The Beatles—forerunners of psychedelic sound and once again at the forefront with their latest album, *Sgt. Pepper's Lonely Hearts Club Band*—are the major tastemakers in hippiedom."[1]

Sgt. Pepper's Lonely Hearts Club Band

After the Beatles played their last concert in Candlestick Park, San Francisco, in August 1966, they took a short break and then, towards the end of the year, gathered at the EMI Recording Studios on Abbey Road in London to record new music. The next time Chicagoans would see the

Beatles was in two films made to promote their double A-sided single, "Strawberry Fields Forever" and "Penny Lane." These introduced a new and slightly unsettling sound and look to the American public. Released in the US on February 13, 1967, McCartney's "Penny Lane" was a rather traditional sounding song about life on a Liverpool street but told with some unconventional lyrical touches, while Lennon's "Strawberry Fields Forever" brought forth stranger psychedelic flourishes and more obscure lyrics. The promotional films used slow motion, reversed film, and other experimental movie techniques. They also featured each Beatle sporting mustaches and exotic-looking clothing.[2]

The sound that the Beatles introduced with "Penny Lane" and "Strawberry Fields" they brought to spectacular fruition with *Sgt. Pepper's Lonely Hearts Club Band* issued on June 2 in the US. Rock 'n' roll provided the foundations for the record, but the Beatles and producer George Martin added innovative architectural flourishes in the form of outside musicians and imaginative studio techniques. The Beatles mixed Indian, music hall, brass band, classical, and psychedelic influences to create a mosaic of soundscapes. On "She's Leaving Home," none of the Beatles played a musical instrument, on "Within You Without You" George played with outside musicians, and on "A Day in the Life" a full orchestra provided a prolonged crescendo of noise at the climax of the song. The many British themes, including mentions of the House of Lords, the Albert Hall, and Blackburn; the use of Northern brass band, fairground, and music hall sounds; and the Victorian imagery that permeated the album, made the disc an even more exotic experience for the American listener. The Beatles had already started to write songs that no longer addressed the joys of romantic relationships, but they now broadened their subject matter even further and used lyrics that were more abstruse. Capitol released no singles from the record, and the tracks ran together in a seamless listening experience, all of which contributed to the focus on the album as a whole, rather than on individual songs.[3]

Sgt. Pepper was important for its innovative use of the possibilities of the studio but was also significant for its packaging. The Beatles employed pop artists Peter Blake and Jann Haworth to design a new kind of album liner with little expense spared. With its gatefold sleeve and a collage of celebrities on the cover, some known and some unknown to a general audience, the album looked unique in the racks of the local record store. Inside the LP sleeve, there were cardboard cutouts of a mustache, a picture card of Sgt. Pepper, some sergeant stripes, two badges, and a stand-up of the Beatles in their *Sgt. Pepper* outfits. It was also the first rock album to print the complete song lyrics on the back cover, inviting listeners to immerse themselves more deeply in the musical experience.

On its release, critics fired off effusive praise for the Beatles' latest creation. *Crawdaddy* called *Sgt. Pepper* "a monument in rock and as such, a revitalization of their career."[4] "All the successes of the past two years were a foreshadowing of *Sgt. Pepper*, which more than anything else dramatizes, note for note, word for word, the brilliance of the new Beatles," *Time* enthused.[5] Thomas Willis reviewed *Sgt. Pepper* for the *Chicago Tribune* and was equally impressed. He believed that "the Beatles newest album is one of the best song records ever.... If this is not universal art as well as good entertainment, one of us is a monkey's uncle."[6] Even the folk and classical communities were won over. A reviewer in the preeminent folk journal *Sing Out!* called it "a masterpiece." *Sgt. Pepper* "is both enigmatic and brilliant, comprised of so many elements that one hardly knows where to begin talking about it."[7] Don Heckman, writing in the classical music magazine *American Record Guide,* described the album as "a major achievement of popular entertainment art."[8]

Not all reviews were as glowing, possibly reflecting the novelty of the music. Richard Goldstein in the *New York Times* believed that George Martin and the Beatles overproduced the album: "like the cover, the overall effect is busy, hip and cluttered. Like an over-attended child 'Sergeant Pepper' is spoiled." Goldstein liked "A Day in the Life," but it was "only a coda to an otherwise undistinguished collection of work."[9]

"It is not a symphony, and it isn't a masterpiece, though the best of its songs are gems," Gene Less in *High Fidelity* wrote in August 1967. "At its best, it is popular music of a high order; at its worst, it is tripe." The reviewer was particularly critical of the "meandering, unstructured, free-association do-it-yourself-Rorschakism that Lennon and McCartney too often pass off as lyric writing." In the end, there are "three, maybe four important songs in this album, a few that are so-so, and a couple that can be considered authentically insignificant."[10]

It had been ten months since the last Beatles LP, and after the success of "Penny Lane" and "Strawberry Fields," anticipation for *Sgt. Pepper* among fans was high. *Sgt. Pepper* garnered advance sales of over one million in the US and sold 2.5 million copies within the first three months of its release.[11] Because of the long wait, many people have vivid memories of hearing *Sgt. Pepper* for the first time. Danny Fields, who now worked for Elektra Records, first heard "A Day in the Life" in the company of Brian Epstein. Epstein visited New York City and invited a few luminaries in the music business to his suite at the Waldorf hotel, including Fields. (Epstein was still unaware of his role in the "bigger than Jesus" controversy.) "As the six of us sat around, Epstein produced the best pot, and we all smoked as he put on the cassette. Nothing ever sounded like 'A Day in the Life.' It was so far from 'I Want to Hold Your Hand.'" Fields eventually heard the whole album with his colleagues at Elektra. "The day the record was released, the coolest people in the company headed to the recording studio on Broadway to hear the album in its full glory. Nothing could beat a private airing with Brian Epstein on pot, though."[12]

Like many, Allen Shaw, the assistant program director at WCFL radio station in Chicago, enjoyed the experience of listening to the album on the latest audio equipment. "I remember taking it home, and I had one of these typical, big stereo systems with an amplifier, turntable, AM/FM tuner, and two giant speakers in the living room. I remember putting that record on and listening to it from start to finish, both sides, and just being amazed at what I was hearing."[13]

It was particularly memorable for nineteen-year-old David Witz, who experienced both LSD (lysergic acid diethylamide) and *Sgt. Pepper* for the first time on the same night. Witz was with a handful of friends in a studio apartment in North Side Lincoln Park listening to the jazz album *Forest Flower: Charles Lloyd at Monterey.* "The apartment owner strolled in, smiling broadly. He took the Charles Lloyd album off the record player and slipped on his new purchase, the new Beatles album. The acid hit. Cellophane flowers. Giant structures of music, of attitudes, towered toward infinity. It had begun." The experience of listening while under the influence of hallucinogenic drugs was life-changing for the young Witz. "I was transformed from just another confused kid to an emissary of the New Age."[14]

"I bought it at a Sears in Oakbrook, Illinois, at a shopping mall, on the day of release," recalled Katie Jones, the dedicated fourteen-year-old Beatles fan who had wound up backstage at the 1966 concert in

Chicago. Katie rushed home and first perused the cover. "We opened up the gatefold sleeve, and here are these guys dressed in this silk stuff and all these colors, and they had mustaches. It was kind of confusing. I was still into the puppy love thing, and the Beatles were safe. We could fantasize about them. We had them all over our walls. And then they grew up, all the sudden. It was like almost overnight. It was confusing to us, especially the girls, because we had in our minds an ideal of what the Beatle boy was like; and when *Sgt. Pepper* came out, that changed." She then placed the record onto her turntable. "I listened to the album start to finish like everybody was doing that day and that week. I loved it. It was hard to get used to in some spots, like with the orchestrations and horns, which they hadn't used that much. It was definitely a different sound. But we loved the story aspect of it, or what we perceived as the story aspect of it, and songs that were very close together or merging; the segues were really close. It was a magical thing. We knew it was the Beatles, but we really kind of bought into that *Sgt. Pepper's Lonely Hearts Club Band* thing, the persona they put on for this record. So, we were looking at it from a slightly different perspective. We weren't looking at it strictly as the Beatles' thing. We were looking at it as the alternate persona of the Beatles."[15]

Sgt. Pepper was a ubiquitous presence in Chicago in the hot, humid summer of 1967. Teenagers lay on their beds listening to the unsettling yet familiar sounds on the revolving disc, examining the cover, trying to make sense of the lyrics. The aural wonderland of *Sgt. Pepper* drifted out of open bedroom windows into the streets and back alleys, while record shops, hairdressing salons, boutiques, bookstores, coffee houses, and craft shops played the record on rotation as the smell of incense filled the air. Katie could not escape hearing the album, not that she wanted to. "When I went to visit the University of Iowa, *Sgt. Pepper* was pouring out of every window that I passed. It was coming out of the dorms. I remember passing a fire station. It was coming out of the fire station. And it was on the radio 24/7 almost. It was like the whole world had stopped and heard the same note at the same time."[16]

The release of *Sgt. Pepper* became a landmark in popular music. The album has spent twenty-eight weeks at the top of the albums chart in the United Kingdom and fifteen weeks at number one in the United States.[17] It cemented the Beatles' place as generational icons. In December 1967,

Newsweek asked its thirty-eight campus correspondents across the US to survey their classmates about their heroes. "The most popular non-ideological idols are the Beatles, particularly John Lennon, and their record *Sgt. Pepper's Lonely Hearts Club Band*," *Newsweek* found.[18] Many still see *Sgt. Pepper* as a cultural milestone. In 1987, *Rolling Stone* named it number one in their Top 100 Albums of the Last 20 Years, and in December 2003, *Rolling Stone* placed it number one in its 500 Greatest Albums of All Time list.[19]

"I find they believe the *Lonely Hearts Band* music has a new, exciting sound, but, more than that, it touches the changing, fitful moods of adolescence today in a world of constant change," Mary Merryfield, columnist for the *Chicago Tribune*, wrote after speaking to a dozen sixteen- to eighteen-year-olds. "Above all," a college freshman told her, "the lyrics fit in with our search for meaning in a pretty complex world. They use drug-oriented words that the hippie uses—the most obvious being the title 'Lucy in the Sky with Diamonds,' that spells out LSD." One girl told Merryfield that the album "puts down the person who is just going about his life, business as usual, too. Shows him as hypocritical or unaware." For one student, "it makes you feel special to understand these lyrics. It's like good poetry that way."

"With a Little Help from My Friends" seemed to have special meaning to many. "Friends are in vogue, sort of tribal units with someone coming in or flowing out, boys and girls together," Ronald Birsa, a freshman at Northern Illinois University, informed Merryfield. "Some pair off, but not so much. More likely you'll have a couple, a girl, and two boys. That's a status quo group today."[20]

Writers like Mary Merryfield believed that *Sgt. Pepper* captured a cultural moment, but for most of those who bought the album, it was simply a collection of rather conventional, melodic sing-along pop tunes. The music may have been more inventive, and the studio gadgetry more prevalent, but the Beatles never alienated their mainstream fans by being too radically complex with their music. There were no extended tracks, no self-indulgent solos, and no experimental pieces. Only "A Day in the Life" could be termed avant-garde, the rest of the songs appealed to parents as well as children. None of the songs dealt with contemporary social issues. The album made no mention of Vietnam, the growing racial problems in the UK, or the inequality that plagued the world; instead, the Beatles highlighted the mundane nature and absurdities of modern life. *Sgt. Pepper* seemed exotic but accessible and safe.

Undeniably, *Sgt. Pepper* helped change the recording industry. The commercial and critical success of the album inspired record labels to devote extra resources into making albums and allowed artists more time in the studio. Before *Sgt. Pepper*, record companies and producers regulated the output of their young artists, but the Beatles inspired other well-known acts to take control of their own destiny by grabbing greater control over the recording process. Musicians now possessed the time and money, and the inspiration of the Beatles, to try new studio techniques; to terminate boundaries between musical styles, and to widen their imaginations. After *Sgt. Pepper*, the music industry divided into those who produced music for listening, mostly found on albums, and music for dancing, mostly found on singles. Partly, but not only, because of *Sgt. Pepper*, rock music increasingly became the subject of serious analysis. The stuffy *Chicago Tribune* began to review rock records and launched a regular music column for young readers, "The Sound."[21] New pop newspapers and magazines appeared on the market to meet the demand for serious-minded writing. *Rolling Stone* was launched in November 1967, *Hullabaloo*, which started in 1966 as a teen magazine, became more serious in its coverage when it changed its name to *Circus* in March 1969, the same month that *Creem* magazine first appeared in the shops. *Jazz* magazine, which began in October 1962, changed its name to *Jazz & Pop* in August 1967 because "1967 has witnessed the birth of a serious American pop music which encompasses jazz, rock, folk and blues," an editorial explained.[22]

The Beatles followed *Sgt. Pepper* with the release of a series of psychedelic-stained counterculturally-aware records. On June 25, 1967, the Beatles and a select group of friends dressed in hippie-style clothes, met at EMI Recording Studios in London, and performed the John Lennon song "All You Need Is Love" in a live global television event to celebrate satellite technology. Over four hundred million people from twenty-four countries watched the program. The Beatles released the song as a single the following month. "All You Need Is Love" quickly became a hippie anthem because of its message of universal love and the communal singing that they similarly used in "With a Little Help from My Friends" and "Yellow Submarine." *Magical Mystery Tour*, released as an album in the

United States in November of 1967, continued the Beatles' psychedelic phase. The album included music from the film of the same name, shown on British TV on Boxing Day, December 26, 1967, and their singles issued earlier in the year. The release of the animated film, *Yellow Submarine*, in the latter part of 1968 and the issue of the album of the same name the following January all but closed out their psychedelic period.

The new musical direction of the Beatles gave other musicians, including some in culturally conservative Chicago, license to experiment and to broaden their musical pallet. Danny Seraphine, drummer with The Big Thing who incarnated into the group Chicago, credited the Beatles with transforming them from a cover band to pioneers of improvisational, horn-driven jazz-rock. "The Beatles had a very profound influence for sure because it was that point *Sgt. Pepper* had hit, and everybody was getting high on *Sgt. Pepper*," he punned. "It was really opening our thought patterns and minds to other music, like Frank Zappa, Cream, and Jimi Hendrix. But the Beatles were kind of at the forefront with *Sgt. Pepper*, really making a statement, musical statement, with the lyrics and the music. We played 'Magical Mystery Tour.' That really changed the band, because it had horns in it."[23] Other Chicago musicians were equally inspired by the Beatles' new output. "When *Sgt. Pepper* hit, I was seriously drinking the Kool-Aid by that time, and that album changed my life," Jim Peterik of the Ides of March remarked. "It actually influenced the Ides of March a great deal to expand our sound. It inspired songs like 'Children' that was on *World Woven*, one of my favorite tracks. We tried to get out of the pop genre a little bit, and it inspired 'Tie-Dye Princess' on *Common Bond*."[24] The Buckinghams was similarly motivated to change their sound from sunshine pop to progressive album-orientated rock. "It influenced us," said Carl Giammarese. "A lot of things we did on that *Portraits* album—*Sgt. Pepper* definitely influenced us when we did that album."[25]

Sgt. Pepper also encouraged new developments in local radio. Deejay Ron Magel, who changed his name to Ron Britain because of his staunch Anglophilia, joined Chicago's WCFL in 1965. Britain visited London in the fall of 1966 where he met Jimi Hendrix, who had just arrived from the US. The ambitious deejay returned to Chicago eager to host a show that featured the innovative music of Hendrix and other album-orientated artists. Britain gained an ally in Allen Shaw, who became the assistant program director at WCFL in February 1966. Shaw, a fan of new rock acts such as the Velvet Underground, Jefferson Airplane, and Vanilla Fudge, found no place on the radio dial to hear the music he loved. "I felt we ought to be playing this somehow on WCFL. We ought to represent it. I remember talking to program director Ken Draper about that idea, and he wasn't wild about it. He was a hit music guy all the way, and a very good one, and he just didn't want to break format by playing some of these long and strange-sounding cuts. We said, 'What if we just did something on a weekend night, or Saturday or Sunday night? Just for a couple of hours play some of these tracks off of these albums, because these groups are beginning to sell very well, and they're just not on the air.' He agreed to give us two hours on Sunday night." On Sunday, October 30, 1966, *Ron Britain's Subterranean Circus* debuted, running from 6-8 p.m. on WCFL.[26] The show was the first to play album-orientated rock on an AM station in Chicago and one of the first in the nation. With the most popular group in the world releasing an album with no singles on it, *Sgt. Pepper* provided an enormous boost to the late-night format pioneered by *Subterranean Circus* and became an inspiration for other Top 40 radio stations to modify their programming.

Sgt. Pepper played an equally important role in aiding FM radio to emerge as an alternative to the AM format. In the '60s, radio stations owned both an AM and FM frequency on the dial. On their money-making AM frequency, stations like WLS and WCFL broadcast a narrow playlist of hit singles, while the less popular FM stations, with their superior sound quality and ability to broadcast in stereo, played classical and jazz or simply carried the same programming as their AM stations. In 1967, however, all this began to change when the Federal Communications Commission imposed a rule that barred the simulcasting of programming. "FM was the perfect solution to the problem of how you get all this music exposed on the radio," said Allen Shaw, who saw an opportunity to play the album-orientated progressive rock ignored on AM daytime programming. "Because FM was doing nothing, it was wide open. None of the FM stations had any audience, so, they had nothing to lose."[27] The replacement of mono with stereo albums, the growing popularity of home Hi-Fi stereo systems, and the increased use of complex studio sounds and technology on records like *Sgt. Pepper,* meant that many preferred the superior sound quality of FM radio. A slightly older demographic was buying albums, not singles, and wanted to hear more natural and intelligent presenters rather than the juvenile deejays heard on Top 40 radio.[28]

The success of *Ron Britain's Subterranean Circus* and the release of *Sgt. Pepper* convinced Allen Shaw at WCFL that radio programming built around album-orientated rock was the future of radio. "I didn't really have a big desire to leave Chicago initially, but I got so convinced that this idea of playing progressive rock albums on FM was absolutely something that has to be done. If I don't do it, somebody else will, because it's such an obvious idea." Many stations refused to

The Seed, February 12, 1968, page 17

The Beatles' music helped to popularize FM radio.

accept the change, including WLS-FM in Chicago. "I actually called on three or four FM station owners in Chicago first before I went to New York," recalled Shaw, who left Chicago in June 1968 and went to work for ABC in New York to program their FM stations. "There was resistance from the general manager at WLS-FM, Gene Taylor. Gene, without even saying it, decided he didn't want to carry any of the things that I was presenting. He wanted to keep what he had. My boss, Hal Neal, president of ABC Radio, finally stepped in and said, 'Allen is now in charge of the programming on all the FM stations, so you got to do what he says.' But it took that to get WLS-FM on board."[29] By the '70s, FM was the undisputed king of American radio.

The Beatles and the Counterculture

The release of *Sgt. Pepper* cemented the Beatles' position as one of the leaders of the counterculture. The counterculture, so-called because it ran counter to the mainstream, was hardly a movement with a unified agenda. It embraced many of those who spurned the restrictions of mainstream society; those who rejected war, organized politics, and work routines; and those who pushed at the boundaries of conventional behavior by embracing mind-altering drugs and sexual promiscuity. Male and female hippies, a term first coined by Beats to refer to the hip or the aware, sported casual clothes, denim jeans, flowered shirts, and long, unkempt hair to signify a rejection of materialism and consumerism. Some hippies may have marched against the Vietnam War or taken part in political action, but most eschewed political involvement, believing that by changing their own behavior, they could make the world a better place. Growing out of the Beat movement of the '50s, the counterculture took hold on the West Coast, particularly in the San Francisco area where activists organized a Human Be-In in January 1967. The event gained extensive media coverage, bringing the ideas of the counterculture to the rest of the United States, encouraging similar events in other cities, and leading to tens of thousands of young people descending on San Francisco during the Summer of Love.

Undoubtedly, the epicenter of the counterculture remained in San Francisco, but a hippie enclave developed in the Old Town neighborhood on Chicago's North Side. Lined with restaurants, bookstores, art galleries, coffee houses, boutiques, craft shops, and nightspots playing folk, blues, jazz, and rock music, Old Town was similar to Greenwich Village in New York and the Haight-Ashbury district in San Francisco. "Old Town is full of conflict, full of life; a sometimes maddening but always exciting place to live," stated Richard Atcheson in *Holiday* magazine in March 1967. The historic area was "probably the most amusing [as in entertaining] neighborhood in the country. It may be, in fact, depending on one's residential proclivities, the nicest place in the world," Atcheson concluded.[30] A guide to Chicago, published in 1968, described Old Town as "six blocks of complete physical and mental derangement."[31]

Out of this milieu emerged several countercultural newspapers, the most successful being *The Seed*. Begun in May 1967 by Don Lewis and Earl Segal, owners of a poster and button shop called the Mole Hole in Old Town, *The Seed's* content was a cross between San Francisco's groundbreaking countercultural *Oracle* newspaper and the left-wing periodicals that had a long history in Chicago. Its covers were provocative, its writing irreverent, and its visuals a mix of psychedelic and surrealistic graphics. The first issue featured a picture of a naked woman on the front cover, and the September 1968 issue included an image of a pig dressed in a Chicago police uniform. The paper advertised concerts, art shows, and literary talks, and published poems and short stories. *The Seed*, and the counterculture in general, exhibited a harder, more political edge in Chicago than it did on the West Coast, as editorials constantly railed against the war, police harassment, and Mayor Daley. Sold by volunteers on street corners and in coffee houses and bookstores, *The Seed* reached a circulation of thirty to forty thousand per issue. [32]

Abe Peck, the editor of *The Seed*, was born in New York in January 1945 and arrived in Chicago in 1967 to work as a textbook rep after dropping out of college and spending time in California. Peck wrote his first article for *The Seed* in October 1967 under the name Abraham Yippie and soon became the editor of the paper. To Peck, the counterculture embraced many different ideas. "It was a confluence. It was the civil rights movement; it was the war, it was rock 'n' roll, it was LSD, you had all these rivulets flowing into a river. People had different accents on where they were at on this stuff," Peck recalled. "But our influences were really Lenny Bruce, Surrealists. I'm talking specifically about *The Seed*. The Music, Tim Leary, Herman Hesse. There were some literary ones, Orwell and stuff like that, a little more recently Thomas Pynchon, and Ken Kesey was a real transitional figure. Those were more the countercultural kind of people that we were into." Peck saw *The Seed* and the counterculture in the US as part of a wider international configuration. "Many, many people started seeing us not as hippies, but as internationalists. If you went internationalist, you weren't alone. You were part of the anti-colonial movements of hundreds of millions of people. You were the people in France, you were the people in Prague, you were the IT [*International Times*, a counterculture journal in England] people. You were part of something much, much bigger. So when Paris happened, for example, in May of '68, that was us. In many ways, we were different from some people, more political or something, but that was us. And there was a sense that the walls of the city were shaking." [33]

The Seed organized Chicago's first be-in at North Avenue Beach on Mother's Day, May 14, 1967. Some early birds arrived on a cold spring morning to watch the sunrise while most reached the beach at a more civilized time after lunch. Griffith Harter Union, the Little Boy Blues, the Dirty Wurds, and Mike Bloomfield performed to the crowd of 3,500 "hippies, would-be hippies and curious spectators," reported the *Tribune*.

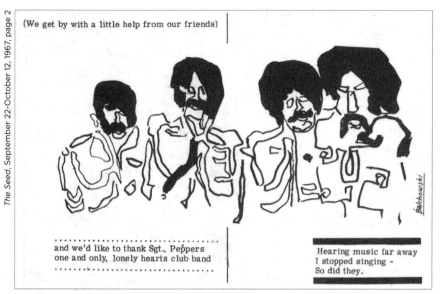

The Seed, September 22–October 12, 1967, page 2

(We get by with a little help from our friends)

and we'd like to thank Sgt. Peppers
one and only, lonely hearts club band

Hearing music far away
I stopped singing –
So did they.

The Seed *gives respect to Sgt. Pepper and the Beatles.*

Participants "had painted their faces with flowers" and wore "dandelions and paper flowers in their hair.... Costumes ranged from zoot suits to army fatigue jackets, togas, Arabian clothing, an old shirt lettered in the back 'property of Joliet State penitentiary,' and even a Cub Scout cap and neckerchief and gingham dress which a tall man wore over his Levis."[34] The police called an end to proceedings at 5 p.m., and the crowd drifted away, leaving behind balloons, kites, and flowers littering the beach.[35] Buoyed by the success of the event, *Seed* organized more be-ins over the summer and fall of 1967. With a substantial student population in the city, the events drew large crowds. Unlike in other US cities, Chicago remained riot-free throughout 1967, which added to the relatively peaceful ambiance in the city.

The leading countercultural nightclub, the Electric Theater (soon renamed the Kinetic Playground), opened in April 1968 in the Uptown neighborhood on the North Side of the city. "Chicago lags behind New York and San Francisco in contemporary music," owner Aaron Russo told *Billboard*. "Our idea is to educate the patrons and promote contemporary music." With a capacity of 2,500, the club cost $300,000 to build and featured "25 carousel projectors, nine 16mm movie projectors, nine overhead projectors and seven strobe mechanisms," casting psychedelic patterns and pictures on the graffiti-stained walls.³⁶ After paying their entrance fee, patrons passed through a maze of mirrors and into an open room of hipsters sitting cross-legged on the floor or dancing to the psychedelic sounds. The Kinetic Playground sold no alcohol, but patrons could score an assortment of drugs from the dealers who stalked the dark subterranean premises. Like the Fillmore in San Francisco, the venue booked up-and-coming rock acts such as Pink Floyd, Led

To celebrate the release of Sgt. Pepper, The Seed July–August 1967 issue, featured George Harrison on the cover.

Zeppelin, Jethro Tull, and Deep Purple from the UK and West Coast bands like Jefferson Airplane, Grateful Dead, and the Doors.³⁷ The venue also held benefits for local community organizations including *The Seed*.

Through their appearance, pronouncements, record sleeves, and songs, the Beatles became a central influence on the counterculture as they connected with the hippies that congregated in Old Town, with the readers of *The Seed,* and with the dancers at the Kinetic Playground. The crowded picture on the front cover of *Sgt. Pepper* played into the countercultural desire, exemplified by the be-ins, to share a communal experience. The marijuana plants and countercultural figures on the cover openly signaled the group's attachment to countercultural values. Songs like "With a Little Help From My Friends" and "Lucy in the Sky with Diamonds," which seemed to allude to a drug trip, strongly resonated with hippies and fellow travelers. The concept of romantic love was a theme in early Beatles songs, but with "The Word," included on the *Rubber Soul* album, and the single "All You Need Is Love," they preached a message of universal love. When the Beatles and their friends dressed in hippie-style flowery clothes and sang "All You Need Is Love" on the *Our World* TV broadcast in June 1967, they captured the spirit of the Summer of Love and the hippie ideal. "I think people tuned in on them as kind of messengers," ventured Abe Peck, indicating how the Beatles' music became an emblem of the countercultural cause so many held dear. "Kind of the State of the Union in a way of global, hip community. I think they were seen as really just, no pun intended, in the groove of exactly what was going on. *Sgt. Pepper* was seen as an acid marker. People would treat this as like the Talmud. It was revelatory. It was like acid on vinyl."[38]

The Seed, January 1968, page 1

The Seed *shows the world their heroes and villains in January 1968.*

Venues frequented by the countercultural crowd, like the Kinetic Playground, began to screen the Beatles' movie, *Magical Mystery Tour.* Shops in Old Town sold Beatles posters and their album sleeves adorned the walls. The language of *Sgt. Pepper* permeated countercultural publications such as *The Seed* and its rival in Chicago, *Fred*, which used the heading "With a Little Help From Our Friends" for their Notices section.[39] In recognition of their elevated status in the counterculture, *The Seed* devoted more space to the Beatles than to any other musical act. Images of the Beatles in Sgt. Pepper-like uniforms, long tresses, and facial hair, as well as lines from their songs, regularly graced its pages. While *Seed* journalists criticized the latest releases from the darlings of the West Coast scene such as the Doors and Jefferson Airplane, all mentions of the Beatles remained invariably positive. *The Seed* printed a George Harrison interview, which the English paper *International Times*

Kaleidoscope Chicago, March 14–27, 1969, page 17

The Beatles may not have performed in Chicago after the summer of 1966, but they were still very much part of the countercultural scene.

had previously published, as if he were a visionary spreading his wisdom to the world.[40]

Distrust of Authority

The counterculture influenced the Beatles and vice versa but, in essence, the philosophy of the four Beatles paralleled that of the hippie movement. John, Paul, George, and Ringo all became musicians because they detested the idea of working for someone else in a conventional job. They disliked taking orders and despised authority figures. "The worst thing was leaving the junior school and going to the big grammar school," recalled Harrison, who with Lennon became the Beatle most closely associated with the counterculture and the most contemptuous of authority. "That's when the darkness began and I realized it was raining and cloudy with old streets and backward teachers and all of that, and that is where my frustrations seemed to start. You would punch people just to get it out of your system…. Be here, stand there, shut up, sit down and always you need those exams, those eleven-plus exams, or scholarships or GCE. That's when the darkness came in. I didn't like school. I think it was awful; the worst time of your life."[41] Harrison maintained his contempt for teachers into his adult years. "I wouldn't let [my child] go to school," he grumpily stated in 1967. "I'm not letting fascist teachers put things into the child's head. I'd get an Indian guru to teach him—and me, too."[42]

The four Beatles held a special disdain for politicians. "The trouble with government as it is," Lennon told Ray Coleman in the spring of 1966, "is that it doesn't represent the people. It controls them. All they seem to want to do - the people who run the country - is keep themselves in power and stop us knowing what's going on." Lennon despised both Labour and Conservative parties equally. "From what you hear, none of the politicians has any intention of giving ordinary people complete freedom. Just keep them down—that's all they really want." Lennon possessed a cynical view of the intentions of all politicians. "They're politicians because they want power. What we need to change things is a bloody revolution."[43] The Beatles often articulated a libertarian position on the relationship between individuals and the state. In October 1969, Lennon told *Penthouse* magazine of his distrust of government. "Just the idea that the individual is capable of looking after himself, that we don't need centralized government, that we don't need father-figures and leaders.... Government was an invention that I think didn't work."[44] Harrison, too, voiced contempt for any form of governmental authority. "You've got to get them hip to all this government bull, all the governments, all the religions, and all that bull that's been going on and on and on, and it'll just keep going on and on and on unless we hip the people," he opined in 1968. "I'm not trying to get a riot going or anything, just a bit of peace and a bit of respect, instead of some fellow sticking out a gun and telling you where to go and what to do, when to pay, and so forth. That's why much of what's going on in San Francisco is great, it's just to show those fellows, 'stuff it, we can do what we want.'"[45]

"They can't make anything work. Buses, trains. None of them work," Ringo told Beatles' biographer Hunter Davies in 1967. "Everything the Government does turns to crap, not gold. The railways made profits when they were private firms, didn't they? It's like Victorian England, our Government. Outdated."[46]

Free Love

All four of the Beatles embraced one of the most discussed and sensationalized aspects of hippie culture, free love. Each had multiple sex partners and paid little heed to prevailing views on monogamy. Fame and life on the road were tests for any dedicated boyfriend or husband, but the Beatles dismally failed the tests as they cheated on wives and girlfriends on a regular and casual basis.[47] They hid much of their touring exploits from public view, but they were more open about their sexual relationships than other public figures of the time. In May 1964, at the height of their fame, Harrison took a vacation in Honolulu with his then-girlfriend Pattie Boyd and with John Lennon and his wife Cynthia, while McCartney and Starr vacationed with their teenage girlfriends, Jane Asher and Maureen Cox, in the Virgin Islands. The British tabloid *Sunday Mirror* was shocked that "even in this with-it age, the golden age of the teenager," that seventeen-year-old Maureen Cox would vacation with twenty-three-year-old Ringo. The newspaper asked her father if he approved of her going on holiday with her boyfriend, and he told them that he had "no qualms," which led to the headline "Seventeen—she's on a month-long holiday with a Beatle. And Maureen's Dad Says 'Why Not?'[48] *Confidential,* an American gossip magazine, broke the same scandalous news to a stunned US public in September 1964 when it ran the headline, "London's Hottest Scandal: Named: The teen-age girls two Beatles took to the Virgin Islands."[49] The first wives of John, Paul, and Ringo were pregnant before they married. George and his first wife, Pattie Boyd, never conceived; but not to be left out, George's second wife, Olivia, gave birth to a son, Dhani, a month before they married in 1978.

While the media condemned the infidelities of Britain's Secretary of State for War, John Profumo, whose affair with a teenage girl gained saturation coverage in the press in 1963, Paul defended the married politician's errant behavior. Profumo was "just an ordinary fellow who sleeps with women. Yet it's adultery in the eyes of the law, and it's an international incident. But in actual fact, if you check up on the statistics, you find that there are hardly any married men who've been completely faithful to their wives." Paul condemned the "Puritan" media for its coverage of the affair and its criticism of Profumo. "But, in actual fact, if you ask the average Briton what they really think of the Profumo case, they'd probably say, 'He was knockin' off some bird. So what?'"[50]

The Beatles' embrace of free love did not extend to allowing their partners the same sexual license. "The northern male chauvinism was quite strong in the group," Cynthia Lennon wrote in her memoirs. "The Beatles were very happy to have their women subservient in the background." They wanted their wives and girlfriends "to be seen and not heard. Very Victorian and totally different to the lives they themselves led and the temptations they succumbed to whilst on tour. It was a question of 'don't do as I do but do as I say,' and we did."[51] The four bachelor Beatles persuaded girlfriends to dye their hair and wear short skirts so that they looked like their fantasy figure of Brigitte Bardot. None of the Beatles wanted their wives to pursue careers, and when Jane Asher continued to work as an actor, it caused friction between her and Paul. "I don't think women like to be equal," Ringo told Hunter Davies. "They like to be protected and in turn they like looking after men."[52] Lennon, who admitted to a history of hitting women, wrote the songs "Run For Your Life" and "You Can't Do That," both of which issued dark threats to straying girlfriends.[53]

Drugs

The Beatles' drug use further tied them to the counterculture. They indulged in amphetamines in their early days, gravitated to marijuana as they rose to fame, and then embraced LSD. The Beatles did not just ingest drugs; they publicly discussed their drug use. "After I took it, it opened my eyes," a *Life* magazine article entitled "The New Far-Out Beatles" quoted Paul's view of LSD in June 1967. "We only use one-tenth of our brain. Just think what all we could accomplish if we could only tap that hidden part! It would mean a whole new world. If the politicians would take LSD, there wouldn't be any more war, or poverty or famine."[54] Paul defended his use of LSD in a British television interview with ITN evening news, and all four Beatles signed a petition to legalize marijuana, which the *Times* published on July 24, 1967. The Beatles wrote songs that contained implicit if not explicit references to drugs. "A song like 'Got to Get You Into My Life,' that's directly about pot, although everyone missed it at the time," Paul McCartney admitted years later. "'Day Tripper,' that's one about acid. 'Lucy in the Sky,' that's pretty obvious. There's others that make subtle hints about drugs." During the recording of *Sgt. Pepper* "we were all into one thing or another.... I did coke for about a year around that time."[55] John was prosecuted for drug possession in October 1968 and George in March the following year. Even years later, George Harrison spoke of the benefits of LSD. "I can't imagine, if I hadn't had it, how many years of normal life it would have taken to get me to the realizations: I might've never got them in this life," he told *Creem* magazine in 1988. "It just opened the door and I experienced really good things. I mean, I never doubted God after that. Before I was a cynic. I didn't even say the word God; I thought 'bullshit to all that stuff.' But after that, I *knew*. It was not even a question of 'Is there possibly a God?'—I knew absolutely."[56]

The Beatles' drug taking coincided with an increase in drug use in the United States. "On campus after campus, scandal and denials follow the revelation that students are 'turning on,'" Richard Goldstein wrote in the *Saturday Evening Post* after he undertook a major investigation into drug use on the college campuses in 1966. "Administrators deny it, and alumni doubt it. But the police know about it. Health officials and school psychiatrists are aware of it. The students themselves are not only sure it exists but they can usually tell you where to find the action."[57] In December 1970, a Gallup poll based on interviews with 1,062 college students on sixty-one campuses found that 42 percent of respondents had tried marijuana. The figure was almost double that for 1969 and eight times higher than for 1967. Some 14 percent had tried LSD in 1970 compared to only 4 percent in 1969.[58] "Drug arrests set record in 7 suburbs," the *Chicago Tribune* noted in October 1968. "The kids tell us marijuana is all over the place," said suburban Wilmette police chief Harold Graf.[59] In November 1968, William Hopf, state's attorney for suburban DuPage County, suggested that four years prior, there was "almost no drug problem here." In 1966, however, twenty-four people were indicted and prosecuted for drug offenses, and in 1967, the number tripled.[60]

It would not be too far a stretch to suggest that the Beatles' drug taking not only coincided with the increased use among young people but also influenced some into experimenting with drugs in the first place. The Beatles may not have encouraged people to take drugs, though some of the fans thought they did, but they certainly legitimized their use. Fans paid close attention to their idols' lifestyles, studied their lyrics, and listened to their every pronouncement. Sue Trusty, nineteen when she saw the Beatles in concert in Chicago in 1966, was typical of many fans who copied the Beatles. "I even started smoking because all the Beatle people smoked, and I wanted to fit in. I smoked for twelve years, yeah, but you know, that was part of the sophistication that I was striving for."[61] Although most fans refused to follow the Beatles into using mind-altering drugs, some admitted that they did. One male fan, who was seventeen when the Beatles released *Sgt. Pepper*, told interviewer Candy Leonard that "Lucy in the Sky with Diamonds" influenced his drug taking. "If nothing else got you interested in trying pot or LSD, that would." Another female fan who was a teenager in the late 1960s told Leonard: "LSD never interested me, but pot did. I would attribute that to the Beatles."[62]

In the summer of 1967, the Beatles publicly announced that they had stopped taking drugs, even if they carried on taking them in private. "It was an experience we went through, and now it's over," Paul told an interviewer in August 1967. "We don't need it any more."[63] In a television interview undertaken the following month, John and George said that they had ceased dabbling in drugs. "We dropped them long before the Maharishi. We'd had enough acid. It had done all it could for us," Lennon said. "There was no going any further."[64]

"I don't need LSD any more. I can get high smelling a bloomin' flower," Harrison stated in January 1968, but along with the other Beatles he stopped short at condemning their use. "In this connection, perhaps the Beatles' most significant recent announcement is that LSD and mysticism don't mix," *Look* magazine suggested in January 1968. "They were made Members of the Order of the British Empire for being 'a national asset' (all those records sold abroad) in 1965. For damning drugs, they should be knighted."[65]

India

A fascination with Indian culture was another factor that attached the Beatles to the counterculture. The Beatles', and particularly George Harrison's, interest in India began in April 1965 when Indian musicians hired for a scene in their film *Help!* introduced Harrison to the sitar.[66] David Crosby of the Byrds claims that he introduced Harrison to Ravi Shankar's music in August 1965. "I had a Ravi Shankar record in my bag when I went to London one time and I gave it to George. George said to people that I had turned him on to Indian music."[67] Crosby's partner, Roger McGuinn, recalled it differently, suggesting that it happened when the Beatles met the Byrds in Los Angeles later in August 1965. "So we told George and John about Indian music. We showed them the licks and they were blown away. They loved it. I guess I also helped them get into Eastern religion, which was strange too. I remember asking George if he believed in God, and he said, 'Well, we don't know about that yet.'"[68] Either way, Harrison became infatuated with Shankar and learned to play the sitar, which he then added to *Rubber Soul*'s "Norwegian Wood." He subsequently used Indian musicians on *Revolver*'s "Love You To" and *Sgt. Peppers*' "Within You Without You;" he also played the sitar and tambura on "Tomorrow Never Knows." George eventually met Shankar in June 1966 at a party he attended as a guest of the Asian Music Circle in London.[69]

Harrison, more than the others, used his worldwide fame to promote Indian music. "You might include this in your article," he told a startled *Detroit Free Press* reporter in August 1966. "For anyone who likes music a lot and has a good understanding of it, let me suggest they listen to Indian classical music," Harrison said, warming to his task. "I'd like to see more people interested in it, honestly interested. Not just to cash in on the sitar boom. On 'Norwegian Wood' on the *Rubber Soul* album I used the sitar like a guitar. On the new album I developed it a little bit. But I'm far from the goal I want to achieve. It will take me 40 years to get there. I'd like to be able to play Indian music as Indian music instead of using Indian music in pop," he continued. "It takes years of studying, but I'm willing to do that." The reporter, Loraine Alterman, like others, was impressed with what she heard. "George's passion for Indian music is so catching he made me want to hear Shankar play right then and there."[70]

There was already a growing interest in India among countercultural devotees in the Western world, but the Beatles undoubtedly popularized South Asian music among a wider audience. Harrison helped make Shankar famous across the globe, and Shankar, in turn, was delighted with the exposure the Beatles brought to India. He was one of the very few non-Western musicians who toured the United States performing in front of young white audiences, and he appeared at the Monterey

International Pop *Festival* in June 1967 along with the luminaries of the British and American rock fraternity.

The Beatles' interest stretched beyond the music as they became interested in India's culture and religion. They first visited India in July 1966 on their way back from their disastrous trip to the Philippines. In September of the same year, Harrison and Pattie Boyd traveled to India and spent six weeks studying yoga. The Beatles started to wear the Nehru jacket, named after Indian Prime Minister Jawaharlal Nehru, which had a straight stand-up collar and a lapel-less button front, together with madras-patterned shirts, beads, and sandals. Among the celebrities and cultural icons featured on the cover of the *Sgt. Pepper* album, are four Indian spiritual figures. The cover also included a figurine of the Hindu goddess Lakshmi. EMI dissuaded the Beatles from including Mahatma Gandhi on the cover in case it gave offense in India.[71] In the summer of 1967, Harrison made his second Indian connection when his wife Pattie saw the Indian guru Maharishi Mahesh Yogi give a talk in London and persuaded George, Paul, and John, to come to hear him speak. Shortly after, all four Beatles were Maharishi's guests at a retreat in Wales; and in February 1968, they journeyed to India to stay with him and study transcendental meditation (TM). "It may have been the most momentous spiritual retreat since Jesus spent those forty days in the wilderness," author Philip Goldberg proposed.[72]

Their attraction to Indian culture led to the Beatles becoming vegetarians at a time when it was virtually unheard of in the West. George was first. "George had been talking about it, and it had been going through my mind, anyway, for a long time," John said in December 1967. "I just started looking at this meat on my plate and I thought: 'Why?'"[73] Paul was probably already dabbling in vegetarianism on their visit to India in February 1968. "I occasionally eat meat," Paul said in December 1967. "John and George feel more like vegetarians than me, but I'm a sympathizer."[74] Ringo, too, adopted a vegetarian diet. He told *Disc and Music Echo* that all four jointly committed to vegetarianism and even veganism before they went to India. "I still eat eggs, but that's about all in that line. I suppose it would be better to call us fruit-atarians than anything else."[75] Beatles biographer Hunter Davies recalls that when he invited Ringo to his house for dinner, Ringo phoned Davies beforehand to remind him that he was a vegetarian. "So my wife bustled around getting and cooking proper vegetarian dishes. Ringo left them all. His idea of being a vegetarian was eating fried eggs and baked beans on toast."[76]

It is easy to see why India would appeal to the Beatles and those immersed in the hippie culture in the West. Westerners saw the Indian people as peaceful, non-materialistic, and contented, everything that those in the counterculture aspired to be. India's music, fashion, and religious beliefs were exotic compared to staid traditional Western culture. While other religions imposed rather rigid guidelines on followers and developed authoritarian institutions, Hinduism appealed to those, like the Beatles, who refused to adhere to strict rules and who sought an individual path to enlightenment.

The Beatles' adoption of Indian culture came at a time when there was little respect for South Asian culture in the West, emphasizing again their enlightened perspective on race. The media and British society in general ignored India's rich history and ridiculed their food, language, and religious beliefs. Newly arrived South Asian immigrants faced hostility. Racist thugs attacked them on the streets in what they called "Paki-bashing," while conservative politicians and far-right organizations called for a halt to nonwhite immigration and the expulsion of those already in the UK. In an interview broadcast on US television in May 1968, John and Paul condemned the racism of Enoch Powell, the conservative politician who had predicted racial strife in Britain and called for a halt to immigration. "We sow what we reap, or whatever it is," John rambled about those who had called for a halt to immigration. "And Britain is paying for what it did to all those countries. And to say, 'Keep out,' is just barking in the garden, you know. Because whatever is going to happen will happen like that." Paul was more forceful and articulate: "You know those people; they don't know a thing. They just hate."[77] Paul wanted to put these thoughts down on record. The early version of "Get Back" satirized Powell and those who wanted to repatriate nonwhites from Britain, but the group decided to abandon the idea of making a protest song and rewrote the lyrics.[78]

Of the four Beatles, Harrison was the most earnest about his love of Indian culture. Alan Smith of the NME compared George and John in June 1968 after their dabbling in meditation. George exhibited "almost that look of holy inner calm (together with a nice, mellow sense of humour) that wouldn't disgrace the most devout of monks." The benefits of TM were less evident on Lennon. "I'm not sure whether it's done anything at all for John. He still looks like the old gum-chewing 'ard case to me. And the way he always seems ready to clobber his enemies, with a few well-chosen words of vitriol, still frightens me off the way it used to."[79] In an interview with *Queen* magazine in July 1967, Paul sounded remarkably like George when he pronounced that "God is in everything. God is in the space between us. God is in that table in front of you. God is everything and everywhere and everyone."[80] A year later, however, Paul seemed less than spiritual when talking about the launch of their new Apple Corps venture. "No, starvation in India doesn't worry me one bit," he told Alan Smith, who wanted to know if the Beatles should give their money to the poor in India rather than to other artists through Apple. "Not one iota. It doesn't man. And it doesn't worry you, if you're honest. You just pose…. If it comes to a toss-up, and getting a new car, you'd get a new car. And don't say you wouldn't—'cos that's the scene, with you and most people."[81]

Harrison helped the Krishna movement to establish itself in the West. In August 1969, Apple Records released the Harrison produced single "Hare Krishna Mantra," the chant sung by devotees at the Radha Krishna Temple in London. George invited *The Beatles Book* to meet the members of the Temple. "I'm just bringing them to the attention of the public," George told the magazine. "If they like them, well and good; if not, it's not for me to say they're wrong."[82] George's patronage seemed to have some effect. The song reached number twelve in the UK and chanting Krishna devotees became a ubiquitous sight on the streets of Central London.[83] "A few months back no one would have taken much notice as they walked up and down Oxford Street with their bald or semi-bald heads and Indian robes, rattling their tambourines and asking passers-by to contribute money for their London temple," *Rave* noted about Hare Krishna. "Today, thanks to George Harrison and Apple, they have a more sophisticated means of catching the attention."[84]

"Are you deliberately using the power of the Beatles to spread the word about transcendental meditation?" journalist and deejay Annie Nightingale asked Lennon in October 1967. "Yes, because we've never felt like this about anything else," he answered unequivocally. "We want the younger generation, especially, to know about it. It's for everyone."[85]

"I go a lot on transcendental meditation—I wish we'd heard about it before we ever went on those tours," Lennon told *Disc and Music Echo* in September 1967. "We got little sleep and some form of mental relaxation is what we missed. Now we know this form of meditation could have helped a lot. This meditation can be used by everyone. It isn't just because we have the freedom that we can do it—people in 9 to 5 jobs can use it, because it can be done any time, and it can help people unwind and do their jobs properly."[86]

On his return from India, Ringo told the world about the benefits of meditation, promising: "if you spend a short while in the mornings and evenings meditating, it completely relaxes you—and it's easier to see your way through problems. If everyone in the world started meditating, then the world would be a much happier place, and there would be less wars and things."[87] The Beatles appeared on television shows in the UK and the US publicizing their new passion. "If just one in every thousand viewers who watched the program was encouraged to look into transcendental meditation then it was well worth doing," John commented after he and George appeared on *The Frost Programme* in October 1967, the second appearance the two had made on the show in a week extolling the virtues of TM. "We want to get the message across to as many people as possible that meditation can help everyone."[88] Lennon and McCartney used their appearance on NBC's *The Tonight Show* broadcast on May 14, 1968, to persuade people to meditate. John told host Joe Garagiola that "meditation is good, and it does what they say. It's like exercise or cleaning your teeth."[89]

When the Beatles spoke, the media listened. Articles appeared on Maharishi Mahesh Yogi in leading newspapers and magazines, and books on his life and beliefs hit the shelves. Art Unger's *Teen Datebook* particularly took the Beatles' pronouncements to heart. In the spring of 1967, the magazine published an interview with George. "I'm not a Christian," he proclaimed, but "I'm very religious."[90] In December, *Teen Datebook* featured a competition in which the winners received a Beatles Indian bead necklace "just like the ones they wear when they visit their favorite swami. If you're hip on what's happening around us, and you want to join the Beatles in meditation, just fill in the coupon." The magazine openly pushed the Beatles' ideas on Indian spirituality. "Remember, the Beatles want to help you learn all about eastern philosophy."[91] In May

1968, the same magazine published a two-page article, "George Tells You All About Meditation," in which Harrison discussed the benefits of TM with Art Unger.[92]

The Beatles' advocacy of Indian culture had some effect, as Americans adopted Indian fashions, registered for yoga and transcendental meditation classes, and dabbled in the Hindu religion. Karma became a commonly used word, and some young people traveled to South Asia as part of their own spiritual journey.[93] "Their announced intention of following the Maharishi Mahesh Yogi to his Academy of Meditation in Kashmir may do more for India's economy than foreign aid," *Look* stated in January 1968. "Brass bells, saris and slim, high-collared Indian shirts are already *de rigueur* gear for the young in Britain and America. A new kind of meditation has become the vogue.... Hindu dancing lessons are 'in.' The kids are burning incense while they do their homework."[94] In January 1971, the International Meditation Society claimed that sixty thousand Americans practiced Maharishi's meditation methods, and the number of meditators had doubled in each of the last four years.[95]

The influence of Indian culture was most pronounced among students and hippies in California, but South Asian styles evidently inspired some young people in the Chicago area. Newspapers in rural Illinois like the *Morris Daily Herald* and the *Alton Evening Telegraph,* not the most obvious of advocates of countercultural values, featured articles on Indian music.[96] The student newspaper for Mundelein College, a private Roman Catholic women's college in Chicago, noted: "a new fad for a century-old sound has been implanted on campuses all over the country. The steep rise in the Indian music craze is related chiefly to two other factors which are not necessarily connected yet widely associated with it: drugs and the new Beatles.... The enormous success of the *Sgt. Pepper* album, not so much to teen-agers as to the college segment, illustrates that the Beatles have brought a popular, sophisticated sound of Indian music to the West."[97]

"A lot of the crusader cats who rushed to the pawnshops and music stores at the beginning of the Beatles' invasion of 1964 to trade in their old trumpets, clarinets, and saxes for a shiny new electric guitar, are starting to do pretty much the same thing, except this time they're trading in 'one' of their guitars and a couple of bucks and getting a flute, or a sax, or even a sitar," an article in *The Seed* stated in 1967.[98] It was no coincidence that Nikhil Banerjee, a sitar player from India, became the first non-Western musician to perform at Northwestern University in October 1967.[99] "They all know who Ravi Shankar is," a surprised *Chicago Tribune* columnist Mary Merryfield found when she talked to a group of teenagers in the summer of 1967. "They know how Shankar is steeped in yoga and discipline and spiritual exercise and that he doesn't like to see drug-using hippies lead the lives they do. Some of them even quote the Swami Satchidananda of the Integral Yoga Institute at 500 West End Ave. in New York."[100]

The Beatles' advocacy of Indian culture similarly led to an upsurge of interest in Indian religion and philosophy in the Chicago area. Books on eastern religions, especially Alan Watts' series on Buddhism, became popular reading material. "Chicago bookstores and libraries report they can't keep them, especially Watts' 'The Way of Zen,' on the shelves," Mary Merryfield reported in March 1968.[101] Devotees of Hare Krishna, sporting shaved heads, yellow and orange clothing, and shaking cymbals and chanting, started to become a common sight on the streets. Disciples established Chicago's first Krishna temple in a Halsted Street storefront in 1970. The temple moved to suburban Evanston before settling into its home in far north Rogers Park in 1979.[102] Articles appeared in newspapers outlining, even in a superficial way, the ideas of meditation.[103] In January 1971, the *Tribune* reported that more than 1,200 Chicagoans had practiced the methods of the Maharishi since it came to the Midwest two years previously.[104]

Yoga, another Indian import, grew in popularity. Earlier in the century, yoga instructors from India journeyed to Chicago, and by the mid-'60s, the local YMCAs and Park Districts started running yoga classes for the devoted few. The advocacy of George Harrison introduced more young people to the discipline. "I started doing yoga in 1968 at age 26," recalled Sharon Steffensen, editor and publisher of *Yoga Chicago*. "My mother had a friend who was taking a yoga class at the YMCA, and she told me she thought I'd like it. I went there for the physical benefits of hatha yoga, and the teacher introduced us to meditation and told us about the Temple of Kriya Yoga in downtown Chicago. I started going there for meditation and philosophy. I was a Beatles fan and was also into the Indian sitar music, which George played. I remember playing Ravi Shankar while doing yoga. The Beatles' music, especially George, definitely influenced me and many others toward spirituality, Indian philosophy, and, of course, yoga. At that time, I was a seeking a spiritual path because I no longer related to the Christian church of my childhood. I was delighted to know that yoga was a spiritual path I could accept and embrace."[105] By February 1970, the *Tribune* featured a twelve-part series on the benefits of hatha yoga, an ancient practice that can turn anyone "into the kind of person our modern-day culture has come to glorify and idealize."[106] When the yoga devotees staged their first major event in Chicago, the Yoga Festival of Joy, at McCormick Place in 1972, one of the organizers of the gathering, the wonderfully named Becky Love, recalled that they never thought they would fill such a large space. "We pushed the chairs closer to the front so it wouldn't look so empty. But when hundreds of people started pouring in, I knew there was nothing to worry about."[107]

Peace and Love

All four Beatles talked of their desire for peace but John Lennon became the greatest exponent of pacifism after he met Japanese avant-garde artist Yoko Ono in London in November 1966. Forever restless and impatient, moving swiftly from one interest to another, the besotted Lennon left his wife, Cynthia, and their young son, Julian, and moved in with Yoko. Yoko calmed some of his aggressive tendencies, introduced him to feminism, reignited artistic ambitions that had lay dormant since he left the Liverpool College of Art, and taught Lennon that art could be a fun public spectacle. The lovebirds courted publicity and overtook Richard Burton and Elizabeth Taylor as the most famous celebrity couple in the world. In November 1968, John and Yoko appeared naked on the cover of their *Unfinished Music No. 1: Two Virgins* LP. When asked why he and Yoko would want the world to see their less than model-like frames, Lennon merely replied: "Truth. We're all naked baby, and ain't that news? And isn't it about time we faced up to it?"[108] If the sight of John and Yoko's genitals wasn't bad enough, a bigger shock lay in store for those fans who bought the album, took it home, and expected Beatles-style harmonies and melodies, only to find self-indulgent noise. John and Yoko followed this up with *Unfinished Music No. 2: Life with the Lions,* where listeners were treated to the heartbeats of their (soon to miscarry) baby followed by two minutes of silence. A third, and mercifully final, experimental album, the *Wedding Album,* included a track in which John and Yoko recited each other's names in a variety of tones and styles for an excruciating twenty-two minutes and forty-one seconds.

"We changed music and short hair and dancing and clothes," commented John Lennon in 1969 on the early impact of the Beatles. "Now what we want to do is change people's minds as well, and change the way they think. If we can do that, then we will have succeeded in changing

Two Virgins. I've kept the brown paper bag over the cover of the album to avoid offending delicate readers.

the pattern of life."[109] To this end, John and Yoko engaged in a series of public events promoting peace. In their first outing in June 1968, they planted acorns for peace at Coventry Cathedral. On July 1, at a joint art show in London, they sent 365 balloons into the air, each containing a card for the finder to send a comment to the Robert Fraser Gallery. The couple married in Gibraltar in March 1969 and spent their honeymoon engaged in a public Bed-In for Peace at a hotel in Amsterdam. Then the couple conducted a press conference in Vienna while sitting in a large white bag. At the end of May, they held another Bed-In in Montreal, where they recorded "Give Peace a Chance," which John and Yoko released under the name the Plastic Ono Band in the summer of 1969. A Bed-In "focuses attention on world peace, and sets an example to people about various methods of protesting against violence," Lennon told the press. "Do something about it, is what we're saying, and give peace a chance. It draws attention to peace, via us."[110] In November 1969, Lennon returned his MBE "in protest against Britain's involvement in the Nigeria-Biafra thing, against our support of America in Vietnam" but then added flippantly "and against 'Cold Turkey' slipping down the charts, referring to the recent single by the Plastic Ono Band."[111]

Their campaign for peace illustrated Lennon's long-held distrust of political engagement. He told *Penthouse* that he was against participating in politics to further his quest for peace because "you've got to play games—political games like compromise." Marching, he told the interviewer, was "outmoded. It was all right for our forefathers to protest, to march; it worked for them. Now it's different. We've got new tools—communication."[112] Rather than protest, Lennon told one interviewer, people should simply move if they disagreed with the policies of Republican Richard Nixon, elected US president in November 1968. "Look, you've got two years to give out propaganda before the next election and if all those minds are working but can't get rid of that guy in two years—then leave and let the guy govern nothing. OK, it sounds hard to just move, migrate, but people have been doing it for millions of years." The interviewer suggested that most people, but especially the poor, would find it rather difficult to simply relocate. "Why can't they move?" Yoko replied. "Even if it's a ghetto, like a Jewish ghetto, you can escape. There are ways of escaping." When the interviewer suggested that some people are starving, Yoko quickly shot back, "If they are starving, they should move."[113]

John and Yoko's peace campaign was certainly creative and brave. He was the first major pop star to devote his time to such a political cause. Many celebrities would prostrate themselves for publicity to sell their latest product, but not many would hold themselves up to such ridicule for an idea. It is possible, and probable, that Lennon influenced some young people to think more deeply about pacifism and the war in Vietnam as he shed light on the anti-war campaign. "John Lennon helped to end the Vietnam War, by assisting in galvanizing the legitimate protests by thousands who felt the war to be illegal and immoral," author Joseph J. Mangano concluded.[114]

In spite of the publicity generated by the Bed-Ins, and the assertions of Mangano, John and Yoko's peace campaigns seemed to have little impact on public opinion. Their comments on the Vietnam war were based on disliking violence in general, not on any great knowledge of the conflict or any critique of the US presence in Southeast Asia. There were no follow-up events to the Bed-Ins, no avocation of nonviolent resistance on the lines of Mohandas Gandhi or Martin Luther King, no attempt to build a movement, and no organization left behind after the Bed-Ins ended.

Huge anti-war protests were already taking place before John and Yoko entered the fray, and opinion polls had already shown that the American public was turning against US involvement in the war. Incidents in Vietnam, such as the Tet offensive in January 1968, and the rise in American casualties, proved far more pivotal in ending the conflict than the pronouncement of two famous hippies lying in bed in Montreal.

John and Yoko's advocacy of pacifism may not have been very successful, but the publicity their exploits generated shows that even though the Beatles quit touring in 1966, they continued to capture the imagination of many young people. As the appearance and concerns of the four Beatles evolved, so too did those of many of their fans who followed their heroes' every move and adopted some of their countercultural ideas. However, while many continued to idolize the Beatles as they embraced the look and the values of the hippie generation, others enjoyed their music but felt alienated from the group because of their countercultural stance. This anti-Beatle sentiment, strongly evident in Chicago, would spread across the nation and help to explain the underwhelming response to the breakup of the once-beloved group in April 1970.

CHAPTER 9

"They Sort of Faded Away"

The Decline of the Fab Four, 1967–70

On September 4, 1968, Republican Richard Nixon launched his presidential campaign in the Chicago Loop. Nixon and his family drove in an open-top car through a blizzard of confetti, surrounded by an enthusiastic crowd of over four hundred thousand people. Unable to contain himself, the agile Nixon climbed onto a motorcade vehicle, spread his arms, and flashed his trademark two-handed V signs with a broad grin on his face. "Veteran observers said they never had seen a Republican candidate for any office get such a welcome here in more than 30 years," the *Tribune* gleefully reported.[1] The *Chicago Daily News* and the *Chicago Sun-Times*, who both endorsed Democrat Lyndon B. Johnson for president in 1964, now joined with the *Tribune* and its sister paper, *Chicago's American*, and urged their readers to vote for Richard Nixon.[2] Nixon, who ran on a law-and-order platform to a background of rising crime, black insurgency, and student radicalism, and claimed to speak for the "great silent majority," duly won the November election by making inroads into Democratic strongholds like Chicago. In the 1964 presidential election, 71 percent of Chicagoans cast their vote for Johnson, but in 1968 only 60.8 percent voted for Democratic candidate Hubert Humphrey. The more conservative suburbs showed a similar pattern with the vote for the Democrats declining from 47.7 percent in 1964 to 33 percent in 1968.[3]

The election of Richard Nixon confirmed that the American public was tiring of the long-haired hippies and their countercultural views.

Condemnation of the counterculture and its most famous adherents, the Beatles, spiked in Mayor Daley's Chicago where the courts, the police, and the media sought to curtail their influence. At the same time, however, the counterculture itself was splintering. As the political climate became more explosive, and the Beatles criticized revolutionary ideals; New Left radicals became more estranged from the group; and African Americans, under the influence of Black Nationalism, sought their own cultural heroes.

Opposition to the Counterculture

The release of *Sgt. Pepper* confirmed what was already evident on the 1966 tour, the Beatles now appealed to more boys. Bernie Biernacki, the high school student on Chicago's Southwest Side who witnessed the conflict the Beatles engendered in the student body in 1964, was now a college student. Previously an outsider to the conflict between pro and anti-Beatles factions, he failed to understand how a pop group could ignite such passion. He bought none of their records nor attended their concerts. As Bernie went off to college, however, he, like many other boys, reappraised his view of the Beatles as they produced more experimental music. "I really got into them at *Sgt. Pepper*," Bernie recalled of the first Beatles record he bought. "Before that, I thought, eh, they're love songs. But when they hit with *Sgt. Pepper* and all the following ones, then I became a fan."[4]

The countercultural Beatles appealed to more older boys but they failed to attract many younger pop fans. Their nicely groomed appearance, so crucial for their early success, had changed to mustaches and psychedelic outfits and then to scraggy, shoulder-length hair, bushy beards, and disheveled clothing, making them look more like Stone Age cavemen or Russian Orthodox priests than teenage heartthrobs. Outraged youngsters wrote to teen magazines complaining about the new Beatles. "I never saw such a ridiculous looking person in my whole life," one girl from Chicago wrote to *TeenSet* in November 1967, criticizing a photo of Ringo printed in the magazine. "I really mean it; he looks—awful. He looked bad before, but now! What's he trying to prove? I think if I ever saw someone with a striped jacket, a polka dot shirt and a paisley tie, I would laugh in his face. The same goes for the rest of the Beatles."[5] In January 1967, fifteen-year-old Andy Willie from Holcomb, a town west of Chicago, wrote to *Datebook* condemning "all those rock n roll groups with almost all members over 20. Where are our teens?" Andy wanted those groups with wives and children to stop behaving like teenagers. "Why don't you old men (like the Beatles) leave the record making to younger groups?"[6] It was clear that a gap in the market existed for a band that could provide the energy and simple songs of the early Fab Four days. *The Monkees*, a TV comedy series starring four zany characters with Beatle-style haircuts, launched in September 1966, catered to teenyboppers who longed for the mop-top Beatles. According to *Billboard*, their second album, *More of the Monkees*, not *Sgt. Pepper*, was the top-performing album of 1967.[7]

Young boys and girls complained that the new Beatles music was less exhilarating and less joyful than their earlier recordings, but most of the objections came from females. "I liked the old Beatles more," said Chicago musician Judy Bloom. "When they got into 'Revolution' and *Sgt. Pepper*, I listened to that, but my love was the first three albums. I like the original Beatles. They got almost too deep. I was drawn to the simplicity, the uniqueness of their style, and, oh, they were cute!"[8] Like many girls, Kathy Mangan, who lived on a farm in rural Illinois and was fourteen years old when she saw the Beatles on *The Ed Sullivan Show*, felt alienated from the new Beatles. "Before they broke up, the music just wasn't the same. The original songs were about love and life. I think maybe they got too big. They had the money, and if you have the money, you can get the drugs. I think that's what destroyed them. I stopped listening to them pretty much when *Yellow Submarine* came out, and *Sergeant Pepper's Lonely Hearts Club Band*."[9] Many of the Beatles fan clubs that formed in the heat of Beatlemania became inactive as older girls went off to high school and away to college, and younger girls failed to take their place.

The Beatles' records continued to sell but their popularity was never just based on their music, and as they became publicly associated with the counterculture, they grew ever more estranged from ordinary Americans. Their music may have stayed close to the mainstream and continued to appeal to the masses but their views certainly did not. The Beatles not only grew their hair long and scruffy, and now wore clothes with less attention to sartorial style, they also shunned Christianity and adopted Indian philosophical traditions, displayed a willingness to experiment with mind-altering drugs, embraced a promiscuous lifestyle, supported pacifist ideals, and voiced not only a dislike for a particular political party or politician but for the whole concept of governmental authority. A *Look* nationwide survey of 550 teenagers undertaken during the height of the Summer of Love in 1967 revealed the gulf between the countercultural values of the Beatles and the values of mainstream America. Some 86 percent of the respondents said they believed in God, 77 percent that they went to a Church or Synagogue in the last month, and 55 percent that their "religious belief is getting stronger." A full 85 percent would not take either LSD or marijuana at a party. Only 46 percent thought it acceptable for a girl to have sex before marriage.[10] Rather surprisingly, polls consistently showed that younger people supported the US war in Vietnam more than older people. In April 1968, for example, 54 percent of those between twenty-one and twenty-nine years of age thought the war was not a mistake, 44 percent of those between thirty and forty-nine, and only 31 percent of those over fifty.[11]

The general public's impression of the counterculture, and the wholesome image of the Beatles, deteriorated further when a group of young people led by Charles Manson, a former Haight-Ashbury resident who was apparently obsessed with the Beatles and claimed that he heard messages on the White album, went on a murder spree in California in December 1969. Fitting the popular stereotype of hippies, the long-haired assailants wrote the words "Healter Skelter" (a misspelling of "Helter Skelter") in blood on the refrigerator in the victim's house. In the same month, Hells Angels, for many a rebellious symbol of the counterculture, killed a man and injured numerous others as many revelers overdosed at the chaotic Altamont Speedway Free Festival, where stars of the counterculture including the Rolling Stones; Crosby, Stills, Nash and Young; and Jefferson Airplane performed.

Chicago, a Midwest working-class city, embraced hippie culture even less than cities on the East and West Coasts. A Gallup poll undertaken in October 1969 confirmed that the South was the most conservative part of the country, but the Midwest followed close behind. Some 78 percent of those in the East opposed the legalization of marijuana, in the West it was 80 percent, and in the South 89 percent. In the Midwest, the figure was 87 percent. Only 2 percent of people in the South and the Midwest had tried marijuana, while 9 percent of those in the West and 5 percent in the East had indulged in the wacky backy.[12] Dennis Johnson, a guitarist in the band The Moving Violation from Chicago Heights, played in his hometown in the summer of 1967 and found little of the West Coast vibes. "It was all squeaky clean, with no booze or drugs, typical of the Midwest in '67. It might have been the summer of love in California, with hippies dropping LSD and smoking pot, but it was still pretty square in Chicago."[13]

The permissive '60s seemed to pass Chicago by. In the '50s, there were so many strip clubs in Chicago that fifty booking agents for exotic dancers operated in the city. Chick Schloss, one of only three booking agents left in Chicago in the late '60s, blamed the Church, city officials, and the media for closing down the strip clubs. "One day, they all got together and started thinking sex was sinful, pretty soon they even convinced others there might be something to the theory, and before long South Wabash and State Street began to look like graveyards. Now there's nothing left but the 606," a strip club on South Wabash Avenue.[14]

"The hookers, hoods and B-girls are hardly to be seen," Arno Karlen wrote rather disappointedly in 1967, comparing the Chicago he encountered then with the one he saw when he first moved to the city ten years earlier. "The many 'topless' clubs there are as topless as sealed tin cans,' pornography and rough shows, aside from a few transvestite bars, are almost nonexistent. This is the influence not only of the police but of the Roman Catholic Church."[15] Police too raided gay-owned establishments arresting people for public indecency and disorderly conduct. "This harassment was as harsh in Chicago as in any American city," wrote Timothy Stewart-Winter in his study of gay politics in the postwar years. "In the 1950s, police raids on gay bars had been sporadic; in the early 1960s, they had become systematic."[16]

For boys with long hair and girls with short skirts, Chicago could be a hostile place. When *The Seed's* Abe Peck arrived in Chicago in 1967, he "found it very racist. It's a much better place now despite all the problems of violence. If you had long hair, you could get jumped."[17]

"They better not come down here," thirteen-year-old Michael Rogers, a neighbor of Mayor Daley's, told the *New York Times,* referring to the long-haired demonstrators at the 1968 Democratic Convention in Chicago. "We'll get scissors and cut all their hair off." His friend, ten-year-old David Cuomo, was even blunter: "We'll take their hippie chains and strangle them."[18]

In the spring of 1968, suburban Chicago schools still forbade long hair on boys and short skirts on girls. In Fenton High School in Northwest suburban Bensenville, the principal told thirty boys to get their hair cut or face suspension. "They have a stupid idea to look like a hippie," said an unsympathetic Nick Mycyk, owner of Nick's Barber Shop. Elynor Reid from a local clothing store said she stocked "a few minis but that the fad hasn't caught on in Bensenville." Even then, miniskirts were still rather modest. "Minis are not as short as it may sound," Terri Ringeisen, of Toni's Conversation Clothes, told the local paper, describing the skirts as "about two inches above the knee."[19] Young women also found it difficult to wear slacks or jeans. Chicagoan Carol Hirsch told the fashion editor of *Chicago's American* that she would prefer to wear pants than a skirt but felt she had to wear the latter. "I don't want to be considered too way out. If you wear pants all the time, some people think you are a hippy."[20]

College students in the Midwest, the people you would expect to be the most supportive of hippie ideals, exhibited a similar hostility to the Beatles' countercultural values. In 1970, the school of business at Indiana University undertook a survey of Midwest college students and found that 75.2 percent believed that disagreement with a law did not justify disobedience to it.[21] There was little sign of free love ideals in a follow-up survey. As few as 14 percent thought it acceptable for a woman to have casual sex before marriage, 26 percent thought it appropriate for dating women to have sex with their partners, and only 41 percent found it acceptable for engaged women to have sex with their fiancés.[22]

The campuses of the Midwest were equally unimpressed with the Beatles' sponsorship of Indian culture. "In recent weeks the fad from the Far East has spread westward to the East Coast of America," the *Daily Northwestern* student newspaper noted in April 1968, but they found their college immune to the trend. "Trying to locate the Northwestern man who will grab the first Nehru jacket to hit Evanston clothing stores this month can be time-consuming." After interviewing several male students, the paper found that most would not wear the jacket or would only wear one with a traditional shirt and tie. The writer suggested that "clothing fads at NU have at best been delayed and diluted with conservatism."[23] The "reaction to TM at Northwestern has been slow," noted the *Daily Northwestern* in November 1970, with as little as 250 people in the Evanston area enrolling in transcendental meditation classes. "TM is associated with the long hair psychedelic lifestyle," the newspaper explained.[24]

Those adults who previously indulged their children's infatuation with the Beatles or who saw them as a benign influence now viewed them in a different light. Donald Jensen, a juvenile officer for suburban Bensenville police, blamed the Beatles and other rock groups for the rise in drug use in the area. "Ever listen to one of those songs?" he asked. "They sing about trips on LSD."[25]

"Marijuana has always been covertly popular," a columnist in the suburban Arlington Heights newspaper wrote disapprovingly on the drug of choice for students, "but the opiates of LSD and the Beatles' drug songs unified students as never before."[26] An editorial in Moline's *Daily Dispatch* criticized the Beatles for calling for the legalization of marijuana. "For whatever influence the Beatles have, it could be put to far better use than pushing pot."[27]

Conservatives, as expected, were the most vocal in their opposition to the Beatles. Gary Allen, of the staunchly anti-communist John Birch Society, wrote an article in their journal, *American Opinion* that condemned their music for promoting drug use and supporting communism. He suggested that "Hey Jude" was a song about the drug methedrine, "Yellow Submarine" alluded to barbiturates, and "Norwegian Wood" was a "British teenagers' term for marijuana." Using his superior analytical skills, Allen also revealed that "Strawberry Fields Forever" was about drugs because "marijuana is often planted in strawberry fields," and the lyrics of "Magical Mystery Tour" contained the advice to "Roll up, roll up [your sleeve] for the mystery tour," an obvious reference to injecting heroin. It probably didn't add to the Beatles popularity among conservatives that they included a picture of Karl Marx on the cover of *Sgt. Pepper*. Even worse, "Back in the USSR" glorified communism, and "Revolution" showed that the Beatles were "on the side of, and working for, revolution."[28]

Many Beatles fans now voiced discontent with their idol's newfound countercultural stance. "In 1970, I was fifteen years old, and although I did enjoy most of their music, I couldn't relate to the *Sgt. Pepper* stuff," Leann Julian from Joliet, mused. "They seemed to be getting into stuff like the Maharishi and drugs, so I was finding other music that I enjoyed more at that time."[29] Chicagoan Linda Milan, who was twelve years old when the Beatles first appeared on *The Ed Sullivan Show*, and who saw them at White Sox Park in 1965, began to temper her devotion. "I started thinking they were too far out, and I just didn't like them anymore." Other artists competed for her affections. "I started liking those groups better than the Beatles just because they didn't have all the baggage the Beatles had, and they didn't have the drug problems either."[30] Many fans expressed disappointment when they found out that the Beatles took drugs. "I must admit I was furious when I read the news in the Chicago papers that you had taken LSD, not because you had taken the drug, but because you went on to explain that it brought you 'closer to God' among other things," eighteen-year-old Kristin Santose wrote to Paul in October 1967. "I was upset knowing that some kids were going to try the drugs because you had."[31]

"I've been an avid Beatle fan from the very beginning," Barb Haig, a music critic on a suburban newspaper wrote in December 1967. "I think it's kind of sad that the Beatles have changed their image so. When they first started out in '64, they were so clean and they really appealed to teens. Now with the beards and weird clothes they look like slobs. They no longer want to appeal to young people, their experiments in LSD proved that. They are out to be the leader of the 'Cool Group.'"[32]

Fran Ugo wrote to her local Chicago newspaper wishing Paul a happy birthday in 1969 but voiced the unease many now felt. "Your seemingly unending list of musical compositions and accomplishments will always challenge new artists, though I doubt that any will ever top you," she wrote. However, Fran suggested that it was not easy to keep following the Beatles. "There did come a time in your career when a marked difference became obvious to your public. Not only did your music change, but the entire Beatle image became (as some might term it) 'less desirable.' Here the teeny-bopper fans who started with you in 1964 were faced with a choice. They could hold your personal life against you and turn to other less talented but more conventional, 'respectable' groups, or they could accept you as the people you are and the musical genius you display and continue to support you for your talents. Needless to say, some of your fans took the easier route."[33]

John Lennon attracted the most criticism as he and Yoko Ono seemed to be doing their utmost to distance the Beatles from their mainstream audience. After their first joint art exhibition, "You Are Here," took place at the Robert Fraser Gallery in London in the summer of 1968, many patrons added their views to the visitor's book. "In six years, nobody has ever written anything in that book," gallery owner Fraser told *Titbits* magazine, but now the book was full of comments. "Opinions ranged from the succinct—'Absolutely pointless,' 'Drivel,' 'Incredible rubbish'— to the incredulous 'You've gotta be joking,'" Fraser told the press, suggesting he was looking for something a little more positive.[34]

The Beatles Book asked people in London for their reaction to the couple's first appearance together on television, when they were guests on the *Frost on Saturday* program in August 1968. On the show, the happy couple talked about vibrations, showed a clip of one of their films, and invited audience members to hammer a nail into a piece of wood. "I watched with my boyfriend," one fan said. "Neither of us could make head or tail of what John and Yoko were on about. At first, I thought I was daft until my boyfriend suddenly said he didn't know what I saw in the Beatles because they talked a load of old rubbish these days." A twenty-year-old female fan was equally unimpressed. "I belong to The Beatles Fan Club," she stated. "I joined five years ago and I collect all their records. I loved *Sgt. Pepper* and even *Magical Mystery Tour*, but I think John is making far too much of this art business. I think he's being influenced too much by Yoko Ono and I think they're both trying to make excuses for the fact that they don't know how to create really important works of art paintings or sculptures... There's no meaning to the things he's doing with Yoko Ono—a film of someone smiling isn't art. Nor can we appreciate knocking nails into a slab of wood—well, I ask you, surely John is losing his touch if he really thinks we ought to be praising him for THAT!"[35]

John and Yoko made more appearances on TV chat shows, each baffling the studio audience and those watching at home, not to mention testing the loyalty of the Beatles fan even further. Appropriately enough, on April Fool's day 1969, they appeared on the *ITV Today* show hosted by Eamonn Andrews. The genial Irishman interviewed the couple while they were inside a white bag and in bed. Two days later, John and Yoko again appeared with Andrews, this time on *The Eamonn Andrews Show*. The host asked the audience if anyone had been inspired to think about peace because of John and Yoko's actions. Only one or two put their hands up, and Andrews asked one to speak. "Yes, I thought it was the biggest piece of rubbish I'd heard this year," the man said as the audience burst into sustained applause. "The fact of you staying in bed was nothing wrong with that. In fact, if you stayed there longer, I think it would better for everybody." Andrews asked Lennon, "Why do you think so many people have turned against the Beatles?" Because "we don't conform to the image" we had before, he replied.[36] At the end of 1969, the *Daily Mirror*, the British newspaper that showered effusive praise on the Beatles in 1963, now named John Lennon "the clown of the year."[37]

John and Yoko's public activities seemed to be just the latest Beatles' activity to bewilder their mainstream audience. Beginning with the broadcast of the disappointing *Magical Mystery Tour* film on Boxing Day 1967 and leading up to the closure of the Apple boutique in London in July 1968, there seemed to be an "increasing number of disasters" befalling the band, a worried *Disc and Music Echo* noted. "Paul's admission that he took LSD; the rotten reception for *Magical Mystery Tour*; the embarrassing Maharishi period; their climb aboard the Flower power bandwagon when previously they had always *set* trends; the clumsily-announced split between Paul and Jane Asher; the publicity surrounding John and Yoko Ono; the vague unreality of Lennon talking about 'vibrations,' and walking around wearing a badge bearing the words: 'You Are Here.' And now a thin public reception for the 'Yellow Submarine' film," all "are hitting the Beatles' image."[38]

For a variety of reasons, John Lennon faced greater criticism in his homeland than he did in the US. While Americans generally admire those who are successful, the British tend to criticize those who move above their allotted station and take a more cynical view of public figures. Additionally, John and Yoko's activities were less visible to the American public. The couple lived in England, and British newspapers, TV, and radio tracked their every move. In contrast, John and Yoko never visited the US together in the '60s, and Americans saw and heard less about their undertakings. American television never aired their appearances on *Frost on Saturday* and *The Eamonn Andrews Show,* and while British television audiences saw the bewildering *Magical Mystery Tour,* American television companies spared their viewers the dubious pleasure.

Even though they gained less negative coverage in the US media, Chicago newspapers joined in the criticism of John and Yoko. The

American mainstream media all but ignored their Bed-Ins for peace, but Irv Kupcinet, columnist of the *Chicago Sun-Times,* could not resist a cutting remark. The couple is "doing their thing," he wrote, "but isn't the public more than a little fed up with such beatle-mania?"[39] The Beatles' old friend, the *Chicago Tribune,* kept up a concerted campaign of negativity. Articles on the couple invariably mentioned that the two appeared naked on the front cover of an album, and that Yoko made a film featuring over three hundred bare bottoms.[40] The "Beatles revived the shoulder length tresses of Elizabethan England, even tho Drake and Raleigh would never have been caught dead in the hair style John Lennon wore for his wedding," a *Chicago Tribune* editorial commented. Even more bizarrely, the *Tribune* compared the hairstyle of the Mohican Indian with those of the newly married couple. "We will take his style in preference to that of Lennon and Yoko," the editorial concluded.[41]

In November 1968, *Tribune* music critic Robb Baker thought he had spotted John and Yoko at the Kinetic Playground in Chicago but "it's hard to recognize John and Yoko these days with their clothes on anyway."[42] When the *Tribune* movie critic described a film with nude scenes, he could not resist a dig at the couple. "In a John Lennon-Yoko Ono dream come true, a stark naked man and woman romp around the bed and on top of it."[43] The *Tribune* described Lennon's visit to Canada in December 1969 as, "Beatle John Lennon, promoting propaganda in Canada against resistance to communist aggression in Viet Nam."[44]

In July 1969, John and Yoko made one of their rare appearances on American TV when they agreed to be interviewed on the newly launched *The David Frost Show.* During the show, which was filmed in England, they threw acorns into the audience, played an extract from their album *Life with the Lions,* and talked of their peace campaign. Under the headline, "John's New Bag," the *Chicago South End Reporter* editorial called the appearance "tragic" and, like many, was baffled by what John and Yoko said, including their slogan of "Love plus peace equals baggism." The paper questioned the couple's sincerity. "Peace and equality are things too great to be purchased at the price of one straight week in bed under the tag of commitment."[45]

"I was like, 'What are they doing?'" recalled Chicago suburban teenager Katie Jones. "Cutting their hair and having the acorns. 'What are they doing? This is crazy stuff.' So the fandom didn't necessarily lend itself to the unit of John and Yoko. I remember when one of John and Yoko's albums came out, like the *Wedding Album* and *Two Virgins*. You got *Two Virgins* for the cover so you could have a naked cover, and the *Wedding Album* actually had all sorts of neat inserts. So if you bought it, you bought it for that. Nobody ever listened to them. I don't know anybody who actually listened to them."[46] The music critic of *The Daily Dispatch* in Moline, Illinois, voiced surprise that the Beatles were still selling records taking into account "their raps on religion, the John Lennon-Yoko thing, and the fact that none of their recent recordings even approaches their earlier efforts…. Personally, we'd like to see them clean shaven once more."[47]

The Beatles themselves recognized that a decline in their popularity had taken place over the length of the '60s. Ringo told an interviewer in December 1968 that he accepted the fact that people admired the Beatles less than before. "[W]hen we first started we were the nice clean mop tops and every mother's son and everyone loved us. And then suddenly there's a few things they don't understand, don't get and don't like and so it turns them off us a bit."[48] In 1987, George, too, noted the wane in the Beatles' popularity in an interview with *US* magazine. "We started out as 'the cute little boys,' and people were telling us how great we were. But then, there was a divorce, someone gets caught smoking reefer, they're wearing weird mustaches, strange things are happening around them. And suddenly, we aren't so loved anymore."[49] "We went from being the cute, lovable mop tops to being these horrible, bearded hippies," George told *Rolling Stone* more bluntly.[50]

Mayor Daley and the Counterculture

Richard J. Daley, elected to a fourth term as mayor in the spring of 1967, emerged as the staunch enemy of the counterculture. He warned "outsiders," whether student demonstrators, hippies, or civil rights activists, to keep out of his city. "As long as I am Mayor, there will be law and order in Chicago. And I don't care who it affects," he added rather ominously.[51] The *Chicago Tribune* opposed Daley's candidacy when he first ran for mayor in 1955 and subsequently criticized his fiscal policies and the corruption of his administration, but in 1967 the paper broke with tradition and endorsed a Democrat for mayor. "His personal honesty has never been questioned. His family life is a model.

He works harder than any other public official we have ever known," they gushed.[52] Daley, who won the support of the hard-working white Chicagoans that resented the antiwar movement, the civil rights marchers, and the counterculture, saw his share of the vote increase from 56 percent in 1963 to 73 percent in 1967. In 1971, he gained 70 percent of the vote; and in 1975, when he won a sixth term of office, 78 percent of voters put their trust in Daley.

Mayor Daley was serious about maintaining traditional standards and keeping any hint of countercultural values out of his domain. When Bobby Kennedy came to Chicago to obtain the mayor's support for his run for president in 1968, Daley received his fellow Irish American with courtesy and respect. To ingratiate himself with the country's most powerful mayor, Kennedy asked Daley if he had any advice for him. As legend would have it, Daley simply replied, "Get a haircut."[53] Deejay Clark Weber, who joined WCFL in 1969 and that November worked at a Rolling Stones concert in the city, recalled how the British reprobates faced the wrath of City Hall when it became known that they had an underage girl in their hotel. "Mayor Daley found out about it and ordered the Rolling Stones to be put into a squad car immediately after the show and driven directly to O'Hare and do not pass go. They were really run out of town by the mayor."[54]

In his book on undercover police work, author Frank Donner called Chicago, "The National Capital of Police Repression." Helped by an authoritarian Democratic machine and a pliant *Chicago Tribune*, the counterculture faced intense scrutiny from the Chicago Police Department's Subversive Unit, or "Red Squad." The Red Squad compiled files on campaigners, closely watched those deemed a threat, infiltrated radical organizations, and raided meetings, arresting many for drug offenses.[55]

In June 1967, Chicago police arrested several bookstore owners for selling the May 1967 issue of the New York underground magazine *The Realist*, which contained a center spread of Disney cartoon characters indulging in an orgy. The police detained *The Seed* editor Abe Peck and reporter Michael Abrahams on obscenity charges after the publication of the Christmas 1968 edition of *The Seed*. In this case, the police objected to a cover that featured an image of Santa Claus crucified on a dollar sign and a center spread collage that included images of nude women and Mayor Daley. The police later dropped the charges.[56]

As the preeminent countercultural venue in the city, the Kinetic Playground became a target of the police department. Within days of its opening, the police arrested the club's manager, Richard Shelton, on drug charges after they raided his apartment in Old Town.[57] In May, during a benefit for the Free City Survival Committee, an affiliate of the Yippies (Youth International Party), officers descended on the club, pulled the plug on the light show and music, arrested the owner Aaron Russo for disorderly conduct, and prosecuted 29 patrons, many for curfew violations.[58] After "numerous complaints had been received that hippies congregated at the theater and created a nuisance," the police raided the club again in July and arrested the new manager, Peter De Blanc, for keeping a disorderly house.[59]

The four most famous symbols of the counterculture could not escape the backlash. After a time-consuming and expensive campaign of surveillance of left-wing organizations, Chicago Police Department undercover operative David Gumaer revealed to the world the secret behind the Beatles' many achievements. The "reason the Beatles and other folk-rock groups received such success in the music field was because they were backed by the Entertainment Section of the Communist Party." Even more revelatory, Gumaer disclosed in a world exclusive, "Paul McCartney of the Beatles was a member of the Young Communist League."[60]

It was no surprise that Chicago became the scene of the first obscenity case involving John and Yoko's *Two Virgins* album. Concerned about

After the police arrested the owners of Head Imports in Chicago, John and Yoko sent a one word telegram to the two men: "Congratulations."

Chicago Kaleidoscope, December 20, 1968–January 2, 1969, page 3

the nude photo on the cover, Capitol refused to handle the disc. Tetragrammaton Records stepped in to distribute *Two Virgins* in the US but enclosed it in a brown paper bag. The album hit the streets in November 1968, but the bags did not stop the controversy. Chicago-based Sears refused to carry it in any of its more than eight hundred stores. "We don't carry any product that might haunt our reputation as a family store," said a spokesman.[61] "We wouldn't sell it to teen-agers," a Chicago store told *Billboard*. "I don't know whether we'll have it out or keep it in the back," surmised another. "I would rather not carry it, but I have to because my competition will

The Seed, March 1, 1969, page 8

After the arrest of the owners of Head Imports, those brave enough to sell the Two Virgins poster in Chicago covered up the offending bits.

have it," said one store owner.[62] On December 3, 1968, police arrested the owners of Head Imports, George Sells and Jonathan Tuttle, after a woman complained to police that the shop displayed a photo of the cover, not the album cover itself, in its front window. "The point is that the police have been out to do us in since we opened last June 1," claimed Sells. "I didn't think we'd get busted for putting that picture in the window." For their troubles, the two men received a telegram containing the single word "Congratulations" from John and Yoko.[63] Sgt. Zarno of the Chicago police department seemed unimpressed. "Who in the hell would want a picture like that, with this Lennon standing there showing his private organs? That Japanese girl—she's nothing to look at. Lennon must be soft in the head."[64] The two men escaped charges of obscenity, but the court fined Sells and Tuttle twenty-five dollars each for disorderly conduct.[65]

John and Yoko's private parts may have caused consternation in Chicago but so too did some of the Beatles' music. Most radio stations played four tracks from the *Sgt. Pepper* album: "A Day in the Life," "She's Leaving Home," "When I'm 64" and the title track; but WLS program director Clark Weber refused to play "A Day in the Life" due to the drug inferences in the lyrics.[66] In the summer of 1969, WLS joined with other Top 40 radio stations in banning the Beatles' single "The Ballad of John and Yoko" because they deemed John Lennon's lyrics that mentioned Jesus Christ and crucifixion to be offensive to Christians.[67]

The New Left and the Beatles

Mayor Daley escalated his campaign against "outsiders" just as the counterculture became more politically charged with the emergence of the New Left. While hippies wanted to drop out of mainstream society and create their own communities, the self-styled New Left, to distinguish themselves from the Old Left supporters of Soviet-style communism, sought to overhaul the economic and political system. Radicals focused their ire on racial disparities and the Vietnam War, and they espoused countercultural views on rock 'n' roll, drugs, and sex. Some admired new flamboyant revolutionary heroes such as Ernesto "Che" Guevara, Ho Chi Minh, and Mao Zedong. Many joined the Students for a Democratic Society (SDS), formed by student activists at the University of Michigan in 1960. In April 1965, the SDS held the first of several mass demonstrations against the Vietnam War, drawing more than fifteen thousand people to Washington, DC. SDS moved its headquarters from New York to Chicago in the summer of 1965. In 1968, the SDS claimed one hundred thousand members in three hundred campus chapters.[68]

The old-style Left may have generally ignored the Beatles but some of the younger elements of the radical Left increasingly found much to admire in the Beatles and the rock explosion. The W.E.B. DuBois Clubs of America, a Communist Party-sponsored youth organization formed in San Francisco in the summer of 1964 and headquartered in Chicago from 1966, praised the Beatles in the first issue of their journal, *Insurgent*. "The Beatles have brought a new vitality to pop music. In their records, their film, and their on- and off-stage comments, they speak for our era with a new voice, a voice of refreshing, light-hearted contempt for the very society that has made them what they are. With zestful wit, infectious rhythm and a sly sophistication they are eating up success, bringing joy to millions of kids, and thumbing their noses at a host of conventional notions ranging from politics to English usage." Their first film, *A Hard Day's Night,* "pulsates with life. It is so filled with spirit and energy that it seems to overflow the screen, and audiences are left glowing," the radicals who campaigned for civil rights and against the Vietnam War gushed. The film was full of "socially pointed innuendos" and "ribs police, TV directors, reporters and stodgy elders." In the end, the Beatles "made so many of us feel more alive in the process."[69]

Many of the New Left viewed rock music as potentially subversive and groups like the Beatles as kindred spirits in the struggle. Students at Chicago's Roosevelt University, dubbed "The Little Red Schoolhouse" because of its reputation of having a radical faculty and student body, expressed admiration for popular culture in their journal, *The Rebel Worker.* "That rock 'n' roll is one of the most important working class preoccupations (among the young, at least) is clearly evident," Franklin Rosemont wrote in a pamphlet issued by *The Rebel Worker* in the summer of 1965. Rosemont saw a particular rebelliousness in the Fab Four. "The Beatles are the most successful group in entertainment history. Their flippant replies to interviewers; their wild, raucous behavior; their riotous and insulting sense of humor remove them far beyond the pale of 'respectable entertainers.' Their first movie, *A Hard Day's Night,* will remain one of the greatest cinematic delights of 1964, a lone cry of uninhibited freedom and irrationality in a cold desert of 'seriousness' and pretentiousness."[70] Gatherings of the New Left organization the Weatherman often sang, "We all live in a Weatherman machine, Weatherman machine, Weatherman machine," to the tune of "Yellow Submarine."[71] Even more elaborately, and less successfully, to the tune of "Nowhere Man," they sang: "He's a real Weatherman, Ripping up the mother land, Making all his Weather plans, For everyone, Knows just what he's fighting for, Victory for people's war, Trashes, bombs, kills pigs and more, The Weatherman."[72]

Many of the radical Left may have initially admired the Beatles' anti-authority attitude, but the era-defining confrontation between Mayor Richard J. Daley's administration and the New Left, which took place in Chicago in August 1968, drew a sharp wedge between the left and the Beatles. Led by Yippie activists Jerry Rubin and Abbie Hoffman, some ten thousand people descended on the city during the Democratic National Convention, calling for an end to the Vietnam war. They nominated a pig for president and rumors spread that they would put LSD in the Chicago River and make love in public. "We knew it would be easy to cause a commotion in Chicago," said Jerry Rubin boasting of their provocative actions. "They're very backward here."[73] Rising to the bait, Mayor Daley refused them a permit to march. After nights of clashes between police and protestors, events climaxed on the night of the presidential nomination in what an independent national commission headed by future Illinois Governor Dan Walker later deemed a "police riot." Police used tear gas, mace, and clubs on the demonstrators, journalists, and bystanders, all seen by a national TV audience of millions.[74] On the last day of the Convention, Abbie Hoffman claimed that the Yippies had won the Battle of Chicago and expressed gratitude to several countercultural heroes. "We thank Lennie Bruce—thanks, Lennie. The Marx Brothers—Karl, too. The Beatles, out there in Lake Michigan in their Yellow Submarine. Bob Dylan."[75]

The reaction of the public to the police riot at the Democratic Convention confirmed the unpopularity of hippies and radical politics. Blue-collar Midwesterners, including the police who enjoyed their night's work, saw the protestors as the pampered sons and daughters of the rich who were unwilling to sacrifice for their country and were using the sanctuary of college to avoid the draft. The *Chicago Tribune* blamed Marxist leaders for the violence and declared that the "bearded, dirty, lawless rabble that followed them used every sort of provocation against police and national guardsmen—vile taunts, lye solutions, bricks, and rubble.... For enforcing law and order, Mayor Daley and the police deserve congratulations rather than criticism."[76]

"A large majority of the hundreds of people telephoning the *Tribune* yesterday in the wake of street rioting praised Mayor Daley and the Chicago police," the newspaper noted.[77] Jack Mabley, now a columnist for the *Tribune*, received a huge amount of mail, of which 80 to 85 percent supported the mayor and the police. "The feeling of the city was anti-hippie. People hated them for what they were and for their lifestyle," Mabley said years later. "The general perception was that the police did a good job beating those yippies."[78] For their troubles, Jerry Rubin and Abbie Hoffman ended up on trial as part of the Chicago 8 (later 7) accused of conspiring to incite a riot at the Democratic Convention. The jury found the defendants not guilty of conspiracy, but guilty of intent to riot, later overturned on appeal.

To the dismay of the political activists on the streets of Chicago, John Lennon, now the most public Beatle, exhibited little sympathy for the protestors. "He said something to the effect that the Chicago Riot had made a name for the leaders, but the kids who followed the leaders and participated in the actual demonstrations just got clobbered, had their heads split open and didn't even make names for themselves," Yoko Ono later told *Instant Karma* fanzine about John's views.[79] While some activists called for a boycott of Chicago, John and Yoko chose to premiere their first experimental films at the Chicago International Film Festival, less than three months after the violence. "I believe a lot of artists and people pulled out their stuff from Chicago as a protest," he told a student interviewer from Keele University in England, "so, they just leave it to the wolves, y'know? To just create the whole atmosphere and keep it so's it, you couldn't even go within a hundred miles of the place without getting uptight, or paranoid, or frightened," he somewhat incoherently continued. "I believe if you just keep sending the gear at them, y'know. You gotta…it's got to be yin yang. If it's all bad in Chicago and all the good guys pull out everything they've got and move away from it, that place would just be completely bad and would be a stronghold for all the baddies" Rather than concern themselves with broader politics, Lennon told the two interviewers that they should change the attitudes of those around them. "Your auntie, your uncle, your parents, your cousin, your brother and everyone. They're the same people as the cops that are beating up people in Chicago. Exactly the same types up in Keele University. And they're living on this hill, they're all around. They're not just in uniform."[80]

To the further irritation of the radicals, the Beatles voiced no support for left-wing politics. Hippie and New Left ideals often overlapped, but the Beatles were careful to embrace the former and its emphasis on personal freedom, but not the latter and its focus on political engagement. "I think young people shouldn't take an active part in political action," John Lennon told Art Unger of *Datebook* on the 1966 tour. "They should know about it and be aware of it and see what it is, then they wouldn't [play an] active part in it."[81] As student radicalism spread across the US, the Beatles increasingly espoused the idea that people should change themselves and not worry about politics. "If everybody just fixes themselves up first, instead of everybody going around trying to fix everybody else up like the Lone Ranger, then there isn't any problem," Harrison told *International Times* in the summer of 1969, reflecting the views of all four Beatles. "The problems are created more, sometimes, by people going around trying to fix up the government, or trying to do something—I mean most of the revolutionaries, who try to change the outward physical structure when really that automatically changes if the internal structure is straight."[82]

The reaction to John and Yoko's two films shown at the Chicago International Film Festival illuminates the weary hostility to the celebrity couple and Lennon's band mates in the Windy City. The Festival hosted the world premiere of the films to a sellout crowd at the Playboy Theater on North Dearborn Street at Midnight on the night of Thursday, November 14, 1968. The films were both shot on a sunny day in Lennon's garden. *Two Virgins*, a nineteen-minute short that blended images of John and Yoko, was described as a "painting of introspection, strangeness and love." Film No. 5, also known as Smile, was a fifty-two-minute film featuring a close-up of John Lennon's face as he periodically smiled in slow motion.[83] "It's a great portrait and it's a great film and it's all that," Lennon told an interviewer about Smile. "It's also a great vibration," meaning that the smiles would communicate good feelings to the audience.[84] Famed film critic Roger Ebert, who had stated that *A Hard Day's Night* was one of his favorite movies, attended the premier and suggested that *Two Virgins* was "one of the lovelier films you could imagine" but Film No. 5 "was more of a put-on."[85] Clifford Terry of the *Chicago Tribune* did not feel the good vibes, calling the films "the biggest con jobs since Yellow Kid Weil was doing his thing." *Two Virgins* was "accompanied by music that sounds like a combination of the Holyoke Piccolo Players and a malfunctioning lathe." That was Yoko's singing.[86]

For the second film, *Smile*, John and Yoko encouraged the crowd to bring their own musical instruments to play during the viewing. The audience duly played "harmonicas, recorders, a cornet, several combs with paper, a musical fan, a trombone, a Halloween noisemaker and things like that."[87] Yet *Smile* did not keep the attention of the increasingly discontented crowd, Ebert reported. Baskets of flowers ringed the stage, and soon, the audience was throwing the flowers into the air. The audience shouted slogans like "Up against the Wall" and "Nixon's the one."

"One piper with a recorder led a parade around the theater. Someone else jumped up on stage and put the microphone upright, so it looked like John was speaking into it. Great applause. John pursed his lips, ever so slowly. Tumultuous cheering." A youngster left the stage on the orders of management, but before he did, "he wiped John's nose with his hankie." By this time, half the audience had walked out of the movie theater.[88]

The Beatles, the Rolling Stones, Bob Dylan, and the New Left

The respect the Beatles enjoyed among student radicals lessened after the Democratic Convention as the New Left increasingly looked to Bob Dylan and the Rolling Stones as musicians that shared their worldview. Many began to realize that the Beatles-inspired rebellion consisted of taking drugs, supporting nonviolence, and learning Indian philosophical and religious practices. It was not questioning the fundamentals of capitalism, materialism, or consumerism, or using their songs to highlight societal problems. "Dylan *sang for us*," president of SDS Todd Gitlin wrote. "We followed his career as if he were singing our song; we got in the habit of asking where he was taking us next."[89] The Weatherman were so enamored with Dylan that they adopted their name from a lyric found in his song, "Subterranean Homesick Blues."

Many on the Left began to compare the Beatles with the Stones, with the latter gaining more approval. Even though Mick Jagger and co. never embraced a coherent political philosophy, and certainly not one that coincided with the beliefs of the New Left, their posturing and attitude appealed to the young radicals. From the beginning, the Rolling Stones seemed scruffier and tougher than the Beatles and were less accepted by the establishment. The Beatles' willingness to wear suits on stage, their acceptance of the MBEs, and their desire to become businessmen and establish Apple Corps made many on the Left uneasy. While the British courts sentenced Mick Jagger to three months in prison and Keith Richards to twelve months for drug offences, both later overturned on appeal, the judge only fined Lennon and Harrison for drug possession in the late '60s. In June 1967, Keith Richards appeared in an English court and told the judge, "We are not old men. We are not worried about petty morals."

With these words, he cemented the Rolling Stones' place in the forefront of countercultural rebels.

On Monday, August 26, 1968, the day the Democratic National Convention in Chicago began, the Beatles released "Revolution" as the B-side of "Hey Jude" in the United States. Written by Lennon, the song was a critique of the New Left, many of whom were about to have their skulls cracked open on the streets of Chicago. The single version of "Revolution," a slightly different version than the one that appeared later on the White Album, was unequivocally against the use of violence for political ends and condemned the anger of social movement activists. Even the *Chicago Tribune* took a dig at the "social copout 'Revolution'" noting that WLS and WCFL refused to air the Rolling Stones single "Street Fighting Man" but that this "one is being played on radio."[90]

While upheaval was spreading across the US, young political militants grew tired of the unwillingness of the Beatles to support left-wing causes and voiced disappointment with the sentiment behind "Revolution." *Rising Up Angry*, a radical paper launched in Chicago in July 1969, laid out their distaste for the Beatles and their admiration for the Rolling Stones. "Unlike the Beatles and their passive resistance with 'All You Need Is Love'…the Stones take a different look at things," the inaugural issue of the newspaper declared. "They know you can't love a pig to death with flowers and love while he kicks the shit out of you…. They don't try to keep the people down with bullshit influence like the Beatles did with 'Revolution.' The Stones talk about real life and how to deal with it—not

By the end of the decade, the Rolling Stones, not the Beatles, were the heroes of young radicals.

Rising Up Angry, Winter 1970, page 5

meditation and cop-out escape." Because of the Stones' drug busts, "Street Fighting Man," and their propensity for paternity suits, smashing up hotels, and urinating on walls, "Youth seems to identify with the Stones," the article rather worryingly suggested.[91] Student radicals at Northwestern University were equally dismissive of the Beatles and their song. "The decidedly non-radical political philosophy typical of most rock culture heroes is in perfect harmony with the system's attempts to channel potential political unrest into various forms of harmless cultural rebellion," William Kaufman wrote in the *Daily Northwestern*. "The most notorious example of this can be found in the Beatles' song, 'Revolution,' which urges us to free our minds rather than attack institutions."[92]

In the fall of 1968, Bill Ayers, a native of the Chicago suburb of Glen Ellyn and one of the founders of the Weatherman faction, and a young activist named Michael Klonsky, began to organize SDS chapters on college campuses throughout the Midwest. "We'd roll into town knowing two or three people, that's all, it didn't take much," Klonsky recalls. "Bill would go to the student union, climb on a table and start rapping, and I'd hand out our fliers. We had some great times together, but we also had our fights. Once we were sitting in some student union and the Beatles' song 'Revolution' came on the jukebox. Bill went berserk. He ripped out the cord to the jukebox. To him, 'Revolution' wasn't radical enough. He wanted 'Street Fighting Man' by the Stones. Now that was revolutionary. I know it sounds crazy, but he wasn't kidding. That's the way it was. There was a lot of anger in the air."[93]

The Beatles' breezy optimism seemed more out of place after the Democratic Convention than the darker sounds and lyrics of the Rolling Stones. In March 1969, *Second City*, a countercultural paper in Chicago, published music critic Jon Landau's review of the Beatles' White Album and the Rolling Stones' *Beggars Banquet*. The two albums "offer conflicting statements about the desirability of politicizing rock," in Landau's estimation. The Stones' lyrics "are direct, violent, political, and often lewd." The Beatles' album "lacks aesthetic direction and flirts with reality only occasionally, and even then from a fairly safe distance." The Stones "strive for realism in contrast to the Beatles' fantasies," he concluded.[94] In a glowing review of the Stones' *Let It Bleed* album, *Rising Up Angry* compared the two groups. "Most of us like the Stones. One of the reasons is that we know the Stones like us. They understand what we are going through, our struggles, our pains, our pleasures." The Beatles, however, have "forgotten where they came from. They're like middle-class rebels: they don't like the government, but they don't want the revolution coming through their plate glass windows...the Beatles use the word 'love' today to argue against struggle."[95]

Many right-wingers, who had previously criticized the Beatles for their countercultural views and condemned Lennon for his more popular than Jesus remarks, now rejoiced at their stance. Writing in the conservative journal the *National Review,* Phillip Abbott Luce defended "Back in the USSR" from its conservative critics, justifiably noting that the song did not "really laud the Communists" and "that the song is a total put-on." Conservatives would later adopt "Taxman" as their anthem against big government, but in the climate of political radicalism, "Revolution"

While criticized by the New Left, the Beatles were adopted by the rising conservative movement. The New Guard, *November 1969, page 16.*

became their favorite song, praised for its condemnation of violence for political ends and for "putting down the antics of the SDS and New Left types."[96]

"As the Left prepares its ultimate orgy of violence and anarchy, all elements of Western society are forced to choose sides: even those Pop culture heroes, the Beatles, have mounted the barricade—on our side," *The New Guard*, magazine of the Young Americans for Freedom, proudly noted in November 1968. "The latest Beatle disc, aptly named 'Revolution,' is a witty, firm condemnation of Leftist activism," the magazine continued. "Both musically and polemically the Beatles urge the generation they helped create to free its mind from revolutionary enticements."[97] The Young Americans for Freedom expressed their delight with "Revolution" by producing a wall poster depicting the Beatles and the song's lyrics. "Turn on your friends and turn off the Left with this revolutionary pulchritude now distributed by YAF," they delightedly exclaimed. It is unknown how many bedroom walls the poster graced.[98]

African Americans

"Too many of our people are hooked on the Beatles," noted the Chicago-based *Negro Digest* in November 1969, a leading voice of the black artistic fraternity who worried about the influence of white culture on the black community.[99] The *Negro Digest* need not have expressed such concern, however, as the previously positive view of the Beatles emanating from the South and West Sides of the city lessened as the end of the decade approached. A new Black Nationalist slogan, "Black Power," first brought to national prominence in 1966 by Stokely Carmichael, head of the Student Nonviolent Coordinating Committee (SNCC), resonated with frustrated African Americans and reflected a changed cultural outlook on the part of the young. Advocates of Black Power suggested that blacks should not integrate but separate from whites and ought to defend themselves against white violence. Instead of admiring white culture, nationalists urged blacks to take pride in their own race and their own cultural achievements, leading to a surge of interest in African history and culture among young black people.[100]

Reflecting this support for Black Power among young blacks, a national poll taken in 1970 indicated that 43 percent of blacks under the age of twenty-one agreed that the revolutionary organization, the Black

Panthers, "represent my own personal views." In a poll of segregated black high schools undertaken in five cities, 29 percent supported the Black Panthers, and only 25 percent the integrationist NAACP.[101] As a result, many young African Americans turned away from white music and style, under the influence of Black Nationalism and its promotion of black culture, and adopted their own musical and cultural heroes.

As the Beatles left behind their rhythm and blues roots and replaced African-derived rhythms with Western melody, classical-style instruments and arrangements, and British folk sounds, they further alienated many young blacks. In the late '60s, the Beatles may have encapsulated the interests and feelings of young white America, but they failed to appeal to black youngsters living in riot-torn ghettoes. "*Sergeant Pepper* is not in the world as black people see it. No doubt about it. It's even ridiculous to speak about it. I mean this is all bullshit intellectualism anyway," black poet Larry Neal said shortly after its release. "Neither the Beatles nor any other white group brings to the black community any experiences that are finally meaningful. There is no pain inside them. Or at least it is pain that we cannot perceive."[102] Unsurprisingly, Neal and other young blacks identified more with James Brown's "Say It Loud, I'm Black and I'm Proud" and Aretha Franklin's "Respect" than with any Beatles song.

In this inflamed atmosphere, many young African Americans became increasingly resentful of the success that the Beatles and other British groups enjoyed with their reworking of black music. "Everybody talks about the Negro being culturally deprived," Stokely Carmichael declared in the summer of 1966. "We got culture! We got to stop the Beatles from stealing it from us!"[103] African-American poet and social critic LeRoi Jones likened the Beatles and other white pop groups to white performers at minstrel shows who dressed up as caricatures of blacks and mimicked them in an unflattering way. "They take from us all the way up the line. Finally, what is the difference between Beatles, Stones, etc., and Minstrelsy. Minstrels never convinced anybody they were Black either."[104] Eldridge Cleaver, an early leader of the Black Panther Party, condemned the Beatles for stealing black music in his memoir *Soul on Ice*. The "popular music of urban Negroes—which was known as Rhythm and Blues before the whites appropriated and distilled it into a product they called Rock 'n Roll—is the basic ingredient, the core, of the gaudy, cacophonous hymns with which the Beatles of Liverpool drive their hordes of Ultrafeminine fans into catatonia and hysteria."[105]

Both Larry Neal and LeRoi Jones questioned the manliness of the Beatles. "To the black community, the Beatles come across as young boys," Neal wrote in 1968. "Everything about them smacks of boyhood. The most consistently asserted value in the black community is the necessity of maintaining one's manhood. In terms of the collective perception, the long hair of the Beatles and other white rock groups gives hints of femininity. In a world where a manly image is highly valued, there is no place for little boys."[106] Jones succinctly described the Beatles as a "group of Myddle-class white boys who need a haircut and male hormones."[107]

Chicago, one of the most segregated cities in the nation, was a hotbed of black self-reliance and activism. The city was home to some of the leading African-American publications of the time, the *Chicago Defender*, *Ebony*, *Jet*, and *Negro Digest*. Elijah Muhammad's Nation of Islam established their headquarters on the South Side of Chicago, as did Jessie Jackson's Operation Breadbasket. The Illinois Black Panther Party, founded in Chicago in June 1968, became one of the strongest chapters of the party in the country. Led by the charismatic Fred Hampton, the Panthers established a strong following among young blacks and the respect of other political radicals in the Midwest as they sought to reach out across racial lines. Worried about Hampton's influence, officers attached to the Cook County State's Attorney's Office shot and killed the twenty-one-year-old as he lay in his bed in the early hours of December 4, 1969.[108]

Indicative of the growth of Black Nationalism among the young and of the racial divide in the city were the disputes that rocked the education system. On October 13, 1968, the Concerned Black Students of Chicago, representing thirteen schools, called for a city-wide boycott of high schools to take place each Monday until the Board of Education met their demands. They demanded black control of black schools, black history classes, black administrators, holidays to honor the achievements of famous black men and women, and black businesses to supply black schools. On Monday October 14, twenty-eight thousand students, more than half of the black high school students in the city, boycotted the schools, and many marched on the Board of Education and City Hall.[109] In the spring of 1969, black students, demanding a stronger minority presence on campus, disrupted classes at the city colleges, Chicago State University, Roosevelt University, and Northwestern University.[110]

African-Americans in this crucible of black militancy became more critical of the Beatles. "The Beatles adapted Negro jazz and made a million before the world knew what was going on," Gordon Hancock stated in the *Chicago Defender* in February 1966. "Stealing our stuff!"[111] Similarly, in September 1969, the music critic of the *Chicago Defender* could not resist criticizing the Beatles in an article on gospel music. When the Beatles broke through, "the entertainment world heralded them as the originators of a new bold musical style," he wrote. "All of this energy, the music, the style, the clapping of the hands, stomping of the feet, the hoopin' and hollerin' are all a part of the sounds the adults of this generation heard when they were children."[112] Poet Larry Neal, writing in *Ebony* about the black struggle, noted that African Americans needed their own cultural heroes. "A revolution that would have Leonard Bernstein, Bobby Dylan or the Beatles at the top of its cultural hierarchy would mean that in the process of making the revolution, the so-called revolutionaries had spiritually murdered Black people."[113]

Those African Americans that still liked the Beatles now had to conceal their enthusiasm from their friends and neighbors. Bonnie Greer, who grew up on the South Side of Chicago, found that her vocal admiration for the Beatles led to criticisms from others in the black community. Greer, a student at DePaul University, was addressing a meeting of the Black Student Union when a black militant walked in and posted a note on the desk, condemning her "in the same style that the French denounced women they called 'collabos' after the Second World War, women who had slept with the enemy. He also put in his sign that I loved the Beatles, which was probably, for him, the ultimate sign of treachery." Soon Greer, like many other young blacks, became less enamored of the group as "the girl who had been astounded by the Beatles was gone. In her place was an entity looking at the panorama of what was beginning to be called 'the black world.'"[114]

The Beatles' Breakup

The criticism of the Beatles and their values may have been more severe in Chicago than in any other major American city, but the underwhelming response to Paul McCartney quitting the Beatles in April 1970 signaled a decline in the group's popularity that was evident across the entire nation. After Brian Epstein's death in August 1967, the Beatles were slow to appoint a new manager and managed themselves for a time. Paul increasingly took leadership of the group, causing friction among the other three. John became distant from the group, partly because of his drug intake and partly because he enjoyed being with Yoko Ono more. He insisted that Yoko be present in the recording studio, angering his bandmates. It may have been disconcerting for those who firmly believed in the Beatles and the hippie ideal, but financial issues brought these differences and tensions to a head. The Beatles became so successful that they had to negotiate financial deals with song publishers, record companies, and their own enterprise, Apple Corps. When they realized that Apple was failing, John convinced George and Ringo, already annoyed at Paul's bossiness, that the hard-nosed New Yorker Allen Klein should manage the group. Paul, however, insisted that his father-in-law, the show business lawyer Lee Eastman, should represent his interests. Uncharacteristically, for a group that prided itself on unanimity in decision-making, John, George, and Ringo went with Klein, leaving Paul out in the cold.[115]

On the morning of April 10, the *Daily Mirror* broke the news with the dramatic front-page headline, "Paul Quits the Beatles." McCartney announced his departure via a question and answer press release he distributed to British journalists with advance copies of his solo album, *McCartney*. In the release, McCartney never actually said he was quitting the group, but he strongly suggested he was. "Are you planning a new album or single with the Beatles?"

"No," he replied.

"Is your break with the Beatles temporary or permanent, due to personal differences or musical ones?"

"Personal differences, business differences, musical differences, but most of all because I have a better time with my family. Temporary or permanent? I don't really know," he concluded.[116]

Many assume that McCartney's announcement gathered "front-page coverage in every corner of the globe."[117] The press reported the statement, but rather than garner front-page headlines, newspapers buried it among other more important news. The *New York Times* ran the story on page 21 and the *Los Angeles Times* on page 7.[118] The *Detroit Free Press* put the report on its front page, but below the far more important story: "State Bans St. Clair Fishing."[119] Under the heading, "Beatle Quits," the news appeared on page 16 of the *Chicago Tribune*.[120] The *Chicago Sun-Times* printed the story on page 5, while the *Chicago Daily News* ran a small item on page 2 under the hopeful headline "McCartney may return to Beatles."[121] Even the music periodicals seemed less than enthralled by the news. *Billboard* ran a matter-of-fact statement at the bottom of its front page, "Beatles Doing Own Things: Paul Quits."[122] *Cashbox* waited until May 2 to announce the story on page 52 and then stated, "So, if the Beatles don't seem too unhappy about the future, or the present for that matter, there is no reason that we should be. Why not just let it be."[123] Even though the group meant so much to many people, there followed no mass outburst of mourning and no letters to the editors expressing either sadness or outrage.

Maybe the public saw Paul's remarks as ambiguous, or maybe they had already been prepared for the day by the frequent rumors of a pending Beatles split; but the lack of interest in Paul's statement suggests that while they were still selling records, the Beatles were no longer the phenomenon they had been six years earlier. The *Chicago Tribune* mentioned the Beatles 919 times in 1964, the year they debuted in the United States, and 749 times in 1965. By 1969, the *Tribune* only mentioned the Beatles on 486 occasions; and in 1970, even with the news of the breakup, they received only 406 mentions in Chicago's leading newspaper. In February 1970, *Chicagoland* magazine asked six people aged from twenty-four to their fifties to discuss their most memorable event from the '60s. None mentioned the Beatles. Three said the moonwalk, two the assassinations of John F. Kennedy and Martin Luther King, and one the Chicago convention of 1968.[124] Most adult Americans felt distanced from the countercultural Beatles. For younger kids, other stars such as the Monkees had taken their place in the teen magazines. "I'm one of the few Beatle fans left in my neighborhood today," Celeste DeYoung dejectedly wrote to the *Tribune* in March 1970. "Too many people judge them by their appearance, not their personalities.... It sounds childish, but the few of us left have joined together. We appreciate what they've done and are trying to offset the people who refuse to see."[125]

A meeting of 125 members of the official Beatles fan club in Chicago's Executive House hotel in March 1970 illustrates how the Beatles now even divided their most ardent followers. There seemed to be friction between younger and older fans, and between those who supported John and Yoko's peace campaign and those who disapproved of their eccentric activities. "It's such a shame how the Beatles have changed," said Joanne Maggio, president of the Official United States Paul McCartney chapter. When organizers showed photos of the newly cropped John and Yoko to the crowd, they groaned. "He was proclaiming 'hair peace' and now he gets it cut. Sort of hypocritical, don't you think?" asked one attendee of John's decision to cut his hair. "Hey, okay! Let's have a Yoko and John party—everybody strip!" joked another. Area secretary Vikki Paradiso had seen enough. "To me there are no more true Beatle fans," she sadly claimed and announced the cancellation of future meetings.[126]

Many of those who hold vivid memories of seeing the Beatles on *The Ed Sullivan Show*, of sitting in the movie theater watching *A Hard Day's Night*, of attending a Beatles concert, or of listening to *Sgt. Pepper* for the first time have retained few recollections of the demise of the Beatles. Bethjoy Borris, the Beatlemaniac who met the Beatles at her father's hotel when they stayed in Chicago in 1965, said she liked other groups, "but not like I loved the Beatles. Still, I don't remember the whole deal about them breaking up."[127]

"At the time there really wasn't that much" coverage in the media, lamented longtime fan Katie Jones, who had sneaked backstage at the 1966 concert. "It's almost as if they sort of faded away quickly. It's not that they weren't popular anymore, but they weren't as popular as they were. They weren't in front of our faces, on our radar as much, especially after they stopped touring." She saw interest in the group decline after the release of the White Album. "A lot of fans were very confused and didn't like the album. It was like, 'Well, they're finished.'"[128]

"I sensed that they were not going to be around, and it hurt a lot when they finally broke up," recalled Cynthia Dagnal, the African-American girl who saw them in Chicago in 1964 and 1965. "I just didn't ever want that to happen. But I could tell they were tired, and I thought they had done enough. There were other bands. There were other sounds. There were other things going on. Things were moving on. You did have Bowie and all these people, and that was a completely different thing. I don't think they'd gotten obsolete. They had just gotten beyond it all. It

Cynthia Dagnal-Myron

Cynthia Dagnal, now a journalist, meets a thrilled looking Ringo Starr in Chicago in 1978.

didn't really matter if they were around because they had already done everything they needed to do."[129]

The lack of interest in the breakup further suggests that the Beatles had ceded ground to other groups. In 1964, the Beatles had no serious rivals, and in 1967, they were undoubted tastemakers with the release of *Sgt. Pepper*, but by 1970 substantial competition had emerged. With an emphasis on musicianship and loud, bluesy rock, Led Zeppelin released their debut album in January 1969 in the US and followed it up with their second long-playing disc in October, which alternated with *Abbey Road* for the number one position on the charts. In the same year, King Crimson pioneered progressive rock with their debut album, psychedelic innovators Pink Floyd released the ambitious *Ummagumma*, and the Who issued the first rock opera, *Tommy*. Starting with *Beggars Banquet* (1968) and *Let It Bleed* (1969), the latter briefly pushing *Abbey Road* off the top of the charts in the UK, the Rolling Stones were finally making albums to rival the Beatles' output. Black Sabbath released their debut album, ushering in heavy metal just weeks before McCartney left the Beatles. New singer-songwriters like Joni Mitchell; Neil Young;

and Crosby, Stills, and Nash produced songs with more introspective confessional lyrics than the Beatles could provide. Their unwillingness to tour hurt the Beatles at a time when better amplification, innovative light shows, and greater showmanship created stars out of such bands as the Who, Cream, and Led Zeppelin. When mass gatherings took on almost spiritual dimensions, the Beatles failed to appear at the major countercultural festivals in Monterey in June 1967 and at Woodstock in August 1969. In the UK, the Rolling Stones played to half a million people in Hyde Park, and Bob Dylan made his concert comeback at the Isle of Wight Festival in front of one hundred and fifty thousand people, watched by the rather glum trio of John, George, and Ringo. *The Seed*, always very supportive of the Beatles even during the "Revolution" days, discussed their "demise as a group" since they gave up live shows. "In their four-year stay in the studio, they became the most polished rock group on the planet, but consequently lost the energy that made people shout 'yeah, yeah' back in 1963."[130]

The release of *Sgt. Pepper's Lonely Hearts Club Band* in June 1967, so often seen as the pinnacle of their success, actually accelerated the Beatles' decline. The album heralded a new direction for the group that aligned them with the emerging counterculture. As the look and concerns of the four Beatles evolved, so, too, did those of many of their fans. Others, however, felt estranged from the group that they had once loved so much. Able to unite generations and tribes when they first appeared in the US, the most famous foursome in the world now alienated the mainstream, who decried their attachment to hippie ideals; young teens, who wanted the old Mop Tops to return; political radicals, who criticized their nonpolitical stance; and African Americans, who sought their own cultural role models. The Beatles were trailblazers when they first arrived in the United States, but by the decade's end, other rock groups had equaled or eclipsed them as musical innovators. When the Beatles broke up in the spring of 1970, they did so with a whisper rather than a scream.

Epilogue

After the Beatles broke up, each member of the group spent some time in Chicago. In May 1972, John and Yoko traveled to the city to talk to the preeminent African-American periodical *Jet,* aiming to calm the storm over their controversial song "Woman is the Nigger of the World." The famous couple checked into the Gold Coast's Ambassador East Hotel on Wednesday, May 10, 1972, and in the evening saw African-American comedian Dick Gregory perform at Mister Kelly's on Rush Street. The following day, they visited the offices of Johnson Publishing Company where they met with journalists from *Jet* for an interview in which Lennon spoke of his love for black music. The same day, they taped an appearance on *Kup's Show,* a late night TV program hosted by *Chicago Sun-Times* columnist Irv Kupcinet, where John and Yoko talked about their music and Lennon's fight to avoid deportation as an undocumented immigrant.[1] The trip, and especially Lake Michigan, left a deep impression on the couple. "We were enchanted with the lake," Yoko recalled years later of her visit to Chicago. "So when I was writing the song, 'Walking on Thin Ice,' I had this lake in my mind. The song is about a girl who tries to walk across a frozen lake, not knowing how big it is. It's funny because that's me! That's something I would do."[2] It would be the last song Lennon worked on before his assassination in New York City on December 8, 1980.

George became the first ex-Beatle to perform solo in Chicago when he played two shows at the Chicago Stadium on November 30, 1974, as part of an extensive North American tour. The shows received some poor reviews, with critics annoyed at the overlong set by the support act, Ravi Shankar and his orchestra, the hoarseness of Harrison's voice, and the rearranging of some of his classic Beatles songs. "Harrison never

292

proved to be much of a showman," the *Tribune* rock critic Lynn Van Matre wrote, "he looked tired and sounded it."[3] George visited Chicago once more in November 1976 as part of a promotional tour for his *Thirty-Three & 1/3* album, but he never again played in the city before his death from cancer in November 2001.

Paul McCartney became a frequent visitor to Chicago. He performed with his new band, Wings, at Chicago Stadium over three nights, May 31, June 1, and June 2, 1976, just under ten years since he had last played in the Windy City with the Beatles. McCartney used Chicago, along with Dallas, New York, and Los Angeles as his base for the tour, returning there after the concerts to spend time with his family. Paul came to Chicago to promote his film, *Give My Regards to Broad Street*, in October 1984, but the next time he performed in the city was as a solo artist at the Rosemont Horizon on the first leg of a world tour in December 1989. On these trips, he was able to venture outside his hotel and enjoy the delights the city had to offer. Chicago became his kind of town. "I find it very surprising actually in a good way. Its image worldwide tends to be as a secondary city to New York, the other New York, I think. I thought it was like amazing it was a real space-age city," he said on his 1984 visit. "I find it very surprisingly modern and a pretty classy place."[4] Paul and his wife, Linda, returned to the Windy City for a press conference to promote Linda's line of frozen dinners in May 1994, but his next concerts in Chicago were not until April 2002 when he played the United Center. After that, he played in the city on several occasions.

One of McCartney's more memorable trips to Chicago occurred during the summer of 2008. The song "Route 66," which name-checked Chicago as the start of the iconic American highway that ran west to California, had a magical ring for the Beatles and other British Invasion acts. In August 2008, Paul, with his girlfriend, Nancy Shevell, fulfilled his long-held ambition to drive Route 66 when they set off from Chicago in a green 1989 Ford Bronco. On their first stop, Paul and Nancy walked into the Route 66 Welcome Center at the Joliet Area Historical Museum and met Elaine Stonich, a volunteer who, unfazed by celebrity, immediately told the lovebirds to move their illegally parked car. After the chastised couple complied, they toured the museum and dropped some money into the collection box. "I froze. It was like seeing Bigfoot," said museum worker Pamela Biesen, who ran into McCartney in the gift shop. "I really just wanted to be polite," she said, not wanting to appear starstruck, but she could not halt impure thoughts from entering her head. "I really just wanted to lick him and say, 'I love you.'" Before leaving, Paul signed an autograph for Elaine and then drove off to the next stop on the Mother Road.[5]

On March 29, 1978, Ringo Starr made his first post-Beatles visit to the city when he recorded an appearance on the Chicago-based *Phil Donahue Show.* Ringo paid another visit in March 1981 to promote the film *Caveman* and again appeared on Donahue's show, this time with his girlfriend, and future wife, Barbara Bach. On July 25, 1989, Ringo played his first show in the Chicago area when he performed at the Poplar Creek Music Theater in the western suburb of Hoffman Estates as part of Ringo Starr and His All-Starr Band tour. Like Paul, he then returned to perform in Chicago on many occasions with various incarnations of his All-Starr Band.

Just like Paul, Ringo's most memorable visit to Chicago came during the summer of 2008. On July 13, he performed at the scenic Charter One Pavilion on Northerly Island on the banks of Lake Michigan and used his stay to publicly celebrate his 68th birthday. Ringo appeared with his wife at the entrance to the Hard Rock Hotel in the Loop at noon on Monday, July 7, to host a "peace and love" moment. About three hundred fans, camera crews, and reporters met outside the hotel to sing "Happy Birthday," flash peace signs, and eat birthday cake courtesy of the hotel. "If you could pan around, you could see Chicago is full of peace and lovers," he told the bemused reporters gathered around him. The Peace and Love event became a yearly tradition, occurring on his birthday in various cities around the world.[6]

The concerts of the ex-Beatles were invariably sold out; even with Paul playing massive sports stadiums like Soldier Field and Wrigley Field, but most came not to listen to them perform their solo material but to hear the old Beatles hits. As others such as Led Zeppelin, Pink Floyd, Bob Marley, David Bowie, and Kraftwerk pushed the boundaries of popular music in the '70s, the solo Beatles increasingly produced music that was mostly unadventurous and seldom matched their '60s output. The sounds of disco, salsa, acid house, reggae, and hip-hop captured the imagination of youngsters like the music of the solo Beatles could not. Paul McCartney and Ringo Starr, at least, knew this. "One thing you have to say is that I've put out an awful lot of records," Paul regretfully told

Uncut magazine in 2004. "Some of them I shouldn't have put out, sure. I'd gladly accept that."[7]

"I've made some really limp records," Ringo Starr admitted even more bluntly in August 1998, and those who heard his output readily agreed with his assessment.[8]

Despite the underwhelming quality of much of their solo work, and as the sold-out shows illustrate, interest in the Beatles endured, particularly in the United States. "The Beatles have gone beyond music in the United States, even beyond legend. They are a religion," Chicago-based music journalist Al Rudis wrote in 1976.[9] Fear of the Fab Four dissipated. Ringo's peace and love pronouncements and Paul's advocacy of vegetarianism now seemed quaint, rather than threatening, as the Beatles became loveable cultural icons. Jeff Griffin, who compiled a radio program in the early '80s about the Beatles' recordings at the BBC, found the show to be more popular in the US than in Britain. "That interest and the subsequent response when the extended programme was aired in the USA has finally convinced me of something that many Americans have told me over the years," Griffin wrote in October 1982. "However proud of the Beatles we are in Britain, probably very few of us have ever realized just how important they were as a source of inspiration to the youth of the world but very especially to the adolescents of America."[10] After the breakup of the Beatles, virtually all their solo albums performed better in the US charts than in the UK hit parade. While all three of the Anthology CDs released in 1995-96 reached number one in the US, only *Anthology 2* topped the charts in the UK.[11]

Chicago, along with the rest of America, had clearly not forgotten about the Beatles. Signaling the enduring popularity of the group, Beatlefest, later called the Fest for Beatles Fans, began in New York in 1974 to celebrate the tenth anniversary of the Beatles' arrival in the US and has taken place in Chicago virtually every year since 1977. The fest attracts musicians, those who befriended the group or worked with them, Beatles authors and, of course, fans both young and old; many trying to recapture their youth, others seeking to uncover the magic that they missed out on the first time around. Beatles tribute bands perform in the local area, while local radio stations broadcast Breakfast with the Beatles shows every week. In the early '70s, the Northwestern University Libraries acquired original lyric sheets for seven Beatles songs, the second largest collection of original Beatles lyrics in the world after the British Library in London.[12] In 1983, Chicago's Peace Museum hosted a Give Peace A Chance exhibition, featuring a number of items donated by Yoko Ono, including John Lennon's guitar inscribed with two of his drawings.[13] At the invitation of the city, in October 2016, Yoko Ono unveiled her first permanent public art installation in North America in Chicago's Jackson Park.[14]

The Beatles are now part of history. Only Paul and Ringo remain from the group, while all of the UK contingent that had traveled with the Beatles on their tours to Chicago have passed away: Brian Epstein, Neil Aspinall, Mal Evans, Alf Bicknell, Derek Taylor, Bess Coleman, Wendy Hanson, Diana Vero, and Tony Barrow. None of the Chicago venues they performed in or the hotels they stayed in are still in service. The International Amphitheatre, where the Beatles played their first and last concerts in Chicago, closed in 1999; the Stock Yard Inn, where the group met the hostile Chicago press for the first time, fell victim to the wrecking ball in 1977; and the sprawling Union Stock Yards that so offended the nostrils of many visitors shut its doors in 1971. The landmarks of the 1965 tour, White Sox Park and the Sahara Inn Hotel, were demolished in 1991. The Astor Tower Hotel, where they stayed in 1966 and John gave his "We're more popular than Jesus" press conference, is now converted into condominiums.

Undoubtedly, the Beatles were a social and cultural phenomenon who set so many precedents for others to follow. They directly inspired the proliferation of guitar groups and, through their example, encouraged many to write their own songs. They motivated musicians to demand more autonomy in the studio, pioneered the marketing and merchandising of pop music, and broke new ground with the first stadium concert tours. They wrote and recorded music that will be played for as long as people play music, and they helped push the boundaries of popular music into previously uncharted waters. When they started out, many viewed the Beatles' music and pop music in general as disposable and ephemeral, but now young and old alike celebrate the music, and scholars see it as an art form worthy of serious study. Myriad British acts can thank the Beatles for opening the door to the US market. The Beatles accelerated the process of cultural globalization as they provided people with a sense of a world beyond the confines of their locality, and they brought aspects of British and Indian culture to American shores. By the end of the '60s, the Beatles' impact was visible on the streets of Chicago and other US cities. Boys sported longer hair and girls shorter skirts, unisex hairdressers became a fixture on Main Street, YMCAs staged yoga classes, the universities taught transcendental meditation courses, long-haired rock musicians played in city clubs watched by pot-smoking enthusiasts, and youngsters listened to album-orientated rock programs on WLS and WCFL and on the burgeoning FM radio stations.

For all their achievements, however, the Beatles were not as influential as is often thought. Most youngsters ignored the Beatles' countercultural pronouncements and simply enjoyed the music. The Beatles' stand on civil rights, and their willingness to give credit to those black musicians who inspired them, was admirable, but they only influenced the African-American community and race relations in a tangential way. The '60s proved to be a momentous decade in the history of Chicago and the US, but the Beatles were not responsible for most of the changes that took place. The most important movements of the '60s—environmentalism, student protests, feminism, civil rights, and gay liberation—had nothing to do with the Beatles and would have happened even if the group had never arrived in the US. Indicative of their lack of sustained impact on Chicago, the most significant histories of the city focus on the civil rights movement, the political dominance of Mayor Richard J. Daley, and the violent events surrounding the Democratic convention of 1968 but fail to even comment on Beatlemania or the cultural influence of the Beatles.[15]

Beatlemania was temporary and the influence of the Beatles on Chicago and the nation rather innocent. The Beatles brought immense pleasure and joy to young people and offered them an alternative to the dull and the sober. Their critics were too quick to fear and condemn the Beatles and Beatlemania, and many of their adherents too eager to overstate their significance. For most, the Beatles were a youthful infatuation, but one that they still fondly remember more than fifty years later. Even today, that generation cannot shake the impact of first hearing "I Want to Hold Your Hand" on the radio, seeing the Beatles on *The Ed Sullivan Show*, watching *A Hard Day's Night* in a dark movie theater, or listening to the innovative sounds of *Sgt. Pepper* during that glorious summer of 1967.

Endnotes

INTRODUCTION

1   *Chicago Tribune,* February 13, 2014, page 7.

2   Joel Whitburn, *Top Pop Singles, 1955-2012* (Menomonee Falls, Wisconsin: Record Research, 2013), 66-67; and Joel Whitburn, *The Billboard Book of Top 40 Albums* (New York: Billboard Books, 1987), 28-29.

3   William Howland Kenney, *Chicago Jazz: A Cultural History, 1904-1930* (Oxford and New York: Oxford University Press, 1993).

4   Robert M. Marovich, *A City Called Heaven: Chicago and the Birth of Gospel Music* (Urbana: University of Illinois Press, 2015).

5   Campbell Gibson and Kay Jung, "Historical Census Statistics On Population Totals By Race, 1790 to 1990, and By Hispanic Origin, 1970 to 1990, For Large Cities And Other Urban Places In The United States" (Washington DC: U.S. Census Bureau, 2005).

6   Mike Rowe, *Chicago Blues: The City and the Music* (London: Da Capo Press, 1973).

7   Nadine Cohodas, *Spinning Blues into Gold: The Chess Brothers and the Legendary Chess Records* (New York: St. Martin's Griffin, 2001).

8   *The Mike Douglas Show,* February 16, 1972, YouTube. https://www.youtube.com/watch?v=lMOgIGWfDZ4. Accessed September 27, 2019.

9   Joel Whitburn, *Top Pop Singles, 1955-2012* (Menomonee Falls, Wisconsin: Record Research, 2013), 77.

10 Robert Pruter, *Chicago Soul* (Urbana: University of Illinois Press, 1991); Aaron Cohen, *Move on up: Chicago Soul Music and Black Cultural Power* (Chicago and London: The University of Chicago Press, 2019); and Robert Pruter, *Doowop: The Chicago Scene* (Urbana: University of Illinois Press, 1996).

11 Tom Dyja, *The Third Coast: When Chicago Built the American Dream* (New York: Penguin, 2013), xxiii.

12 Diane Pecknold, *The Selling Sound: The Rise of the Country Music Industry* (Durham: Duke University Press, 2007), 160-161; and *Variety,* March 3, 1965, pages 55 and 58.

13 Jeremy Geltzer, *Dirty Words & Filthy Pictures: Film and the First Amendment* (Austin: University of Texas Press, 2015), 23-27, 161-164, and 188-190.

14 Lenny Bruce, *How to Talk Dirty and Influence People: An Autobiography* (New York: Simon & Schuster, 1992), 96.

15 *Chicago Tribune,* December 8, 1963, page 8.

16 *Dixon Evening Telegraph,* April 1, 1955, page 1.

17 *The Pantagraph*, March 1, 1957, page 1; and *Billboard*, March 16, 1957, page 20.

18 Clark Weber interview with the author March 6, 2015.

19 *Chicago Tribune*, May 13, 1966, section 2, page 13.

20 *Time*, July 1, 1966, page 57.

21 Ron Smith, *Chicago Top 40 Charts 1960–1969* (New York: Writers Club Press, 2001), 77; and Jeff Lind, "History of Chicago Rock," *Illinois Entertainer*, February 1981.

CHAPTER 1

1 *New Musical Express*, December 6, 1963, page 2.

2 Mark Lewisohn, *All These Years. Volume 1, Tune In, Extended Special Edition* (London: Little, Brown, 2013).

3 *Viva*, March 1975, page 51.

4 *Radio Times*, May 28–June 3, 2011, page 20.

5 Cameron Steagall (2014), "George Harrison Recalls The Influence American Culture Had On The Beatles In 1987 Interview." http://newyork.cbslocal.com/top-lists/george-harrison-recalls-the-influence-american-culture-had-on-the-beatles-in-1987-interview/. Accessed May 23, 2017.

6 *Inner-View*, August 28, 1977, *The Beatles Ultimate Experience*. http://www.beatlesinterviews.org/db1976.00rs.beatles.html. Accessed May 23, 2015.

7 Mark Lewisohn, *All These Years. Volume 1, Tune In, Extended Special Edition* (London: Little, Brown, 2013), 646.

8 *The Paul McCartney World Tour program* (London: MPL, 1989), 44.

9 *Rolling Stone*, January 22, 1981, pages 38-39.

10 *You*, August 1971, pages 32-33.

11 *Disc Weekly*, Beatles Supplement, October 12, 1963, page iv.

12 Chas McDevitt, *Skiffle: The Definitive Inside Story* (London: Robson, 1997), 6.

13 Charlie Gillett, *The Sound of the City: The Rise of Rock and Roll* (New York: Outerbridge and Dienstfrey, 1970); and Ed Ward, *The History of Rock & Roll: Volume 1: 1920-1963* (New York: Flatiron Books, 2016).

14 Peter Guralnick, *Last Train to Memphis: The Rise of Elvis Presley* (New York: Little, Brown, 1994).

15 *New Musical Express*, August 30, 1963, page 10.

16 *The Beatles Anthology* (London: Cassell and Co. and San Francisco: Chronicle Books, 2000), 21.

17 *Mojo*, September 2005, page 90.

18 Max Weinberg and Robert Santelli, *The Big Beat: Conversations with Rock's Great Drummers* (New York: Billboard Books, 1991), 183.

19 *Let It Rock*, BBC Radio 2 interview by Joe Brown, July 5, 1999, *Let It Rock Around the World* (Yellow Cat CD, 2002).

20 *The Ultimate Music Guide: Lennon* (*Uncut* magazine special, 2010), page 146.

21 Frank Allen interview with the author, June 13, 2015.

22 Cynthia Lennon, *A Twist of Lennon* (New York: Avon, 1978), 167.

23 *Rock Compact Disc*, Volume 1 Number 4, 1992, pages 12-13.

24 Ray O'Brien interview with the author, February 21, 2015.

25 Ray O'Brien interview with the author, February 21, 2015.

26 Ray O'Brien interview with the author, February 21, 2015.

27 Chris Hutchins interview with the author, February 9, 2015.

28 Ray Coleman, *Brian Epstein: The Man Who Made the Beatles* (London: Viking, 1989).

29 *Eye,* September 1968, page 88.

30 *Beatlefan,* January-February 1994, page 14.

31 David Pritchard and Alan Lysaght, *The Beatles: An Oral History* (New York: Hyperion, 1998), 319.

32 *Good Day Sunshine,* Spring 1987, page 9.

33 *The Word,* March 2012, page 65.

34 *Uncut,* October 2015, page 43.

35 *New Musical Express,* October 5, 2013, page 24.

36 *The Beatles Anthology* (London: Cassell and Co. and San Francisco: Chronicle Books, 2000), 11.

37 *Disc,* November 14, 1964, page 5.

38 *The Beatles Anthology* (London: Cassell and Co. and San Francisco: Chronicle Books, 2000), 160.

39 *Billboard,* March 9, 1996, page 87.

40 Kevin Howlett, *The Beatles at the Beeb, 62-65: The Story of Their Radio Career* (Ann Arbor, MI: Pierian Press, 1983), 10.

41 *Bass Player,* October 2005, pages 42-43.

42 Mark Lewisohn, *The Complete Beatles Recording Sessions: The Official Story of the Abbey Road Years: Introductory Interview with Paul McCartney* (London: Hamlyn, 1988), 7.

43 *Record Mirror,* February 29, 1964, page 14.

44 *Cashbox,* March 2, 1963, page 25.

45 *New Musical Express,* August 9, 1963, page 10.

46 Tony Barrow, *Meet the Beatles: Star Special, Number 12* (Manchester: World Distributors, 1963), page 6.

47 Ray Coleman, *Brian Epstein: The Man Who Made the Beatles* (London: Viking, 1989), 110.

48 Pete Goodman, *Our Own Story by the Rolling Stones* (New York: Bantam Books, 1965), 104.

49 *The Beatles Ultimate Experience.* http://www.beatlesinterviews.org/db1964.0211cj.beatles.html. Accessed May 23, 2015.

50 *The Beatles Book,* March 1964, page 27.

51 *The Beatles Book,* January 1965, page 15.

52 *Daily Express,* October 15, 1963, page 16.

53 *The Beatles Ultimate Experience.* http://www.beatlesinterviews.org/db1963.1016.beatles.html. Accessed May 23, 2015.

54 1963 TV interview, YouTube. https://www.youtube.com/watch?v=1tvdJYxqxWM. Accessed May 23, 2015.

55 *Melody Maker,* December 3, 1969, page 20.

56 Christine Paine interview with the author, October 9, 2014.

57 Christine Paine interview with the author, October 9, 2014.

58 *New Musical Express,* November 22, 1963, page 10.

59   *Beatlefan,* December 1981/January 1982, page 3.
60   *The Observer,* November 10, 1963, page 29.
61   *Evening Standard* (London), December 24, 1963, page 1.

CHAPTER 2
1   MemyselfandI (2013) Interview with Ian and Lauren Wright, *4d5 rpm* http://4d5rpm. blogspot.com/2013/05/happy-birthday-tommy-roe.html. Accessed May 27, 2017.
2   *Record Mirror,* February 1, 1964, page 3.
3   *Not Just the Beatles: The Autobiography of Sid Bernstein* as told to Arthur Aaron (Teaneck, NJ: Jacques and Flusster Publishers, 2000), 125-126.
4   Piers Hemmingsen, *The Beatles in Canada: The Origins of Beatlemania* (Toronto: Hemmingsen publishing, 2015), 92-96.
5   Bruce Spizer, *The Beatles Records on Vee-Jay: Songs, Pictures and Stories of the Fabulous Beatles Records on Vee-Jay* (New Orleans, LA: 498 Productions, 1998).
6   Clark Weber interview with the author, March 6, 2015.
7   WLS surveys provide documented evidence that Biondi played the Beatles first, but other American deejays may have broadcast the Beatles' music before Biondi. Parlophone released "Love Me Do" in the UK in October 1962 and "Please Please Me" in January 1963, and other radio stations, besides WLS, could have played imported copies of these records even though they may not appear on any surviving radio survey. For example, deejay Dave Hull from California claims that he first heard "Love Me Do" on WVKO in Ohio in 1962. Harvey Kubernik, *It Was Fifty Years Ago Today: The Beatles Invade America and Hollywood* (Los Angeles: Other World Industries, 2014), 50.
8   Bruce Spizer, *The Beatles Records on Vee-Jay: Songs, Pictures and Stories of the Fabulous Beatles Records on Vee-Jay* (New Orleans, LA: 498 Productions, 1998), 4.
9   Bob Wilson interview with the author, March 1, 2015.
10   *South Bend Tribune,* August 7, 2014, page D7.
11   WYNR Top 40 Disks Survey, July 19, 1963; and Bruce Spizer, *The Beatles Records on Vee-Jay: Songs, Pictures and Stories of the Fabulous Beatles Records on Vee-Jay* (New Orleans, LA: 498 Productions, 1998), 12.
12   Louise Harrison interview with the author, May 9, 2015.
13   *El Paso Herald-Post,* October 14, 1963, page 5; *Eureka Humboldt Standard,* October 14, 1963, page 24; *Tucson Daily Citizen,* October 14, 1963, page 24; and *Ogden Standard Examiner,* October 14, 1963, page 5.
14   *Los Angeles Times,* October 6, 1963, page 3; *Washington Post,* October 29, 1963, page 3; and *Detroit Free Press,* October 29, 1963, page 11.
15   *Time,* November 15, 1963, page 66; and *Newsweek,* November 18, page 104.
16   Bruce Spizer, *The Beatles Are Coming!: The Birth of Beatlemania in America* (New Orleans, LA: 498 Productions, 2003).
17   Val Camilletti interview with the author, February 17, 2015.
18   Ron Smith, *Chicago Top 40 Charts, 1960-1969* (New York: Writers Club Press, 2001), 9.
19   *Billboard,* January 18, 1964, page 1; and *Billboard,* February 1, 1964, page 20.
20   *You,* August 1971, pages 32-33.
21   *The Beatles Book,* May 1997, pages 7-8.

22 *Billboard,* February 15, 1964, pages 1 and 8.

23 *Daily Herald,* February 2, 2014, page 1.

24 Bill Ehm interview by Melanie Monbrod, May 5, 2019, Joliet Junior College Library Archives.

25 *Beatlefan,* January-February 2004, page 15.

26 Katie A. Jones interview with the author, April 27, 2019.

27 Hillary Rodham Clinton, *Living History* (New York: Simon & Schuster, 2003), 18.

28 Fox News (2015), "'Angst'-Ridden Hillary Clinton Found Answers in the Beatles." https://www.foxnews.com/story/angst-ridden-hillary-clinton-found-answers-in-the-beatles. February 20, 2009. Accessed May 24, 2017.

29 Terry Cessna interview by Jacqueline Marquez, December 9, 2014, Joliet Junior College Library Archives.

30 *Chicago Tribune,* February 18, 1964, section 2, page 1.

31 Thefab40.com. http://www.thefab40.com/alltimetop75.html. Accessed January 23, 2017.

32 *Billboard,* February 18, 2012, page 16.

33 *Billboard,* February 15, 1964, pages 1 and 8.

34 *Billboard,* February 22, 1964, page 38.

35 *Chicago Daily News,* February 11, 1964, page 3.

36 Terry Crain, *NEMS and the Business of Selling Beatles Merchandise in the US, 1964-1966* (USA: FaBgear company, 2019).

37 *The Lincolnwood Life,* September 16, 1965, page 1.

38 *Q* magazine, September 1989, page 34-35.

39 *The Realist,* November 1968, page 15.

40 *Q* magazine, September 1989, page 34-35.

41 *Rolling Stone,* February 15, 1969, page 22.

42 *Daily Mirror,* March 27, 1978, page 18.

43 *Billboard,* February 22, 1964, page 38.

44 Louise Harrison interview with the author, May 9, 2015.

45 Stew Salowitz, *Chicago's Personality Radio: The WLS Disc Jockeys of the Early 1960s* (Normal, IL: Chicago Radio Book, 1993), 79.

46 Clark Weber interview with the author, March 6, 2015.

47 *Chicago Tribune,* August 29, 1964, page 7.

48 *Chicago Sun-Times,* August 29, 1964, page 20.

49 Cynthia Dagnal-Myron interview with the author, July 12, 2017.

50 Kathy Holden interview with the author, March 13, 2015.

51 *The Pantagraph,* February 4, 1984, page 19.

52 *Chicago Tribune,* September 3, 1964, section 2, page 10.

53 *Chicago Daily News Panorama* magazine, August 29, 1964, page 17.

54 *Chicago Sun-Times,* August 30, 1964, section 3, page 1.

55 *Daily Northwestern,* September 17, 1964, pages 21-22.

56 *Chicago Tribune,* March 18, 1964, page 2.

57 *Sterling Daily Gazette,* December 6, 1965, page 4.

58 Steve Gillon, *Boomer Nation: The Largest and Richest Generation Ever, and How It Changed America* (New York: Free Press, 2004), 19.

59 David Farber, *The Age of Great Dreams, America in the 1960s* (New York: Hill and Wang, 1994), 8.

60   David Halvorsen, *Chicago: A Profile of Greatness* (Chicago: Chicago Tribune, 1966), 1.

61   Linda Milan interview by Jennifer Raymond, December 3, 2014, Joliet Junior College Library Archives.

62   *Chicago's American,* February 9, 1964, page 28.

63   George H. Gallup, *The Gallup Poll: Public Opinion, 1935-1971 Volume 3, 1959-1971* (New York: Random House 1972), 1598, 1940-41, 2010, and 2211.

64   The Interuniversity Social Research Committee-Chicago Metropolitan Area, *Militancy For and Against Civil Rights and Integration in Chicago: Summer 1967* (Chicago: University of Chicago, 1967), 5.

65   *Time,* November 15, 1963, page 64.

66   Julius Fast, *The Beatles: The Real Story* (New York: G.P. Putnam's Sons, 1968), 102.

67   William L. Schurk, B. Lee Cooper, and Julie A. Cooper, "Before the Beatles: International Influences on American Popular Recordings, 1940–63," *Popular Music and Society* (May 2007), 227–66.

68   The *Pantagraph*, November 24, 1963, page 15.

69   *Chicago Tribune,* February 3, 1963, section 5, page 14.

70   Barry Miles, *The British Invasion* (New York: Sterling, 2009), 174.

71   *Newsweek,* March 21, 1966, page 60.

72   *Chicago Defender,* April 11, 1964, page 16.

73   *Chicago Defender,* March 28, 1964, page 9.

74   *Chicago Defender,* February 16, 1966, page 23.

75   Cynthia Dagnal-Myron interview with the author, July 12, 2017.

76   Cynthia Dagnal-Myron interview with the author, July 12, 2017.

77   *Chicago Defender,* August 18, 1964, page 17.

78   *Chicago Defender,* September 8, 1964, page 12.

79   *Chicago Defender,* September 5, 1964, page 16.

80   *Photoplay*, August 1964, page 91.

81   *Daily Express,* September 8, 1964, page 2.

82   *Soul,* April 28, 1966, page 6.

83   *Motown 25: Yesterday, Today, Forever* (DVD, 2014).

84   Black artists covered far more Beatles numbers than the blues-influenced music of the Rolling Stones or the folk songs of Bob Dylan. The abundance of Beatles songs covered by black artists is evident by the release of a number of compilations devoted to the phenomenon: *Motown Meets the Beatles* (1995), *Stax Does the Beatles* (2008), *Come Together: Black America Sings Lennon & McCartney* (2011), *Let It Be: Black America Sings Lennon, McCartney & Harrison* (2016) and *Glass Onion: Songs of The Beatles from the Atlantic & Warner Jazz Vaults* (2003).

85   Charles Shaar Murray, *Boogie Man: The Adventures of John Lee Hooker in the American Twentieth Century* (New York: St. Martin's Press, 2000), 262.

86   *New Musical Express,* April 30, 1977, page 30.

87   Stew Salowitz, *Chicago's Personality Radio: The WLS Disc Jockeys of the Early 1960s* (Normal, IL: Chicago Radio Book, 1993), 90.

88   "Official Beatles Fan Club" enrollment letter, April 1964.

89   Vicki Thom to Mayor Richard J. Daley September 2, 1964, Richard J. Daley collection, Series I, subseries 3: the Colonel 'Jack' Reilly Papers, Box 2, "Beatles Buffs, 1964" folder, Special Collections and University Archives, University of Illinois at

Chicago; *Chicago's American,* August 28, 1964, *Chicago's American,* September 6, 1964, page 3; and *Chicago Sun-Times Midwest* magazine, August 30, 1964, page 9.

90 Margaret McGahan to Mayor Richard J. Daley 1964, Joanne Abrams to Mayor Richard J. Daley 1964, Marianne O'Laughlin to Mayor Richard J. Daley 1964, Richard J. Daley collection, Series I, subseries 3: the Colonel "Jack" Reilly Papers, Box 2, "Beatles Buffs, 1964" folder, Special Collections and University Archives, University of Illinois at Chicago.

91 *Chicago Tribune,* May 23, 1964, page 9 and *Chicago's American,* May 25, 1964 page 3.

92 *Chicago Tribune,* November 20, 1964, page 16.

93 Arthur Unger Papers, The State Historical Society of Missouri. Beatles, Lennon Controversy, 1966, f718.

94 Marti Edwards and Joe Carroccio, *16 in '64: The Beatles and the Baby Boomers* (2016).

95 *Teen World,* June 1965, page 29.

96 *Teen Life,* June 1965, page 22.

97 Pat Meyers interview with the author, February 25, 2015.

98 *Beatle Hairdos and Setting Patterns* (1964).

99 *Spec Magazine,* Winter 1967, page 26.

100 *Newsweek,* March 21, 1966, pages 74-75.

101 Claudia Chalden interview by Andy Okroi, November 21, 2014, Joliet Junior College Library Archives.

102 *Datebook,* August 1966, page 52.

103 *Ebony,* February 1965, page 118.

104 *Chicago Defender,* April 2, 1966, page 36.

105 Cynthia Dagnal-Myron interview with the author, July 12, 2017.

106 Bonnie Greer, *A Parallel Life* (London: Arcadia Books, 2014), 132-133 and 149.

107 *Chicago Tribune,* July 18, 1967, page 20.

108 Terry Cessna interview by Jacqueline Marquez, December 9, 2014, Joliet Junior College Library Archives.

109 *Chicago Sun-Times Midwest* magazine, August 15, 1965, page 13.

110 Hugh Willoughby, *Amid the Alien Corn: An Intrepid Englishman in the Heart of America* (Indianapolis: Bobbs-Merrill, 1958), 104.

111 Marjorie Banks and Edward Ward, *The U.S. and Us* (London: Allan Wingate, 1952), 149 and 151.

112 Bill Adler, *Dear Beatles* (New York: Wonder Books, 1966), 4.

113 Bill Adler, *Love Letters to the Beatles* (New York: Putnam, 1964), 78.

114 Linda Milan interview by Jennifer Raymond, December 3, 2014, Joliet Junior College Library Archives.

115 *Datebook,* Winter 1965, page 46.

116 Ginny Venson Greninger interview with the author, April 20, 2015.

117 *Datebook,* September 1966, page 51.

118 Jeanne Yorke interview with the author, May 18, 2015.

119 *Life,* May 13, 1966, page 82.

120 *Hullabaloo,* October 1966, page 3 and December 1966, page 7.

121 Jeffrey S. Miller, *Something Completely Different: British Television and American Culture* (Minneapolis and London: University of Minnesota Press, 2000), 35.

122 David Wangerin, *Soccer in a Football World: The Story of America's Forgotten Game* (Philadelphia: Temple University Press, 2006), 127.

123 *Chicago Tribune*, September 30, 1965, page 8.

124 *Chicago Tribune*, October 10, 1965, page 19.

125 Joel Whitburn, *Top Pop Singles, 1955-2012* (Menomonee Falls, Wisconsin: Record Research, 2013), 1109-1110 and 170.

126 Pete Shelton interview with the author, March 11, 2016.

127 Pete Shelton interview with the author, March 11, 2016.

128 *Billboard,* September 11, 1965, page 37.

129 Pete Shelton interview with the author, March 11, 2016.

CHAPTER 3

1 *Chicago Tribune,* January 9, 1964, page 16.

2 Val Camilletti interview with the author, February 17, 2015.

3 Leann Julian interview with the author, February 12, 2015.

4 Kathy Mangan interview by Jon Mangan, December 7, 2015, Joliet Junior College Library Archives.

5 *Daily Northwestern*, April 2, 1964, page 14.

6 Bob Smith interview by Bobby Smith, May 1, 2014, Joliet Junior College Library Archives.

7 Tom Ruddy interview by Shawn Ruddy, May 1, 2015, Joliet Junior College Library Archives.

8 *Chicago Tribune*, December 8, 2001, page 25.

9 Bernard Biernacki interview with the author, May 29, 2018.

10 *Chicago Garfieldian*, February 19, 1964, page 2.

11 *Photoplay*, July 1964, pages 1, 38-39, 41 and 79-80.

12 David A. Noebel, *Communism, Hypnotism and the Beatles* (Tulsa, OK: Christian Crusade Publications, 1965), 15.

13 *Chicago Austin News*, May 6, 1964, page 27.

14 *Chicago Austin News*, July 22, 1964, page 18.

15 *Chicago Austin News*, October 14, 1964, page 15.

16 *Amarillo Globe Times*, August 20, 1965, page 18.

17 *New York Times*, June 16, 1964, page 43.

18 Timothy Stewart-Winter, *Queer Clout Chicago and the Rise of Gay Politics* (Philadelphia: University of Pennsylvania Press, 2016).

19 *Chicago Tribune*, November 3, 1964, page 3; and *Chicago's American*, November 1, 1965, section 6, page 8. The *Chicago Daily News* and the *Chicago Sun-Times* both endorsed Democrat Lyndon B. Johnson (*Chicago Daily News*, November 2, 1964, page 1 and 8 and *Chicago Sun-Times*, November 2, 1964, page 6). The *Los Angeles Times* also endorsed Republican Barry Goldwater, the *New York Times* backed Johnson, and the *Washington Post* refused to officially endorse either candidate but clearly supported the Democratic ticket.

20 *Chicago Tribune*, May 23, 1975, page 1.

21 *Chicago Tribune*, May 25, 1975, page 14.

22 *Los Angeles Times*, February 10, 1964, page 2 and *New York Times*, February 10, 1964, page 53.

23   *Chicago Tribune,* February 11, 1964, page 16.

24   *Chicago Tribune TV Week,* February 29, 1964, page 6.

25   *Chicago Tribune,* February 23, 1964, page 22.

26   *Chicago Garfieldian,* February 26, 1964, page 24.

27   Popboprocktiludrop. "Buggin' the Beatles," https://kimsloans.wordpress.com/about-2/skipped-a-beat/. Accessed September 5, 2017.

28   *Chicago Tribune,* October 4, 1965, page 16.

29   John Sebastian interview with the author, June 25, 2015.

30   Louise Harrison interview with the author, May 9, 2015.

31   *Chicago Daily News,* February 13, 1964, page 6.

32   *Chicago's American,* September 5, 1964, page 13.

33   *Chicago's American,* September 4, 1964, page 28.

34   *Chicago's American,* September 9, 1964, page 14.

35   *Chicago Tribune,* September 9, 1966, section, 2, page 14.

36   Dora Loewenstein and Philip Dodd (eds) *According to the Rolling Stones: Mick Jagger, Keith Richards, Charlie Watts, Ronnie Wood* (San Francisco: Chronicle Books, 2003), 168-169.

37   Pete Shelton interview with the author, March 11, 2016.

38   *Record Mirror,* October 7, 1965, page 2.

39   *Chicago Tribune,* February 14, 1965 section 5, page 7.

40   *Chicago Sun-Times Midwest* magazine, August 15, 1965, page 13.

41   *The Spire,* June 1966, page 9, St. Willibrord High School collection, Archdiocese of Chicago's Joseph Cardinal Bernadine Archives and Records Center, Chicago, IL.

42   *Berwyn Life,* August 15, 1965, page 8.

43   *Datebook,* Winter 1965, page 49.

44   *The DePaulia,* April 27, 1966, page 2.

45   *The Spire,* November 1964, page 5, St. Willibrord High School collection, Archdiocese of Chicago's Joseph Cardinal Bernadin Archives and Records Center, Chicago, IL.

46   *Daily Mail,* May 7, 1965, page 16.

47   *The Height Herald* (Peoria), February 14, 1964, page 5.

48   *The Lowdown,* July 1964, pages 31-32.

49   *Chicago Garfieldian,* February 19, 1964, page 12G.

50   *Chicago Tribune,* August 26, 1964, page 17.

51   *Christianity Today,* February 28, 1964, page 27.

52   *Chicago Tribune,* March 24, 1964, page 24.

53   Nicholas Schaffner, *The Beatles Forever* (New York: McGraw-Hill, 1977), 16

54   *Chicago Daily News,* September 4, 1964, page 8.

55   *Boston Globe,* September 13, 1964, page 3.

56   *Chicago Daily News,* February 10, 1964, page 37.

57   *Chicago's American,* January 14, 1964, page 32.

58   *Chicago's American,* February 10, 1964, page 20.

59   *Chicago's American,* September 4, 1964, page 3.

60   *Chicago's American,* September 7, 1964, page 1.

61   *Chicago's American,* September 8, 1964, page 3.

62   *Chicago Tribune magazine,* March 15, 1964, page 12.

63   *Chicago Tribune,* February 29, 1964, page 12.

64 *Chicago Tribune,* February 23, 1964, page 22.

65 *Chicago Tribune,* August 17, 1964, page 16.

66 *Chicago Tribune,* August 29, 1964, page 14, and August 21, 1964, page 14.

67 Otis L. Graham, Jr. (2004), "A Vast Social Experiment: The Immigration Act of 1965." http://npg.org/library/forum-series/a-vast-social-experiment-the-immigration-act-of-1965.html. Accessed December 1, 2017.

68 Michael Roberts, "A Working-Class Hero is Something to be: The American Musicians' Union's Attempt to ban the Beatles, 1964," *Popular Music* (January 2010), pages 1-16.

69 Cushing Strout, *The American Image of the Old World* (New York: Harper and Row, 1963), 230; and Henry Steele Commager (ed) *Britain Through American Eyes* (New York: McGraw-Hill, 1974).

70 Jeffrey Richards, *Hollywood's Ancient Worlds* (New York: Continuum, 2008); and Maria Wyke, *Projecting the Past: Ancient Rome, Cinema, and History* (New York and London: Routledge, 1997).

71 *Billboard,* March 28, 1964, page 10, April 4, 1964, page 3, June 6, 1964, page 1.

72 *Variety,* March 25, 1964, page 49.

73 *Billboard,* September 19, 1964, page 15.

74 *Billboard,* December 12, 1964, page 1.

75 Curt Johnson with Craig Sautter, *Wicked City: Chicago From Kenna to Capone* (Highland Park, IL: Da Capo Press, 1998), 218.

76 Richard Norton Smith, *The Colonel: The Life and Legend of Robert R. McCormick* (Boston and New York: Houghton Mifflin, 1997).

77 *Chicago Tribune*, October 7, 1947, pages 1 and 12; October 8, 1947, pages 1-2; and October 9, 1947, pages 1 and 19.

78 *Chicago Tribune*, July 17, 1951, page 1, and January 17, 1949, page 3.

79 *Chicago Sun-Times,* February 10, 1964, page 23.

80 *Loyola News,* December 9, 1964, page 1.

81 *TeenSet,* February 1966, page 5.

82 *Tiger Beat,* September 1966, page 65.

83 *Bridgeport News,* February 19, 1964, page 1.

84 Nicholas Schaffner, *The Beatles Forever* (New York: McGraw-Hill, 1977), 53.

85 Soviet Propaganda Film, YouTube. https://www.youtube.com/watch?v=7V0wR8V-JsyY. Accessed December 18, 2018.

86 *Chicago's American,* September 2, 1964, page 1.

87 *The Nation,* March 2, 1964, pages 221-222.

88 Fielding Buck (2012), "RIVERSIDE: Q&A with Roger McGuinn." http://www.pe.com/articles/years-665279-chicago-judy.html. Accessed August 22, 2016.

89 John Einarson with Ian Tyson and Sylvia Tyson, *Four Strong Winds* (Toronto: Emblem, 2011), 151-152.

90 Cynthia Dagnal-Myron interview with the author, July 12, 2017.

91 *Billboard,* February 22, 1964, page 38.

92 *Chicago Defender,* February 8, 1964, page 16.

93 *Chicago Defender,* February 26, 1964, page 15.

94 *Chicago Defender* (city edition), May 30-June 5, 1964, page 26.

95 *Chicago Defender,* May 9, 1964, page 16.

96   Charles Colbert interview with the author, March 16, 2016.
97   Sylvester Cottrell interview with the author, November 29, 2015.

CHAPTER 4

 1   Marlene Bendt to Mayor Richard J. Daley, February 2, 1964, Katherine Preiser to Mayor Richard J. Daley, February 10, 1964, Kathy White to Mayor Richard J. Daley, February 15, 1964, Beatle Fan Club in Portage Park School to Mayor Richard J. Daley, February 13, 1964, Cathy Ann Kennedy to Mayor Richard J. Daley, February 23, 1964, Richard J. Daley collection, Series I, subseries 3: the Colonel "Jack" Reilly Papers, Box 2, "Beatles Buffs, 1964" folder, Special Collections and University Archives, University of Illinois at Chicago.

 2   Joan Marek to Mayor Richard J. Daley, February 8, 1964, Richard J. Daley collection, Series I, subseries 3: the Colonel "Jack" Reilly Papers, Box 2, "Beatles Buffs, 1964" folder, Special Collections and University Archives, University of Illinois at Chicago.

 3   *Chicago Tribune,* April 14, 1964, section 2, page 4.

 4   Frank Fried, *From Lenin to Lennon: My Unlikely Life in Show Business and Revolution* (Morrisville, North Carolina: Lulu, 2013); and Dan La Botz (2015) Frank Fried, 1927-2015, Presente!. http://newpol.org/content/frank-fried-1927-2015-presente. Accessed January 23, 2015.

 5   Frank Fried, *From Lenin to Lennon: My Unlikely Life in Show Business and Revolution* (Morrisville, North Carolina: Lulu, 2013), 106-107.

 6   Chad Mitchell interview with the author, August 24, 2016.

 7   Chad Mitchell interview with the author, August 24, 2016.

 8   *Chicago Tribune,* April 23, 1964, page 18.

 9   CPI Inflation Calculator. http://www.govspot.com/ask/inflation.htm. Accessed June 14, 2015.

10   *Chicago Tribune,* June 25, 1964, page 21.

11   *Chicago Sun-Times,* June 28, 1964, pages 3 and 60.

12   *The Write Thing,* February/March 1984, page 5.

13   Q magazine, January 1988, page 60.

14   Derek Taylor, *Fifty Years Adrift* (Surrey, England: Genesis, 1984), 193.

15   Art Schreiber and Hal Simmons, *Out of Sight Blind and Doing All Right* (Los Ranchos, New Mexico: Nuevo Books, 2014), 36-37.

16   *Leicester Mercury,* June 30, 2009. http://www.leicestermercury.co.uk/Fab/story-12054304-detail/story.html. Accessed January 27, 2015; and *Teen Life,* November 1966, page 18.

17   *Record Mirror,* September 11, 1964, page 4.

18   *Datebook,* Fall 1965, page 14.

19   *The Write Thing,* February/March 1984, page 4.

20   *The Beatles Anthology* (London: Cassell and Co. and San Francisco, Chronicle Books, 2000), 155.

21   George Harrison interview by Arthur Unger, Arthur Unger Papers, The State Historical Society of Missouri. Beatle Interviews, 1-5, f704.

22   Clarence 'Frogman' Henry interview with the author, March 6, 2015.

23   Lillian Walker interview with the author, September 12, 2016.

24   Bob Tucker interview with the author, February 26, 2015.

25   Lillian Walker interview with the author, September 12, 2016.
26   Lillian Walker interview with the author, September 12, 2016.
27   Lillian Walker interview with the author, September 12, 2016.
28   *New York Post,* September 16, 1964, page 21.
29   *Chicago Tribune,* August 28, 1964, section 2, page 13.
30   *Chicago's American,* September 4, 1964, page 15.
31   *Chicago Sun-Times Midwest* magazine, August 30, 1964, page 9.
32   Adam Cohen and Elizabeth Taylor, *American Pharaoh. Mayor Richard J. Daley: His Battle for Chicago and the Nation* (Boston: Little Brown and Company, 2000).
33   *Chicago Tribune,* July 5, 1988, page 7; and *Sunday Tribune* magazine, May 4, 1969, pages 44-54, quote on page 44.
34   Donna Sharkozy to Mayor Richard J. Daley, July 12, 1964, Sandra Hossin to Mayor Richard J. Daley, Mary Beth Simmons to Mayor Richard J. Daley, July 28, 1964, Sharon Fuldoon to Mayor Richard J. Daley August 31, 1964, Janice Erwin to Mayor Richard J. Daley August 31, 1964, Linda Cerven to Mayor Richard Daley September 1, 1964, Richard J. Daley collection, Series I, subseries 3: the Colonel "Jack" Reilly Papers, Box 2, "Beatles Buffs, 1964" folder, Special Collections and University Archives, University of Illinois at Chicago.
35   Marilyn Everhart to Mayor Richard J. Daley, July 1964, Richard J. Daley collection, Series I, subseries 3: the Colonel "Jack" Reilly Papers, Box 2, "Beatles Buffs, 1964" folder, Special Collections and University Archives, University of Illinois at Chicago.
36   Jack Reilly to Marilyn Everhart, July 27, 1964, Richard J. Daley collection, Series I, subseries 3: the Colonel "Jack" Reilly Papers, Box 2, "Beatles Buffs, 1964" folder, Special Collections and University Archives, University of Illinois at Chicago.
37   Ruth Tully and Annette Moody to Mayor Richard J. Daley July 20, 1964, Richard J. Daley collection, Series I, subseries 3: the Colonel "Jack" Reilly Papers, Box 2, "Beatles Buffs, 1964" folder, Special Collections and University Archives, University of Illinois at Chicago.
38   Susan Dembek to Mayor Richard J. Daley, August 20, 1964, Richard J. Daley collection, Series I, subseries 3: the Colonel "Jack" Reilly Papers, Box 2, "Beatles Buffs, 1964" folder, Special Collections and University Archives, University of Illinois at Chicago.
39   "Beatlemaniacs of Chicago" to Richard J. Daley, June 11, 1964, Richard J. Daley collection, Series I, subseries 3: the Colonel "Jack" Reilly Papers, Box 2, "Beatles Buffs, 1964" folder, Special Collections and University Archives, University of Illinois at Chicago. See also Diana Riches to Mayor Richard J. Daley, August 5, 1964, Kathy Clarke to Mayor Richard J. Daley, August 5, 1964, Linda Nygren to Mayor Richard J. Daley, August 18, 1964, Ann Gerace to Mayor Richard J. Daley, August 21, 1964, Richard J. Daley collection, Series I, subseries 3: the Colonel "Jack" Reilly Papers, Box 2, "Beatles Buffs, 1964" folder, Special Collections and University Archives, University of Illinois at Chicago.
40   Jack Reilly letter, August 19, 1964 Richard J. Daley collection, Series I, subseries 3: the Colonel "Jack" Reilly Papers, Box 2, "Beatles Buffs, 1964" folder, Special Collections and University Archives, University of Illinois at Chicago.
41   Fran Sanocki to Jack Reilly September 6, 1964, Richard J. Daley collection, Series I, subseries 3: the Colonel "Jack" Reilly Papers, Box 2, "Beatles Buffs, 1964" folder, Special Collections and University Archives, University of Illinois at Chicago.

42 *Chicago Tribune,* August 28, 1964, section 2, page 13.

43 *New York Times,* February 13, 1964, page 26.

44 *Chicago's American,* September 5, 1964, page 3.

45 Chuck Gunderson, *Some Fun Tonight!: The Backstage Story of How the Beatles Rocked America: The Historic Tours of 1964 to 1966: Volume 1 1964* (San Diego, California: Gunderson Media, 2013), 36 and 267.

46 1964 TV interview, YouTube. https://www.youtube.com/watch?v=kFriNh0axwU. Accessed April 18, 2017.

47 Alan B. Anderson and George W. Pickering, *Confronting the Color Line: The Broken Promise of the Civil Rights Movement in Chicago* (Athens, GA: University of Georgia Press, 1986), 157; *Chicago Sun-Times,* October 23, 1963, page 1; and *Integrated Education* 1 (December 1963–January 1964), 10-11 and 2 (April-May 1964), 23.

48 *Chicago's American,* September 5, 1964, page 1.

49 *Chicago Tribune,* August 26, 1964, page 18.

50 *Melody Maker,* September 12, 1964, page 3.

51 *Chicago Tribune,* September 4, 1964, page 10.

52 Frank Sullivan, *Legend, the Only Inside Story About Mayor Richard J. Daley* (Chicago: Bonus Books, 1989), 33.

53 *Chicago Sun-Times,* September 5, 1964, page 23.

54 *Chicago Sun-Times,* June 28, 1964, pages 3 and 60.

55 Anthony Scalise, Chief of Staff of Finance Chairman John P. Daley, email to the author on August 23, 2016.

56 *Chicago Sun-Times,* June 28, 1964, pages 3 and 60.

57 Merrilee Clark Redmond, telephone conversation with the author, October 8, 2016.

58 *Chicago Tribune,* September 5, 1964, page 1.

59 *Chicago Daily News,* September 5, 1964, page 5.

60 Beatles in Chicago, YouTube. https://www.youtube.com/watch?v=dy9O8osIOSQ. Accessed December 19, 2014.

61 *Melody Maker,* September 5, 1964, page 3.

62 *Chicago's American,* September 6, 1964, page 3.

63 Louise Harrison interview with the author, May 9, 2015.

64 *Chicago Tribune,* September 14, 1964, section 2, page 3.

65 *The New York Times,* July 6, 2010, Arts section, page 7.

66 *Music Trades,* February 2014, page 44.

67 Paul William Schmidt, *History of the Ludwig Drum Company* (Fullerton, CA: Centerstream, 1991), 75-76.

68 *Chicago Heights Star,* September 10, 1964, page 18.

69 *Daily Mail,* September 18, 1964, page 8.

70 Larry Kane, *Ticket To Ride: Inside The Beatles' 1964 & 1965 Tours That Changed The World* (Philadelphia: Running Press, 2003), 93.

71 The Beatles Ultimate Experience. http://www.beatlesinterviews.org/db1964.0905.beatles.html. Accessed November 26, 2014.

72 *How the Brits Rocked America* (BBC TV documentary, 2012).

73 Derek Taylor, *Fifty Years Adrift* (Surrey, England: Genesis, 1984), 181.

74 *Rolling Stone,* February 4, 1971, page 37.

75 John Lennon interview with Arthur Unger, summer 1966, Beatle Interviews, 1-5, f704, Arthur Unger Papers, The State Historical Society of Missouri.

76 "Food in the Life of Sir Paul McCartney," *The Food Programme*, BBC Radio 4, January 27, 2013.

77 *New York Post*, September 16, 1964, page 21.

78 *Daytrippin,'* Summer 2002, page 6.

79 *Billboard*, May 26, 2001, page 4.

80 Denny Somach, *A Walk Down Abbey Road* (Hertford, NC: Crossroad Press, 2020), 34.

81 Kevin Howlett, *The Beatles: The BBC Archives, 1962-1970* (London: BBC Books, 2013), 89.

82 *TV Week* (Australia), June 13, 1964, page 2.

83 *Ready, Steady Go*, March 20, 1964.

84 *Daily Mail*, October 11, 1955, page 1.

85 *Daily Mirror*, June 30, 1959, page 24.

86 *Daily Express*, May 16, 1961, page 11.

87 *Daily Mail*, September 4, 1962, page 1.

88 *Time*, April 3, 1964, page 47.

89 *Chicago Daily News*, September 5, 1964, page 5.

90 The Beatles Ultimate Experience. http://www.beatlesinterviews.org/db1964.0823.beatles.html. Accessed May 25, 2015.

91 The Beatles Ultimate Experience. http://www.beatlesinterviews.org/db1964.0828.beatles.html. Accessed May 25, 2015.

92 *Chicago Sun -Times*, September 6, 1964, page 14.

93 Ginny Venson Greninger interview with the author, April 20, 2015.

94 *The Skokie Life*, September 17, 1964, page 3.

95 *Chicago's American*, September 6, 1964, pages 1 and 3.

96 Scotty Moore website (2011). http://www.scottymoore.net/Chicago.html. Accessed June 5, 2015.

97 Louise Harrison, *My Kid Brother's Band a.k.a. the Beatles* (Morley, MO: Acclaim Press 2014), 233.

98 Mary Mack Conger, *Sweet Beatle Dreams: The Diary of Mary Mack Conger* (Kansas City, MO: Andrews and McMeel, 1989), 40-41.

99 Cynthia Dagnal-Myron interview with the author, July 12, 2017.

100 *Chicago's American*, September 8, 1964, page 3; and *Chicago's American*, September 5, 1964, page 3.

101 *Chicago's American*, September 1, 1964, page 3.

102 *The Pantagraph* (Bloomington), September 7, 1964, page 7.

103 *Chicago's American*, September 7, 1964, page 1.

104 *Chicago Tribune*, June 8, 1976, page 4.

105 *Arlington Heights Herald*, September 10, 1964, page 14.

106 Mary Mack Conger, *Sweet Beatle Dreams: The Diary of Mary Mack Conger* (Kansas City, MO: Andrews and McMeel, 1989), 41.

107 A. J. S. Rayl and Curt Gunther, *Beatles '64: A Hard Day's Night in America* (New York: Doubleday, 1989), 164-166.

108 *Chicago Tribune*, June 18, 1978, section 6, page 3.

109 *Chicago Daily News,* September 7, 1964, page 7.

110 *Chicago Tribune,* November 20, 1964, page 16.

111 Larry Kane, *Ticket To Ride: Inside The Beatles' 1964 & 1965 Tours That Changed The World* (Philadelphia: Running Press, 2003), 94.

112 *The Skokie Life,* September 17, 1964, page 3.

113 Ginny Venson Greninger interview with the author, April 20, 2015.

114 *Chicago's American,* September 6, 1964, page 1.

115 *Datebook,* Winter 1965, page 63.

116 *Chicago Sun-Times,* September 2, 1964, page 30.

117 Andee Levin interview with the author, February 6, 2015.

118 Louise Harrison, *My Kid Brother's Band a.k.a. the Beatles* (Morley, MO: Acclaim Press 2014), 234.

119 *Albuquerque Journal Sun,* February 9, 2014, page B6.

120 Jim O'Boye interview with the author, April 2, 2015.

121 *Modern Drummer,* November 2005, page 70.

122 No recordings of the Chicago shows have surfaced, so I've depended on fans who attended the concerts for the setlists. Marti Edwards and Joe Carroccio, *16 in '64: The Beatles and the Baby Boomers* (2016), 78.

123 *Fabulous,* November 28, 1964, page 5.

124 Larry Kane, *Ticket To Ride: Inside The Beatles' 1964 & 1965 Tours That Changed The World* (Philadelphia: Running Press, 2003), 95.

125 *The Realist,* November 1968, page 16.

126 Mary Mack Conger, *Sweet Beatle Dreams: The Diary of Mary Mack Conger* (Kansas City, MO.: Andrews and McMeel, 1989), 44.

127 Marc A. Catone, *As I Write This Letter: An American Generation Remembers The Beatles* (Ann Arbor, MI: Greenfield Books, 1982), 134.

128 Frank Fried, *From Lenin to Lennon: My Unlikely Life in Show Business and Revolution* (Morrisville, North Carolina: Lulu, 2013), 109.

129 *Chicago Sun-Times,* September 6, 1964, page 14.

130 *Chicago Tribune,* September 6, 1964, page 1.

131 *Chicago Tribune,* September 6, 1964, page 2.

132 *Daily Mail,* September 18, 1964, page 8.

133 *Melody Maker,* December 19, 1964, page 24.

134 *Daily Mirror,* March 5, 1965, page 5.

135 *Melody Maker,* November 7, 1964, page 7.

136 *Datebook,* Fall 1965, page 11.

137 Derek Taylor, *Fifty Years Adrift* (Surrey, England: Genesis, 1984), 224.

138 *Teen Life,* December 1966, page 24.

139 *Leicester Mercury,* June 30, 2009. http://www.leicestermercury.co.uk/tour-Fab/story-12072644-detail/story.html. Accessed January 27, 2015.

140 Frank Fried, *From Lenin to Lennon: My Unlikely Life in Show Business and Revolution* (Morrisville, NC: Lulu, 2013); and *Pollstar,* March 3, 2008, pages 6-7.

141 Jack Reilly to Benita Gooby July 9, 1964, Richard J. Daley collection, Series I, subseries 3: the Colonel 'Jack' Reilly Papers, Box 2, "Beatles Buffs, 1964" folder, Special Collections and University Archives, University of Illinois at Chicago.

CHAPTER 5

1   *Disc Weekly*, September 11, 1965, page 5.

2   *Chicago Sun-Times*, February 5, 1984, page 5.

3   *Berwyn Life*, August 25, 1965, page 21.

4   *Chicago Tribune*, August 8, 1965, section 10, page 6 and August 15, 1965, section 10, pages 2 and 4.

5   *Chicago Tribune*, June 5, 1965, page 14.

6   *Chicago Tribune*, August 21, 1965, page 2. *Chicago's American*, August 21, 1965, page 1, puts the figure nearer to 60,000.

7   *Chicago Tribune*, July 21, 1965, page 16.

8   *Chicago Tribune*, January 17, 1964, page 1.

9   *Chicago Tribune*, December 23, 1964, page 11.

10 *Chicago Tribune*, August 14, 1965, page 15. Skar was gunned down on September 11, 1965 for unpaid gambling debts.

11 Nathan Godfried, *WCFL, Chicago's Voice of Labor, 1926-78* (Urbana: University of Illinois Press, 1997).

12 Val Camilletti interview with the author, February 17, 2015.

13 Ken Draper interview with the author, March 25, 2016.

14 *Chicago's American*, August 22, 1965.

15 *Datebook*, Winter 1966, page 22.

16 *Chicago Tribune*, August 27, 1965, section 2, page 11.

17 *Fabulous*, January 8, 1966, page 9.

18 Richard Houghton, *I Was There: The Beatles* (London: Red Planet, 2016), 333-334.

19 No photos or interviews have surfaced from the Beatles' visit to the club. The meeting Clark describes may well have taken place at White Sox Park.

20 Clark Weber interview with the author, March 6, 2015.

21 Clark Weber interview with the author, March 6, 2015.

22 Smoking Gun, December 11, 2008. http://www.thesmokinggun.com/documents/crime/van-halens-legendary-mms-rider; and Amy Blumsom, October 13, 2015. https://www.telegraph.co.uk/music/news/craziest-music-rider-demands/. Accessed March 25, 2018.

23 Chuck Gunderson, *Some Fun Tonight!: The Backstage Story of How the Beatles Rocked America: The Historic Tours of 1964 to 1966: Volume 2 1965-1966* (San Diego, California: Gunderson Media, 2013), 13.

24 *Chicago Daily News*, August 19, 1965, page 25.

25 Larry Kane, *Ticket To Ride: Inside The Beatles' 1964 & 1965 Tours That Changed The World* (Philadelphia: Running Press, 2003), 234.

26 Denise Mourges interview with the author, June 12, 2015.

27 Denise Mourges interview with the author, June 12, 2015.

28 Denise Mourges interview with the author, June 12, 2015.

29 Ben Quiñones, *Naa Na Na Na Naa*, December 29, 2005. https://www.laweekly.com/news/naa-na-na-na-naa-2141348. Accessed October 12, 2017.

30 *The Playing Beatles 2: The Houston Complete Concert* (Great Dane Records, 1993) and *The Beatles and the Great Concert at Shea* (Great Dane Records, 1993).

31 *Detroit Free Press*, November 7, 1965, page 12.

32 *Record Mirror*, May 30, 1964, page 16.

33   Alan "Boots" Holmes interview with the author, February 27, 2015.
34   Denise Mourges interview with the author, June 12, 2015.
35   Alan "Boots" Holmes interview with the author, February 27, 2015.
36   Alan "Boots" Holmes interview with the author, February 27, 2015.
37   *Green Bay Press-Gazette*, August 22, 1965, page 3.
38   This set list is from Sharon Simons, who attended the afternoon show. *Green Bay Press-Gazette*, August 22, 1965, page A-3. On the same tour, the concerts at Shea Stadium, Houston, Texas, and Atlanta, Georgia, were recorded, and in those shows the Beatles played "Everybody's Trying to Be My Baby" followed by "Can't Buy Me Love," which they also performed at the evening show, suggesting Simons may have slightly mixed up the order.
39   *Chicago Sun-Times,* August 21, 1965, page 3.
40   *The Beatles Book*, May 1998, page 13.
41   *Musician*, July 1996, page 54.
42   Alan "Boots" Holmes interview with the author, February 27, 2015.
43   Dee Elias, *Confessions of a Beatlemaniac: A True Story of a Fan who Broke all the rules to Meet the Beatles* (AuthorsBound.com, 2014), 104.
44   *Green Bay Press-Gazette*, August 22, 1965, page A-3.
45   *Waukesha Daily Freeman,* September 2, 1965, page 22.
46   *Green Bay Press-Gazette*, August 22, 1965, page A-3.
47   Cynthia Dagnal-Myron interview with the author, July 12, 2017.
48   Alf Bicknell and Alasdair Ferguson, *Ticket to Ride: The Ultimate Beatles Tour Dairy* (London: Glitter Books, 1999), 69.
49   *Datebook,* Winter 1966, pages 22-23.
50   *Melody Maker*, August 28, 1965, page 7.
51   The Beatles Ultimate Experience. http://www.beatlesinterviews.org/db1965.0820.beatles.html. Accessed January 18, 2017
52   Beatles chauffeur Alf Bicknell told an elaborate story in his memoirs about meeting Lovin' Spoonful singer John Sebastian at White Sox Park in Chicago in 1965. Sebastian told me he was not there. Alf Bicknell and Alasdair Ferguson, *Ticket to Ride: The Ultimate Beatles Tour Dairy* (London: Glitter Books, 1999), 69. John Sebastian interview with the author, June 25, 2015.
53   Stuart Wolf interview with the author, August 17, 2018.
54   *Chicago Tribune*, August 21, 1965, page 1.
55   1965 Chicago press conference, YouTube. https://www.youtube.com/watch?v=VZd-MEk7yaNc. Accessed March 25, 2018.
56   Katie MacLeod Davidson interview with the author, September 2, 2019.
57   Katie MacLeod Davidson interview with the author, September 2, 2019.
58   *Datebook,* Winter 1966, page 5.
59   *Datebook,* Winter 1966, page 31-32.
60   *Chicago Tribune,* August 20, 1965, page 12.
61   Clark Weber interview with the author, March 6, 2015.
62   This set list is from Fab4 Mania. http://fab4mania.blogspot.com/. Accessed August 22, 1965. Carol Tyler attended the evening show at White Sox Park and wrote this setlist independent of her sister who attended the same show and verified the list. Email from Carol Tyler to author, August 22, 2015.

63   *Chicago Daily News*, August 21, 1965, page 4.

64   *The Pantagraph*, August 23, 1965, page 1.

65   *Beatlefan*, August/September 1980, page 18.

66   Clark Weber interview with the author, March 6, 2015.

67   *Belvidere Daily Republic*, August 23, 1965, page 8.

68   *Chicago's American*, August 21, 1965, page 1.

69   Larry Kane, *Ticket To Ride: Inside The Beatles' 1964 & 1965 Tours That Changed The World* (Philadelphia: Running Press, 2003), 235.

70   Bob Mitchell interview with the author, May 17, 2016.

71   Chuck Dingée interview with the author, November 24, 2015.

72   Ruby Wax, *How Do You Want Me?* (London: Ebury Press, 2002), 61-62.

73   *Chicago Sun-Times*, February 12, 1993, page 7. Photos from the night have yet to surface. Consequently, some doubt that the Beatles ever visited Margie's.

74   David Cacioppo Sr., "Chicago rock concerts 1960's and 1970's Facebook Group," May 5, 2012.

75   Bethjoy Borris interview with the author, August 6, 2018.

76   Bethjoy Borris interview with the author, August 6, 2018.

77   Louise Harrison interview with the author, May 9, 2015.

78   *The Southern Illinoisan*, February 2, 1995, page 5.

79   Janis Esch, "Remembering George Harrison's 'American friend,' Gerald 'Gabe' McCarty of Benton," July 14, 2016. http://thesouthern.com/news/local/remembering-george -harrison-s-american-friend-gerald-gabe-mccarty-of/article_d596165b-813f-5bc0- be97-f813b5d258a2.html. Accessed July 28, 2016.

80   Bethjoy Borris interview with the author, August 6, 2018.

81   *Rolling Stone*, January 21, 1971, page 39.

82   *Observer*, October 14, 2007. https://www.theguardian.com/music/2007/oct/14/pop androck5. Accessed February 20, 2017.

83   *GQ* magazine, October 2018, page 124.

84   Bethjoy Borris interview with the author, August 6, 2018.

85   *TeenSet*, February 1966, page 29.

86   *Chicago Tribune*, August 28, 1965, page 6.

87   Denise Mourges interview with the author, June 12, 2015.

88   Alan "Boots" Holmes interview with the author, February 27, 2015.

CHAPTER 6

1   Cary Baker, "Where Are the Punks of Yesteryear?" *Triad*, December 1976, page 17.

2   Ronnie Rice interview with the author, September 11, 2015.

3   *Chicago Tribune*, August 5, 1965, section 2, page 1.

4   Dean Milano interview with the author, February 17, 2015.

5   *Billboard*, July 1, 1967, page WS-47.

6   *Record Beat*, March 1, 1966, page 7.

7   *Music Trades*, February 2014, page 44, and *Music Trades*, September 2014, page 146.

8   Walter Carter, *The Gibson Electric Guitar Book: Seventy Years of Classic Guitars* (New York: Backbeat Books, 2007), 65.

9   *Jacksonville Daily Journal*, April 24, 1965, page 7.

10 Adam Langer, "Glory Days," *Chicago Reader*, January 13, 1989, page 14.

11   Bruce Mattey interview with the author, February 17, 2015.

12   Ron Smith, *WCFL Chicago Top 40 Charts, 1965-1976* (New York: iUniverse, 2007), 73, and Ron Smith, *Chicago Top 40 Charts 1960-1969* (New York: Writers Club Press, 2001), 83.

13   Bruce Mattey interview with the author, February 17, 2015.

14   Ronnie Rice interview with the author, September 11, 2015.

15   Joel Whitburn, *Top Pop Singles, 1955-2012* (Menomonee Falls, Wisconsin: Record Research, 2013), 609.

16   Jimy Sohns interview with the author, March 12, 2015.

17   Jimy Sohns interview with the author, March 12, 2015.

18   *Arlington Heights Herald,* March 24, 1966, page 25.

19   The Shadows of Knight, *Back Door Men* (Sundazed CD, 1998).

20   Laura E. Hill, "When the Northwest Suburbs Rocked," *Chicago Tribune,* section 17, December 31, 1995, page 1.

21   The Shadows of Knight, *Alive in '65* (Sundazed CD, 2018) and *Chicago Tribune,* October 31, 1965, section 10, page 3.

22   The Shadows of Knight, *Back Door Men* (Sundazed CD, 1998).

23   *Omnibus,* June 1967, page 50.

24   *Chicago Tribune,* October 31, 1965, section 10, page 3.

25   Dave Grundhoefer interview with the author, September 11, 2015.

26   *Arlington Heights Herald,* November 3, 1966, page 3.

27   Jimy Sohns interview with the author, March 12, 2015.

28   *Arlington Heights Herald,* July 8, 1965, page 11.

29   *Here 'tis,* Number 6 (1994), page 15.

30   Jim Peterik interview with the author, May 4, 2015.

31   Jimy Sohns interview with the author, March 12, 2015.

32   Ron Smith, *WCFL Chicago Top 40 Charts, 1965-1976* (New York: iUniverse, 2007), 92; Ron Smith, *Chicago Top 40 Charts 1960-1969* (New York: Writers Club Press, 2001), 104; and Joel Whitburn, *Top Pop Singles, 1955-2012* (Menomonee Falls, Wisconsin: Record Research, 2013), 753.

33   *Arlington Heights Herald,* May 5, 1966, page 27.

34   Adam Langer, "Glory Days," *Chicago Reader,* January 13, 1989, page 24.

35   *Arlington Heights Herald,* September 2, 1965, page 1; and *Arlington Heights Herald,* October 7, 1965, page 5.

36   Adam Langer, "Glory Days," *Chicago Reader,* January 13, 1989, page 28.

37   *Here 'tis,* Number 6 (1994), page 17.

38   *Here 'tis,* Number 9 (1999), page 62.

39   Various Artists, *If You're Ready! The Best of Dunwich Records…Volume 2* (Sundazed CD, 1994).

40   Email from Jimy Sohns to the author, December 2, 2015.

41   Joel Whitburn, *Top Pop Singles, 1955-2012* (Menomonee Falls, Wisconsin: Record Research, 2013), 753.

42   *Daily Herald Suburban Chicago,* January 8, 1984, page 7.

43   Curt Bachman interview with the author, August 1, 2016.

44   Carl Giammarese interview with the author, February 10, 2015.

45   Curt Bachman interview with the author, August 1, 2016.

46   Carl Giammarese interview with the author, February 10, 2015.

47   Adam Langer, "Glory Days," *Chicago Reader,* January 13, 1989, page 24.

48   Joel Whitburn, *Top Pop Singles, 1955-2012* (Menomonee Falls, Wisconsin: Record Research, 2013), 122.

49   Marty Grebb interview with the author, September 21, 2015.

50   Marty Grebb interview with the author, September 21, 2015.

51   Joel Whitburn, *Top Pop Singles, 1955-2012* (Menomonee Falls, Wisconsin: Record Research, 2013), 122.

52   *Tiger Beat,* March 1969, pages 48-49.

53   Gary Loizzo email to the author December 15, 2015.

54   Charles Colbert interview with the author, March 16, 2016.

55   Gary Loizzo interview with the author, February 24, 2015.

56   Charles Colbert interview with the author, March 16, 2016.

57   Charles Colbert interview with the author, March 16, 2016.

58   Joel Whitburn, *Top Pop Singles, 1955-2012* (Menomonee Falls, Wisconsin: Record Research, 2013), 33; and Official Charts. http://www.officialcharts.com/artist/13167/american-breed/. Accessed January 21, 2016.

59   *KRLA Beat,* January 13, 1968, page 13.

60   Charles Colbert interview with the author, March 16, 2016.

61   Tom Doody interview with the author, January 26, 2015.

62   Tom Doody interview with the author, January 26, 2015.

63   Adam Langer, "Glory Days," *Chicago Reader,* January 13, 1989, page 28.

64   Laura E. Hill, "When the Northwest Suburbs Rocked," *Chicago Tribune,* December 31, 1995, section 17, page 1.

65   The Beat (2017), "Sharing a cuppa tea with Jim Pilster–JC Hooke." http://beat-magazine.co.uk/2017/sharing-a-cuppa-tea-with-jim-pilster-jc-hooke#.W8UEAWhKjZs. Accessed October 15, 2017.

66   Clark Weber interview with the author, March 6, 2015.

67   Various Artists, *2131 South Michigan Avenue* (Sundazed CD, 2009).

68   Jimy Sohns interview with the author, March 12, 2015.

69   Clark Weber interview with the author, March 6, 2015.

70   Tom Doody interview with the author, January 26, 2015.

71   Ron Smith, *WCFL Chicago Top 40 Charts, 1965-1976* (New York: iUniverse, 2007), 26; Ron Smith, *Chicago Top 40 Charts 1960-1969* (New York: Writers Club Press, 2001), 30; and Joel Whitburn, *Top Pop Singles, 1955-2012* (Menomonee Falls, Wisconsin: Record Research, 2013), 206.

72   Jim Peterik interview with the author, May 4, 2015.

73   Jim Peterik interview with the author, May 4, 2015.

74   Jim Peterik interview with the author, May 4, 2015.

75   Joel Whitburn, *Top Pop Singles, 1955-2012* (Menomonee Falls, Wisconsin: Record Research, 2013), 403.

76   UK Official Charts http://www.officialcharts.com/artist/14064/ides-of-march/. Accessed January 21, 2016.

77   Allan Vorda interview with Ted Nugent, February 24, 1988, Briscoe Center for American History, The University of Texas at Austin. http://av.cah.utexas.edu/index.php/Vorda:Da_00117. Accessed December 15, 2017.

78 *Illinois Entertainer*, August 2016, page 6.

79 *Alton Telegraph*, August 24, 1999, section 3, page 5.

80 Dave Grundhoefer interview with the author, September 11, 2015.

81 Jeff Lind, "History of Chicago Rock," *Illinois Entertainer*, May 1977, page 7.

82 Warren Willingham interview with the author, March 21, 2016.

83 Warren Willingham interview with the author, March 21, 2016.

84 Warren Willingham interview with the author, March 21, 2016.

85 *Here 'Tis*, Number 8 (1997), page 60.

86 *Here 'Tis*, Number 8 (1997), pages 61-62.

87 David Kell Blanchard interview with the author, December 20, 2016.

88 *Here 'Tis*, Number 6, (1994), pages 9-10.

89 David Kell Blanchard interview with the author, December 20, 2016.

90 David Kell Blanchard interview with the author, December 20, 2016.

91 *Here 'Tis*, Number 8 (1997), pages 62-69.

92 *Here 'Tis*, Number 8 (1997), pages 62-69.

93 Debi Pomeroy interview with the author, January 25, 2015.

94 Andee Levin interview with the author, February 6, 2015.

95 Debi Pomeroy interview with the author, January 25, 2015.

96 Debi Pomeroy interview with the author, January 25, 2015.

97 Andee Levin interview with the author, February 6, 2015.

98 Andee Levin interview with the author, February 6, 2015.

99 Debi Pomeroy interview with the author, January 25, 2015.

100 Andee Levin interview with the author, February 6, 2015.

101 Various Artists, *Oh Yeah! The Best of Dunwich Records* (Sundazed CD, 1991).

102 Donna Smolak interview with the author, August 31, 2015.

103 *The Roselle Register*, December 27, 1967, page 8.

104 Donna Smolak interview with the author, August 31, 2015.

105 Debi Pomeroy interview with the author, January 25, 2015.

106 Donna Smolak interview with the author, August 31, 2015.

107 Donna Smolak interview with the author, August 31, 2015.

108 Judy Bloom interview with the author, July 19, 2015.

109 Judy Bloom interview with the author, July 19, 2015.

110 Various Artists, *2131 South Michigan Avenue* (Sundazed CD, 2009).

111 Various Artists, *Oh Yeah! The Best of Dunwich Records* (Sundazed CD, 1991).

112 Carl Giammarese interview with the author, February 10, 2015.

113 Jim Peterik interview with the author, May 4, 2015.

114 Danny Seraphine interview with the author, September 14, 2015.

115 *Here 'Tis*, Number 6 (1994), page 14.

116 Jimy Sohns interview with the author, March 12, 2015.

117 John Rook interview with the author, September 27, 2015.

118 Jeff Lind, "History of Chicago Rock," *Illinois Entertainer*, June 1978, page 7.

119 *Chicago Tribune*, June 26, 1966, section 10, page 1, and July 3, 1966, section 10, page 1.

120 Jeff Lind, "History of Chicago Rock," *Illinois Entertainer*, June 1978, page 7.

121 Various Artists, *If You're Ready! The Best of Dunwich Records... Volume 2* (Sundazed CD, 1994).

122 Various Artists, *If You're Ready! The Best of Dunwich Records...Volume 2* (Sundazed CD, 1994); and Jeff Lind, "History of Chicago Rock," *Illinois Entertainer,* June 1978, page 7.

CHAPTER 7

1   *Rave,* February 1966, page 39.
2   *Billboard* Top 100, http://billboardtop100of.com/1964-2/, http://billboardtop100of.com/1965-2/, http://billboardtop100of.com/1966-2/ All accessed August 19, 2017.
3   *Newsweek,* March 21, 1966, page 60.
4   *Chicago Tribune,* March 23, 1966, page 18, and March 24, 1966, page 18.
5   *Teen Circle,* February 1966, pages 9-10.
6   *Prospect,* January 2009, page 32, and *Risen,* July/August/September 2007, page 19.
7   Beatles Interviews. http://www.beatlesinterviews.blogspot.com/2009/02/beatles-press-conference-boston.html. Accessed March 7, 2015.
8   The Beatles Ultimate Experience. http://www.beatlesinterviews.org/db1965.0813.beatles.html. Accessed May 29. 2015.
9   Larry Kane, *Ticket To Ride: Inside The Beatles' 1964 & 1965 Tours That Changed The World* (Philadelphia: Running Press, 2003), 177.
10 *Disc and Music Echo,* July 23, 1966, page 2.
11 *Evening Standard* (London), March 18, 1966, page 8.
12 The Beatles Ultimate Experience. http://www.beatlesinterviews.org/db1966.0630.beatles.html. Accessed May 25, 2015.
13 *Pittsburgh Press,* April 26, 1966, page 61, *Pittsburgh Press,* May 2, 1966, page 48; and *Melody Maker,* June 4, 1966, page 4.
14 *Evening Standard* (London), March 4, 1966, page 10.
15 *Playboy,* February 1965, page 58.
16 *Evening Standard* (London), March 18, 1966, page 8.
17 Michael Braun, *"Love Me Do!": The Beatles' Progress* (Harmondsworth: Penguin, 1964, 1995 edition), 42-43.
18 *Sunday Mirror,* December 15, 1963, page 5.
19 *Newsweek,* March 21, 1966, page 52.
20 *The San Francisco Chronicle,* April 13, 1966, page 26.
21 *Detroit Free Press,* April 24, 1966, pages 18, 20, and 23; May 1, 1966, pages 18, 19, and 23; May 8, 1966, pages 28, 30, 32 and 37; and May 22, 1966, pages 27, and 30-31.
22 *The New York Times* Magazine, July 3, 1966, page 30.
23 Tony Barrow to Arthur Unger, March 9, 1966, Beatles Correspondence, 1964-1971, f703, Arthur Unger Papers, The State Historical Society of Missouri.
24 Arthur Unger to Maureen Cleave, March 22, 1966, Beatles Correspondence, 1964-1971, f703, Arthur Unger Papers, The State Historical Society of Missouri.
25 Maureen Cleave to Arthur Unger, March 24, 1966, Beatles Correspondence, 1964-1971, f703, Arthur Unger Papers, The State Historical Society of Missouri.
26 Arthur Unger to Tony Barrow, April 4, 1966, Beatles Correspondence, 1964-1971, f703, Arthur Unger Papers, The State Historical Society of Missouri.
27 *Evening Standard* (London), March 25, 1966, page 8.
28 Eric Cohen (2016), "Rock, Punk, Photography and Lore: A Conversation with Danny Fields." https://www.adorama.com/alc/rock-punk-photography-and-lore-a-conversation-with-danny-fields. Accessed April 24, 2017. See also Team Rock.com.

http://teamrock.com/feature/2016-04-21/danny-says-how-danny-fields-changed-music-forever. Accessed April 24, 2017; and *Danny Says* documentary (DVD 2016).

29   Danny Fields interview with the author, June 28, 2018. For more on the controversy see Brian Ward, "'The 'C' is for Christ': Arthur Unger, *Datebook* Magazine and the Beatles," *Popular Music and Society* 35 (October 2012), 541-560; and Steve Turner, *The Gospel According to the Beatles* (Louisville and London: John Knox Press, 2006).

30   Terry Magoon to *Datebook,* August 12, 1966, Beatles, Lennon Controversy, 1966, f711, Arthur Unger Papers, The State Historical Society of Missouri and *Teen Life,* October 1966, pages 1, and 6-10.

31   *Alabama Journal,* August 4, 1966, page 31.

32   *Datebook,* August 1966, page 60.

33   Art Unger C4027_ac_51_side_B_Beatles, Audiovisual Series, Arthur Unger Papers, The State Historical Society of Missouri.

34   Russell Wells (2015), *Birmingham Rewound.* http://www.birminghamrewound.com/radio-tv2.htm. Accessed July 16, 2018.

35   Danny Fields interview with the author, June 28, 2018. The two Alabama deejays remained quiet on how they received their copy of the magazine.

36   *Abilene Reporter News* (Texas), August 16, 1966, page 10.

37   *Longview News-Journal* (Texas), August 14, 1966, page 17.

38   Brian Ward, "'The 'C' is for Christ:' Arthur Unger, *Datebook* Magazine and the Beatles," *Popular Music and Society* 35 (October 2012), 552, *Kittanning Simpson Leader Times* (Pennsylvania), August 4, 1966, page 2; and *Kilmarnock Rappahannock Record* (Virginia), August 11, 1966, page 13.

39   *KRLA Beat,* August 27, 1966, page 16.

40   *Kingsport Times-News* (Tennessee), August 7, 1966, page 12.

41   *KRLA Beat,* August 27, 1966, page 16.

42   *The Tennessean,* August 17, 1966, page 12.

43   George Gallup, *The Gallup Poll, 1935-1971: Volume 3* (New York: Random House, 1972), 2174.

44   George Gallup, *The Gallup Poll, 1935-1971: Volume 3* (New York: Random House, 1972), 2059.

45   *KRLA Beat,* August 27, 1966, page 16.

46   *The Baltimore Sun,* August 15, 1966, page 3.

47   Letter and petition from James M. Featherstone to Detroit City Council, Jerome P. Cavanagh Papers, Box 278, Folder 16, Walter P. Reuther Library, Detroit, MI.

48   *New York Times,* August 6, 1966, page 13; *Chicago Tribune,* August 5, 1966, page 3; *Chicago Tribune,* August 7, 1966, page 22; *The Republic* (Columbus, Indiana), August 6, 1966, page 13; *The Troy Record* (New York), August 4, 1966, page 2; *Appleton Post Crescent* (Wisconsin), August 4, 1966, page 1; and Bryn Bagenstose to *Datebook,* August 6, 1966, Beatles, Lennon Controversy, 1966, f712, Arthur Unger Papers, The State Historical Society of Missouri.

49   *The Republic* (Columbus, Indiana), August 6, 1966, page 13.

50   Beatles, Lennon Controversy, 1966, f709. Arthur Unger Papers, The State Historical Society of Missouri.

51   *KRLA Beat,* August 27, 1966, page 16; *New York Times,* August 6, 1966, page 13; *The Daily Journal* (Franklin, Indiana) August 11, 1966, page 9; *The Republic* (Columbus, Indiana), August 6, 1966, page 13; *Victoria Daily Colonist* (British Columbia,

Canada), August 6, 1966, page 13; *Hammond Times* (Indiana), August 7, 1966, page 1; and *Chester Delaware County Daily Times* (Pennsylvania), August 27, 1966, page 1.

52 *Record Mirror*, February 25, 1967, page 10.

53 *The Daily Dispatch*, August 19, 1966, page 20.

54 *The Daily Sikeston Standard* (Missouri), August 31, 1966, page 12.

55 *The Hillsdale Daily News* (Michigan), August 24, 1966, page 8.

56 *Chicago Defender,* August 22, 1966, page 13.

57 Barry Tashian, *Ticket to Ride: The Extraordinary Diary of The Beatles' Last Tour* (Nashville, Tenn: Dowling Press, 1997), 26-27.

58 *Chicago's American,* August 5, 1966, page 1.

59 *Chicago Daily News,* August 6, 1966, page 10.

60 *Chicago Tribune,* August 7, 1966, page 22.

61 *Christianity Today,* September 2, 1966, page 54.

62 *Moody Monthly*, October 1966, page 12.

63 *New York Times,* August 6, 1966, page 52.

64 *New World,* August 12, 1966, page 1.

65 Adam Cohen and Elizabeth Taylor, *American Pharaoh. Mayor Richard J. Daley: His Battle for Chicago and the Nation* (Boston: Little Brown and Company, 2000), 387-391.

66 *Daily Telegraph,* August 2, 1966, page 18.

67 *Chicago Daily News*, August 5, 1966, page 1.

68 *Chicago Sun-Times*, August 3, 1966, page 44.

69 *Chicago Police Statistical Report 1966* (Chicago Police Department), pages 4 and 6.

70 *Chicago Tribune*, August 2, 1966, page 5.

71 *New Musical Express,* August 12, 1966, page 2.

72 *Disc and Music Echo*, August 20, 1966, page 7.

73 *Newsweek, August 22, 1966, page 94.*

74 Chris Hutchins and Peter Thompson, *Elvis Meets the Beatles* (London: Neville Ness House, 2016), 175-178.

75 Frank Fried, *From Lenin to Lennon: My Unlikely Life in Show Business and Revolution* (Morrisville, North Carolina: Lulu, 2013), 108 and 112.

76 George Harrison, *I, Me, Mine* (San Francisco: Chronicle Books, 1980), 39.

77 *The Beatles Book,* August 1986, page 4.

78 Tony Barrow, *John, Paul, George, Ringo and Me: The Real Beatles Story* (London: Carlton Press, 2005), 202.

79 The Beatles Ultimate Experience. http://www.beatlesinterviews.org/db1966.0811. beatles.html and 1966 Chicago press conference, YouTube. https://www.youtube. com/watch?v=SBOgJx51Vy8. Both accessed May 24, 2018.

80 Frank Fried, *From Lenin to Lennon: My Unlikely Life in Show Business and Revolution* (Morrisville, North Carolina: Lulu, 2013), 114.

81 *Daily Mirror,* August 13, 1966, page 4.

82 *Moody Monthly*, October 1966, page 12.

83 Danny Fields interview with the author, June 28, 2018.

84 *Chicago Tribune*, April 10, 1966, section 5, page 9.

85 *Chicago Tribune*, August 4, 1966, page 6.

86 *Chicago Sun-Times*, August 10, 1966, page 48.

87 Martin 'Mike' Koldyke interview with the author, May 14, 2018.

88 Vern Miller interview with the author, February 22, 2015.

89 Bill Briggs interview with the author, March 2, 2015.

90 Vern Miller interview with the author, February 22, 2015.

91 Bill Briggs interview with the author, March 2, 2015.

92 Earle Pickens interview with the author, September 8, 2016.

93 Earle Pickens interview with the author, September 8, 2016.

94 *Chicago's American*, August 13, 1966, page 7.

95 "Pre-Concert Amphitheatre Interviews Pt 3," *Beatles Tapes VI - Rock And Religion 1966* (Jerden CD, 2005).

96 *TeenSet*, December 1966, page 35.

97 *Datebook*, February 1967, page 19.

98 *Chicago Sun-Times Family Magazine*, August 13, 1966, page 25.

99 *Chicago Tribune*, August 13, 1966, page 13.

100 *Daily Mirror*, August 13, page 4.

101 Earle Pickens interview with the author, September 8, 2016.

102 Keith Badman, *The Beatles Off the Record* (London: Omnibus, 2000), 234-235.

103 *Chicago Tribune*, August 13, 1966, page 13.

104 *Melody Maker*, August 20, 1966, page 14.

105 *Daily Express*, August 13, 1966, page 2.

106 *Chicago's American*, August 13, 1966, page 1.

107 *The Plain Dealer*, August 19, 1966, page 14.

108 *Teen Life*, November 1966, page 40.

109 Set list provided by *Chicago Sun-Times Family Magazine*, August 13, 1966, page 25.

110 Kathy Whitgrove interview with the author, February 2, 2015.

111 Pat Meyers interview with the author, March 9, 2015.

112 Allen Shaw interview with the author, April 3, 2017.

113 *Telegraph Herald* (Dubuque), February 8, 2004, page 34.

114 Katie A. Jones interview with the author, April 27, 2019.

115 Katie A. Jones interview with the author, April 27, 2019.

116 *Daily Mirror*, August 13, page 4.

117 *The Beatles North American Tour Diary August 1966* (Lazy Tortoise CD, 2007).

118 *Chicago's American*, August 13, 1966, page 1.

119 *Chicago's American*, August 13, 1966, page 7.

120 *Beatlefan*, May-June 1996, page 18.

121 *State Journal-Register*, August 21, 1966, page 48.

122 Mike Love and James S. Hirsch, *Good Vibrations: My Life As a Beach Boy* (New York: Blue Rider Press, 2016), 184.

123 *State Journal-Register*, August 21, 1966, page 48.

124 *Chicago Sun-Times*, December 10, 1980, page 4. Spink claims that this incident took place in 1965, but the Beatles stayed in the Gold Coast in 1966 not 1965, so if the meeting did take place, it took place in August 1966.

125 *Chicago Tribune*, June 3, 1976, page 16.

126 George Harrison interview by Arthur Unger, Beatle Interviews, 1-5, f704, Arthur Unger Papers, The State Historical Society of Missouri.

127 *Mojo*, October 2000, page 80

128 George Harrison interview on UK TV-AM, October 20, 1987.

129 Earle Pickens interview with the author, September 8, 2016.

130 *Billboard,* September 3, 1966, page 12.

131 *Disc and Music Echo,* October 15, 1966, page 2.

132 *The Beatles Anthology* (London: Cassell and Co. and San Francisco: Chronicle Books, 2000), 155.

133 *Daily Mirror,* July 5, 1969, page 7.

134 *The Beatles Anthology* (London: Cassell and Co. and San Francisco: Chronicle Books, 2000), 228.

135 *Datebook,* January 1967, page 4.

CHAPTER 8

1   *Time,* July 7, 1967, page 21.

2   *Chicago Tribune, TV Week,* February 25, 1967, page 4.

3   For more on the album see Allan F. Moore, *The Beatles: Sgt. Pepper's Lonely Hearts Club Band* (Cambridge: Cambridge University Press, 2007).

4   *Crawdaddy,* September/October 1967, page 8.

5   *Time,* September 22, 1967, page 61.

6   *Chicago Tribune,* June 18, 1967, section 5, page 11.

7   *Sing Out!* October/November 1967, page 37.

8   *The American Record Guide,* October 1967, page 169.

9   *New York Times,* June 18, 1967, page 24.

10 *High Fidelity,* August 1967, page 94.

11 Olivier Julien (ed) *Sgt. Pepper and the Beatles It Was Forty Years Ago Today* (Aldershot, Hampshire, England: Ashgate, 2008), 8.

12 Danny Fields interview with the author, June 28, 2018.

13 Allen Shaw interview with the author, April 3, 2017.

14 *Chicago,* August 1978, page 128.

15 Katie A. Jones interview with the author, April 27, 2019.

16 Katie A. Jones interview with the author, April 27, 2019.

17 UK Official Charts. https://www.officialcharts.com/chart-news/the-beatles-iconic-sgt-pepper-album-returns-to-the-top-on-its-50th-birthday__19326/ Accessed January 23, 2018; and Joel Whitburn, *The Billboard Book of Top 40 Albums* (New York: Billboard Books, 1987), 29.

18 *Newsweek,* December 4, 1967, page 54.

19 *Rolling Stone,* December 11, 2003.

20 *Chicago Tribune,* September 17, 1967, section 5, page 4.

21 *Chicago Tribune,* August 30, 1967, section 2, page 18.

22 *Jazz & Pop,* August 1967, page 5.

23 Danny Seraphine interview with the author September 14, 2015.

24 Jim Peterik interview with the author, May 4, 2015.

25 Carl Giammarese interview with the author, February 10, 2015.

26 *Chicago Tribune,* October 30, 1966, section 5, page 15.

27 Allen Shaw interview with the author, April 3, 2017.

28 Michael C. Keith, *Voices in the Purple Haze: Underground Radio and the Sixties* (Westport, CT: Praeger, 1997).

29   Allen Shaw interview with the author, April 3, 2017.

30   *Holiday,* March 1967, page 67.

31   Jory Graham, *Chicago: An Extraordinary Guide* (Chicago: Rand McNally, 1968), 89.

32   Abe Peck interview with the author, April 5, 2017.

33   Abe Peck interview with the author, April 5, 2017.

34   *Chicago Tribune,* May 15, 1967, section 2, page 19.

35   *The Seed,* May-June, 1967, page 3.

36   *Billboard,* December 21, 1968, pages 14 and 46.

37   Corry342 (2010), Kinetic Playground, Chicago, IL 4812 N. Clark Street: Performance List 1968-69. http://rockprosopography101.blogspot.com/2010/03/kinetic-play-ground-chicago-il-4812-n.html. Accessed April 4, 2017.

38   Abe Peck interview with the author, April 5, 2017.

39   *Fred,* June 16, 1969, page 45.

40   *The Seed,* July 21-August 20, 1967, pages 18-19.

41   George Harrison, *I, Me, Mine* (San Francisco: Chronicle Books, 1980), 21-22.

42   *Melody Maker,* September 9, 1967, page 13.

43   *Disc Weekly,* April 2, 1966, page 6.

44   *Penthouse,* October 1969, pages 29, 30 and 34.

45   *Holiday,* February 1968, page 142.

46   Hunter Davies, *The Beatles: The Authorized Biography* (New York: Dell, 1968), 375.

47   See Larry Kane, *Ticket To Ride: Inside The Beatles' 1964 & 1965 Tours That Changed The World* (Philadelphia: Running Press, 2003); and Ivor Davis, *The Beatles and Me on Tour* (Los Angeles: Cockney Kid Publishing, 2014) for some of their infidelities on the North American tours. Even more revealing is Glenn A. Baker, *The Beatles Down Under: The 1964 Australia and New Zealand Tour* (Ann Arbor, Michigan: Pierian Press, 1985).

48   *Sunday Mirror,* May 10, 1964, page 1.

49   *Confidential* September 1964, page 1.

50   *Playboy,* February 1965, page 58.

51   Cynthia Lennon, *A Twist of Lennon* (New York: Avon, 1978), 146.

52   Hunter Davies, *The Beatles: The Authorized Biography* (New York: Dell, 1968), 376.

53   In 1980, Lennon told *Playboy* magazine: "I used to be cruel to my woman, and phys-ically — any woman. I was a hitter. I couldn't express myself and I hit. I fought men and I hit women." David Sheff, *All We Are Saying: The Last Major Interview With John Lennon and Yoko Ono* (New York: St. Martin's Griffin, 2000), 182.

54   *Life,* June 16, 1967, page 105.

55   *Uncut,* July 2004, page 52.

56   *Creem,* January 1988, page 59.

57   *Saturday Evening Post,* May 21, 1966, pages 40-62, quote on page 40.

58   *New York Times,* January 17, 1971, page 52.

59   *Chicago Tribune,* October 28, 1968, section 3, page 11.

60   *Chicago Tribune,* November 10, 1968, section 1B, page 1.

61   Sue Trusty interview with the author, February 6, 2015.

62   Candy Leonard, *Beatleness: How the Beatles and Their Fans Remade the World* (New York: Arcade Publishing, 2014), 144 and 151.

63   *Washington Post,* August 28, 1967, page 3.

64   *Frost Programme*, September 1967, YouTube. https://www.youtube.com/watch?-time_continue=3&v=gXuN1Y6vaUY. Accessed January 12, 2018.

65   *Look,* January 9, 1968, page 41.

66   Ronald Lee Zigler, "Realizing It's All Within Yourself: The Beatles as Surrogate Gurus of Eastern Philosophy" in Michael Baur and Steven Baur (eds), *The Beatles and Philosophy: Nothing You Can Think That Can't Be Thunk* (Chicago: Open Court, 2006), 139-150.

67   *Uncut*, October 2016, page 81.

68   Denny Somach, Kathleen Somach, and Kevin Gunn, *Ticket to Ride* (New York: Morrow, 1989), 212.

69   *The Beatles Book,* August 1998, page 4.

70   *Detroit Free Press*, August 19, 1966, page 4C.

71   David Reck, "The Beatles and Indian Music," in Olivier Julien (ed) *Sgt. Pepper and the Beatles It Was Forty Years Ago Today* (Aldershot, Hampshire, England: Ashgate, 2008), 68.

72   Philip Goldberg, *American Veda: From Emerson and the Beatles to Yoga and Meditation—How Indian Spirituality Changed the World* (New York: Harmony Books, 2010), 7.

73   *Disc and Music Echo,* December 9, 1967, page 9.

74   *Disc and Music Echo,* December 9, 1967, page 9.

75   *Disc and Music Echo,* March 16, 1968, page 24.

76   Hunter Davies, *The Beatles: The Authorized Biography* (New York: McGraw-Hill, second revised edition 1985), liv.

77   The Beatles Ultimate Experience. http://www.beatlesinterviews.org/db1968.0514.beatles.html. Accessed December 13, 2016.

78   Doug Sulpy and Ray Schweighardt, *Get Back: The Unauthorized Chronicle of the Beatles' Let It Be Disaster* (New York: St. Martin's Griffin, 1999), 153 and 188.

79   *New Musical Express,* June 1, 1968 page 11.

80   *Queen,* July 19, 1967, pages 25-28.

81   *New Musical Express,* August 17, 1968, page 3.

82   *The Beatles Book,* October 1969, page 8.

83   UK Official Charts. https://www.officialcharts.com/search/singles/hare%20krishna. Accessed May 24, 2018.

84   *Rave,* December 1969, page 54.

85   *Daily Sketch,* October 9, 1967, page 12.

86   *Disc and Music Echo*, September 1967, page 16.

87   *Record Mirror,* March 23, 1968, page 7.

88   *The Beatles Book,* November 1967, page 25.

89   The Beatles Ultimate Experience. http://www.beatlesinterviews.org/db1968.05ts.beatles.html. Accessed July 7, 2017.

90   *Teen Datebook,* Spring 1967, pages 34-35.

91   *Teen Datebook,* December 1967, page 60.

92   *Teen Datebook,* May 1968, pages 12-13.

93   Philip Goldberg, *American Veda: From Emerson and the Beatles to Yoga and Meditation—How Indian Spirituality Changed the World* (New York: Harmony Books, 2010), 7.

94 *Look,* January 9, 1968, page 41.

95 *New York Times,* January 11, 1971, page 33.

96 *Morris Daily Herald,* October 7, 1967, page 4 and *Alton Evening Telegraph,* October 5, 1967, page 8.

97 *The Skyscraper,* January 11, 1968, page 2.

98 *The Seed,* Volume 1 Number 1, 1967, page 9.

99 *Daily Northwestern,* October 5, 1967, page 2.

100 *Chicago Tribune,* September 17, 1967, section 5, page 4.

101 *Chicago Tribune,* March 17, 1968, section 5, page 3.

102 *Chicago Tribune,* September 3, 2004, section 2, page 10.

103 *Chicago Tribune,* February 14, 1968, page 14, and *Chicago Tribune magazine,* December 1, 1968, pages 34-35.

104 *Chicago Tribune,* November 7, 1971, section 10, page 6.

105 Email from Sharon Steffensen to the author, October 23, 2018.

106 *Chicago Tribune,* February 8, 1970, section 5, page 7.

107 Sharon Steffensen, "History of Yoga in Chicago, 1893-1998," *Yoga Chicago,* May-June 1998, page 18.

108 *Circus,* December 1969, page 18.

109 *Fiesta,* November 1969, page 56.

110 *Circus,* December 1969, page 18.

111 Chip Madinger and Scott Raile, *Lennonology: Volume 1, Strange Days Indeed, A Scrapbook of Madness* (Missouri: Open Your Books, 2015), 159.

112 *Penthouse,* October 1969, pages 29, 30 and 34.

113 *RAT Subterranean News,* June 12-18, 1969, page 18.

114 Joseph J. Mangano, *Living Legacy: How 1964 Changed America* (Lanham: University Press of America, 1994), 85.

CHAPTER 9

1 *Chicago Tribune,* September 5, 1968, page 1.

2 *Chicago Daily News,* November 4, 1968, page 3 and *Chicago Sun-Times,* November 4, 1968, page 47.

3 Peter W. Colby and Paul Michael Green, "Voting Patterns in the 96 Downstate Counties," *Illinois Issues,* August 1978, page 15.

4 Bernard Biernacki interview with the author, May 29, 2018.

5 *TeenSet,* November 1967, page 54.

6 *Datebook,* January 1967, page 70.

7 Billboard.com. https://web.archive.org/web/20080124153225/http://www.billboard.com/bbcom/charts/yearend_chart_display.jsp?f=The%2BBillboard%2B200&g=-Year-end%2BAlbums&year=1967. Accessed May 20, 2018.

8 Judy Bloom interview with the author, July 19, 2015.

9 Kathy Mangan interview by Jon Mangan, December 7, 2015, Joliet Junior College Library Archives.

10 *Youth Quake: Look Special,* 1967, pages 55-57.

11 William L. Lunch and Peter W. Sperlich, "American Public Opinion and the War in Vietnam," *The Western Political Quarterly* (March 1979), pages 25, 28, 31 and 33.

12 George Gallup, *The Gallup Poll, 1935-1971: Volume 3* (New York: Random House, 1972), 2220-2221.

13 Dennis Johnson and R. J. Furth, *The Moving Violation, A Rock and Roll Memoir, 1966-68* (North Charleston, SC: Create Space, 2014), 52-53.

14 *Chicago Sun-Times,* June 1, 1969, page 69.

15 *Holiday,* March 1967, page 158.

16 Timothy Stewart-Winter, *Queer Clout Chicago and the Rise of Gay Politics* (Philadelphia: University of Pennsylvania Press, 2016), 5 and 56.

17 Abe Peck interview with the author, April 5, 2017.

18 *New York Times,* August 24, 1968, page 20.

19 *Addison Register,* March 1, 1968, page 1.

20 *Chicago's American,* November 17, 1968, page 2.

21 *Chicago Tribune,* January 15, 1970, section A1, page 1.

22 *Chicago Tribune,* April 11, 1970, section 1, page 2.

23 *Daily Northwestern,* April 10, 1968, page 3.

24 *Daily Northwestern,* November 6, 1970, page 7.

25 *Arlington Heights Daily Herald,* August 2, 1968, page 48.

26 *Arlington Heights Daily Herald,* May 5, 1968, page 78.

27 *The Daily Dispatch,* July 27, 1967, page 46.

28 *American Opinion,* February 1969, pages 49-62.

29 Leann Julian interview with the author, February 12, 2015.

30 Linda Milan interview by Jennifer Raymond, December 3, 2014, Joliet Junior College Library Archives.

31 *The Beatles Book,* October 1967, page 19.

32 *Arlington Heights Daily Herald,* December 13, 1967, page 15.

33 *South End Reporter,* June 18, 1969, page 13.

34 *Titbits,* August 31, 1968, page 9.

35 *The Beatles Book,* October 1968, page 24 and 31.

36 The Eamonn Andrews Show, April 3, 1969, YouTube. https://www.youtube.com/watch?v=vjw_WfrfpVA Accessed September 11, 2017.

37 *Daily Mirror,* December 18, 1969, page 13.

38 *Disc and Music Echo,* August 10, 1968, page 24.

39 *Chicago Sun-Times,* March 27, 1969, page 122.

40 *Chicago Tribune,* October 9, 1968, section 1B, page 27.

41 *Chicago Tribune,* March 22, 1969, page 10.

42 *Chicago Tribune,* November 19, 1968, section 2, page 19.

43 *Chicago Tribune,* January 27, 1969, section 2, page 12.

44 *Chicago Tribune,* December 24, 1969, page 3.

45 *Chicago South End Reporter,* July 16, 1969, page 4.

46 Katie A. Jones interview with the author, April 27, 2019.

47 *The Daily Dispatch,* February 14, 1970, page 20.

48 *The Beatles Tapes from the David Wigg Interviews* (Polydor album, 1976).

49 *US,* November 30, 1987, page 52.

50 *Rolling Stone,* October 22, 1987, page 41.

51 *Chicago Tribune,* March 21, 1967, page 5.

52 *Chicago Tribune,* March 26, 1967, page 22. Its sister paper, *Chicago's American*, also endorsed Daley, April 2, 1967, page 16.

53 *Saturday Evening Post,* August 24, 1968, page 70.

54   Bob Sirott Interviews Clark Weber, YouTube. https://www.youtube.com/watch?v=4 VvvZS0Smgk Accessed December 28, 2019.

55   Frank J. Donner, *Protectors of Privilege: Red Squads and Police Repression in Urban America* (Berkeley: University of California Press, 1992), chapter 4.

56   *Second City*, February 1, 1969, page 6.

57   *Chicago Tribune*, April 24, 1968, page 14.

58   *Chicago Tribune*, May 21, 1968, section 2 page 7.

59   *Chicago Tribune*, July 19, 1968, section 3 page 14.

60   *American Opinion*, February 1969, page 61.

61   *Billboard*, December 14, 1968, page 4.

62   *Billboard*, January 18, 1969, page 100.

63   *Billboard*, December 21, 1968, page 46.

64   *Rolling Stone*, March 15, 1969, page 12.

65   *Chicago Tribune*, April 1, 1969, page 10.

66   *Chicago Daily News,* June 10, 1967, page 25.

67   *Rolling Stone,* July 26, 1969, page 8.

68   Kirkpatrick Sale, *SDS* (New York: Vintage, 1973).

69   *Insurgent*, Volume 1 Number 1, 1965, pages 10-12.

70   Franklin Rosemont and Charles Radcliffe, *Dancin' in the Streets: Anarchists, IWWs, Surrealists, Situationists and Provos in the 1960s as Recorded in the Pages of Rebel Worker and Heatwave* (Chicago: Charles H Kerr, 2005), 127-128.

71   Thai Jones, *A Radical Line: From the Labor Movement to the Weather Underground, One Family's Century of Conscience* (New York: Free Press, 2004), 208.

72   Kirkpatrick Sale, *SDS* (New York: Vintage, 1973), 438.

73   *New York Times*, September 15, 1968, page 31.

74   Abe Peck, *Uncovering the Sixties The Life and Times of the Underground Press* (New-York: Citadel Underground, 1991), 106-107.

75   *New York Times Magazine*, September 15, 1968, page 28.

76   *Chicago Tribune,* August 30, 1968, page 1.

77   *Chicago Tribune,* August 30, 1968, page 12.

78   *Daily Herald,* section 3, June 19, 1996, page 3. See also Frank Kusch, *Battleground Chicago: The Police and the 1968 Democratic National Convention* (Westport, CT: Praeger, 2004).

79   Yoko Ono to *Instant Karma*, October 9, 1986, *Instant Karma* No. 29 (Winter 1986), page 4.

80   John Lennon interview with Maurice Hindle, December 1968, transcript part 1, page 15, Hard Rock website. http://www.hardrock.com/promo/lennon/. Accessed April 19, 2017.

81   John Lennon interview by Arthur Unger, Arthur Unger Papers, The State Historical Society of Missouri. Beatle Interviews, 1-5, f704.

82   *International Times,* August 29-September 11, 1969, page 3.

83   *Chicago Tribune*, November 10, 1968, section 5, page 17.

84   John Lennon interview with Maurice Hindle, December 1968, transcript part 1, page 15, Hard Rock website. http://www.hardrock.com/promo/lennon/. Accessed April 19, 2017.

85   *Chicago Sun-Times*, November 16, 1968, page 21.

86   *Chicago Tribune*, November 24, 1968, section 5, page 16.

87 *Chicago Sun-Times*, November 16, 1968, page 21.

88 *Chicago Sun-Times*, November 16, 1968, pages 21 and 33.

89 Todd Gitlin, *The Sixties: Years of Hope, Days of Rage* (Toronto: Bantam Books, 1989, originally published in 1987), 197-198.

90 *Chicago Tribune*, August 26, 1968, section 3, page 12.

91 *Rising Up Angry*, July 1969, page 6.

92 *Daily Northwestern*, October 14, 1969, page 3.

93 *Chicago Reader*, November 8, 1990. https://www.chicagoreader.com/chicago/the-long-strange-trip-of-bill-ayers/Content?oid=876592. Accessed May 15, 2017.

94 *Second City*, March 1969, page 14.

95 *Rising Up Angry*, Winter 1970, page 5.

96 Phillip Abbott Luce, "Are the Beatles Termites? The Great Rock Conspiracy," *National Review*, September 23, 1969, page 959.

97 *The New Guard*, November 1968, page 20.

98 *The New Guard*, November 1969, page 16.

99 *Negro Digest*, November 1969, page 30.

100 William L. Van Deburg, *New Day in Babylon: The Black Power Movement and American Culture, 1965-1975* (Chicago and London: University of Chicago Press, 1992).

101 Daniel U. Levine, Norman S. Fiddmont, Robert S. Stephenson, and Charles Wilkinson, "Differences Between Black Youth Who Support the Black Panthers and the NAACP," *Journal of Negro Education* 42 (Winter 1973), 19-32.

102 Edward E. Davis, *The Beatles Book* (New York: Cowles, 1968), 139 and 143.

103 *Jet,* August 18, 1966, page 30.

104 LeRoi Jones, *Black Music* (New York: William Morrow, 1967), 205-206.

105 Eldridge Cleaver, *Soul on Ice* (New York: Delta, 1992, originally published in 1968), 235.

106 Edward E. Davis, *The Beatles Book* (New York: Cowles, 1968), 138.

107 LeRoi Jones, *Black Music* (New York: William Morrow, 1967), 205-206.

108 Jakobi Williams, *From the Bullet to the Ballot: The Illinois Chapter of the Black Panther Party and Racial Coalition Politics in Chicago* (Chapel Hill, University of North Carolina Press, 2013).

109 *Chicago Tribune*, October 15, 1968, pages 1-2.

110 *Chicago Defender*, March 24, 1969, page 4 and April 16, 1969, page 2.

111 *Chicago Defender*, February 19, 1966, page 7.

112 *Chicago Defender*, September 4, 1969, page 18.

113 *Ebony*, August 1969, page 56.

114 Bonnie Greer, *A Parallel Life* (London: Arcadia Books, 2014), 195 and 197.

115 Peter Doggett, *You Never Give Me Your Money: The Battle for the Soul of The Beatles* (London: Bodley Head, 2009); Stan Soocher, *Baby you're a Rich Man: Suing the Beatles for Fun and Profit* (Lebanon, NH: ForeEdge, 2015); and Peter Brown and Steven Gaines, *The Love You Make: An Insider's Story of the Beatles* (London: Macmillan, 1983).

116 *Daily Mirror*, April 10, 1970, page 1.

117 Ken McNab, *And in the End: The Last Days of the Beatles* (Edinburgh: Polygon, 2019), 301.

118 The *New York Times*, April 11, 1970, page 21 and *Los Angeles Times*, April 11, 1970, page 7.

119 *Detroit Free Press,* April 11, 1970, page 1.

120 *Chicago Tribune,* April 11, 1970, page 16.

121 *Chicago Sun-Times,* April 11, 1970, page 5, and *Chicago Daily News,* April 10, 1970, page 2.

122 *Billboard,* April 18, 1970, page 1.

123 *Cashbox,* May 2, 1970, pages 52 and 54, with quote on page 54.

124 *Chicagoland,* February 1970, pages 34-39.

125 *Chicago Tribune,* March 29, 1970, section 10, page 4.

126 *Chicago Tribune,* March 12, 1970, section 2A, page 12.

127 Bethjoy Borris interview with the author, August 6, 2018.

128 Katie A. Jones interview with the author, April 27, 2019.

129 Cynthia Dagnal-Myron interview with the author, July 12, 2017.

130 *The Seed,* June 15, 1970, page 14.

EPILOGUE

1 Chip Madinger and Scott Raile, *Lennonology: Volume 1, Strange Days Indeed, A Scrapbook of Madness* (Missouri: Open Your Books, 2015), 324.

2 *Chicago Sun-Times,* June 23, 1986, page 10.

3 *Chicago Tribune,* December 2, 1974, section 3, page 6.

4 Paul McCartney interview promoting *Give My Regards to Broad Street,* YouTube. https://www.youtube.com/watch?v=GEnO4HQP8os. Accessed May 15, 2018.

5 *Chicago Tribune,* August 5, 2008, section 2, page 1, and August 6, 2008, page 2C.1.

6 *Chicago Tribune,* July 8, 2008, section 2, page 2.

7 *Uncut,* July 2004, page 56.

8 *New Musical Express,* August 15, 1998, page 24.

9 *Sounds,* June 26, 1976, page 22.

10 Kevin Howlett, *The Beatles at the Beeb, 62-65: The Story of Their Radio Career* (Ann Arbor, MI: Pierian Press, 1983), 7.

11 *The Ultimate Music Guide The Beatles* (*Uncut* magazine special, 2013).

12 Hunter Davies, *The Beatles Lyrics: The Stories Behind the Music, Including the Handwritten Drafts of More Than 100 Classic Beatles Songs* (New York, Boston and London: Little Brown and Co, 2014), 8.

13 *Chicago Tribune,* September 9, 1983, section 5, page 4.

14 Nick Blumberg and Marc Vitali (2016), "Yoko Ono Unveils 'Sky Landing' in Jackson Park." https://news.wttw.com/2016/10/17/yoko-ono-unveils-sky-landing-jackson-park. Accessed August 28, 2018.

15 Robert G. Spinney, *City of Big Shoulders: A History of Chicago* (DeKalb, Ill: Northern Illinois University Press, 2000), Dominic A. Pacyga, *Chicago A Biography* (Chicago: University of Chicago Press, 2009), Andrew J. Diamond, *Chicago on the Make: Power and Inequality in a Modern City* (Oakland, CA: University of California Press, 2017) and Whet Moser, *Chicago: From Vision to Metropolis* (London, UK: Reaktion Books, 2019).

Acknowledgments

Librarians and archivists provided invaluable help with my research: the Special Collections and University Archives at the University of Illinois at Chicago, the State Historical Society of Missouri in Columbia, the Rock & Roll Hall of Fame Library & Archives in Cleveland, Ohio, the Northwestern University music library in Evanston, Illinois, the Archdiocese of Chicago's Joseph Cardinal Bernardin Archives and Records Center in Chicago, and the Walter P. Reuther Library at Wayne State University in Detroit, Michigan. I would like to send a special thanks to Amy Chellino and the wonderful staff at the Joliet Junior College Library for fulfilling my many esoteric requests, always with a smile.

A number of people helped me gather the oral interviews for the book. I would like to extend my gratitude to my students who I shamelessly exploited by sending them near and far to interview people about their memories of the Beatles. The *Herald-News* in Joliet helped me find interviewees. Guy Arnston, Clark Besch, Ivor Davis, Jeff Jarema, Mat Irvine, Dean Milano, Bob Stroud, John Trusty, Linda Ulreich, and Ken Voss pointed me in the right direction. A special thanks to those I interviewed for the book: Abe Peck, Alan Holmes, Allen Shaw, Andee Levin, Barry Tashian, Bernie Biernacki, Bethjoy Borris, Bill Briggs, Bob Tucker, Bob Wilson, Bruce Berry, Bruce Mattey, Carl Giammarese, Carolyn Dillon, Chad Mitchell, Charles "Chuck" Colbert, Cheryl "Pinkie" Jennings, Chris Hutchins, Christine Paine, Chuck Dingée, Clarence "Frogman" Henry, Clark Weber, Curt Bachman, Cynthia Dagnal-Myron, Dan Pietrzyk, Danny Fields, Danny Seraphine, Dave Grundhoefer, David Kell Blanchard, Dean Milano, Debi Pomeroy, Denise Mourges, Donna J. Smolak, Earle Pickens, Frank Allen, Gary Loizzo, Ginny Greninger, Ivor Davis, Jean Etsinger, Jeanne Yorke, Jeff Augsburger, Jim O'Boye,

Jim Peterik, Jimy Sohns, Joel Geier, John Grochowski, John Rook, John Sebastian, Judy Bloom, Katie A. Jones, Katie MacLeod Davidson, Kathy Holden, Kathy Whitgrove, Ken Draper, Ken German, Leann Julian, Lillian Walker, Lois Easter, Louise Harrison, Lynn Mullaney, Lynn Thurmaier, Marty Grebb, Mary Towey, Melvyn "Deacon" Jones, Mike Koldyke, Mike Losekamp, Mindy Brickhandler, Pat Meyers, Pete Shelton, Ray O'Brien, Robert Mitchell, Ronnie Rice, Steve Moroniak, Stuart Wolf, Sue Trusty, Sylvester Cottrell, Tom Doody, Val Camilletti, Vern Miller, Warren Willingham, and Wendy Calcanas. Due to space limitations, the words of some of the interviewees are not included in the study, but their views have still been invaluable in influencing the content of the book.

I want to acknowledge the contributions of my agent, Joe Perry, who provided sage advice and found an excellent home for the book, and my editors Jacob Hoye and Holly Layman, who offered valuable and constructive suggestions that immensely improved the finished work. Giorgia Fiorani provided tennis lessons and vital help with the photographs. Finally, heartfelt thanks to Mike and Mary, and the extended "Fam," Enrico, Michele, Giorgia, Mike, Dorothy, and Eddie. My wonderful wife, Joanie, and fabulous daughter, Sinead, suffered the most during the writing of this book. The former had to put up with her husband disappearing into the attic for long periods of time while the latter would cry out in pain on the drive to school, "No Daddy, please don't play another Beatles song!"

Index

About the Author

John F. Lyons is a Professor of History at Joliet Junior College in Illinois where he teaches classes in British and American history. He was born in London, England, and lives in Chicago. *Joy and Fear* is his fifth book.